The Economic Way of Thinking

THIRD EDITION

Paul Heyne
University of Washington

SCIENCE RESEARCH ASSOCIATES, INC.
Chicago, Palo Alto, Toronto
Henley-on-Thames, Sydney, Paris

A Subsidiary of IBM

Acquisition Editor	David Bruce Caldwell
Project Editor	James C. Budd
Compositor	Dharma Press
Text and Cover Designer	Michael Rogondino
Photo Researcher	Audrey Ross
Cover Photographer	Chuck Place

ACKNOWLEDGMENTS

Chapter opener photographs are used by permission of: *Chapter 1*, Charles Harbutt © 1970 Magnum Photos; *Chapter 2*, Copyright © 1968 Margaret Durrance, Photo Researchers; *Chapter 3*, Ken Heyman, N.Y.C.; *Chapter 4*, © Cartier-Bresson, Magnum; *Chapter 5*, © Alex Webb, Distributed by Magnum; *Chapter 6*, Frank Siteman Copyright © Stock, Boston; *Chapter 7*, © B. Kliewe, Jeroboam; *Chapter 8*, Doug Wilson, Black Star; *Chapter 9*, Eva Demjen, Copyright © Stock, Boston 1977; *Chapter 10*, Bruce Davidson © 1965 Magnum Photos; *Chapter 11*, © Carl Weese, Photo Researchers, 1975; *Chapter 12*, Cary Wolinsky © 1977 Stock, Boston; *Chapter 13*, Jack Prelutsky Copyright © 1977 Stock, Boston; *Chapter 14*, John Running, Copyright © 1977 Stock, Boston; *Chapter 15*, Burk Uzzle © 1967 Magnum Photos; *Chapter 16*, Burt Glinn © Magnum Photos, Inc.; *Chapter 17*, Lawrence Cameron, Jeroboam; *Chapter 18*, Roy Zalesky, Black Star; *Chapter 19*, Copyright 1979 Barrie Rokeach, Berkeley, CA; *Chapter 20*, © Bruce Roberts from Rapho/Photo Researchers, Inc.; *Chapter 21*, Kent Reno, Jeroboam; *Chapter 22*, Cornell Capa, Magnum Photos.

Library of Congress Cataloging in Publication Data

Heyne, Paul T.
    The economic way of thinking.

    Includes index.
    1. Economics. I. Title.
HB171.5.H46 1980 330 79-21656
ISBN 0-574-1925-6

10 9 8 7 6 5 4 3

Preface

Introductory economics has long been an easy subject to teach. It's been a hard subject to *take*, but that's another matter. Moreover, the amount of learning that comes out of principles courses bears no reasonable relationship to the amount of teaching that goes in.

Principles of economics has been an easy course to teach, because we have used it largely to regurgitate the bits of technique acquired during our own training in economics. There are so many such bits and pieces, and they are so hard for students to grasp, that principles teachers need never worry about what to do today. They can always introduce a new complication or spend the hour clarifying the complication introduced yesterday. And they don't even have to prepare the complications. A single phrase—elasticity, total-average-marginal revenue, long-run competitive equilibrium, marginal-value-product, IS-LM, the multiplier—will serve as an adequate text for an entire class session.

What Are We After?

What should be the learning goal in the beginning economics course? It is clear from what has already been said that the present author has little use for what he takes to be the usual learning goal: introducing the student to bits and pieces of technique. Why should we want a beginning student to be familiar with the concepts of average variable, average total, and marginal cost, their downward-then-upward shapes, the necessary intersection of marginal cost at the low point of average cost, and everything else contributing to the demonstration that in the long run, under perfectly competitive conditions, price will be equal to average total and marginal cost for all firms after quasi-rents have been capitalized? To ask the question is to answer it. We have no good reason for wanting a beginning student to know all this. Then why have we continued to teach it?

Part of the explanation lies in our commendable concern to teach *theory*. It is economic theory that gives to economics almost all its predictive or clarifying power. Without theory, we must grope our way blindly through economic problems, conflicting opinions, and opposing policy proposals.

But economic theory has proved itself unusually difficult to communicate. So those responsible for teaching undergraduate economics, struck by the apparent failure of theory-oriented principles courses, have sometimes opted instead for a problems and issues course. In such a course, students typically read and discuss statements by labor leaders, industry representatives, agricultural lobbyists, politicians, and a few domestic radicals or foreign socialists. They look at figures on income distribution, gross national product, employment, prices, and rates of economic growth. They read and discuss the arguments for guaranteed incomes and against planned obsolescence, for free enterprise and against unregulated competition, for nuclear power and against uncontrolled economic growth. And when it is all over, what have they learned? They have learned that opinions abound, with data to support every one of them, that "it's all relative," that every American is entitled to an opinion, and that economics is not a science and probably a waste of time.

The insistence upon teaching theory is correct insofar as it is a denial of the significance of facts without theories. Theory is essential! But what theory? Economic theory, of course. But that begs the real question. What *kind* of economic theory? And in what *context*? Before we can answer we must know what we're after.

Concepts and Applications

The author of this book wants beginning students to master a set of concepts that will help them think more coherently and consistently about the wide range of social problems that economic theory illuminates. The principles of economics make sense out of buzzing confusion. They clarify, systematize, and correct the daily assertions of newspapers, political figures, ax grinders, and barroom pontiffs. And the applicability of the economist's thought tools is practically unlimited. Students should come to appreciate all of this in a beginning course.

But they won't unless we, the teachers and textbook writers, persuade them. And we can only persuade them by showing them. *The principles of economics must therefore be taught as tools of analysis.* The teaching of a concept must take place in the context of application. Better, the potential application should be taught first, then the tool. There is so much evidence from pedagogy to support this approach that it's hard at first to understand how any other approach could ever have conquered the field.

"Here is a problem. You recognize it as a problem. What can we say about it?" That's step one.

"Here is how economists think about the problem. They employ the concept of such and such." Step two entails the exposition of some concept of economic theory.

After the applicability of the concept to the original problem has been demonstrated and some of the implications examined, the concept should be applied to additional problems. That's step three.

It isn't as easy as one-two-three, of course, and we don't mean to imply that it is. The teaching of economic principles requires imagination, insight, a knowledge of current events, and a sense of perspective, as well as familiarity with the formal techniques of economic analysis. Those are all scarce goods. And it presupposes a conviction on the part of the teacher that economic theory really is useful for something more than answering artificial questions and passing equally artificial examinations.

The Virtue of Restraint

Perhaps no one would disagree in principle with any of the above. If so, our practice has been far out of step with our precept. One reason is undoubtedly the obsession with formal technique that characterizes so much teaching of economic theory at all levels. The disciple will very rarely rise above the master. And if the masters in our profession are more concerned with form than content, the effects will be felt at the principles level. We need not debate here the question of how much of the material taught in intermediate and advanced theory texts really belongs there, or what balance should be struck in graduate theory courses between the logic-mathematics and the economics of theory. For the question of what should go into a beginning course can be answered without resolving the other questions. And that answer is: *Very little.*

For very little indeed of what might go into a Compleat and Current Compendium of Economic Theory is actually useful in enabling us to make sense of the real world and to evaluate policy proposals. Almost all the genuinely important things that economics has to teach are elementary concepts of relationship that people could almost figure out for themselves if they were willing to think carefully.[1]

The challenge is getting people to *appreciate* these few, simple concepts. To do that, we must practice the virtue of

---

1. A compelling statement of this view was provided by Ely Devons in the first two of his *Essays in Economics* (London: George Allen and Unwin, 1961), pp. 13–46.

restraint. We must attempt less and thereby accomplish more. An introductory course should distinguish itself as much by what it excludes as by what it incorporates. Unless it is our aim to impress students with the esoteric quality of economists' knowledge, we should teach no theory in the introductory course that cannot be put to work immediately. Otherwise we drown beginning students; they are made to thrash about so desperately that they don't learn to swim a single stroke. Our aim should be to get them swimming and to instill in them the confidence that through practice they can learn to swim better.

Every introductory economics teacher ought to read a short essay by Noel McInnis, entitled "Teaching More with Less." Here are three excerpts:

> I dare say that all of us who teach have been guilty of telling our students much more than they cared—or needed—to know. In fact, I would theorize that we have probably been telling them more about our subjects than *we* care to know. That is one reason why we feel compelled to rely on notes to deliver lectures.
>
> Our present methods of communicating often obscure meaning rather than reveal it. . . . We often see the tragic results of this in our "best" students, who can repeat what we have told them but cannot apply it in a new context so that it means something. Their learning may have been comprehensive, but it has not been comprehend*ing*.
>
> Survey courses in almost all disciplines are becoming increasingly impractical because of their compulsive attempt to cover all relevant information. They could be made highly practical once again—or perhaps for the first time—if they were organized to convey the five or six most fundamental organizing and conceptual principles of the discipline, utilizing only the most immediately relevant information to bring the principles to life.[2]

The author of this book agrees wholeheartedly with McInnis. Our implementation of this vision will undoubtedly be found far from perfect. But the teacher who wonders why this or that topic is not treated in the book, or why there is no complete exposition of some familiar portion of theory, should remember that knowledge is imparted by what is left out as well as by what is included. Judgments on relevance and relative importance will, of course, vary. But the argument of McInnis should be faced every time we are tempted to add another jot or tittle to the corpus of what we teach in beginning principles courses.

---

2. *Change: The Magazine of Higher Education* (January–February 1971), pp. 49, 50, 51.

Every economics teacher, whether of graduates or undergraduates, knows how disconcertingly little most students bring with them from principles courses into subsequent studies. Sometimes they don't seem to remember anything except that they've "heard of it." Is the solution more credit hours of introduction? Should we detain them longer so that we can drill them more thoroughly in the fundamentals of our discipline? In this teacher's judgment the solution lies rather in the direction of fewer hours spent in the introductory course.

What is true and relevant tends to get lost when a beginning course is extended over two quarters or semesters. The student gets many fuzzy ideas of what the subject is *about*, but little grasp of what it *is*.

Moreover, there are too many pedagogical and administrative problems associated with the truncated unity of a two-term single course. Teachers change, textbooks change, micro comes before macro and then macro is put before micro, students drop out after the first term and return two years later for the second term. Why have we nonetheless persisted? It sometimes seems as if we're afraid to teach it all in one term for fear that we'll cut our demand in half. If we can persuade the curriculum makers, especially in the business schools, that two terms is the absolute minimum, we can better maintain the demand for our services.

But a single *worthwhile* term can leave the beginning student eager for more. And economic education doesn't have to end with the introductory course. It won't, at least for many of the students whom we want to continue, if we do a better job of getting them started. The demand for economic principles may even prove to be elastic: if we cut the hourly cost in half, the number of customers may more than double.

Some economists have argued in discussions with the author that although a one-term course may be adequate for the general student, two terms are the essential minimum for economics or business majors. But isn't a brief and lively introduction to economics the best start for everyone, for those who plan never to take another course and for those who intend to go on to graduate school in economics? Ater all, a one-term principles course does not preclude subsequent courses in theory, courses that could be required or strongly recommended for majors. And more students might enroll in the theory courses if the introductory course managed to persuade them that economic theory is a worthwhile and occasionally even an exciting study.

Notes on the Third Edition

A reader who compares the length of this third edition with the length of the second by counting pages will conclude that the new edition is substantially longer. That conclusion is probably mistaken. I have taken seriously the admonitions of some friendly critics that "short writing often makes for long reading." I have added no new concepts in this edition. But I have tried, through "longer writing," to clarify those parts of the discussion that students and teachers have found obscure. I believe and hope that the result will be a book that can be understood in less time, even if it takes slightly longer to read.

The third edition of *The Economic Way of Thinking* has been extensively revised. Users of earlier editions may find the following summary of changes helpful.

Three broad changes or shifts in emphasis run throughout the present edition. First of all, the theme of social cooperation is now in sharper and more frequent focus. The economy is depicted as a social system, by means of which people secure cooperation in using what is available to achieve their infinitely varied goals. The complexity of this challenge and the consequent complexity of the coordinative mechanisms that have evolved to meet it are continually emphasized.

Second, no human purposes are allowed to be exogenous to the economic system. Government in particular is presented as a constellation of people with particular expectations and interests rather than as a *deus ex machina*. Government joins large corporations, trade associations, citizen activists, professional economists, and other "private interests" in being part of the problem as well as part of the solution.

Finally, a persistent effort has been made to show that economic theory offers a coherent, unified perspective on human behavior and social interaction, rather than a set of *ad hoc* theorems. Much of the subject matter reorganization within and among chapters has been undertaken with the objective of making the coherence of economic theory more visible to the student.

Many significant changes of a more specific nature have also been made. Here are some of the principal ones. Chapter 1 has been greatly enlarged in an effort to introduce the reader to the problem of social cooperation and to economic theory as a systematic way of thinking.

The concept of supply has been introduced in Chapter 3, right after the concept of demand, in order to emphasize the common dependence of both supply and demand upon people's choices among alternatives.

Chapter 11 now includes a discussion of discounting and a set of tables for use in determining present values. Almost all of the old Chapter l3 (now Chapter 12) has been eliminated in favor of new material focusing on the measurement and determination of the distribution of income. Chapters 11 and 12 also introduce and start to show the implications of the fact that people's expectations about what they will be able to do guide their behavior. Chapter 13 (on pollution) asks what can happen when people's expectations conflict. Chapter 14 looks at the expectations citizens have of government and the expectations of those in government, which in turn determine what government will actually accomplish.

Chapters 15 through 21 represent a thorough rethinking, reorganization, and rewriting of the material on inflation, recession, and unemployment. Some standard topics have been excluded, in the belief that they contribute little or nothing to understanding these problems. Considerable effort was also expended, in planning and writing the chapters, to ground all explanations in the fundamental principles introduced in the first two-thirds of the book. The hope underlying this effort was that much light—and relatively little doctrinal controversy—could be produced by staying in close touch with basic facts and elementary principles.

Borrowings and Acknowledgments

Anyone who teaches introductory economics for more than twenty years has numerous opportunities to borrow good ideas from others and time enough to forget from whom they were borrowed. This nourishes a pleasant illusion of originality but becomes embarrassing when acknowledgments must be made. I can't even remember who inspired all of the changes in the third edition, much less the people who contributed good ideas to earlier editions. I do still remember my original debt to Armen A. Alchian and William R. Allen, whose *University Economics* first showed that introductory economics could be a useful and exciting course. I'm still grateful to Thomas Johnson, of North Carolina State University, who was such a valuable source of ideas, criticism, and encouragement before we veered off toward opposite coasts. And I know that my thinking has often been clarified, corrected, and extended through continuing conversations with colleagues, students as well as faculty, in the Economics Department at the University of Washington. I am deeply grateful especially to Douglass North, for the opportunity to work with so many people who genuinely care about both teaching and research.

The third edition has been improved in numerous ways through the comments of Robert Bish, University of Maryland; Ronald Brandolini, Valencia Community College; William Brown, California State University, Northridge; Henry Bruton,

Williams College; P. J. Hill, Montana State University; L. Jill Mellick; Donald A. Wells, University of Arizona; Sidney Wilson, Rockland Community College; G. Winston, Princeton University; and Harvey Zabinsky, University of Kentucky. Marian Bolan deserves a special word of thanks for making so much of it legible, often on short notice and always with good humor.

My largest debt in connection with the third edition is to Judith Cox, whose critical insights as both an economist and a teacher have improved every chapter. None of the above should be blamed for the book's errors and shortcomings, except possibly Judy. She probably ought to have supplemented rational arguments with threats in a few cases. For the forms and colors whose primacy I too often forget, I am grateful to my wife, Juliana.

Paul Heyne

Contents

With gratitude to my joint authors, Wallie and Ruth

The Theory of Economics does not furnish a
body of settled conclusions immediately applicable
to policy. It is a method rather than a
doctrine, an apparatus of the mind, a technique
of thinking which helps its possessor to draw
correct conclusions.

John Maynard Keynes

Chapter 1

The Economic Way of Thinking

Good mechanics can locate the problem in your car because they know how your car functions when it *isn't having any problems*. A lot of people find economic problems baffling and perplexing because they do *not* have any clear notion of how an economic system works when it's working well. They are like mechanics whose training has been limited entirely to the study of malfunctioning engines.

When we have long taken something for granted, it's hard even to see what it is that we've grown accustomed to. That's why we rarely notice the existence of order in society and cannot recognize the mechanisms of social coordination upon which we depend every day. A good way to begin the study of economics, therefore, might be with astonishment at the feats of social cooperation in which we daily engage. Rush-hour traffic is an excellent example.

Recognizing Order

You are supposed to gasp at that suggestion. "Rush-hour traffic as an example of social *cooperation*? Shouldn't that be used to illustrate the law of the jungle or the *breakdown* of social cooperation?" Not at all. If the association that pops into your mind when someone says "rush-hour traffic" is "traffic jam," you are neatly supporting the thesis that we notice only failures and take success so much for granted we aren't even aware of it. The dominant characteristic of rush-hour traffic is not jam but movement, which is why people venture into it day after day and almost always reach their destinations. It doesn't work perfectly, of course. (Name one thing that does.) But the remarkable fact at which we should learn to marvel is that it works at all. Think about it.

Thousands of people leave their homes at about eight in the morning, slide into their automobiles, and head for work. They all choose their own routes without any consultation. They have diverse skills, differing attitudes toward risk, and varying degrees of courtesy. As these passenger automobiles in their wide assortment of sizes and shapes enter, move along, and exit from the intersecting corridors that make up the city's traffic veins and arteries, they are joined by an even more heterogeneous mixture of trucks, buses, motorcycles, and taxicabs. The drivers all pursue their separate objectives with an almost single-minded devotion to their own interests, not necessarily because they are selfish but simply because none of them knows anything about the objectives of the others. What each one does know about the others is confined to a few observations on the position, direction, and velocity of a changing handful of vehicles in the immediate environment. To this they add the important assumption that other drivers are about as eager to avoid an accident as they themselves are. There are general rules, of course, which everyone is expected to obey, such as stopping for red lights and staying close to the speed limit. That's about it, however. The entire arrangement as just described could be a prescription for chaos. It ought to end in heaps of mangled steel.

What ensues instead is a smoothly coordinated flow, a flow so smooth, in fact, that an aerial view from a distance can almost be a source of aesthetic pleasure. There they are—all those independently operated vehicles down below, inserting themselves into the momentary spaces between other vehicles, staying so close and yet rarely touching, cutting across one another's paths with only a second or two separating a safe passage from a jarring collision, accelerating when space opens before them and slowing down when it contracts. The movement of rush-hour traffic, or indeed of urban traffic at any time of day, really is an astounding feat of social cooperation.

The Importance of Social Cooperation

The traffic example is particularly effective in making us see how much social cooperation we totally fail to notice, because everyone is familiar with traffic but almost no one thinks of it as a cooperative endeavor. But the example is also useful in making the point that we are dependent on mechanisms of coordination for far more than what we usually think of as "economic" goods. If we had no working procedures to induce cooperation, we could enjoy none of the benefits of civilization. "In such a condition," as Thomas Hobbes (1588–1679) observed in an often-quoted passage of his *Leviathan*:

> . . . there is no place for industry, because the fruit thereof is uncertain; and consequently no culture of the earth; no navigation, nor use of the commodities that may be imported by sea; no commodious building; no instruments of moving and removing such things as require much force; no knowledge of the face of the earth; no account of time; no arts; no letters; no society; and, which is worst of all, continual fear, and danger of violent death; and the life of man, solitary, poor, nasty, brutish, and short.[1]

Because Hobbes believed that people were so committed to self-preservation and personal satisfaction that only force (or the threat of it) could keep them from constantly assaulting one another, his writings emphasize only the most basic form of social cooperation: abstention from violence and robbery. He seems to have supposed that if people could be induced not to attack one another's persons or property, then positive cooperation—the kind that actually produces industry, agriculture, knowledge, and art—would develop of its own accord. But will it? Why should it?

How Does It Happen?

By what means do the members of a society induce one another to take precisely those complexly interconnected actions that will eventually produce the multitude of goods, tangible and intangible, that we all enjoy? Even a society of saints must use some procedures for inducing positive cooperation *of the right kind* if the life of each saint is to be more than "solitary, poor, nasty, brutish, and short." Saints must, after all, somehow find out exactly what ought to be done and when and where it ought to be done before they can play an effective part in helping others.

Hobbes probably failed to see the importance of this question for understanding life in the "commonwealth," because the society he knew was far simpler, more bound by custom and tradition, and less subject to rapid and disruptive change than the societies in which we have grown up. Not until late in the eighteenth century, as a matter of fact, did any significant number of thinkers begin to wonder why it was that society "worked"—that individuals pursuing their own interests

1. Hobbes, *Leviathan, or the Matter, Forme and Power of a Commonwealth Ecclesiastical and Civil*, 1651.

on the basis of extremely limited information nonetheless managed to produce, not chaos, but a remarkably ordered society.

One of the most perceptive and surely the most influential of these eighteenth century thinkers was Adam Smith (1723–1790). Smith lived in an age when most educated people believed that only the diligent attentions of political rulers could prevent a society from degenerating into disorder and poverty. Smith did not agree. But in order to refute the accepted opinion of his day, he had to describe the mechanism of social coordination that he saw operating in society, a mechanism that not only functioned, in his judgment, without the constant attention of government, but worked so powerfully that it often cancelled the effects of contrary governmental policies. Adam Smith published his analysis in 1776 as *An Inquiry into the Nature and Causes of the Wealth of Nations*, and thereby established his claim to the title, *Founder of Economics*. He did not *invent* "the economic way of thinking." But he developed it more extensively than any of his predecessors had done, and he was the first writer to use it in a comprehensive analysis of social change and social cooperation.

An Apparatus of the Mind

What exactly do we mean by *the economic way of thinking*? To begin with, it is exactly what the term suggests: an approach, rather than a set of conclusions. John Maynard Keynes phrased it aptly in the statement quoted on the frontispiece to this book:

> The Theory of Economics does not furnish a body of settled conclusions immediately applicable to policy. It is a method rather than a doctrine, an apparatus of the mind, a technique of thinking which helps its possessor to draw correct conclusions.

But what is this "technique of thinking"? It is, most fundamentally, an assumption about what guides human behavior. The theories of economics, with surprisingly few exceptions, are simply extensions of the assumption that individuals take those actions which they think will yield them the largest net advantage. Everyone, it is assumed, acts in accordance with that rule: miser or spendthrift, saint or sinner, consumer or seller, politician or business executive, cautious calculator or spontaneous improviser.

But don't misunderstand. Economic theory does not assume that people are selfish, or materialistic, or short-sighted, or irresponsible, or interested exclusively in money. None of these is implied by the statement that people try to secure for themselves the largest possible net advantage. Everything depends on what, in fact, people find in their own interest. As we know, some derive enormous satisfaction from helping people. A few, unfortunately, seem to derive satisfaction from actually hurting others. Some find their keenest pleasure in the sight of roses blooming. Others would far rather speculate on urban real estate.

But if people are all that different, how can economic theory explain or predict anything about their behavior merely by assuming that they all try to maximize their own interests? What does the assumption imply except that people do what they want to do, whatever that is?

Matters aren't quite that hopeless, for people do not really seem to be as different in their interests as the contrasts above would suggest. All of us regularly and successfully predict the behavior of people whom we have never even met, and we could not function effectively in society without the ability to do so. (Rush-hour traffic flow, for example, would be impossible if we could not predict the actions of others completely unknown to us.) Moreover, in any society that uses money extensively, just about everybody prefers more money to less, because money offers a general command over the resources that can be used to advance one's interests, whatever they may be. This is a most useful fact to know when we are trying to predict the behavior of others.

It is also a useful piece of information when we want to *influence* the behavior of others. And that brings us back to the issue of social cooperation and to a second prominent characteristic of the economic way of thinking. Economic theory asserts that the actions people take in the pursuit of their own interests create the alternatives available to others, and that social coordination is a process of continuing mutual adjustment to the changing net advantages that their interactions generate. That is a very abstract argument. We can make it more concrete by referring once more to traffic flow.

Cooperation through Mutual Adjustment

Picture a four-lane freeway, with all the entrances and exits on the right. Why don't all the drivers stay in the far right lane? Why do some of them go to the trouble of driving all the way over to the far left when they know they'll have to come back to the right lane to exit? Anyone who has driven on a freeway knows the answer: the traffic flow is impeded in the right-hand lane by slow-moving entrants and exiters, so people in a hurry get out of the right-hand lane as quickly as possible.

Which of the other lanes will they choose? Although we can't predict in the case of any single driver, we know that they will disperse themselves quite evenly among the three other lanes. But why does this happen? How does it happen? The answer is also the explanation of what we meant just now by *a process of continuing mutual adjustment to the changing net advantages that their actions generate*. Drivers are alert to the net advantages of each lane and therefore try to move out of any lanes that are moving slowly and into ones that are moving faster. This speeds up the slow lanes and slows down the fast lanes until all lanes are moving at the same rate, or, more accurately, until no driver perceives any net advantage to be gained by changing lanes. It all happens quickly, continuously, and far more effectively than if someone at the entrances passed out tickets *assigning* each vehicle to a particular lane.

That, according to the economic way of thinking, is how the social world works. Individuals choose their actions on the basis of the net advantages they expect. Their actions alter, however minutely, the relative benefits and costs of the options that others perceive. When the ratio of expected benefit to expected cost for any action increases, people do more of it. When the ratio falls, they do less. The fact that almost everyone prefers more money to less is an enormous aid in this process, an extremely important lubricant, if you will, in the mechanism of social coordination. Modest changes in the monetary cost and monetary benefit of particular options can induce large numbers of people to alter their behavior in directions more consistent with what other people are concurrently doing. And this is the primary system by which we obtain cooperation among the members of society in using what is available to provide what people want.

How Much Does Economic Theory Explain?

Some might object that the preceding paragraph claims too much. "You have not given a description of 'how the social world works' but only of how the economic part of its works. You have described the market system. But that's not the whole of society. In addition to the market or economic sector, we have other institutions (such as the government sector) that operate by different principles and procedures."

That sounds like a reasonable objection, or at least one consistent with the traditional ways in which we have learned to divide up the world. But the economic way of thinking is subversive when it comes to those traditional distinctions. If it makes sense to explain the output of the Bethlehem Steel Company and the Chrysler Corporation as the product of competing interests mutually adjusted, why won't it make sense to explain the output of the United States Congress or the Department of Energy in the same way? Why draw a line between "the economy" and "the government"? Isn't every branch and agency of government made up, just like any other social group, of ordinary mortals with a wide variety of interests? The necessity of inducing others to cooperate does not stop when the capital city is reached! Or if it does, someone has neglected to communicate that fact to the lobbyists, legislative leaders, staff assistants, and executive agents who struggle daily to shape the directions of government action.

To tell the embarrassing truth, economic theorists are highly imperialistic. They tend to think that their way of looking at society explains everything, or at least explains more occurrences more adequately than does any other approach. And so economists have been venturing out in recent years to raid territories traditionally occupied by sociologists, political scientists, historians, and others. Economists don't all agree (and representatives of the raided disciplines *surely* do not all agree) that these excursions have always captured valuable terrain. Some critics of the imperialistic ambitions of economics have even accused it of saying nothing about everything. We won't try to resolve those disputes at this point. But you should be aware in advance that this book will draw no clear lines to mark the boundaries of economics. Instead we shall fall back upon the vague but sensible principle that economic theory should be used wherever it successfully explains or predicts and abandoned for something else whenever it sheds no light.

The Biases of Economic Theory

The admission that economics has imperialistic ambitions may not disturb you as much as our admission now that *the economic way of thinking is a biased perspective*. Economic theory does not offer an unprejudiced view of society, in which all the facts are presented and each is given the same weight. On the contrary, the economic way of thinking selects a few facts to emphasize out of a vast array of possibilities and discards most of what remains.

To begin with, economic theory focuses on the *choices* people make. It largely neglects the factors responsible for the restricted range of choices available to them. Economic theory is so centrally concerned with choice, in fact, that some critics have accused it of assuming that people choose to be poor or choose to be unemployed. When we come to the issues of poverty and unemployment, you can decide for yourself whether this is a fair criticism or a misunderstanding. But there can be no doubt that economic theory attempts to explain the social world by assuming that events are the product of people's choices.

Closely related to this focus on choice is the emphasis

People choose.

Only individual persons choose.

People choose rationally.

All interactions among people's choices can be viewed as market processes.

economic theory gives to the *individual*. Because only individuals actually choose, economists try to dissect the decisions of such collectivities as governments, universities, or corporations until they locate the choices of the individual persons who make them up. This analytical individualism looks suspiciously like certain other kinds of individualism that some people dislike, such as ethical individualism or "rugged" individualism. Does economic theory miss the significance of group action and social bonds by unduly emphasizing the individual? Whatever the merit or lack of merit in this charge, the economic way of thinking definitely does make the individual the ultimate unit of explanation.

Economic theory is also criticized by some as false or misleading because of its emphasis on *rationality*. Economists assume that people do not act capriciously, that they compare the expected costs and benefits of available opportunities before they act, and that they learn from and therefore do not repeat their mistakes. But are people really that rational? Aren't our actions guided more by unconscious urges and unexamined impulses than all this would admit? The question is again a hard one to answer, because it is a hard question even to pose in any clear and testable form. But while economists do not claim that people know everything or never make mistakes, the economic way of thinking does indeed assume that people's actions follow from calculations of costs and benefits.

Another charge often leveled against the economic way of thinking—or perhaps against the way in which it is sometimes used, as in this book—is that it harbors a *promarket* bias. This criticism, too, calls attention to a genuine and significant characteristic of economic theory, although a characteristic that may not be altogether what it seems to be. Economic theory does not really assume that markets work better than alternative institutions, notably government. Rather it assumes, as we have already indicated, that however poorly or well *any* institution functions, its functioning can best be understood as a consequence of market processes. Exaggerating somewhat for emphasis, we could say that economic theory does not find market solutions better (or worse) than government solutions, because it insists that government solutions *are* market solutions. The actions of government are the outcomes of market processes: individuals pursuing their own interests and mutually adjusting to one another's behavior, but doing so in the context of the special "rules of the game" that apply to the institutions that we call government.

Biases or Conclusions?

These are four prominent (and interrelated) biases inherent in the economic way of thinking. But are they really biases or prejudices? Why couldn't we call them convictions (or even conclusions), and simply say that economists explain social phenomena by postulating interaction among the rational choices of individuals, because this enables them to understand those phenomena? Do we say that astronomers are biased because they assume that all the light they observe has traveled toward them at 186,000 miles per second, or that biologists are biased because they assume that DNA molecules control the development of organisms?

The questions we are raising now are important and interesting.[2] But we cannot follow them further without pushing this chapter to an intolerable length. It has long seemed obvious to the author, however (a prejudice or a conclusion?), that the search for knowledge of any kind necessarily begins with some *commitments* on the part of the inquirer. We cannot approach the world with a completely open mind, because we were not born yesterday. And completely open minds would in any event be completely empty minds, which can learn nothing at all. All discussion, every inquiry, and even each act of observation is rooted in and grows out of convictions. We cannot begin everywhere or with everything. We must begin somewhere with something. We proceed from where we find ourselves and on the basis of what we believe to be true, important, useful, or enlightening. We may, of course, be wrong in any of these judgments. Indeed, we are always wrong to some extent, since every "true" statement necessarily leaves out a great deal else that is also true and thus errs by omission.

We cannot avoid this risk, as some people suppose, by steering clear of theory. People who sneer at "fancy theories" and prefer to rely on common sense and everyday experience are often in fact the victims of extremely vague and sweeping hypotheses. Consider this actual letter to a newspaper from a young person in Pennsylvania who was once "one of a group of teenage pot smokers. Then a girl in the crowd got pregnant. Her baby was premature and deformed and needed two operations." The newspaper's adviser to the teenage lovelorn printed that letter approvingly, as evidence that the price of smoking marijuana is high.

Perhaps it is. But suppose the writer of that letter had written: "Then the Pittsburgh Steelers won the Super Bowl, and the Philadelphia Flyers took the Stanley Cup." Everyone would object that those events had nothing to do with the group's pot smoking. *But how do we know that?* If the mere

---

2. The thoughtful student who would like to pursue these issues further should be sure to read *The Structure of Scientific Revolutions* by Thomas S. Kuhn (Chicago: University of Chicago Press, 1962). This highly readable essay on the history and philosophy of science has had an enormous influence in recent years on the thinking of social scientists about the respective roles of assumption and evidence in their investigations.

fact that the young girl's misfortunes followed her pot smoking is evidence of a causal relationship, why can't we also infer a causal relationship in the case of the Steelers and the Flyers?

No Theory Means Poor Theory

The point is a simple but important one. We cannot discover, prove, or even suspect any kind of causal relationship without having a theory in mind. Our observations of the world are in fact drenched with theory, which is why we usually can make sense out of the buzzing confusion that assaults our eyes and ears. Actually we observe only a small fraction of what we "know," a hint here and a suggestion there. The rest we fill in from the theories we hold, small ones and broad ones, vague and precise ones, well tested and poorly tested, widely held and sometimes peculiar, carefully reasoned and dimly recognized.

I. M. D. Little is a distinguished British economist who worked for a time as an adviser to the British treasury. He later wrote an article describing his experiences and discussing the usefulness of economic theory in the world of policymaking. Here is an interesting paragraph:

> Economic theory teaches one how economic magnitudes are related, and how very complex and involved these relationships are. Noneconomists tend to be too academic. They abstract too much from the real world. No one can think about economic issues without some theory, for the facts and relationships are too involved to organize themselves: they do not simply fall into place. But if the theorist is untutored, he is apt to construct a very partial theory which blinds him to some of the possibilities. Or he falls back on some old and over-simple theory, picked up from somewhere or other. He is also, I believe, apt to interpret the past naively. *Post hoc ergo propter hoc*[3] is seldom an adequate economic explanation. I was sometimes shocked by the naive sureness with which very questionable bits of economic analysis were advanced in Whitehall. Of course, economists may be too academic in another sense: they may not appreciate administrative difficulties, or may lack a sense of political possibility. But, then, there is no danger of these things being overlooked.[4]

"Noneconomists tend to be too academic. They abstract too much from the real world!" That isn't the way you usually hear it. But Little is probably correct. "I don't know anything about fancy economic theory," the confident amateur begins, "but I do know this. . . ." And what he says next demonstrates all too

"*People's incomes rise on average when they move from rural to urban areas. They also become more likely to commit a crime. Why not reduce the crime rate by taxing the income of those who migrate from the country to the city?*"

---

3. Literally, "After this, therefore because of this"; the logical fallacy of assuming that A must have caused B if A preceded B in time. The argument of the penitent Pennsylvania pot smoker is an example.

4. I. M. D. Little, "The Economist in Whitehall," *Lloyds Bank Review* (April 1957).

often that he was quite right in denying any knowledge of economic theory, but quite wrong in supposing that this preserved him from error. Those who try to reason about complex economic interrelationships without theory usually manage only to reason with very poor theory.

None of this should be interpreted as a wholesale defense of economists, who sometimes like to dazzle the public with complex theorems and exercises in pure logic instead of addressing the questions people are actually asking. Even in the teaching of economics, we have often behaved as if all the students enrolled in an introductory course were aiming at a Ph.D. in the subject, and that it was our duty to begin their preparation for the doctoral exams. That's probably why introductory courses typically serve up so many more ideas than students can possibly digest.

This textbook developed out of a growing suspicion that when students found economic theory mystifying and tedious, it was largely because we economists were trying to teach them too much. This book very consciously sets out, therefore, to achieve more by attempting less. It is organized around a set of concepts that collectively make up the economist's basic kit of intellectual tools. The tools are all related to the fundamental assumptions discussed above and are surprisingly few in number. But they are extraordinarily versatile. They unlock such mysteries as foreign exchange rates, business firms that make profits by accepting losses, the nature of money, and different prices charged for "identical" goods—mysteries that are generally conceded to be in the economist's province. But they also shed light on a wide range of issues that are not ordinarily thought of as economic at all—traffic congestion, environmental pollution, the workings of government, and the behavior of college administrators—to mention just a few which you will encounter in the chapters ahead.

The primary goal of this book is to start you thinking the way economists think, in the belief that once you start you will never stop. Economic thinking is addictive. Once you get inside some principle of economic reasoning and make it your own, opportunities to use it pop up everywhere. You begin to notice that much of what is said or written about economic and social issues is a mixture of sense and nonsense. You get in the habit of sorting the sense from the nonsense by applying the basic concepts of economic analysis. You may even, unfortunately, acquire the reputation of being a cynic, for people who habitually talk nonsense like to cry "cynic" at anyone who points out what they are doing.

Substitutes Everywhere: The Concept of Demand

You must have read or heard statements like these many times in your life:

1. Fire safety requires that there be two exits from each apartment unit.

2. We need a new car.

3. Our state will need large amounts of additional water in the coming decade.

4. Traffic surveys have established the need for a new expressway.

5. All citizens should be able to obtain the medical care they need regardless of ability to pay.

6. There is no substitute for victory.

Fire safety, water, the smooth and rapid movement of traffic, medical care, victory, and even automobiles are all "goods." We say "even" automobiles because some doubts have begun to be expressed about the goodness of automobiles in our congested cities. But you can ask the man who owns one, and a lot of young people who don't. They will assure you that a new car is very much a good. Then what's wrong with those statements?

The element common to all six is the notion of *necessity*. And that is what makes each statement seriously misleading.

Take the first one. Will apartment dwellers who live with only one exit all be injured or killed by fires? Of course not. It's just that the risk is greater with one exit than with two. But then why not three exits? Or four? Why not go the whole route and make the outside walls nothing but doors? The answer is that, while fire safety is a good, it isn't the only good apartment dwellers are interested in. Low rental costs and low heating and cooling costs are also goods, to say nothing of protection from burglars who notice that multiple exits are also multiple entrances. Moreover, there are other and perhaps better ways to increase fire safety. Extinguishers, alarm sprinklers, and large ashtrays also reduce the risk to apartment dwellers of injury or death from fire. If more than one exit is required, why not also require a fire extinguisher on every wall?

That sensible-sounding statement about apartment exits overlooks three interrelated facts: (1) Most goods are not free but can be obtained only by sacrificing something else that is also a good. (2) There are substitutes for anything. (3) Intelligent choice among substitutes requires a balancing of additional costs against additional benefits.

Costs and Substitutes

Now go back and look at the other five statements. "We need a new car." Who *needs* a new car? Obviously only those who value a new car more than what they must sacrifice to obtain one. That might be a vacation trip this year, new clothes, a lot of movies, and a stereo set. Is it worth it? There are, after all, plenty of substitutes for a new car: an overhaul of the present one, a used car, a bicycle, a car pool, public transportation, moving closer to work, or staying home more. The intelligent consumer tries to determine his or her preferences after considering these various costs and benefits. (Of course, once a man has made up his mind, he might still want to say "We *need* a new car" in the hope that the definitive tone of his statement will dissuade his wife from making her own comparison of the costs and benefits of a new one.)

Consider statement 3: "Our state will need large amounts of additional water in the coming decade." Does any state really need large amounts of additional water? Dams and reservoirs, pipelines, and desalinization plants are ways of obtaining more water. But they have costs. Do the benefits justify the costs? If you think there are no substitutes for water, then you are thinking too academically. You have abstracted in a seriously misleading way from the real world. Probably you are assuming that water is used primarily for drinking, whereas in fact the overwhelming bulk of the water consumed in the United States goes for other uses. Since we shall use the case of water a bit later as an extended working exercise, we can pass this problem by for now. You might want to begin thinking, though, about the substitutes for water in such places of chronic scarcity as Arizona and Southern California.

You will be able to make much more sense out of the water problem and the expressway issue we take up next if you keep in mind that entities like *states* or *cities* never really want anything. Wants and goals are always attached ultimately to individuals. What does the person who says "The people want . . ." really mean? That all the people want it? A majority? Those who count? It is usually a good rule in analyzing statements like those above to ask: *Who* wants more water, or more expressways, or more fire safety?

> Things are seldom what they seem.
> Skim milk masquerades as cream.

The fourth of our misleading propositions—"Traffic surveys have established the need for a new expressway"—leads into one of the vexing issues in city planning. Perhaps it would never have become such a troublesome issue had we realized that expressways have costs as well as benefits, that there are excellent substitutes for more expressways, and that intelligent city planning calls for the weighing of additional benefits against additional costs. Those who hope to derive most of the benefits from a new expressway while paying only a small percentage of the costs will not want others to notice the full costs of the expressway or how many substitutes there really are. That is why they pretend that a traffic survey can establish "needs." But a traffic survey only shows how many cars travel given routes *at existing costs to the drivers*, including such nonmonetary costs as delay, danger, and ulcers. Suppose that the cost of downtown parking increased 500 percent. What do you think would happen to rush-hour traffic? Commuters would form car pools and begin using public transportation. If the cost *to drivers* of commuting were made high enough, through parking charges, toll fees, or some other device, the need for a new expressway could turn overnight into a "need" for a rapid transit system. It's a strange kind of need that can vanish so quickly in the face of a price change.

It's amazing what people will want--- if they think they won't have to pay for it.

The fifth statement sounds humanitarian and liberal. "All citizens should be able to obtain the medical care they need regardless of ability to pay." But how much medical care does any person need? We might all agree that a woman with an inflamed appendix and no money should have an appendectomy completely at the taxpayers' expense if she is unable to meet any of the costs herself. But what of the man with a splinter in his finger? The services of physicians are not free goods, and they would not become free goods even if every physician treated patients without charging a fee. There just would not be enough physicians to go around if everyone consulted a doctor for every minor ill. The lower the price of visiting a physician, the more frequently will people substitute a trip to the doctor for such other remedies as going to bed, taking it easy, or waiting and hoping. One could rather confidently predict that lower monetary fees would result in higher fees of other sorts, like waiting in line for many hours.

What about the sixth statement: "There is no substitute for victory"? It just isn't so. That may be a good battle cry, but it's unrealistic political analysis. Victory is usually obtained by making sacrifices. If the sacrifices reach a certain intensity, people choose compromise or even defeat, although they are then inclined to *say* that they have "no choice." Once again we notice that the intelligent formulation of policy, including foreign policy, flows from a careful balancing of additional expected costs and additional expected benefits.

The word *expected* should be stressed. We live in a world of uncertainty, forced to make choices that will affect our future without knowing for sure just how they will do so. A common mistake in reasoning about economic problems is to assume that there is no uncertainty or that economic decision makers are omniscient. At last report, omniscience was still a virtue denied to mortals. Condemned as we are to living with uncertainty, we can at least keep from making matters worse by pretending otherwise. Be alert for statements, in this book and elsewhere, which assume that completely adequate information is always available. You might even notice that information, too, is a good which has costs of acquisition and for which there are substitutes available.

The Concept of Demand

"Needs" turn out to be mere "wants" when we inspect them closely. That's an important difference, for in the case of wants we may ask: "How *urgently* are they wanted?" Economists get at this question through the concept of *demand*. Demand is a concept that *relates amounts that are purchased to the sacrifices that must be made to obtain these amounts.*

Ask yourself the following questions: How many records do you want to own? How many times do you want to go out to dinner in a year? What grade do you want from this course?

If you can answer any of those questions, it is because you have assumed some cost in each case. Suppose you said you want an A from this course and plan to get one. What difference would it make if the price of an A went up? The teacher isn't taking bribes; the price of an A *to you* (that's what counts) is the sacrifice you must make to obtain it. Would you still want an A if it required twenty hours of study a week, whereas a B could be had for just one hour a week? You might still want it, but you would probably not be willing to buy it at such a high price when a fairly good substitute, a B, is so much cheaper. And that is what counts. Human wants seem to be insatiable. But when a want can only be satisfied at some cost—that is to say, by giving up the satisfying of some other wants to obtain it—we all moderate our desires and accept less than we would like to have.

The phenomenon of which we're speaking is so fundamental that some economists have been willing to assign it the status of a law: *the law of demand*. This law asserts that there is a negative relation between the amount of anything that people will purchase and the price (sacrifice) they must pay to obtain it. At higher prices, less will be purchased; at lower prices, more will be purchased.

Would you agree that this generalization can be called a law? Or can you think of exceptions? Genuine exceptions, if they exist at all, are rare. Why would people be indifferent to the sacrifices they must make? Or prefer more sacrifice to less? That is what a person would be doing who took *more* of something as the cost of obtaining it *increased*.

Alleged exceptions to the law of demand are usually based on a misinterpretation of the evidence. Masochists, for example, would not provide an exception, because pain is for them a good and not a sacrifice. But what of the familiar case where the price of something rises and people increase their purchases in anticipation of further price rises? If you think about it carefully you will see that this is not an exception to the law of demand. The expectation of higher prices in the future, created by the initial price rise, has increased people's current demand for the item. They want to buy more now so they can buy less later. It is not the higher price but the changed *expectations* that have caused people to buy more at the present time. We would observe something quite different if the initial price increase did *not* create those changed expectations. Moreover, those whose expectation of further price increases has prompted them to purchase sooner than they otherwise would have will still consider the sacrifice they must make in deciding how much to buy.

Let's stock up now before the price goes even higher!

It has sometimes been argued that certain prestige goods are exceptions to the law of demand. For example, people supposedly buy mink coats because their price is high, not low. No doubt there are people who buy some items largely to impress others with how much they can afford to pay. And people sometimes, in the absence of better information, judge quality by price, so that over a limited range, at least, their willingness to purchase may be positively rather than negatively related to price.

Even these seeming exceptions can be explained, however,

in a way consistent with the law of demand. People may be purchasing prestige rather than mere mink, or judging quality by price because they have no better information. But cases such as these are rare curiosities at most. Whether or not you are willing to call it a law, the fact is undeniable and extremely important: increases in the price of goods will characteristically be accompanied by decreases in the total amount purchased, and decreases in price will characteristically be accompanied by increases in the amount purchased. It is a serious mistake to overlook this relationship.

Misperceptions Caused by Inflation

There is another reason why many people think that the law of demand doesn't operate: they have forgotten to take the effects of inflation into account. In an era of rapid inflation, such as the United States and much of the rest of the world have been experiencing in recent years, most apparent price increases are not real price increases at all. The nature, causes, and consequences of inflation will be examined in detail later on in this book (beginning with Chapter 15), but inflation so distorts our perceptions of relative price and cost changes that we had better think about it before going any further. An ounce of anticipation may prevent a pound of confusion.

Inflation means an increase in the average *money* price of goods. But because we're accustomed to think of the price of anything as the quantity of money we have to sacrifice to get it, we easily conclude that twice as much money means twice as large a cost or sacrifice. That isn't the case, however, if twice as many dollars have only half as much purchasing power. If the money price of each and every good, including human labor and whatever else people sell or rent to obtain money, were to double, then *no* good would have changed in real price—except money, of course, which would have fallen by one half. And so a doubling of the price of gasoline won't necessarily induce people to use any less gasoline—*if* at the same time their incomes and the prices of all the other goods they use have also doubled.

Money prices do not, in fact, all change in equal proportion as a result of inflation—which is one of the reasons inflation is a problem. But they do tend to move together. Consequently, if we want to examine the effect of a particular price increase, we must first abstract from the effects of a general increase in prices. For example, we must not expect to discover the impact of OPEC's hikes in the price of petroleum simply by comparing the quantity of oil demanded by the U.S. in 1974 at a price of $10.95 per barrel with the quantity demanded in 1979 when the price was $13.34 per barrel. We must first adjust those dollar prices to compensate for the fall over this period in the value of a dollar. We can do that by dividing each year's oil price by some index of the U.S. price level, such as the Consumer Price Index which the Bureau of Labor Statistics calculates each month. (You will learn more about the Consumer Price Index when we take up the study of inflation.)

When we run through that procedure, we discover that from January 1974 to January 1979, the real price of a barrel of Saudi Arabian light crude actually declined about 17 percent. In other words, we had to sacrifice 17 percent less to obtain a barrel of oil at the beginning of 1979 than we had to sacrifice in 1974. Surely that fact says something about the failure of Americans to reduce their rate of oil consumption over those years. (We don't want to give you a false impression. From January 1973 to January 1974, the real price of OPEC oil *did* increase, by an impressive 310 percent.)

Demand and Quantity Demanded

There is a general lesson to be drawn from all of this. In using the concept of demand, you must remain alert for the possibility that something else has changed in addition to the price. Your best protection is a clear grasp of the distinction between *demand* and *quantity demanded*. Commentators on economic events often use the word *demand* as a shorthand term for *quantity demanded*. That can and often does lead to error, as we shall see in a moment.

Demand in economic theory is a relationship between two specific variables: price and quantity demanded. You cannot state the demand for any good simply as an amount. Demand is always a series of prices and a series of quantities (or amounts) that people would want to purchase at each of those prices. We express that fact by saying that demand is a schedule. A movement from one row of the schedule to another should always be called a change in the quantity demanded, not a change in the demand.

A short editorial in the *Wall Street Journal* in November 1977 revealed the perils awaiting those who think such verbal distinctions are too trifling to bother with. The editorial writer wanted to chide an Agriculture Department economist for his ignorance of economics, an ignorance supposedly revealed by his stating that "the power of the U.S. consumer movement" had brought the price of coffee down again after it had hit a high of $4.42 a pound. Not so, said the *Journal's* editorial writer: "The coffee market is behaving the way the basic textbooks say a market behaves: Prices go up, demand falls, and prices come down."

The basic textbooks say nothing of the sort. On the con-

A demand schedule:

Price	Quantity demanded
50¢	125,000
40¢	160,000
30¢	175,000

trary, they say that the editorial writer has confused the quantity demanded and the demand. When the price of coffee went up, the quantity demanded fell. Period. If the consumer movement managed to change people's attitudes toward serving and drinking coffee (some people got so angry about the price rises that they wouldn't drink coffee for a while at *any* price), then the consumer movement did succeed in changing the demand. And if the demand falls, *then* the price comes down. The *Journal's* mistaken logic implies, if you think about it carefully, that the price will bob up and down indefinitely, since when the price comes down again, demand ought to increase once more, causing the price to go up, whereupon the demand will fall, causing the price to go down. . . .

But it's all just a confusion of thought introduced by a careless use of terms. Think of price and quantity demanded as objects on the opposite ends of a see-saw, and demand as a large, lighter-than-air balloon to which the see-saw is attached. When price goes one way, quantity demanded goes the opposite way. Changes in the demand (movements of the balloon up or down) will exert simultaneous pressure in the same direction on both the price and the quantity demanded. The demand for any good is the product of biological realities, social relationships, psychological factors, and a broad assortment of economic variables, such as income and the price, quality, and general availability of substitutes. All these forces combine to create the demand for a particular good, the relationship that will exist between changes in its money price and changes in the quantity people will decide to obtain. Unless the demand is changing (the balloon is ascending or descending), price and quantity demanded will always move in opposite directions.

To put it most simply: The change that will *not* cause a change in the demand for bicycles is a change in the price of bicycles. If a combination of rising incomes, environmental concern, and new interest in outdoor exercise induces more people to want bicycles, the demand for them will increase. And both the price and quantity demanded may well increase as a consequence. (This actually occurred in 1971.) You have grasped the distinction between demand and quantity demanded if you see clearly why this in no way contradicts the law of demand. An increase in demand, or a shift upward and to the right in the demand curve, will pull up both price and quantity demanded. But it was still true with the high demand of 1971—as it had been with the low demand of 1969—that a smaller quantity of bicycles was demanded at higher than at lower prices. And this is what the law of demand asserts. Economic theory isolates the money price of goods for special attention because of the exceptionally important role that

money prices play in adjusting and coordinating people's behavior.

Money Costs and Other Costs

None of this implies, however, that the price in money that
must be paid for something is a complete measure of its cost to
the purchaser. Indeed sometimes it is a very inadequate measure (as in the case of the student who wanted an A). Economists know this at least as well as anyone else. The concept of
demand definitely does not suggest that money is the only thing
that matters to people. Confusion about this point has done so
much to create misunderstanding that we might profitably take
a moment to clarify the matter.

Consider the case of a woman buying soft drinks. Assume
that she can purchase them in either returnable or throwaway
bottles, and that a liter of her favorite drink is priced at $1 in the
throwaway bottle, whereas a liter in a returnable bottle is 80
cents plus a 40-cent deposit. Which will she buy? Which is
cheaper? It depends on the cost to her, of which the retailer's
price is only one element. If she doesn't mind saving and returning bottles—that is, if the cost to her of doing so is low—she
will probably find the returnable bottles cheaper and will buy
them. On the other hand, if she lives in an apartment with very
limited storage space, gets to the store rarely, consumes large
quantities of soft drinks, and has a waste-disposal chute a few
steps from her door, she may well find the throwaway bottles
cheaper and will purchase them in preference to returnable
bottles.

Now suppose that our hypothetical apartment dweller
with a passion for pop attends an ecology conference and
comes away convinced that we must recycle to survive. The
cost to her of using throwaway bottles suddenly jumps, for now
she suffers pangs of guilt every time she tosses a bottle in the
waste-disposal chute. The added cost in moral regret may be
sufficient to induce her to switch to returnable bottles.

Or it may not. Suppose that she is going on a camping trip
and wants to take along a dozen bottles of pop. She must
backpack them in to her camp site, and backpack the empties
out again if she returns the bottles. The added cost of carrying a
dozen empties may be enough to overcome the added cost of
an uneasy conscience, so that, in this case at least, she reverts to
throwaway bottles. (Of course, she will throw them in a trash
can.)

But let's change the last situation. Suppose the price of
throwaways is not $1 but $1.25, with the price of the returnable
bottle still $.80 but the deposit raised to 65¢. At *some* price we

may confidently expect that the cost of transporting empties will become less than the combined cost of buying throwaway bottles and living with guilt.

There are several lessons to be drawn from this tale of the pop bottles. To assert that people purchase less of anything as the cost to them increases does *not* imply that people pay attention only to money, or that people are selfish, or that concern for social welfare does not influence economic behavior. It *does* imply that people respond to changes in cost and—a crucial implication—that a sufficiently large change in price can be counted on to tip almost any balance. When someone says that Americans won't give up the convenience of throwaway bottles and cans unless the government outlaws them, he overlooks several possibilities. A widespread change in attitude toward the environment could overcome the cost of being inconvenienced. And a sufficiently large tax on throwaway containers (call it a deposit if you wish) would make convenience a luxury too expensive to enjoy very frequently.

The essential point in all this is that the money price of obtaining something is only one part, and occasionally even a very small part, of its cost. What the law of demand asserts is that people will do less of what they want to do as the cost to them of doing it increases, and do more as the cost decreases. But at the same time we want to remember that money is a common denominator, and therefore a most useful device for securing widespread changes in behavior. That's why economists give it so much of their attention.

Who Needs Water?

People are creatures of habit, in what they think as well as what they do. Perhaps this also explains why so many have trouble recognizing the significance of substitutes and hence such difficulty in appreciating the law of demand. Water provides an excellent example.

Back in the mid-sixties there was much concern over a serious water shortage in New York City. Several years of less than normal rainfall had depleted the city's reservoirs, and there was great fear that New York would run short of water during the summer unless consumption could be sharply reduced. A few brave souls suggested that the city should install more water meters and raise the price of water. The suggestion was not taken very seriously because, as everyone supposedly knows, water is a necessity. "People won't go thirsty just because the price of water goes up a little, or even a lot," said the critics. And so New York launched a massive campaign of education plus legal threat to try to get its citizens to be more sparing in their use of water.

Lawn sprinkling and car washing were condemned. Restaurants were told not to give customers a glass of water with their meals unless they specifically asked for it. The ornamental fountains of the city were turned off—largely as a symbolic gesture, since the water in the fountains is recirculated. Citizens were asked to refrain from keeping their beer cool by letting the shower drip on it. One of the most amusing aspects of the campaign was a set of ads for a particular Scotch whiskey that urged people to drink their Scotch with water. The word *water* was crossed out in the advertisement and *soda* was written above it, with an appended admonition to save water by drinking soda.

The water shortage was not relieved by any of these measures but by a providential end to the drought. "Man proposes but God disposes." Even man might have disposed, however, had he proposed more intelligently. The basic error lay in the assumption that water is a necessity. The truth is that there are many substitutes for water, a fact which becomes glaringly obvious as soon as we break loose from the habit of assuming that people do nothing with water except drink it.

Here are just a few of the substitutes for water in New York City: dirty automobiles, brown lawns, plumbers, migration, deodorant, larger refrigerators (to hold the beer that would otherwise be cooled in the shower), plus a host of small inconveniences. The trick is to persuade people to *use* these substitutes: to call the plumber, for example, and have that leaky toilet repaired rather than allow it to continue wasting fifty gallons of water a day. To spend money on a larger refrigerator. To tolerate a dirty automobile. To put an ice cube in their glass of drinking water, rather than let the tap run for several minutes to cool it. In the case of industries using huge quantities of water, to sacrifice the advantages of a New York location in favor of locating near more plentiful water supplies. Or to install recycling equipment.

But what is the best way to induce the use of substitutes? Educational campaigns and moral exhortation can help. But how much? Most people are expert rationalizers when their own interest is involved, and it is all too easy to put off calling the plumber until the end of the month, or next month, or the month after that. Always fully intending, of course, to do one's civic duty and get that leak repaired.

What about criminal penalties for wasting water? Enforcement becomes a problem here. Are the police to stage surprise raids to catch people cooling their beer in the shower? Shall we fine a person for rinsing a glass too many times before taking a drink? What constitutes *criminal* waste?

A quite different approach is available. Is there any way to enlist almost everyone in a conscientious effort to seek out and

PLUMBER'S BILL	WATER BILL
$ 26.00	$ 42.00

use substitutes for water? A sizable increase in the price of water just might do the job. Wouldn't the careless householder call the plumber more quickly if that leaky toilet cost more per month than the plumber would charge to fix it? Wouldn't people accept dirty automobiles more readily, or at least not let the hose run the whole time they were washing the car, if water became very expensive? There is some price for water at which it becomes cheaper to buy a new refrigerator than to use the shower as a cooler. Industries that use large quantities of water will tend to locate elsewhere if the price of water is high in their area of first choice.

And so it goes. There are substitutes for anything. A higher money price will induce some people to find and use some of those substitutes. And the higher the price, the more will substitutes be used.

A Useful Device

Many of the most useful concepts in economics can be conviently expressed by means of graphs.

Suppose that we somehow obtained the following data on the relation between the price per gallon of water and the number of gallons that would be consumed (not swallowed!) per day in New York City at each of these different prices:

Price Charged the Consumer per Gallon	Millions of Gallons Consumed per Day
$.0035	60
.0028	80
.0021	120
.0016	160
.0012	200
.0009	240
.0003	360
.0001	450
.0000	510

We graphed these values in Figure 2A. The dots express graphically the data from the demand schedule above. If you are not accustomed to working with graphs, study Figure 2A until you understand exactly how it was constructed from the demand schedule.

The graph of Figure 2A also *adds* something to the information contained in the schedule. We have connected the dots by means of straight lines. The assumption underlying this procedure is that the price can be changed by very small amounts and that, as a result, there will be small continuous changes in the daily consumption of water. When dealing with the total demand of a large number of consumers, it will be easy to find an individual who makes no response to a small

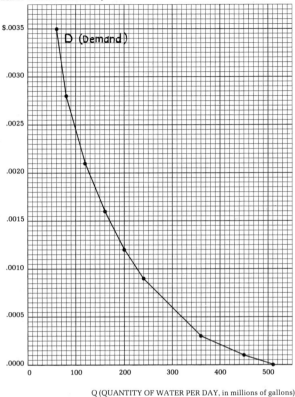

P (PRICE OF WATER PER GALLON)

Q (QUANTITY OF WATER PER DAY, in millions of gallons)

Figure 2A Demand curve for water

price increase. But for others the small increase will be the straw that breaks the camel's back: the new expense that finally prompts a call to the plumber, for example, and an end to the leaking toilet.

Now use the demand curve in thinking through the following questions. (By the way, it is called a demand *curve* even though it is composed exclusively of straight lines.)

1. How much water do New Yorkers "need"? How much will they consume per day if the price of water is zero? Is there an important difference between the two questions?

2. If the price of water has been set for many years at $.0008 per gallon, how much water will the city authorities say that New Yorkers need per day? What are they assuming when they say this?

3. Suppose that New York's reservoirs are being rapidly depleted, and experts predict that the supply will become critically low before fall unless daily consumption is reduced to 180 million gallons. How could the city's water managers obtain this desired reduction in consumption?

4. Notice by how much water consumption would increase if the price were originally $.0035 and were then decreased to $.0003. Do you think that residents of the city would increase their *drinking* by this amount? How might the additional 300 million gallons per day be used?

Time Is on Our Side

If you are at all the suspicious sort of person, you will have wondered whether water consumption really would or could change in response to price changes by as much as the demand curve indicates. Changes take time. And that is an important observation. Changes in the amount purchased will be greater for any given price change the longer the time period allowed for adjustment.

Check this out for yourself with a mental experiment. Suppose the price of water has been $.0003 a gallon for twenty years and it is raised overnight to $.0028. What substitutions for water will be made *right away*? What substitutions would you expect to observe after a month or two had passed? What substitutions would you expect to observe over the next ten years—assuming that everyone expects the price to remain at the higher level?

But an even better example is gasoline. How high will the price of gasoline have to go before Americans reduce their consumption? Don't answer without first noting that the price hasn't gone up by nearly as much as the newspaper headlines suggest. It's the *relative* price that matters, and much of the increase in the price of gasoline since 1972 is merely an infla- tion-induced rise in its *money* price. The 1972 price of 38¢ per gallon for regular would have been 62 cents at the beginning of 1979 if gasoline prices had merely gone up at the rate of infla- tion. The question is nonetheless a good one: How large a relative price increase will it take to cut gasoline consumption by 10 percent or 25 percent or even 50 percent? The answer clearly depends on time: both the time allowed for adjustments and the time period over which these higher prices are expected to remain in force. People will buy cars that use less fuel, will move closer to work, and will arrange carpools if the price of gasoline rises far enough, but they won't do so at once. More- over, they will delay such decisions longer the less sure they are that the higher price is going to stick. If every belligerent statement against OPEC by a prominent political figure fans the hope for lower prices soon, it will induce some to live just a little longer with their much-loved gas guzzlers.

By taking our examples almost entirely from the area of household decisions, we may have obscured the important fact that customers include producers as well as consumers. Business firms use water and gasoline, too, and they sometimes use so much that they are exceptionally sensitive to price changes. You'll be neglecting some of the major factors that cause demand curves to slope downward if you overlook the contribution producers make to the demand for many goods. In the case of water, location decisions are often made on the basis of the expected price of water, and those decisions then affect the quantities demanded in different geographic areas.

But it takes time for customers to find and begin to use substitutes. It also takes time for producers to devise, produce, and publicize substitutes. As a result, the amount by which people increase or decrease their purchases when prices change depends very much on the time period over which we are observing the adjustment. Occasionally even a rather large price increase (or decrease) will lead to no significant decrease (or increase) in consumption—*at first*. And this sometimes causes people to conclude that price has no effect on consumption. A very mistaken conclusion! Nothing in this world happens instantaneously. People, creatures of habit that they are, must be allowed time to prove that there are substitutes for anything.

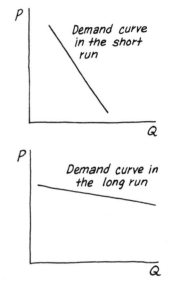

Price Elasticity of Demand

It is extremely cumbersome to talk about "the amount by which people increase or decrease their purchases when the price changes." But this is an important relationship with many useful applications. So economists have invented a special phrase that summarizes the relationship. The formal title of the concept is *price elasticity of demand*.

That's an appropriate name. Elasticity means responsiveness. If the amount of any good that people purchase changes substantially in response to a small change in price, demand is said to be elastic. If even a very large price change results in little change in the amount purchased, demand is said to be inelastic.

Price elasticity of demand is defined precisely as *the percentage change in quantity demanded divided by the percentage change in price*. Thus, if a 10 percent increase in the price of eggs leads to a 5 percent reduction in the number of eggs sold, the elasticity of demand is 5 percent divided by 10 percent, or .5. To be completely accurate, it is *minus* .5, since price and amount purchased vary inversely. But for simplicity we shall ignore the minus sign and treat all coefficients of elasticity as if they were positive.

Whenever the coefficient of elasticity is greater than one (ignoring the sign)—that is to say, whenever the percentage change in quantity purchased is *greater* than the percentage

$$\frac{\% \ change \ in \ Q}{\% \ change \ in \ P}$$

change in price—demand is said to be elastic. Whenever the coefficient of elasticity is less than one, which means whenever the percentage change in quantity purchased is *less* than the percentage change in price, demand is said to be inelastic. Compulsive learners will want to know what is said when the percentage change in quantity is exactly equal to the percentage change in price, so that the coefficient of demand elasticity is exactly one. You may file away the information that demand is then *unit elastic*. (Economics is a very systematic discipline.)

You can begin to familiarize yourself with the uses of this concept by asking whether demand is elastic or inelastic in each case below. Each case is discussed in the subsequent paragraphs.

1. "People aren't going to buy much more no matter how far we cut the price."

2. "This is a competitive business. We would lose half our customers if we raised our prices by as little as 2 percent."

3. The demand for salt.

4. The demand for Morton's salt.

5. The demand for Morton's salt at the Kroger store at Fifth and Main.

6. "The university's total receipts from tuition would actually increase if tuition rates were cut by 20 percent."

7. "It's odd but true. Wheat farmers would gross more money if they all got together and burned one-quarter of this year's crop."

8. If the statement in 7 is true, does it follow that wheat farmers could gross even more money by burning one-half of the crop?

Thinking about Elasticity

1. "People aren't going to buy much more no matter how far we cut the price." If a businessman doubts that even a very large price decrease will do much to increase his sales, he believes that his demand is highly inelastic. He will obviously not want to lower his price under such circumstances, for he will lose more through the lower price than he will gain through the larger volume. But if people don't respond very much to a price cut, will they also be relatively insensitive to a price hike? If they are, a businessman out to increase his income will want to raise his price. Businessmen typically complain that prices are too low. Then why don't they raise their prices? It's a free country, isn't it? The answer, of course, is that they would usually lose too many customers if they did so. It is the elastic-

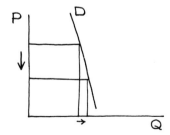

ity of demand that determines whether or not a businessman can add to his money receipts by raising his prices.

2. "This is a competitive business. We would lose half our customers if we raised our prices by as little as 2 percent." The businesswoman making this statement is saying in effect that she faces a highly elastic demand: a 50 percent decline in quantity demanded would follow a mere 2 percent increase in price. The coefficient of elasticity is 25. The demand is very elastic indeed. Another way of putting it would be to say that her customers are extremely sensitive to any price change. And that makes it difficult for her to raise her prices, however eager she might be to do so.

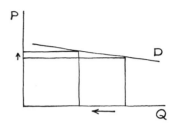

3. The demand for salt. What makes demand curves elastic or inelastic? The availability of good substitutes is clearly an important factor. Another is the importance of the item in the budget of purchasers. If the expenditure on some good is large relative to the income or wealth of the purchaser, he will be more sensitive to any change in its price. Isn't that true from your own experience? Suppose you smoke and also attend movies twice a week. A book of matches costs a penny and movies $4. It is not likely that a 200 percent increase in match prices will have much effect on your smoking. But a 50 percent increase in the price of movie tickets would substantially affect your movie going if you have a typical student's income.

Apply this to table salt. One pound of salt lasts a long time and costs little more than a penny an ounce. So who cares? Shoppers will be relatively insensitive to any change in the price of salt. Moreover, salt has few good substitutes. You would not be inclined to put sugar on your eggs if the price of salt rose dramatically, just as you would not cut the pepper and double the salt if the price of salt fell substantially.

Adam Smith observed in *The Wealth of Nations* that "salt is a very ancient and very universal subject of taxation. . . . The quantity annually consumed by any individual is so small, and may be purchased so gradually, that nobody, it seems to have been thought, could feel very sensibly even a pretty heavy tax upon it." Moreover, salt was one of "the necessaries of life" in Smith's terminology. We can object to the term *necessary* and express Smith's meaning more accurately: salt has few good substitutes. The result is a highly inelastic demand and an apparently irresistible temptation to some governments to levy taxes on salt.

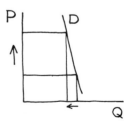

But it's possible to exaggerate the inelasticity of even the demand for salt. Householders in wintry regions sometimes sprinkle table salt on their sidewalks or porch steps to melt the ice. If salt were ten times as expensive, many would substitute chopping and scraping for salt.

4. The demand for Morton's salt. Why would the demand for Morton's salt be less inelastic than the demand for salt? Because there are substitutes—namely, other brands of salt. The Morton Salt Company is not in the privileged position of ancient governments, which could raise the price of *all* salt. If someone in the marketing department at Morton chanced to read Adam Smith and was inspired by him to double the price, the grocery stores that are Morton's customers would tend to make their purchases from other salt manufacturers.

5. The demand for Morton's salt at the Kroger store at Fifth and Main. If there are more good substitutes for Morton's salt than for salt, there are even more good substitutes for the Morton's salt sold at the local Kroger store. We have moved from a very inelastic to what is probably a highly elastic demand for the same quantity. And that is why you aren't victimized when you purchase salt. You might be willing to pay $5 a pound if salt were not available at a lower price. But fortunately for you, there are many options. Sellers who tried to take advantage of that fact that the total demand for salt is highly inelastic would lose customers. The demand for *the salt they sell* will be quite elastic.

　　People often make the mistake of assuming that those who sell "vital necessities" can get away with charging almost any price they choose. We have learned to be suspicious of the phrase *vital necessities*. Now we see again the grounds for this suspicion. Food has as good a claim as anything to the title "vital necessity." But the relevant fact is that *no one buys food*. Shoppers do not purchase a pound of "food"; they buy a pound of hamburger, or bacon, or calf's liver. And there are many sellers selling many kinds of food. All of which means that there are excellent substitutes for specific food commodities, and hence demand curves are highly elastic. So sellers are for the most part closely constrained in the prices they can charge.

Elasticity and Total Receipts

6. "The university's total receipts from tuition would actually increase if tuition rates were cut by 20 percent." The university's total receipts from tuition are the product of the tuition rate and the number of students who enroll. If a 20 percent decrease in the tuition rate results in an increase in tuition receipts, then there must have been a more than 20 percent increase in enrollment. The percentage change in quantity demanded is greater than the percentage change in price, so demand is elastic.

　　This suggests a simple way of thinking about elasticity. Keep in mind that the quantity demanded will always move in the opposite direction from the price. *If the price change causes*

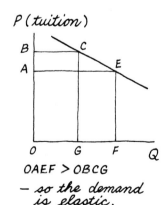

$OAEF > OBCG$
— so the demand is elastic.

total receipts to move in the opposite *direction from the price change, demand must be elastic*. The change in the quantity purchased has to be larger in percentage terms than the price change, because total receipts are nothing but the product of price and quantity. And that is the definition of an elastic demand. *If a price change causes total receipts to move in the* same *direction as the price change, demand must be inelastic*. The change in amount purchased was not large enough to outweigh the change in price. And that is the meaning of an inelastic demand. You can satisfy yourself that this relationship holds by running through a numerical example.

Assume that 1000 students will enroll if the tuition is $500 per term, but only 900 will enroll if the tuition is $600 per term. Is the demand elastic or inelastic within this range of tuition charges? We notice that the university's total receipts change *in the same direction* as the price change: 1000 × 500 is less than 900 × 600. So the demand is inelastic by the rule given above. We can confirm this with a little arithmetic. The percentage change in quantity demanded is 100 enrollments divided by 950. (A percentage change is the change divided by the base: we chose 950, the average of 1000 and 900, as the base because we want to get the same answer whether we raise the price from $500 to $600 or lower it from $600 to $500). The percentage change in price is $100 divided by $550—where we again use the average of the two values between which we're moving as the base. The coefficient of elasticity is $^{11}/_{19}$, or .58.

$$\frac{\frac{100}{950}}{\frac{100}{550}}$$

Now assume instead that enrollment falls from 1000 to 800 as a result of the tuition increase from $500 to $600. In this case total receipts and price are moving *in opposite directions*: 1000 × 500 is greater than 800 × 600. So the demand must be elastic. A few calculations will verify this conclusion. The percentage change in quantity is now 200 divided by 900; the percentage change in price is again 100 divided by 550. (The units don't matter; they cancel out.) The coefficient of elasticity is $^{11}/_{9}$, or 1.22.

$$\frac{\frac{200}{900}}{\frac{100}{550}}$$

Do not jump to the conclusion that the university will always be in a better financial position, given an elastic demand, if it lowers its tuition. True, lower tuition charges will mean larger receipts whenever demand is elastic; but a larger enrollment probably also means larger costs. The university must decide in such a case whether the addition to total receipts will be larger than the addition to total costs. (But problems of pricing strategy must be deferred until we reach Chapter 9.)

7. "It's odd but true. Wheat farmers would gross more money if they all got together and burned one-quarter of this year's crop." The logic of number 6 applies also here. Farmers can only gross more money while selling less wheat if the percent-

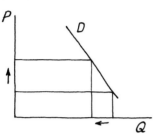

Demand between these two prices is inelastic.

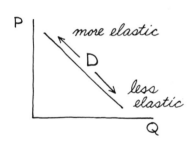

more elastic

D

less elastic

The higher price change is a smaller percentage change

age change in price is greater than the percentage change in the amount sold. Demand would have to be inelastic. The only difference is that we have reversed the causal relationship assumed up till now. We have been tacitly assuming that sellers set the price and buyers respond. This is not always the best way to look at the price-quantity relationship. In some industries, such as agriculture for the most part, it is more useful to assume that the quantity available for sale will determine the price. We'll be talking a lot about this later on. For now it is only important to notice that the relationship between changes in total sales and changes in price depends on the elasticity of demand.

Farmers may never have heard about elastic or inelastic demands. But when they lobby for government controls on production, they are usually very much aware of the relation between price and the amount that is sold. You can, like Molière's famous M. Jourdain, who spoke prose for forty years without knowing it, make good use of demand elasticities without ever having heard the term.

8. Could wheat farmers do even better by burning one-half of the crop? The elasticity of demand will almost certainly not be the same at all points along a demand schedule or curve. As a general rule, demand will be more elastic at higher prices (and smaller quantities) than at lower prices (and larger quantities). Why? Basically because people tend to be more sensitive to price changes when the price in question is large (relative to their incomes) than when it is small. Consequently, if farmers somehow agreed upon a scheme for destroying wheat in order to raise its price, at some point they would run into an elastic demand. And as soon as the demand turned from inelastic to elastic, total receipts would go down as a consequence of further price increases.

This relationship may become clearer to you if you examine a straight-line demand curve. Along the upper left portion of the demand curve, any price change of a given amount will be a *smaller percentage change* than it will be along the lower right portion of the curve. At the same time, the *percentage change* in quantity demanded will be getting *larger* as we move from the lower right portion of the curve to the upper left. Since elasticity of demand is the ratio of these percentage changes, the coefficient of elasticity must be increasing continuously as we move up and back along a straight-line demand curve.

The Myth of Vertical Demand

But enough of such technicalities. In the six statements with which we began this chapter, what was implicitly assumed about the elasticity of demand? Our objection to each statement, you recall, was that it ignored the fact that all goods have substitutes and that substitution does occur when prices change. In other words, demand curves are *not* completely inelastic. A completely inelastic demand curve would graph as a vertical line. You would be wise not to look for such demand curves in the real world.

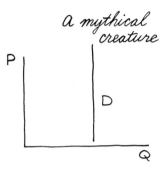

You would also be wise to look out for people who argue as if completely inelastic demand curves are the rule. Here are some additional examples to give you practice in being wary.

"The Mona Lisa is a priceless painting."

Don't believe it. If the French government decided to sell the Mona Lisa at auction, it would be bought at a finite price. No doubt wealthy collectors would be eager to buy it and might even carelessly say something like "I'd give *anything* to get it." The inaccuracy of their speech would be demonstrated as the bidding proceeded, and the collectors, one by one, dropped out of the auction.

"National security requires four million soldiers in uniform."

That sounds like a Pentagon statement. We might put the Pentagon to a hypothetical test by asking the chairman of the Joint Chiefs of Staff whether he would still insist on four million servicemen if the cost of maintaining a military establishment of this size rose to $200 billion annually. If he refused to budge and kept insisting that the Pentagon demand is completely inelastic at four million soldiers, we could shrug our shoulders and recall what the law of demand does and does not assert. It asserts that people find substitutes for anything when the cost *to them* increases. It does not assert that people become willing to reduce their purchases when *someone else* must pay a higher price. If the salaries of generals were made to vary inversely with the total number of people in the army, the military demand for personnel would prove to be far more elastic than the Pentagon is now willing to admit.

"Cleaning up air pollution will be costly. But we cannot weigh money against clean air."

The assumption once again is that the demand for some good, in this case clean air, is completely inelastic. But it obviously is not to anyone who thinks about it for a moment. There are degrees of clean air. How clean do we want the air to be? "As clean as possible" is no answer because we can always make the air cleaner. We could get rid of all factories, all cars, and all home heating systems. If we wanted still more cleanliness in our air, we could start getting rid of people who perspire excessively. But long before this point we would all have noticed that the demand for clean air is not perfectly inelastic. Clean air is a good. But there are costs involved in obtaining it. Intelligent pollution-control programs seek to balance the benefits of clean air against the additional costs that must be incurred to get it.

Once Again with Emphasis

The law of demand can be expressed in the language of elasticity: *There is no such thing as a completely inelastic demand* over the entire range of possible prices. Most purchasers will respond at least a little to changes in the cost to them, and all purchasers will respond to a sufficiently large change. If this seems too obvious to bother mentioning, consult your daily newspaper for evidence that it is by no means obvious to everyone. Well-intentioned people and some not so well-intentioned talk constantly of basic needs, minimum requirements, and absolute necessities.

Demand curves are rarely as inelastic as orators suppose. That does not imply, of course, that they are always elastic. That is a more difficult question to be answered by looking at each case. But as we shall subsequently discover, it is a very important question for anyone who wants to decide how well our economic system functions.

Once Over Lightly

Every good has substitutes: other goods which will be used in its stead when the cost of using the original good rises, goods for which the original good will become a substitute when their cost rises. Pork replaces beef when the price of beef goes up, and a restaurant beef-steak takes the place of a movie when theater tickets become more expensive.

By talking about "needs," we can sometimes win arguments we might otherwise lose. Needs are actually wants of many different urgencies.

People want more or less of a good as the cost those people must pay decreases or increases.

The concept of *demand* is preferable to the concept of *need*, because demand relates the amounts that are purchased to the sacrifices that must be made to obtain these amounnts.

The "law of demand" asserts that more will be purchased at lower prices, less at higher prices—assuming that something in addition to the price has not changed to offset this consequence.

The money cost of a good is only one part of the cost that affects people's decisions.

A sufficiently large change in money cost (price) can usually overcome the effects that nonmoney costs exert on people's decisions.

A change in price will usually induce a larger change in amounts purchased when more time is allowed for consumers and producers to learn about and invent new substitutes.

Price elasticity of demand is a measure of the percentage

change in the quantity of a good demanded relative to the percentage change in its price.

Demand is (price) elastic when the percentage change in quantity demanded is greater than the percentage change in price. Demand is inelastic when the percentage change in quantity demanded is smaller than the percentage change in price.

Price elasticity of demand depends upon the importance of the price relative to one's income, but even more upon the quality and price of available substitutes.

More separate sources of supply for a good imply better substitutes for any particular good and hence a more elastic demand.

Total receipts or expenditures move in the opposite direction from price when demand is elastic and in the same direction as price when it is inelastic.

The concept of "needs" implies a perfectly inelastic demand curve—an extremely rare phenomenon.

The demand for a good refers to the *schedule of relationships* between price and quantity demanded and must be distinguished from the quantity or amount that is demanded. The quantity of a good demanded changes with its price. But a true change in demand will alter both price and quantity demanded.

QUESTIONS FOR DISCUSSION

1. Most systems of hospitalization insurance substantially reduce the cost to the patient of hospitalization, sometimes to zero. How does this affect hospital use? Why? Evaluate the argument that it does not affect hospital use since "no one gets sick just because hospitals are cheap, or avoids getting sick because they're expensive."

2. In 1967 the president of the American Medical Association was quoted as saying that medical care was a privilege and not a right. Today the AMA officially proclaims that "health care is the right of everyone." What quantity and quality of health care do you suppose they're talking about?

3. The contention that certain goods are "basic human needs" carries a strong suggestion that access to those goods should be a matter of right, not of privilege. But the assertion of rights logically entails the assertion of obligations. Your right to vote, for example, entails the obligation of election officials to accept and count your ballot; your right to use your own umbrella implies an obligation on the part of others not to borrow it without your permission. If "health care is the right of everyone," who has the obligation to provide health care to everyone? Who currently accepts this obligation? How will the appropriate persons be persuaded to accept it?

4. Although the combined population of Washington and Oregon was slightly

less in 1975 than the population of Massachusetts, over three times as many kilowatt-hours were sold in Washinton and Oregon during that year as in Massachusetts. How would you account for the enormous difference? (Hint: Over 92 percent of the kilowatt-hours sold by electric utilities in Washington and Oregon were generated by falling water, in comparison with slightly more than 1 percent in Massachusetts.) What persuaded aluminum companies, who are very heavy users of electricity, to locate in the Pacific Northwest? How were so many home builders persuaded to install electric spaceheating?

5. Here is a classroom exercise that might be fun and also sharpen your ability to recognize substitution possibilities. Let one person come up with two goods that seem to have no connection and challenge others to construct a plausible set of circumstances in which one would be a substitute for the other. (Avoid the easy, though correct, answer that all goods are in the last analysis substitutes inasmuch as the acquisition of each uses up scarce time or income.)

6. If a prestigious store (Neiman-Marcus in Dallas, for example) were to put its Chanel Number 5 perfume on sale for one-fourth the current price, do you think customers would purchase more? What do you think would happen if a drugstore in a modest-income neighborhood did the same thing? Suppose that each store sold Chanel Number 5 under another label, one that customers had never heard of, and offered it successively at each of the two prices. At which price do you think each store would sell more perfume?

7. If the government forbids motorists to drive more than 55 miles per hour, does everyone stay within the 55-mile limit? What are the costs of going faster? What are some of the costs of going faster that do not fall on the speeding motorist? Do these latter costs affect motorists' decisions? Why might the fact that faster driving uses up more of the nation's scarce petroleum reduce the speed of some drivers but not others?

8. Why do people live in New York City if the costs of doing so—high rents, noise, dirt, congestion, the risks of being robbed or assaulted—are so high? Is it true that most of them "have no choice"? What do you think would happen if the costs listed above were significantly reduced?

9. A change in expectations can cause a change in demand. Explain how this could lead to a situation where a price decline was followed by a decrease in the amount purchased.

10. Higher prices for beef, automobiles, or television sets will lead to a reduction in the *amount of each demanded*. Think of some specific changes (such as in tastes, prices of substitutes, quality of complementary goods) that would cause the *demand* for each to increase so that more might actually be demanded at higher prices. Why is this completely consistent with the law of demand?

11. These were the prices per (U.S.) gallon of regular gasoline in U.S. dollar equivalents in selected countries in October 1975:

Italy	$1.65	Spain	1.16
France	1.49	Canada	.65
Japan	1.28	U.S.	.59

Why would we *not* have a demand schedule if we obtained data on the gasoline purchased during October 1975 in each of those countries?

12. John loves butter and thinks that margarine tastes like soap. George can't tell the difference. Whose demand for butter is likely to be more elastic?

13. Would the elasticity of a crowd's demand for cold lemonade be affected by the proximity of a drinking fountain?

14. How do you think the development of other copying machines affected the elasticity of demand for Xerox machines?

15. Is the demand for prescription drugs elastic or inelastic? Why? Do you agree with the statement sometimes made that the prices charged for prescription drugs can be freely set by the manufacturers, since people must buy whatever the doctor prescribes?

16. How does ignorance affect elasticities of demand?

17. How might the development of science and technology affect demand elasticities?

18. Does a society's transportation system in any way affect elasticities of demand? How?

19. What is the elasticity of demand for water in New York City, according to Figure 2A? (Be careful: the elasticity varies.)

20. The demand for aspirin at currently prevailing prices seems to be highly inelastic. What do you think would happen to the elasticity of demand if the price of aspirin relative to everything else were five times as high? Fifty times as high? Why?

21. In 1977 Brazil was supplying about a third of the world's coffee exports. When a frost wiped out about 75 percent of Brazil's 1976–77 crop, the price of green (unroasted) coffee rose 400 percent. What was the approximate price elasticity of demand for coffee? Why was it so low?

22. Harvest-time rains in California in the spring of 1978 destroyed a portion of the lettuce crop. As a result, the price for a 24-head carton loaded in California hit a record of $18 on May 1, 1978. On June 29, after new crops had come in, the price was $2.75. What does all this suggest about the demand for lettuce? What attitudes and practices on the part of households and restaurants contribute toward making the demand for lettuce very inelastic with respect to price?

23. Why do airlines so often extend sizable discounts only to passengers who buy round trip tickets and stay at least seven days? What difference does it make to the airline how long a passenger stays? (Hint: Airlines would like to reduce fares *only* for people who otherwise would not fly but not for passengers whose demand is quite inelastic with respect to price.)

24. What would you say is the price elasticity of demand for the rewards of criminal activity? Would increasing the price of crime (that is, raising its cost to the criminal) significantly reduce the crime rate?

25. See if you can straighten out the following analysis. "If half of our forests were destroyed in a fire, the value of the remaining lumber would be greater than the value of all the lumber in the country before the fire. This absurdity—that the whole is worth less than a half—shows that values are distorted in a market economy."

PRICE OF STRAWBERRIES PER CASE

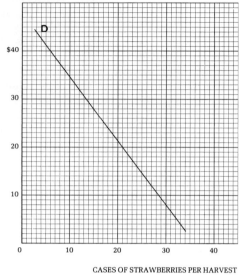

CASES OF STRAWBERRIES PER HARVEST
(in thousands)

Figure 2B Demand curve for strawberries

26. Figure 2B shows a hypothetical demand curve for strawberries.
    a. What price per case would maximize the gross receipts of strawberry growers? (Peek at part *d* of this question rather than waste too much time trying all sorts of different prices. The price that maximizes gross receipts will be found at the midpoint of a straight-line demand curve when the curve is extended to the axes. If you see why, good. If not, it's a bit of knowledge with only academic usefulness anyway.)
    b. If the price of strawberries is determined by the total quantity harvested in conjunction with the demand, what size crop will result in the price quoted in part *d*?
    c. What would the gross receipts of strawberry growers be if the crop turned out to be 30,000 cases?
    d. Can you prove that the demand for strawberries is elastic above a price of $24 per case and inelastic below that price?
    e. If strawberry growers can make more money by selling fewer than 30,000 cases, why would they ever market that much? Why wouldn't they destroy some of the crop rather than "spoil the market"?
27. Assume that Congress has decided to reduce consumption of nonreusable containers in order to preserve Spaceship Earth. Evaluate the following arguments that might be used in the discussion of how to go about achieving this goal.
    a. "We know we cannot survive unless we stop using things and then discarding them. The only sensible approach, therefore, is a legal ban on all nonreusable containers of any kind."
    b. "People will do the right thing once they understand the problem. I don't

think we should start passing laws. We should assume that the American people are public-spirited and we should educate them to the facts."

c. "It has been proposed by some that we place a tax on the manufacture of disposable containers to encourage the use of deposit-and-return. This would not work because people just would not care about the tax. Moreover, a tax says in effect that it's all right to pollute if you're rich, but not if you're poor."

Opportunity Cost and the Supply of Goods

You have already been introduced to the central concept of this chapter. If you failed to notice, that's because we didn't call it by its proper name. But several times in the preceding chapter, in talking about the relationship between price and quantity demanded, we pointed out that the amount of any good that a person will want to purchase is determined by the good's cost to that person, or the value of the sacrifice required to obtain it. That is the definition of *opportunity cost*, a concept which ties together the law of demand and the principles governing supply. We shall try to convince you in this chapter that it makes sense to think of cost as *the value of sacrificed opportunities*.

Costs are Valuations

Everyone will concede that demand reflects people's values. But supply, many believe, is the material side of economics, governed by costs of production which are objective realities, in contrast with such subjective factors as people's values and preferences. That belief is an error. Supply and cost are also based on valuations. To help you see that, we shall detour through a college dormitory on a Monday night in the fall, where the following exchange takes place.

"Hey, Jack, do you want to go see the new Bergman movie? It closes after tonight."

"I'd like to, but I can't. We've got a Russian test tomorrow, and I'll flunk if I don't cram some vocabulary."

"Forget it. You can borrow my vocabulary cards in your free period tomorrow. An hour with the cards right before class is a B for sure."

"Well—trouble is the Redskins and Miami are on TV tonight and I'd rather watch the game if I don't have to study."

"We'll go at six and be back for the kickoff."

"All right. Just let me see how much money I've got—five, six, seven, eight dollars—to last until I get paid on Thursday. And I'm out of meal tickets!"

"Eat peanut butter sandwiches! I thought you wanted to see the movie."

"I do. O.K. I'll let my stomach shrink until Thursday. Should we leave at quarter to six?"

The real cost of any action (going to a movie, buying a pair of jeans, manufacturing a lawnmower, moving to Halifax, raising beef cattle, building a hardware store, taking out an insurance policy) is the value of the alternative opportunity that must be sacrificed in order to take the action. The cost for Jack of going to the movie was at first calculated as a passing grade (given up!) in Russian. When his friend showed him how to reduce that cost, Jack looked at the next most valuable opportunity he would have to sacrifice if he went to the movie: watching the Monday night football game, a game he particularly wanted to see. His friend eliminated that cost for him and Jack turned to the money cost. But money wasn't the real cost. The real cost that dollars and cents represent are the opportunities given up when the money is spent in one way rather than another. The two dollars Jack will spend for the movie represent some meals he would have liked to eat but is willing to sacrifice in order to see the film.

Producers' Costs as Opportunity Costs

The theory of supply in economics is not essentially different from the theory of demand. Both assume that decision makers face alternatives and choose among them, and that their choices reflect a comparison of the benefits anticipated from the alternatives. The logic of the economizing process is the same for producers as it is for consumers.

When we think about producers' costs, asking ourselves for example why it costs more to manufacture a ten-speed bicycle than a redwood picnic table, we tend to think first of what goes into the production of each. We think of the raw materials, of the labor time required, perhaps also of the machinery or tools that must be used. We express the value of the inputs in monetary terms and assume that the cost of the bicycle or the table is the sum of these values. That isn't wrong. But it leaves unanswered the question of why the inputs had those particular monetary values. The concept of opportunity cost asserts that those values reflect the value of the inputs in their next best uses, or the value of the opportunities forgone by using the inputs in the production of bicycles and picnic tables.

The manufacturer's cost of producing a bicycle will be determined by what he must pay to obtain the appropriate resources. And, because these resources have other opportunities for employment, he must pay a price that matches the "best opportunity" value. The value of forgone opportunities thus becomes the cost of manufacturing a bicycle. This makes excellent sense, for the meaningful cost of obtaining one more bicycle is the value of what must be given up or sacrificed or forgone in order to obtain that bicycle.

Consider the case of the picnic table. Part of its cost of production is the price of redwood. Assume that the demand for new housing has increased recently, and that building contractors have consequently been purchasing a lot more redwood lumber. If this causes the price of lumber to rise, the cost of manufacturing a picnic table will go up. Nothing has happened to affect the physical inputs that go into the table, but its cost of production has risen. Because houses containing redwood lumber are now more valuable than formerly, the table manufacturer must pay a higher opportunity cost for the lumber he wants to put into his picnic tables.

The concept of opportunity cost explains also how labor enters into production costs. Workers must receive from their employers a wage that persuades them to turn down all other opportunities. A skilled worker will be paid more than an unskilled worker because and only insofar as those skills make the skilled worker more valuable somewhere else. Workers who can install wheel spokes while standing on their heads and whistling "Dixie" are marvelously skilled. But our bicycle manufacturer will not have to pay them additional compensation for that skill unless their unusual talent makes them more valuable somewhere else. That could happen. A circus might bid for their talents. If the circus offers them more than they can obtain as bicycle producers, their opportunity cost to the manufacturer rises. In that case the manufacturer will probably wish them goodbye and good luck and replace them with other workers whose opportunity cost is lower.

When the National Basketball Association and the American Basketball Association merged into one league, what happened to the opportunity cost of physically coordinated seven-footers? With two leagues, each player has two teams bidding for his services. What either team must pay to get him is determined by what the other team is willing to pay, and both will be willing to pay a lot if they think he will make a big difference in ticket sales. If the leagues merge, however, the right to hire a particular player is assigned to a single team, and the opportunity cost of a well-coordinated seven-footer will fall to the presumably much lower level of his value in other lines of work. It's not surprising that owners of professional basketball teams prefer one league to two.

Let's take a more common case. If a large firm employing many people moves into a small town, the cost of hiring grocery clerks, bank tellers, secretaries, and gasoline station attendants in the town will tend to go up. Why? Because grocery stores, banks, offices, and gasoline stations must all pay the opportunity cost of the people they employ, and these people may now find better opportunities for employment in the new firm. Suppose the new firm is interested in hiring women exclusively; only the opportunity cost of hiring women will increase at first. But that will pull women out of some jobs, thereby creating additional opportunities for men and causing the opportunity cost of male workers to rise.

The resource that most clearly illustrates the opportunity-cost concept is probably land. Suppose you want to purchase an acre of land to build a house. What will you have to pay for the land? It will depend on the value of that land in alternative uses. Do other people view the acre as a choice residential site? Does it have commercial or industrial potentialities? Would it be used for pasture if you did not purchase it? The cost you pay for the land will be determined by the alternative opportunities that people perceive for its use.

Case Studies in Opportunity Cost

Let's examine some other cases of varying costs to see how the concept of opportunity cost explains familiar but often misunderstood phenomena.

Why, in the last 40 years, has the cost of getting a haircut gone up so much more than the cost of goods generally? It's because people who want barbers to cut their hair must be willing to pay them enough to keep them in the trade. If productivity in haircutting had kept pace over the last 40 years with productivity in manufacturing, barbers would have been able to maintain their incomes by trimming more heads per hour. But with productivity virtually unchanged, only a higher price per head could keep them working in the barber shop. We who want our hair cut by professionals have bid up the price of haircuts to meet the rising opportunity cost to barbers of working at a job in which productivity never increases.

Why is it often so much harder to find a teenage babysitter

in a wealthy residential area than in a low-income area? The frustrated couple unable to find a babysitter may complain that all the kids in the neighborhood are lazy. But that is a needlessly harsh explanation. Teenage babysitters can be found by any couple willing to pay the opportunity cost. That means bidding the babysitters away from their otherwise most valued opportunity. If the demand for babysitters in the area is large because wealthy people go out more often—and if the local teenagers receive such generous allowances that they value a date or leisure more than the ordinary income from babysitting, why be surprised to find that the opportunity cost of hiring a babysitter is high?

Why did the cost of obtaining a college education rise so steeply during the 1960s? A very large part of the explanation lies in sharply increased instructional costs, made up partly of higher faculty salaries and partly of reduced teaching loads. But how did these developments come about? Ask your friendly neighborhood professor and he will probably tell you about the long years that must be spent getting a Ph.D. and the impossibility of doing research while teaching twelve hours. Any good member of the professorial guild will assent to the virtues of those arguments. But no good economics professor will be much impressed with their cogency as an explanation of why professors earned more and taught less at the end of the decade than at the beginning.

The rapidly rising demand for professors provides the explanation. State legislatures poured money into building new colleges and expanding old ones; the federal government responded to the fear of Soviet scientific superiority by appropriating vast sums for higher education and for research, which gave teachers new opportunities; the World War II baby boom became a college-student boom in the 1960s; and a larger percentage of the population became persuaded that a college degree was a passport to the good life. The government and private industry meanwhile increased their demand for the services of highly trained persons, widening the range of opportunities for people with extensive education. The net result was a vastly increased demand for the services of college professors. College professors, too, are scarce resources with opportunity costs. A larger number of them were obtained by bidding them away from alternative employments with the offer of higher salaries and reduced teaching loads. (All college professors know that it is easier to raise their incomes by finding a better opportunity elsewhere than by reciting their virtues to their current deans. Deans are more attentive to the recitals of professors with alternative opportunities.)

Why does the high school dropout rate decrease during a recession? The opportunity cost of remaining in high school varies with the job market for teenagers. A decline in job opportunities reduces the opportunity cost of remaining in school for some young people; therefore fewer drop out.

Why are poor people more likely to travel between cities by bus and wealthy people more likely to travel by air? A simple answer would be that taking the bus is cheaper. But it isn't. It's a very expensive mode of transportation for people for whom the opportunity cost of time is high; and the opportunity cost of time is typically much lower for poor people than for those with a high income from working.

Do you have the idea? Figure out for yourself the cost of going to college. If you include in your calculations the value to yourself of whatever you would be doing if you were not in college, you have grasped the principle of opportunity cost.

A final example. Consider the case of a woman who runs a small grocery store all by herself. She says that she does pretty well because she has no labor costs. Is she right? The cost of her own labor is not a monetary outlay, but it certainly is a cost. And that cost can be measued by the value of the opportunities she forgoes by working for herself.

Costs and Actions

The economic way of thinking recognizes *no* objective costs. That offends common sense, which teaches that things do have "real" costs, costs that depend on the firm laws of physics, rather than the vagaries of the human psyche. It's hard to win a battle against common sense, but we must try.

Perhaps we can disarm common sense most quickly by pointing out that "things" have no costs at all. We are talking about costs relevant to supply, of course—costs that have an effect on people's decisions to make goods available. "Things" cannot have costs in that sense. Only actions can. If you think that things do indeed have costs and are ready with an example to prove it, you are almost certainly smuggling in an unnoticed action to give your item a cost.

For example: What is the cost of a baseball? "Four dollars," you say. But you mean that the cost of *purchasing* a baseball at the local sporting goods store is four dollars. Since purchasing is an action, it can entail sacrificed opportunities and thereby have a cost. But note the smuggled-in action. With other actions, the cost of a baseball changes. The cost of *manufacturing* a baseball is quite different. *Selling* one has yet another cost. And what about the cost of *catching* one at the ball park by spearing a line drive foul with your bare hand, where the sacrifice may be the opportunity to wear an unbroken nose the rest of your life?

Let's return to the case of a college education. What does it cost? The answer is that "it" cannot have a cost. We must at least distinguish between the cost of *obtaining* a college education and the cost of *providing* one. As soon as we make that distinction, we should also notice something that has been implicit in everything we've said so far about costs, either in this or the preceding chapter; namely, that costs are always costs *to someone*. The cost of obtaining an education usually means the cost to the student. But it could mean the cost to the student's parents, which is not the same. Or, if that student's admission entailed the rejection of some other applicant, it could even mean the cost to John (who was refused admission) of Marsha's obtaining entrance to the first-year class. Those will all be different.

A great deal of fruitless argument about the "true cost" of things stems from a failure to recognize that only actions have costs, and that actions can entail different costs for different people. The intensifying debate at this writing about reinstituting the military draft is an excellent example. Let's take a look.

The Cost of a Volunteer Military Force

Selective service, as it is euphemistically called, has been around for a long time. While almost everyone regards it as an evil, many Americans still seem to think of it as the only way to secure an adequate supply of military personnel at an acceptable cost.

There may be good arguments for the draft, but the familiar argument that an adequate volunteer army would cost too much is not one of them. The Department of Defense and others who worry about the relative costs of a conscripted and a volunteer military are conveniently by-passing the question, cost to whom? Are we talking about the cost to taxpayers, enlisted personnel, Congress, or the Pentagon? They are very different.

What is the cost to a young person of becoming a soldier? The best way to find out would be to offer a bribe and to keep raising it until it was accepted. If Marshall would enlist for $5000 per year, Carol for $8000, and Philip for no less than $60,000, these represent the opportunity costs of Marshall, Carol, and Philip. The cost of drafting all three, *to them*, would then be $73,000, even though the government can conceal this fact by offering far less in wages and then compelling each to serve.

The opportunity cost is a function of forgone alternative employment opportunities and all sorts of other values: preferences with respect to life-style, attitude toward war, degrees of cowardice or bravery, and so on. When the government bids for military personnel, raising its offer until it can attract just the desired number of enlistments, the government in an important sense actually minimizes the cost of its program. For it pulls in those with the lowest opportunity costs of service—everyone like Marshall but no one like Philip. Under a draft, this could occur only through the most unlikely of coincidences. Figure 3A provides a simple way to grasp the argument.

There is a supply curve of military volunteers. The argument that people won't voluntarily risk their lives is refuted by the fact that people do—not only military volunteers but also police, steeple jacks, and even skiers. Whatever its precise position and slope, the supply curve will certainly incline upward to the right. Some people (those who assign low value to their available alternatives) will volunteer at a very low wage. But three million volunteers can be secured, on our assumptions, only if the wage offer is at least $8000 per year. That would mean a wage bill of $24 billion annually. But because taxpayers don't like to have their taxes raised, Congress is reluctant to approve such a huge appropriation. And the people in the Department of Defense care very much about the likes and dislikes of the people in Congress. They can cut that upsetting bill in half by offering only $4000 and compelling enlistments. The published cost will now be only $12 billion. Hurrah for cost savings!

But what of the costs to those who make up the armed forces? The cost of the *volunteer* army (to the volunteers) under our assumptions would be $15 billion. That is the value of the area under the supply curve up to 3 million men and women, or the sum of the values of the opportunities forgone by those who enlisted. The other $9 billion paid out by the government is a transfer of wealth from taxpayers to members of the military who would have enlisted at a lower wage but who nonetheless receive the higher wage that is required to induce the enlistment of the 3 millionth volunteer.

What will be the cost to those who are drafted of a *conscripted* army? We can't say, except that it will certainly be larger. Only if the draft happened to hit exactly those and only those who would have enlisted under a volunteer system would the cost be as low as $15 billion. But that is most unlikely. The more draftees who are grabbed from the upper, rather than the lower, end of the supply curve, the higher will be the cost to the conscripts. For example, a man who would have volunteered at a wage of $4500 is offered $4000. He rejects the offer, and he is subsequently not drafted. Instead, a person who would only have volunteered at $12,000 is drafted. There was a saving of $500 annually to taxpayers but a loss of $8000 to the draftee.

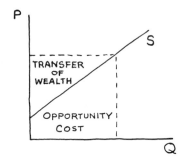

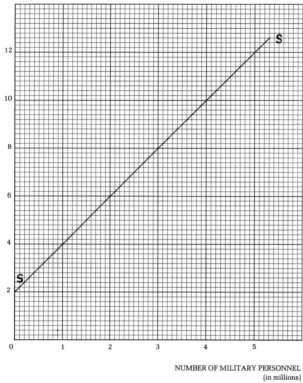

ANNUAL WAGE (in thousands of dollars)

NUMBER OF MILITARY PERSONNEL
(in millions)

Figure 3A   Supply curve of military volunteers

The military draft does *not* reduce the cost of maintaining
a military establishment. It rather transfers that cost from the
shoulders of taxpayers to the shoulders of the draftees. That
may in your judgment be one of the least of its faults; or it may
be outweighed in your mind by presumed advantages. But at
least it's a consequence that economists can point out.

Costs and Ownership

Everyone who has been in the armed forces knows horror
stories about the inefficient ways the military makes use of its
personnel. A highly skilled accountant is put to work painting
barracks, and the commissary books are kept by someone who
counts on his fingers. The stories are probably exaggerated.
Nonetheless, we have grounds for predicting that personnel
will tend to be used in such wasteful ways in the military more
often than in civilian life.

Why? Because in civilian life, those who employ people are
usually compelled to pay them their opportunity cost. When
you have to pay accountants the wages of accountants, you

don't have them paint barracks—at least not if you're an employer with regard for the profitability of your enterprise. On the other hand, what is the cost to a sergeant of assigning a highly skilled recruit to a task that requires no skill at all? If the sergeant happens to resent the recruit for his air of superiority—real or imagined—transferring him to a job more suited to his abilities might actually entail the sacrifice of a valuable opportunity for the sergeant—the opportunity to humiliate someone he dislikes.

Two conclusions emerge from the above analysis. First, resources tend to be utilized more efficiently when users must pay the opportunity cost, or the value of the resources in their next best use. Second, users are more often compelled to pay the opportunity cost of resources when those resources are clearly and definitely owned by someone. A man who is drafted does not "own his own labor," because the law has deprived him of the power to decide where and for whom and on what terms he will work. And so he can't insist upon receiving his opportunity cost when Uncle Sam beckons—as he can when United Soapchips wants his services.

The point also applies, of course, to nonhuman resources. If no one owns a resource, there is no one to insist that potential users of that resource pay the value of the opportunities sacrificed by their use. The resource will consequently tend to be underpriced. And underpriced resources, as we shall see time and again in a variety of situations, tend to be used wastefully. The incentive to economize is weak when the cost of using is low.

A Note on Alternative Systems

Don't fail to notice that the concept of opportunity cost is fully applicable to a socialist society, in which resources are allocated by government planners. To economic planners in the Soviet Union, the cost of building a railway from Lubny to Mirgorod is the value of whatever could otherwise have been done with the resources. But if government officials have the power to obtain valuable resources without having to bid for them, how will they discover the value of the resources in alternative uses? Recall the remarkable workers who could install bicycle wheel spokes while standing on their heads and whistling "Dixie." In the absence of circus owners willing to bid for their services, how would central planners ever find out that they were too valuable to be assigned to bicycle production?

A distinguishing characteristic of different economic systems is the way in which they assign costs to alternative actions. Where resources are privately owned, competing bids and offers generate prices that approximate opportunity costs. Where resources are not clearly owned by anyone, this process cannot operate. What takes its place? Who determines the relative value of this railway line and that one, or of using steel for railroad tracks versus using it to build trucks, or of improving transportation versus improving the quality of what is transported, or of more and better consumer goods versus additional leisure? We'll leave that question for you to think about. But remember that intelligent choices presuppose good information. An effective economic system will be one that transmits reliable information to decision makers.

Do Costs Determine Prices?

When sellers announce a price increase to the public, they like to point out that the increase was compelled by rising costs. The business press publishes frequent announcements of this kind, and it's rare indeed when the announcement fails to include an expression of regret that higher costs made this unfortunate step necessary. In Chapter 9 we'll explore more fully the principles that guide sellers when they're setting prices. All we want to do now is use the concept of opportunity cost to examine critically the basic notion that prices are determined by costs. We want to show you that it makes as much sense to assert that costs are determined by prices. More accurately, we shall argue here that costs are always dependent upon demand. They are not something independent of demand as we often carelessly assume.

Demand and Cost

We can begin with an example discussed earlier in this chapter. Does it make sense to claim that the price of getting a haircut has gone up because barbers' wages have risen? If people weren't willing to pay high prices for haircuts, how could barbers' wages rise? The price people are willing to pay to have their hair cut professionally is one important factor that causes costs, that is, wages, to be what they are.

Plastic surgeons receive high wages for their services. Is this why it costs so much to have a face lift? Not exactly. The causal relationship also runs in the opposite direction. It's the fact that people are willing to pay a high price for cosmetic surgery that makes the cost of hiring a plastic surgeon so high. Few people have the requisite skills, of course, and their acquisition is difficult and time-consuming. That's why the demand for cosmetic surgery raises the income of the surgeons rather than merely increasing the number of people willing and able to provide the service. But the cost of obtaining the services of a plastic surgeon is obviously not independent of the demand for plastic surgery.

When the owners of professional football teams announce in the summer that ticket prices will be raised in the fall, they like to blame the increase on rising costs, especially the high wages that must be paid to the players. But why do the players receive such high wages? It can't be that their work is so dangerous and grueling because it was just as dangerous and grueling in the days when players received only a few hundred dollars for the season. It's the demand, the willingness of many people to pay high prices to watch, that has made football players such valuable resources. Soccer players in the United States receive far less, not because they work less hard, but because soccer isn't that popular in this country.

One of the most interesting cases of the relationship we're stressing is found in agriculture. The average price per acre of farm real estate in the United States rose by more than 200 percent from 1967 to 1978, just about doubling the rate of increase in the general price level. Anyone who decides to go into farming today will find that he has to pay a high price to obtain productive land. It would clearly be misleading to assert that the high cost of land is a cause of high food prices. It was the demand for land, determined in large part by the demand for agricultural products, that pulled up the cost of farming land. When farmers argue for higher government support prices for their crops because land costs so much, they are ignoring the fact that higher support prices will tend to pull up the price of the land on which those crops can be grown. It will do so by enhancing the value of the opportunities available to one who owns the land.

The most dramatic case of misleading reasoning is the argument of a farmer whose land lies near a large city. As the suburbs expand, residential developers offer to buy the land for a price that is three or four times higher than the price it can command as agricultural property. If the farmer refuses to sell because he wants to stay in farming, it is very unlikely that he will complain about the rising cost of land. But farmers who *rent* land near large cities often do just that. The landowner will understandably want to sell the land to developers unless the tenant farmer is willing to pay three or four times more rent. We can certainly sympathize with the tenant farmer dispossessed by the growth of the suburbs. But it's important that we see why he's being asked to pay a rent so much higher than before: it is the demand for land that is raising its cost.

Note that if *tax assessments* are based on what is called "highest and best use," then the owner who wants to remain in farming can legitimately complain that he can't afford *not* to sell. In those circumstances he is required to pay taxes based not on his own use of the land, but on the use to which the land would be put by the highest bidder.

Consumer Prices as Opportunity Costs

In all these examples we've tried to show that the costs of productive resources like labor and land are prices determined by demand. That, in fact, is what's meant by calling them opportunity costs. We can just as easily argue that the prices of consumer goods are, in reality, costs—opportunity costs that measure the value of the goods in alternative uses. Take, for example, the case of lobster.

Sad to relate, so few lobsters come to market that it just isn't possible for all of us to have as many as we could enjoy. More are brought to market as higher prices offer larger incentives to lobster fishermen; but the demand in recent years has increased considerably faster than the supply, and the price has consequently risen sharply.

The higher price can be viewed as the opportunity cost of the resources engaged in bringing lobsters to market. But when the lobsters have all been brought to market on a given day, so that the supply is, for that day at least, completely fixed, then the price should be viewed as the opportunity cost of the last potential purchaser who was persuaded by the high price to do without lobster. Think of it as follows: lobsters have many alternative uses, at least as many as there are potential lobster eaters. Lobsters have only one function, it is true, from the aggregate point of view. (We're notorious for ignoring the values and preferences of the lobster.) But the consumption of a lobster by one gourmet prevents its consumption by another. Lobster lovers in effect bid against one another for the limited supply. As the price rises, more and more potential consumers are reluctantly persuaded to do without. The price that clears the market, that makes the quantity demanded equal to the quantity supplied, will be the price that just barely persuades the most reluctant of the disappointed lobster lovers to go home from the seafood market with ocean perch or flounder fillets. It is *that person's* opportunity cost that is expressed by the market clearing price.

The point of all this is that people don't pay what lobster is worth to them, but rather what lobster is worth in its most valued alternative use: as food for the consumer who was just barely deterred by the price from making a purchase. It's the opportunity cost of this disappointed lobster lover that the price reflects, as well as the opportunity costs of the resources that might have been used to bring additional lobsters to market.

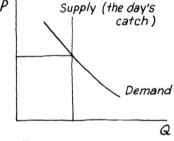

The demand for lobster determines the cost of bringing lobster home.

How many people realized in 1977 when they were paying over $4 for a pound of ordinary coffee that the price was equal to the cost? Not the growers' cost, of course, but the opportunity cost of those coffee lovers who were finally persuaded by the rising price to sacrifice the caffeine they coveted.

But now we have moved into the question of scarcity and its social management. That is the topic for Chapter 4.

Once Over Lightly

Supply curves, as well as demand curves, reflect people's estimates of the value of alternative opportunities. Both the quantities of any good that are supplied and the quantities that are demanded depend on the choices people make after assessing the opportunities available to them.

Supply depends on cost. But the cost of supplying is the value of the opportunities forgone by the act of supplying. This concept of cost is expressed in economic theory by the assertion that all costs relevant to decisions are opportunity costs—the value of the opportunities forsaken in choosing one course of action rather than another.

Insofar as the resources utilized in producing goods can be obtained only through competitive bidding, costs of production will reflect the value of the alternative uses of the resources. This implies that producers will want to suppress competitive bidding for the resources they use, if they can find an effective way to do so.

The value of a human being may be infinite, but the wages of human beings in any task will be much closer to the value of their services in alternative employments than to infinity.

Many disagreements about what something or the other "really costs" could be resolved by the recognition that "things" cannot have costs. Only actions entail sacrificed opportunities, and therefore only actions can have costs.

Costs are always the value of the opportunities that particular people sacrifice. Conflicting assertions about the cost of alternative decisions can often be reconciled by agreement on whose costs are under consideration.

Prices rise to the level of opportunity costs insofar as the owners of resources insist on being paid their value in the next best use. This discourages using resources wastefully; that is, in ways that are less valuable than available alternatives.

Supply curves slope upward to the right because higher prices must be offered to resource owners to persuade them to transform a current activity into an opportunity they are willing to sacrifice.

Demand curves slope upward to the left because higher

prices persuade resource users to sacrifice a current activity for their next best opportunity.

Demand helps determine costs. Costs contribute to the determination of prices. The prices of goods affect the demand for other goods that they complement or for which they can substitute. From the perspective of opportunity cost, everything depends on everything else.

QUESTIONS FOR DISCUSSION

1. What effect would the expectation of a continuing high price for soybeans have on the price of field corn? How does the concept of opportunity cost aid us in seeing the relationship?
2. What is the cost per ticket to a professional baseball club that offers 50 "free" tickets to an orphanage? Does it matter for what game the tickets are offered?
3. Why did the cost of hiring domestic servants increase dramatically during World War II? What would you have replied to people who said that servants "just weren't available"?
4. Some people contend that the ending of the military draft reduced college enrollments. Use the concept of opportunity cost to defend this argument. How did organized draft resistance and mounting public hostility to the Vietnam war affect Congressional perceptions of the relative cost of a conscripted and a volunteer army?
5. Jim Teen, a high school junior, can caddy at the local country club for as many hours as he chooses each weekend. His father insists, however, that Jim mow the lawn each week. It takes Jim one hour to mow the lawn; it takes his younger brother Bill two hours. Can you explain why it might be more efficient for Jim to pay Bill to take over his lawn chore even though Bill is a far less skilled yardman? What sense does it make, if any, to say that it costs more when Jim mows the lawn than when Bill mows it?
6. If the federal government and private foundations allocate large sums for research, will this tend to benefit or harm a small college whose faculty either does no research or cannot land any research grants? Why?
7. By taking an airplane one can go from D to H in one hour. The same trip takes five hours by bus. If the air fare is $30 and the bus fare is $10, which would be the cheaper mode of transportation for someone who could earn $2 an hour during this time? For someone who could earn $10 an hour? Five dollars an hour?
8. At a sufficiently high price for gasoline, almost everyone would choose to leave the car at home and use public transportation to commute to and from work. But that price will differ vastly from one person to another. Why might it be higher for self-employed than for salaried people? For executives than for clerks?
9. What would be the effect on the cost to students of completing high school if legislation denied drivers' licenses to anyone under the age of 18?

10. How do income tax rates affect the cost to a self-employed professional woman of painting her own house?

11. Why might a multinational corporation with identical plants in different countries pay different wage rates to workers in the two countries even though their skill levels were the same? Does this strike you as unjust? Why might the higher-paid workers object?

12. Think about the cost of television commercials. What enters into the cost of a 30-second commercial plugging Friendly Fred's Ford Dealership? How do you explain the fact that the same commercial will cost $90 on Wednesday morning but $1600 right before "All in the Family"? Local television stations are often asked to donate time for public service spots. Does this cost the station anything? Do you think that station owners' religious beliefs make them more willing to donate time on Sunday mornings than on weekday mornings?

13. **a.** It has been argued that a volunteer army would discriminate against poor people, because they tend to have the lowest value alternatives to military service and hence would dominate the ranks of volunteers. Do you agree with the analysis and the objection?

   b. Some critics have argued that if the military relied exclusively on volunteers, the armed forces would be filled with people of such low intelligence and skills that they could not operate sophisticated weapons (such as the ABM). International Business Machines relies exclusively on "volunteers," and *its* employees are not predominantly people of low intelligence and skills. What's the difference between the armed forces and IBM? How would you reply to the argument of these critics?

   c. Another frequent criticism of a volunteer military is that we don't want "an army of mercenaries." How high does the military wage have to be before the recipient becomes a mercenary? Are officers compelled to remain in the armed services? Why do they stay in? Are they mercenaries? Is your teacher a mercenary? Your physician? Your minister?

14. A number of American cities have passed rent control ordinances in recent years. These ordinances often try to restrict rent increases to the amount of cost increases. Use the analysis of this chapter in thinking about these questions:

   a. What is the cost to a landlord of renting an apartment to you for $150 if someone else is willing to pay $250?

   b. What is the cost to this other person of the landlord's renting to you for $150?

   c. What determines the cost to a potential landlord of purchasing an apartment building?

   d. What effect will a rent control ordinance have on the cost of purchasing an apartment building?

   e. What effect will a rent control ordinance have on the cost to landlords of letting an apartment unit stand idle, or of using it themselves, or of allowing relatives to live in it rent-free?

   f. What is the cost to a member of the city council of voting against a rent-control ordinance? How will this cost be affected if the city in question is a small one with a large student population, and students are granted the right to vote in municipal elections?

g. What concept of cost do you think supporters of rent controls have in mind when they speak of basing maximum rents on landlords' costs?

Chapter **4**

Scarcity and the Price System

Economic theory is useful because it helps us understand how the members of a large, complex society cooperate in using the infinitely varied resources available to them in satisfying their equally varied wants. Put more briefly, economic theory explains the interactions of supply and demand. The preceding two chapters looked first at demand, then at supply, and tried to show how each is the product of people's choices among alternative opportunities. This chapter begins the task of putting supply and demand together.

The Precarious Balance

An item in the *Wall Street Journal* of April 30, 1979 described an experiment in organized hitchhiking that was to be launched the next day in Novato, California, near San Francisco. Here is how the program was expected to work. Commuters pay $5 and receive credentials identifying them as members of "Commuter Connection." Drivers then advertise their willingness to take riders by displaying the credentials on their windshields, while would-be hitchhikers solicit rides by holding up their credentials at one of a dozen designated pickup points. Drivers and riders negotiate their own financial arrangements when they make a connection. It all amounts to a carpooling program, but one that is far more flexible than the usual carpooling arrangement. People don't have to commit themselves in advance to share transportation with a particular set of people each day and be bound by their schedules.

The program would seem to offer an attractive combination of economy and convenience. In order for it to work, however, there must be an adequate balance between drivers and riders. The executive director of "Commuter Connection" told the *Journal* reporter that it would take time to achieve the right balance of drivers and riders, but she had high hopes. An official of the federal government, which donated money to support the experiment, called it an innovative solution but also warned that "only time will tell."

By the time this chapter is published, we will probably know whether those offering transportation and those looking for it balanced out adequately and the experiment succeeded. But in view of the fact that we achieve thousands of much more complicated balances between supply and demand every day, why was there so much doubt in the minds of the program's supporters? No one worries that lawn rakes will disappear from the garden shops, or that you won't be able to buy lunch downtown on a week day, or that the recordings of a popular rock star won't be available for sale to the faithful. Each of these depends upon a whole series of balances between those willing to sell and those offering to buy. Nonetheless, we're all fairly confident that rakes, lunches, and records will be supplied when and where they're demanded. Why aren't we nearly as sure about the supply of and demand for commuter transportation to and from San Francisco?

As soon as you imagine yourself actually participating in "Commuter Connection," all sorts of problems come to mind. Will there be enough drivers for all the riders? Or should there be about three riders for each driver to hold down the costs? Will they all be satisfied with the financial arrangements they can negotiate? What about the embarrassment of asking for too much or offering too little? Won't some people consent to compensation that they really think is unfair, to avoid embarrassment, and then just not participate again? But financial arrangements are only one part of a satisfactory transaction. "He drove so fast I was terrified all the way." "She let me off ten blocks from my office." "How do I get home at night?" "One of the passengers lit up a cigar." "He talked incessantly." "She blasted rock music at us all the way." "I'm uneasy. How do I know some guy isn't a sex maniac? How thoroughly did 'Commuter Connection' screen people before handing out credentials?" "I guess I'd rather drive than sit in the back of a sports car with my knees in my face."

Some of these problems were anticipated. Participants were told, for example, to hold up "Commuter Connection" cards labeled FD for the financial district or CC for the civic center area. And in principle none of the problems is unmanageable. HR could mean "hate rock." CD could stand for "cautious driver," NS for "no smokers," LL for "long legs." Drivers and riders could display their monetary offers and bids. And with a sufficient investment in screening, "Commuter Connection" could probably reduce any commuter's chance of encountering a sex maniac on the Golden Gate bridge to that of meeting one on the supermarket parking lot. But all of these arrangements add costly complications and create legitimate grounds for wondering whether the experiment will, in the long run, succeed.

Whatever its ultimate fate, however, the initial uncertainty about the Novato-to-San Francisco experiment points up the complexity of the central problem that faces every economic system: inducing people to cooperate effectively in using what is available to provide what is wanted. There are so many potential dimensions to each side of the equation—to supply and to demand—that the everyday availability of satisfactory garden rakes, noon lunches, and musical recordings really is a minor marvel. How do we manage to pull it off?

We do it primarily through an extensive, continuous exchange of information, in which the central bits of information are money prices. The beginning of all wisdom in economics may be the recognition that *prices are first and foremost information*. They are information about the fundamental fact that makes choice unavoidable and social cooperation so beneficial: the fact of *scarcity*.

Prices and Scarcity

No one blames the thermometer for low temperatures or seriously proposes to warm up the house on a cold day by holding a candle under the furnace thermostat. People do, however, often blame high prices for the scarcity of certain goods and act as if scarcity could be eliminated by pushing down prices through legislation or by moralizing.

To the lover of lobster, its high price does indeed look like the cause of its scarcity. Lobster rarely appears in our house because its price is high. But what would happen if the lobster lovers' lobby pushed a bill through Congress that placed a ceiling price on lobster well below the current prevailing price? Would lobster be any less scarce? Lobster fans would now *want* to buy more lobster. But would they succeed? The low ceiling price might in fact cause lobster to disappear from most of the stores in the country.

Contrary to the doctrine now being propounded by some who are impressed with the enormous wealth of the United States, even we, the wealthiest people in the world, have not ended scarcity. Nor is it likely that we ever shall. We may learn to be more content with fewer material goods, or we may manage to produce and distribute material goods in such abundance that no one any longer gives much thought to acquiring more. But even then we would not have abolished scarcity. For the present and in the foreseeable future, we shall have to live with the fact that the means of satisfying our wants fall far short of the wants themselves.

So we must economize. We must allocate our resources intelligently, trying to obtain from what we have as much as possible of what we want. We must learn to manage scarcity, since we cannot hope to abolish it. The management of scarcity does include scaling down or otherwise altering wants, as well as expanding production. It's often possible to loosen the pinch of scarcity merely by reevaluating one's objectives and discovering that a particular goal really isn't worth the cost of attaining it, or that the want behind the desire for some good can actually be satisfied in another and less difficult way. But the management of scarcity, especially in an economy as large and diversified as ours, with so many different resources and varied preferences, will remain an enormously complex social task. Its successful performance requires, above all else, a social system that facilitates the rapid exchange of accurate information about relative scarcities.

Let's take a closer look at the phenomenon of scarcity. We shall notice, as we do so, that scarcity is quite different from shortage, and that something can be scarce even when a surplus of it exists.

The Consequences of Scarcity

The climate of Gazebo, a fictitious South Sea island, is perfect for growing both oranges and pineapples. But since there are far more pineapple plants than orange trees on the island, 50,000 pineapples are harvested each month and only 5000 oranges. Which is scarcer?

We cannot tell from the information given. Scarcity is a *relationship*. If the people of Gazebo love pineapples and hate oranges, pineapples could be more scarce despite their greater abundance. Scarcity is a relationship between availability and desirability, or between supply and demand. If pineapples in Gazebo were considered unfit for human consumption, and there was no way to sell them to others, they would not be scarce at all. No one speaks of the scarcity of garbage—except perhaps hog farmers, for whom garbage is not garbage.

If people can have all that they want of some good without being required to sacrifice anything else that is also wanted, that good is not scarce. It is a *free good*. There are obviously not many free goods available in our society, despite the song that says the best things in life are free. Perhaps the best things in life cannot be purchased with money; but that does not make them free goods.

If anything is scarce, it must be rationed. That means that a criterion of some kind must be established for discriminating among claimants to determine who will get how much. The criterion could be age, eloquence, swiftness, public esteem, willingness to pay money, or almost anything else. We characteristically ration scarce goods in our society on the basis of willingness to pay money. But sometimes we use other criteria in order to discriminate.

Scarcity makes rationing unavoidable.

Harvard College each year has many more applicants than it can place in the freshman class, so Harvard must ration the scarce places. It discriminates on the basis of high school grades, test scores, recommendations, and other criteria.

Only one person at a time can be president of the United States. Since many more people than that want the position, we have evolved an elaborate system of discrimination in the form of conventions and elections. Although there is considerable doubt about just what the criteria for discrimination are, the system does discriminate. We end up every fourth year with only one satisfied candidate.

Joe College is the most popular man on campus and has young women clamoring for his favor. He must therefore ration his attentions. Whether he employs the criterion of beauty, intelligence, geniality, or something else, he must and will discriminate in some fashion.

But the other side of discrimination is competition. Once Harvard announces its criteria for discrimination, freshman applicants will compete to meet them. The criteria for selecting a president are studied carefully by the hopefuls who begin competing to satisfy those criteria long before the election year. If the women eager to go with Joe College believe that beauty is his main criterion, they will compete with one another to seem more beautiful.

Rationing results in competition.

Competition is obviously not peculiar to capitalist societies or to societies that use money. The point is of fundamental importance: *competition results from scarcity* and can only be eliminated with the elimination of scarcity. Whenever there is scarcity, there must be rationing. Rationing is allocation in accord with some criteria for discrimination. Competition is merely what occurs when people strive to meet the criteria that are being used.

Of course, the criteria used do make a difference. If a society rations on the basis of willingness to pay money, members of that society will strive to make money. If it uses physical strength as a primary criterion, members of the society will do bodybuilding exercises. And if the better colleges and universities use high school grades as an important criterion for selection, high school students will compete for grades. They might be competing for grades to acquire other goods as well (status among classmates, compliments from teachers, use of the family car); but it is odd for colleges to complain of grade grubbers when their own rationing criteria promote grade grubbing.

Monetary prices are the most common rationing device in our society. The high price of lobster both reflects the fact that it is scarce *and* rations to eager gourmets the limited quantity available. What happens when the price of lobster is not allowed to rise to the level that reflects its actual scarcity? Suppose that our lobster lovers' lobby managed to get a law through Congress setting $1 a pound as the maximum price that could be charged for lobster.

The quantity demanded would immediately increase. Lobster lovers would race to the grocery store in anticipation of inexpensive epicurean delights. But many would find only frustration. Someone else would have gotten there first. The lower price does nothing to increase the number of lobsters available, and, in the long run, it will reduce the amount of lobster that reaches the grocery stores and fish markets as lobster catchers find it more profitable to do something other than trap lobsters. The lobster lovers' lobby did nothing to make lobster less scarce. They only suppressed the rationing device. They put ice cubes on the thermometer, so to speak; they did not turn on the air conditioning. They mistook a symptom (the high price) for the cause of their discontent (the scarcity of lobster).

But since lobster is still scarce, it must still be rationed. When price was prevented from serving as the discriminatory criterion, swiftness took its place. Those who were first to the stores took home the lobster, and the rest had none. Later on we might expect friendship with the butcher or fishmonger to become an important discriminatory criterion. And if this happens we would expect the social popularity of these tradesmen to increase as lobster lovers start competing to satisfy the new rationing system. Fishmongers will be seen at all the more glittering social events, and party givers will call months in advance to be sure of their butcher's presence.

Our discussion has emphasized the demand side. But prices ration simultaneously on the supply side. The low lobster prices, which mislead consumers into thinking that lobsters are less scarce than they actually are, also transmit misleading information to the suppliers of it. Low prices tell these people that their scarce time, energy, and other resources are not as valuable in lobster production as they had previously supposed. Sooner or later they act on the basis of this information, and fewer lobsters arrive at the stores. With New Englanders now willing to buy all that becomes available, no one will have any incentive to pay the cost of shipping lobster to the hungry hinterland. Proximity to Maine will thus become another rationing device. When the lobsters no longer come to the people, the people will have to go to the lobsters.

From Scarcity to Shortage

Scarcity is an inescapable fact of life. Shortages, however, are avoidable. *A shortage is defined by economists as a situation in which the quantity demanded is greater than the quantity supplied.* Since the quantity demanded varies inversely with the price, and the quantity supplied varies directly, any shortage can be eliminated merely by allowing the price to rise.

An Instructive Example

Let's take the case of gasoline as an illustration. Figure 4A presents a hypothetical demand curve for gasoline in the U.S., labeled DD, with the price per gallon on the vertical axis and the number of gallons demanded per month on the horizontal axis. The demand is very inelastic within the range shown: a large percentage increase in the price will lead to a much smaller percentage decrease in the quantity demanded. That's a reasonable assumption, well supported by experience. The substitutes for gasoline are not very attractive to most of the people who use it. Moreover, gasoline remains a relatively manageable item in most people's monthly budgets, even at a dollar a gallon.

But there *are* substitutes for gasoline: joining a carpool, moving closer to work, buying a smaller car, taking the bus, planning ahead, getting more frequent tune-ups, or staying at home. As the price of gasoline rises, so do the sacrifices people must make in order to buy it. And as a result, although a few may choose not to reduce their consumption at all, most will find ways to economize at least a little, and some will decide to curtail their purchases substantially as the price goes up. The demand for gasoline is not totally inelastic.

Figure 4A also shows a relatively inelastic supply curve of gasoline, labeled SS.[1] The element of time, which plays such a large role in determining the price elasticity of demand for most goods, performs an even larger part in determining the price elasticity of supply. Gasoline in storage can be quickly released for sale if a higher price makes selling more attractive than storing. But time is required to import gasoline from abroad in response to a higher price. Still more time is required

---

1. Price elasticity of supply is analogous to price elasticity of demand: the percentage change in quantity supplied divided by the percentage change in price.

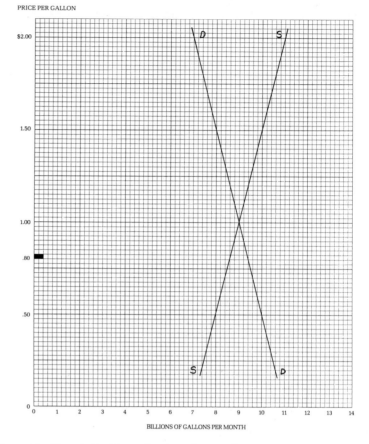

PRICE PER GALLON

BILLIONS OF GALLONS PER MONTH

Figure 4A Hypothetical demand and supply curve for gasoline

to increase the flow of gasoline from the refineries by switching over from the production of other refined products, such as heating oil. And far more time will necessarily elapse before additional refinery capacity can be created in response to the higher price of gasoline.

What about the availability of crude oil? Were not the gasoline shortages of 1973–74 and 1979 the result of inadequate supplies of the basic raw material? We must answer carefully if we are to avoid begging the question. Iran's political turmoil in 1978 and 1979 certainly disrupted the flow of oil imports into the United States. But other OPEC countries had the capacity to step up their rate of production and thereby compensate for the Iranian cutbacks. They did not do so, because they wanted the price of crude oil to rise. But that is precisely our point. More than enough oil could have been supplied in 1979 to keep the refineries running at 100 percent of capacity if the refineries—and ultimately the consumers of refined products—had been willing and able to pay the price. We must add the word *able*, because the ability of consumers and refiners to offer more money for gasoline and for crude petroleum was restricted by U.S. law.

Given our assumed (but plausible) demand and supply curves in Figure 4A, will Americans experience a shortage of gasoline? Not if the price is $1 a gallon. At that price, but only at that price, the quantity of gasoline Americans want to buy is exactly balanced by the quantity offered for sale: 9 billion gallons per month.

Now suppose that the price of gasoline in this situation is fixed by law so that it cannot exceed 80 cents a gallon. At 80 cents the quantity demanded per month will be 9.4 billion gallons. But the quantity supplied will be only 8.6 billion gallons. A shortage will exist: the quantity demanded will exceed the quantity supplied by 800 million gallons per month.

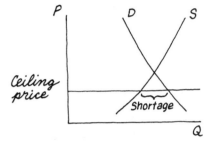

On the graph of Figure 4A, the shortage appears as a gap between the demand curve and the supply curve at the 80 cents per gallon price. In what form would the shortage appear in real life? What would we observe?

When Prices Do Not Change

Inevitably we would see increases in the nonmonetary costs of purchasing gasoline; for gasoline is scarce and therefore *must* be rationed. If by law we suppress the rationing device of monetary price, other rationing criteria will have to be used, whether by drift or by design. Potential purchasers of gasoline will attempt to discover the new criteria being used to discriminate among buyers, and they will compete against one another in trying to satisfy those criteria. Their competition will raise the total cost—price plus nonmonetary costs—and will continue raising it until the quantity demanded no longer exceeds the quantity supplied.

The gas line is probably the best example. When people think they may be unable to purchase as much gasoline as they would like to buy at 80 cents a gallon, they try to get to the station early before the stocks have all been sold. But others have the same idea, so that the lines form earlier and grow longer. Waiting in line is unquestionably a cost. As this cost rises, the law of demand comes into play: consumers drive less when they have to pay $12 plus half an hour's wait for a fill-up than when they can fill their tanks for a straight $12.

Some drivers may decide to hunt around rather than wait in line. They will pay their additional cost in time and gasoline spent on searching. Others will strike deals: a fill-up out of reserved supplies in return for a tip to the station operator, or the payment of a special fee for parking at the station, or an agreement to have service work performed there, or maybe tickets to the theater for the station owner. All these ways of competing for gasoline raise the cost of obtaining it. And the cost will continue rising until it finally reduces the quantity demanded to match the quantity supplied.

Competition among people—whose combined desires to purchase a good cannot all be fully satisfied at the prevailing money price—will bid up the cost of purchasing it. Usually it will be the money price that rises in such a situation. Whenever other components of the cost of purchasing a good start to climb, we can be fairly certain that some kind of social pressure (such as legislated price controls) is holding down the money price. And when that occurs—that is, when lengthening lines, longer searching, or special arrangements come into play to ration a good (because the quantity demanded is greater than the quantity supplied *at the prevailing money price*)—we are then observing a shortage of that good.

Shortages and Money Prices

Go back a few paragraphs to our original definition of the word *shortage* and notice that *we have changed the definition slightly*. A shortage, we are now maintaining, exists when the quantity demanded is constrained to match the quantity supplied by an increase in some component of the cost of purchasing *other than the money price*. That's an essential addition to our original definition, because the quantity demanded really cannot exceed the quantity supplied for more than a very short period of time. Do you see why? A scarce good will inevitably be rationed by some criteria, intended or unintended. To prospective purchasers, those criteria become a part of the cost of acquiring the good and therefore reduce the quantity that they demand.

The economist's concept of shortage, as it now turns out, zeroes in on the money price. Shortages exist only when money prices are not able to perform the function of rationing scarce goods to competing demanders. We spot a shortage in real life whenever we find nonmoney costs rising to ration scarce goods. The justification for this focus on money prices is the central role that prices play in the coordination of activity between demanders and suppliers.

The Supplier's Role in Rationing

We expect the money price of a good to rise when the good becomes scarcer. Why? Because it is almost always in the interest of suppliers to raise the money price rather than see some other component of the acquisition cost increase. What does the gas station owner gain, after all, when customers wait in line for 30 minutes? Nothing (and maybe less than nothing if they are all less pleasant people to serve by the time they get to the pump). But a 20 cents increase in the money price of purchasing a gallon of gasoline is simultaneously a 20 cents per gallon addition to the station owner's wealth. It is usually the case that an increase in nonmoney costs entails an increase in what the economist calls *deadweight costs*. These are *costs to the purchaser that are not simultaneously benefits to the seller*. The cost of waiting in line is a perfect example.

If sellers have it in their power to transform a deadweight cost into a benefit for themselves, they will want to do so. And whenever sellers are free to raise the money price of the good they are supplying, they have ready at hand a simple tool for making that transformation. Notice what a handy and versatile tool it is. Everyone values money because its possession confers command over a whole universe of other goods. Everyone is accustomed to paying money for goods. The seller is usually the owner or agent of the owner with an acknowledged right to change the money price. The money price can be minutely adjusted, up or down, in a search for the price that most completely converts the buyer's cost of acquisition into the seller's benefit from supplying.

All of this explains why changes in money prices are the usual response to changes in relative scarcities, and why economists view changing money prices as such a crucial means for securing social coordination. There are goods that cannot and other goods—most people would agree—that should not be rationed by means of changing money prices.[2] But it is a fact well worth noting that where this mechanism for achieving social coordination is not available, cooperation on any extensive scale becomes much more difficult to achieve.

Appropriate and Inappropriate Signals

What will suppliers do if the law prevents them from raising their prices in a situation of obvious shortage? They will probably look for alternative ways to turn the situation to their advantage. Gasoline retailers may decide to lower the cost *to them* of selling by reducing their daily hours of operation and closing altogether on weekends. If they can sell their entire weekly allocations in 20 hours, why should they bother to stay open for 120 hours a week? This response to the shortage will tend further to increase the cost *to buyers* of purchasing gasoline: they will face even longer lines, will be forced to cancel or curtail weekend traveling, will more frequently find themselves stranded because of the inability to obtain fuel, and will pay

---

2. It would be difficult to assign all residents on a city block the precise amount of street illumination for which each is willing to pay. And we apply a variety of derogatory terms to people who ration their affections by the criterion of money price.

additional costs through searching, worrying, and even endangering their lives by improperly siphoning and storing gasoline.

Those who supply or demand gasoline are not peculiarly selfish or inconsiderate. The costly chaos that we have actually witnessed in recent years at the gasoline pumps simply demonstrates how dependent we are upon changing money prices to secure effective cooperation in our complex, interdependent society and economy. When prices are not permitted to signal a change in relative scarcities, suppliers and demanders receive inappropriate signals. They do not find, because they have no incentive to look for, ways to accommodate one another more effectively. It is important that people receive some such incentive, because there are so many little ways and big ways in which people *can* accommodate—ways that no central planner can possibly anticipate, but which in their combined effect make the difference between chaos and coordination. Changing money prices, continuously responding to changing conditions of demand or supply, provide just such an incentive.

Is There a *Better* System?

To say that money prices perform this function is not to say that they perform it perfectly. They certainly don't. In subsequent chapters we'll be looking at the limitations of social coordination through a price system as well as at its accomplishments. We'll ask under what circumstances money prices are less likely to reflect people's preferences in an adequate way, and we'll discover that ignorance, market power, collusive arrangements, disagreements about property rights, and inequalities in society all interfere with the "ideal" operation of the price system. But we do not discard the first law of motion (which says that bodies in motion tend to remain in motion) just because there is friction in the actual world. It would be a similar mistake to overlook the achievements of the price system just because it fails to coordinate flawlessly.

A system that rations scarce goods by means of money prices will, of course, allocate the goods to those who are willing to pay. Consequently, when rationing occurs by means of price, poor people tend to get less than the rich people. That, in fact, is the very meaning of *rich* and *poor* when used in an economic context. But it is not the whole picture. Price rationing accommodates all sorts of other differences among people as well, differences that will prove extremely difficult to handle fairly under any other form of rationing.

Suppose we decide to ration gasoline by means of specially issued coupons. How will the government allocate those coupons? It would not be fair to allocate the same number to a single person as to a family of seven, but neither would it be fair to give seven times as many coupons to the family. It wouldn't be fair to allocate an equal number of coupons to each licensed driver, and it wouldn't be fair to assign coupons to each owner of an automobile. (This would encourage people to stock their driveways with clunkers.) People who live in dense metropolitan areas probably travel shorter distances on average and also are more likely to have access to public transportation. Fairness therefore suggests that they should receive fewer coupons than those who live in thinly populated regions of the country. But some people in New York City regularly drive farther than some people in Silverton, Colorado. Would a system that ignored the special circumstances of individuals be fair? How could coupons be awarded fairly to a traveling sales representative in west Texas and an elderly woman in Cedar Rapids who drives only to church? Should the person who hates to drive receive as many coupons as someone who enjoys driving?

And what about business users? (An adequate rationing system must take account of the fact that diesel fuel and gasoline compete for scarce petroleum and scarce refinery capacity.) If farmers, taxicab companies, commercial fishermen, and trucking firms—to mention just a handful of businesses that use large amounts of motor fuel—are allotted "all that they need," they will turn out to "need" more than anyone had anticipated. If we therefore create a government agency charged with determining the specific quantities to which each individual firm is entitled, what criteria will it use to make its decisions? Past consumption? Probably. But in an economy where new firms are continually born and old ones die, where some businesses expand and others decline, where technology is constantly changing and so is demand, how can past consumption be an adequate guide to current allocation?

The unfairness of its decisions might be the least of the agency's worries. Because business firms supply inputs to other business firms, as well as final goods to consumers, mistakes that were not quickly caught and corrected could have a domino effect. An error in allocation could close down an entire industry by inadvertently preventing the manufacture or transportation of some seemingly minor but actually indispensable input. The intricate interdependence of a modern, industrialized economy could not long be maintained in the face of arbitrary allocations of motor fuel among business firms.

Inflation and Rent Controls

Popular hostility to rationing by means of money prices builds in periods of inflation, because people mistakenly assume that an increase in money prices means a decline in their level of living. It's hard for most of us to see that our money incomes tend to rise right along with the prices of the goods we buy. When expenditures on a particular good take up a large percentage of our monthly budget, we become especially sensitive to increases in that good's price. If in addition the price of the good changes infrequently, and therefore by large jumps when it does change, we grow even more indignant about increases in its price. And popular indignation is fertile ground for the growth of legislative interference in the movement of money prices.

Rent controls are far and away the best example. While grocery and clothing prices creep slowly upward in a period of inflation and are therefore commonly ignored, rents tend to remain fixed for longer periods of time—and then to do their advancing with a bound. A rent increase from $150 to $225 makes a big dent in the budget and seems unreasonably steep, even when the average prices of the other goods we buy have increased by more than 50 percent since the last rent increase. People look for scapegoats in such circumstances, and landlords (the word itself stirs resentment) are prime candidates.

There is an unusual irony in the case of residential rents, an irony that greatly aggravates the problem. Because residential rents are exceptionally "sticky" prices, tending to lag behind the rate of change in other prices, the average level of rents tends actually to fall during rapid inflations. Thus while the average level of prices paid by consumers more than doubled from 1967 to the end of 1978, rents increased slightly less than 70 percent. That means that rents actually declined by about 15 percent.[3]

But this fall in rental prices was caused by a malfunction of the price system, not by any change in underlying conditions of demand or supply. The result in one American city after another has been *declining vacancy rates*, the initial form always taken by a shortage of rental units. These low vacancy rates, themselves a result of underpriced housing, then become a further argument for rent controls. "We cannot permit rent-gouging when the vacancy rate is less than 1 percent." Or even better: "We must impose rent controls until the vacancy rate rises to an acceptable 3 percent." Since the low vacancy rate is the product of low rents, that is an argument, whether recognized or not, for permanent rent controls. Note that the suppliers who are thus singled out and specifically forbidden to raise their prices are suppliers whose prices are already failing to keep pace with inflation.

When law or custom keeps rents below the level at which the quantity demanded equals the quantity supplied, other ways of rationing will evolve. Landlords might discriminate on the basis of age, sexual preference, personal habits, family size,

---

3. The ratio of rents to all consumer prices, which by definition was 100/100 in 1967, had become 170/200 in 1978; so rents in 1978 were at only 85 percent of their 1967 levels when measured in relative prices. That constitutes a 15 percent decline.

letters of reference, pet ownership, length of residence in the community, or willingness to abide by petty regulations. Tenants who were lucky enough to be in a rent-controlled apartment when the controls were imposed will hang on to as much space as possible for as long as they can and will try to pass the unit on to a friend or to sublease when they do vacate. Landlords will lower the quality of the services they provide, since they know that there is a long line of tenants waiting to move in if any current tenant becomes dissatisfied.

All of these responses will lead to demands for costly administrative review boards and for additional legislation prohibiting particular landlord responses. The long-term result will be the eventual disappearance of landlords, as existing buildings are allowed to deteriorate or are turned into condominiums, and new rental units are not constructed. But even the most unrelenting foe of landlords must concede that it will be hard to find apartments to rent when none is being offered.

Surpluses and Scarcity

It still remains to introduce the concept of a surplus. Many people use the word *surplus* to suggest that a particular good is not scarce. In economic theory, however, *a surplus exists when, at the prevailing price, the quantity supplied is greater than the quantity demanded.*

Agricultural surpluses haven't been much talked about in recent years, but they were a perennial economic problem in the United States for many years after World War II. Farmers and their supporters maintained that the prices of agricultural products should go up at about the same rate as the prices of other goods. They persuaded Congress to establish parity prices: prices that preserved the ratio which farmers had enjoyed from 1910 to 1914 (prosperous years for farmers generally) between the prices they received for their crops and the prices they paid for the goods they bought. A common policy goal was 90 percent of parity.

Through the Commodity Credit Corporation, an agency of the Department of Agriculture, the federal government offered to store for farmers, free of charge, any crops for which they could not find a market at the established parity price, meanwhile loaning the farmers the value of the crops they chose to store. These were nonrecourse loans, which means that farmers could simply pocket the loan and let the Commodity Credit Corporation keep the stored produce. In effect farmers could use the government as a buyer of last resort in order to be sure of receiving the target price for any "supported" crop. The resulting surpluses did not mean that wheat, corn, cotton, and other supported crops were not scarce. They simply meant that Congress was unwilling to let key farm

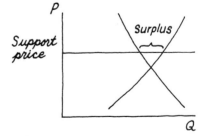

prices fall to the level at which the quantity demanded for current consumption would match the quantity farmers wanted to produce.

The American Medical Association has begun to warn us about an imminent surplus of physicians. There were 149 doctors for every 100,000 people in the United States in 1966 and 189 per 100,000 of population in 1976. By 1990, according to the AMA, there will be 242 physicians for every 100,000 Americans, or 25,000 to 50,000 more than will be "needed." But how many physicians do people "need"? San Francisco reportedly had 525 doctors per 100,000 population already in 1978. Do you suppose that physicians are not scarce in San Francisco? When members of a profession talk about the number "needed," they almost always mean the quantity that would be demanded *at the present price*. They would rather not contemplate any reduction in the price of their services, of course.

Surpluses of teachers have also become a problem in recent years, at least for the teachers. From the standpoint of school boards and local taxpayers, the problem often looks more like an opportunity. At lower wage rates, school districts would be willing to hire more teachers. And at lower wage rates, some of those now offering to teach would decide to seek careers elsewhere. If salary scales cannot be reduced, either because of union contracts or just because it "wouldn't be right" to lower the pay of those to whom we entrust the hearts and minds of our youth, other ways will be found to balance the quantity supplied and the quantity demanded. Salary scale increases that are less than the rate of inflation reduce the real wage. School boards can also add to the duties of teachers, lowering the wage per unit of product by getting more product for a given salary.

If these measures are insufficient to balance quantity supplied with quantity demanded, other criteria will of necessity be used to ration out the scarce supply of teaching positions. (A surplus of teachers is a shortage of teaching positions.) Seniority is an obvious and common rationing criterion. It's one that appeals to long-established teachers, but not one that younger or prospective teachers find very attractive. And certainly it does little to promote a situation in which those most eager or apt to teach are also most likely to end up in the classroom.

Hard as it may be to remember at this time, we have even seen surpluses of gasoline in the not too distant past. How could we recognize gasoline surpluses at the retail level? By quantities of gasoline offered for sale in excess of the quantities demanded *at prevailing prices?* No. The evidence would show up in the techniques used by competing sellers to capture the custom of scarce consumers, techniques that increase the cost to retailers of selling. Station owners might, for example, offer rapid, friendly service, rushing to clean the windshield and check the battery water, tire pressure, and oil level. They might provide road maps at no charge. They might offer clean, comfortable restrooms in an effort to make their stations a more pleasant place to buy gasoline. They might offer premiums, trading stamps, or free car washes with every fill-up. (They might and they did, of course.) The disappearance of all these extras marked the transition from surplus to shortage, but always *at the prevailing price*. Even in the days of spectacular service and bonus gifts, gasoline was scarce. Can anyone doubt that at a high enough price we would again "enjoy" surpluses of gasoline?

A Return to Novato

Why do you suppose we chose to introduce this chapter with that long account of "Commuter Connection"? The key terms in the chapter—*scarcity, shortage, surplus*—weren't even used in our discussion of the organized hitchhiking scheme devised for Novato commuters. The reason we began with that account and now return to it is that we wanted to set our entire analysis in the context of *the central economic problem: securing cooperation among people in using what is available to obtain what is wanted*. The more carefully you reflect on the "Commuter Connection" plan, the more likely is it that you will appreciate the magnitude of the challenge and the extraordinary effectiveness of the social machinery through which we meet it every day.

What is missing in the Novato arrangements? Perhaps by the time you read this, nothing at all, or at least nothing very important. "Commuter Connection" may by now be a stunning success. But if that is so, it will be because *the terms of exchange became sufficiently clear, simple, standardized.* That's exactly what the organizers of the scheme were trying to do through their initial arrangements: reduce the myriad dimensions of a satisfactory transaction to just a handful of issues for participants to negotiate. But it's hard to anticipate all the relevant possibilities. Most of the time that can be done successfully only through the evolving interactions, the experimental give and take, of the individuals who choose to involve themselves.

Money prices are a device of extraordinary effectiveness for simplifying, clarifying, and standardizing. Have you ever wondered why committees achieve so little while consuming so much of their members' time and energy? It's because committees are such poor devices for simplifying, clarifying, and standardizing the available options. If a committee does manage to evolve procedures for performing these tasks, it ceases to behave like a committee—instead it becomes a cooperative venture.

There's another method for getting work done through committees, of course: by letting one person make all the decisions. Dictators do get things done quickly. And dictatorial decision making can also perform, in the larger society, many of the simplifying, clarifying, and standardizing functions of the price system.

The other side of the coin is that the price system makes social cooperation possible in the absence of dictators. That's a definite plus for all those who don't like dictators much.

Once Over Lightly

Scarcity is a relationship between availability and desirability —or between supply and demand. A good ceases to be scarce only when people can obtain all that they want at no cost.

Scarce goods must be rationed in some way.

Every rationing system must employ discriminatory criteria of some kind.

Competition is the attempt to satisfy whatever discriminatory criteria are being used to ration scarce goods.

Monetary prices are by far the most common rationing device used in our society. If the money cost of acquiring a good is not able to rise when the good becomes scarcer, competition among demanders will raise other components of its acquisition cost.

A shortage is a situation in which the quantity demanded exceeds the quantity supplied at the prevailing money price. A shortage can always be eliminated by a sufficiently large price increase.

When prices do not rise in response to a shortage, the other costs of acquisition that rise in their stead are often deadweight costs. These are costs to demanders that, unlike monetary payments, are not benefits to suppliers.

Suppliers have an incentive to convert deadweight costs into benefits for themselves by raising money prices in response to a shortage.

A surplus is a situation in which the quantity of a good supplied exceeds the quantity demanded at the prevailing money price. Any good, whatever its scarcity, will exist in surplus supply if its price is fixed at a high enough level.

Monetary prices are important informational signals in a society characterized by extensive specialization and interdependence. Changing money prices reflect changing circumstances of availability and desirability. They simultaneously provide suppliers and demanders with incentive to alter their behavior in directions more compatible with the new and altered circumstances.

Rationing a good by means of monetary price discriminates in favor of those who receive high monetary incomes,

whether through diligence, luck, genius, or knavery. But it also
discriminates in favor of those who want the good more and
are therefore willing to give up a larger portion of their income
to obtain it. It is not a completely fair system of rationing, but
its fairness should (in fairness?) always be compared with that
of whatever system is proposed to take its place.

   A price system enormously facilitates social cooperation
by making it much easier for people to arrange satisfactory
exchanges.

QUESTIONS FOR DISCUSSION

1. Many ceiling prices were fixed by law in World War II. How were scarce goods rationed?
2. New York City has maintained a system of rent controls since World War II. How do people obtain possession of rent-controlled apartments?
3. State colleges and universities usually set very low tuition. How do they ration scarce facilities? Who do you think gains from this system? Why might professors and administrators of state schools prefer *not* to have scarce facilities rationed by means of higher price (tuition)?
4. There are no toll charges for driving on many urban expressways during the rush hour. How is the scarce space rationed?
5. Parking space is often sold on college campuses at a zero price. How is the scarce space rationed? If all students who bring cars onto the campus are charged $10 a year by the college as an automobile registration fee, is that fee a rationing device?
6. If the supply of turkeys in a particular November turned out to be unusually small, do you think a turkey shortage would result? Why or why not?
7. **a.** There is currently much concern about a growing surplus of college teachers. How could the surplus be reduced or eliminated? Do you think this will happen? Why or why not?
   b. Note that a surplus of college teachers can be viewed as a shortage of college teaching positions. How will the scarce supply of positions be rationed if price (salary of teachers) is not allowed to perform this function?
8. How do you account for the fact that so many people were concerned about world food shortages in 1974 when only five years earlier the governments of Australia, Canada, and the United States had been worrying about surpluses?
9. If you travel through the Western states in the summer, you are much more likely to encounter a shortage of camping spaces than of motel rooms. Why?
10. When motels raise their rates "during the season" and reduce them "off season," are they exploiting customers or promoting a better allocation of resources?
11. The government did not impose controls on sugar prices in 1974, and the price per pound rose about 600 percent. Did the high price cause any more sugar to be available in 1974 than would have been available at a lower, controlled price? Do you think there would have been any refined sugar

available on grocers' shelves if the government had frozen the price near its original level? Where would it have gone?

12. What do you think would have happened had the government imposed price ceilings in 1977 when the price of coffee increased about 400 percent? What do you think would have happened had the government imposed price controls in 1978 when lettuce prices increased by about the same percentage?

13. A letter to the editor recommends: "Gasoline should be rationed, if it becomes necessary, according to need—real need." How will the rationing authorities determine *real need*?

14. Evaluate for its fairness toward single-car and multiple-car families the following proposed systems for rationing gasoline:
    a. People whose license plates end in odd numerals can buy only on odd-numbered days, people whose plates end in even numbers buy on even-numbered days.
    b. People are required to choose one day of the week on which each car will *not* be driven. They are assigned numbers (1 through 7) that they must display. Any car being driven on the prohibited day is ticketed by police.
    c. No one may buy gas on Sundays.
    d. No one may buy less than $10 worth of gasoline.

15. Should parents with one television set and three children allocate program choice to the sibling who submits the highest bid? How do parents ration scarce strawberries, served as dessert at dinner, among competing children? If it is better for parents to allocate these scarce goods according to their sense of justice and fairness, wouldn't it also be better if the Department of Energy allocated scarce energy resources among competing citizens according to the Department's sense of justice and fairness? What is the difference between the two cases?

16. The sign in the cafeteria says: "Please conserve napkins during the paper strike." Suggest some ways in which the cafeteria could ration paper napkins to its customers by raising the cost of taking one (in addition to charging for them). Who will conserve if the cafeteria does nothing except post the above sign?

17. In 1972, to celebrate an anniversary, a Chicago bank offered to sell $100 bills for $80 cash to each of the first 35 customers who appeared at opening time (9 A.M.) on its birthday. How do you suppose the bills were rationed? What kind of people do you think managed to buy the cut-rate $100 bills?

18. Think about a registration scheme under which students would have to pay more tuition for 10 o'clock classes and receive discounts for taking 8 o'clock classes. Would you favor such a plan? Why do colleges *not* charge higher prices for the hours in greater demand? A student willing to pay a friend $5 to stand in line for him and grab a 10 o'clock section might protest vigorously if he were charged an extra $3 to take a 10 o'clock class—even though the $3 fee gets rid of the line which he was willing to pay $5 to avoid. If you think these apparently inconsistent responses are plausible, how would you explain the contradiction?

19. If a ceiling price of $1 per pound was placed on lobster sold at retail, where could you go to eat a lobster?

20. A May 1979 wire service story reported that a San Diego Chargers' football player got so upset about waiting in line to buy gasoline for his Rolls Royce that he purchased a gas station. "I bought it for my friends' convenience, too," Johnny Rodgers said. Do price controls keep the wealthy from obtaining more than the poor?

21. If the distribution of income were completely equalized, would everyone purchase the same quality automobile? Against whom do automobile prices discriminate? Under an equal income distribution, would all families of the same size want to own or rent the same quantity and quality of housing space? Against whom do rental prices discriminate?

22. Are dragons that eat people scarce today? Is smallpox virus rare today? Is it scarce?

23. In many cities, tennis players can reserve municipal courts by phoning early in the week for a reservation. What will occur if there is no charge for reservations? If you think you might want to play later in the week, will you make a reservation? What will you do if you later change your mind and decide not to play? Why do people "waste" free goods? Who bears the cost of such waste?

24. Surpluses seem to be less common or at least less frequently noticed and talked about than shortages. What does this suggest? Why would you expect shortages to be more frequently observed than surpluses during an extended period of inflation?

25. The text maintains that the price system is an institution that secures social cooperation in large part by simplifying options. Another institution that does this effectively is the traffic light. Are traffic lights fair? How much attention do they pay to the special circumstances of the drivers who approach them? Would you prefer a system of traffic control that always gave the right of way to the motorist on the more urgent errand?

26. Would scheduled airline flights continue to be bunched at the popular hours if airports based landing fees on the time of day as well as weight? What are the costs created by the present system with its alternating shortages and surpluses of landing and takeoff times?

27. The table below presents data on total energy consumption in the the United States, in quadrillions of British thermal units, for every other year from 1966 through 1976, along with the percentage increase over each two-year period. Why did the rate of increase drop so sharply after 1972?

Year	BTUs	Increase
1966	56.4	
		9.4%
1968	61.7	
		8.4%
1970	66.9	
		7.0%
1972	71.6	
		1.5%
1974	72.7	
		1.8%
1976	74.0	

Sunk Costs, Marginal Costs, and Economic Decisions

Supply is the more interesting side of the demand and supply interaction. It is on the supply side that farmers rotate crops, wildcatters drill for oil, electricians wire houses, pharmacists compound prescriptions, semiconductor companies design digital circuits, and colleges hire faculty to teach economics.

Supply is limited by cost. In order to obtain a larger quantity of any good, we must offer potential supliers some inducement to move resources from their current use into the production of the good we want. We must make the benefit of doing so greater than the cost—greater than the value to potential suppliers of the opportunities they will have to forgo.

But what counts as cost? More precisely, what are the costs that influence the decisions of suppliers? We will be able to thread our way more confidently through the complexities of cost if we keep in mind three characteristics of all costs capable of affecting decisions to supply. Call them *maxims on cost*. The first two were introduced in Chapter 3.

1. Costs belong to actions, not to things.
2. Costs are costs to particular persons; there are no impersonal costs.
3. Costs always lie in the future.

The first part of this chapter focuses on the third maxim. The last part of the chapter will put the three maxims together to see whether they can shed some useful light on debated public issues.

The Irrelevance of Sunk Costs

If the quantity of a good that is supplied depends on opportunity costs, as we tried to show in Chapter 3, then costs that are not opportunities forgone will not determine the quantity supplied and hence will have no way of affecting price. This is summed up in the economist's dictum: *Sunk costs are irrelevant.* It is a simple but important principle in economic analysis as well as a valuable guide to decision making for both businessmen and consumers. But what exactly is a sunk cost?

When you go into a restaurant and order the 16-ounce steak for $10, you incur a cost: the value of whatever you would have done with the $10 had you not ordered that steak. Now suppose that after eating awhile you realize you overestimated your appetite. You eat half the steak and find that you just don't want any more. You wish that you had ordered the 8-ounce steak listed on the menu at $6. What is the cost of leaving the restaurant with half the steak still on your plate?

It is *not*, as many would erroneously suppose, the difference between the price of the 16-ounce and the 8-ounce entree, or $4. You do not give up $4 in the value of forgone opportunities by leaving half the steak on your plate. You incurred the full cost of the larger steak when you ordered it; you committed yourself at that time to pay the price of the large steak and in that moment you incurred all your costs. The opportunity to spend your money on something else disappeared at that moment.

Then what is the opportunity cost of leaving half your dinner behind? That depends. What opportunity will you thereby forgo? If you have a dog, it might be a chance to see its eyes light up and its tail wag, which will be the value of the opportunity forgone when you choose not to ask for a doggie bag.

Bygones are bygones; sunk costs are sunk.

> The Moving Finger writes; and, having writ,
> Moves on: nor all your Piety nor Wit
> Shall lure it back to cancel half a Line,
> Nor all your Tears wash out a Word of it.

Of course, we must be certain that a cost is really sunk, or fully sunk, before we decide to regard it as irrelevant to decision making. If you were to purchase a new motorcycle and immediately afterward regret your decision, what would be the cost to you of continuing to own the motorcycle? Clearly, you would not be forced to say, "I did it and now I'm stuck." You could resell the motorcycle. By not doing so you would incur a cost (a benefit forgone) equal to its resale value. The genuine sunk cost would therefore be only the difference between what you paid for it and what you can get by selling it. That is the irrelevant part of your cost. *In the economist's way of thinking it is no cost at all, for it represents no opportunity for choice.* It may be cause for bitter regret and the occasion of some education in the dangers of impulse buying, but it is no longer a cost in any sense relevant to the economics of present decisions.

Yet we all know that people do not consistently reason things out in this way. Many people who made such a purchase and then regretted it would be tempted to retain possession of the motorcycle rather than sell it for substantially less than the original price. They might justify this action by saying "I can't afford to take the loss." But they already took the loss! They made a mistake, and their full loss occurred when they made it. If they nonetheless choose to keep the motorcycle, they are probably practicing self-deception. They persuade themselves that a motorcycle gathering cobwebs in the garage has the same value as the money they paid to put it there, and more value than the opportunities forgone by keeping it there. But the only relevant cost now is the opportunity forgone *by not selling*.

The Case of the Las Vegas Caper

Let's take an example now that is more closely related to the business world. You own a television retail store, and one of your suppliers is sponsoring a gigantic Dealers Contest. For every television set you buy (no returns allowed), you receive one day in Las Vegas with all expenses paid. You gleefully order 28 sets, and your wife starts planning your two-week holiday together.

Upon your return from Las Vegas you begin wondering how you will sell all those television sets. One month later you're still wondering. It seems that none of your customers is interested in that brand or model. You are about ready to give up and store the whole lot in the back workroom.

Then you get an offer from an orphanage in some distant city to take all those sets off your hands for $2000. You know that a businessman can't make money by selling below cost, so you sit down to figure out the cost of the sets. You paid $70 apiece to the supplier. Moreover, you have had them in your store for a month tying up valuable floor space. You borrowed the money to buy them from the bank at 12 percent annual interest. You also had various handling costs that you estimate at $200. And you spent $80 on advertising in a vain effort to move the sets. By estimating $140 as the opportunity cost of

$ 1960.00	Wholesale cost
19.00	Interest for 1 month
200.00	Handling costs
80.00	Advertising expenditures
140.00	Display space
$ 2399.60	

display space tied up for a month, you arrive at a figure of $2400. You write back to the orphanage that you would be willing to sell the lot at cost for $2400, forgoing any profit on the transaction in the interest of charity. The orphanage replies that $2000 is their top price since they can get the sets they want somewhere else for that price. But you are a good businessman, you know that losses don't make profits, and you refuse.

You were actually a rather poor businessman. Every one of the "costs" you enumerated in arriving at your total of $2400 was a *past expenditure* and hence no cost at all. *The proper stance for making cost calculations is not looking back to the past, but forward to the future.* Your costs, if you sell, will be the opportunities thereby forgone, or what you can get for the sets if you do not sell to the orphanage. You know the market fairly well and you estimate you could get $560 by selling them for junk. The cost of selling to the orphanage is therefore $560. Your gain from selling to the orphanage is consequently $1440. Any loss that you're worrying about should be assigned to experience and the glorious memories of Las Vegas. It is irrelevant for decision-making purposes.

Value of opportunity forgone by selling to the orphanage: $560

Cost of selling to the orphanage: $560

Net benefit from selling to the orphanage: $1440

Building Bridges

This way of looking at matters is important enough for us to spend time on one further example. Naomi Ballistics is an enterprising engineer who decides to build a bridge across the river. She owns both the access land and the bridge-building rights over the river, so she is free to build her own bridge and charge whatever tolls she pleases. After the bridge has been constructed, at a cost of $10,000, Naomi starts to think about the tolls she should charge. How should she calculate the proper toll, assuming that she is interested in the bridge exclusively as a profit-making enterprise? How does the cost of constructing the bridge enter into her pricing calculations?

The answer is *not at all.* Sunk costs are sunk and therefore irrelevant. The questions Naomi should now ask are future-oriented questions: What will people be willing to pay to use the bridge? What will it cost her to collect the tolls? What will she have to pay for bridge maintenance? What will she get if she sells the bridge for scrap metal? If it turns out that the demand for crossing the bridge is so small that no schedule of rates will yield revenue greater than the costs of toll collection plus maintenance, or that the annual net revenue is less than Naomi could get by selling the bridge for scrap and putting the proceeds in the local savings and loan bank, she should scrap the bridge (assuming, remember, that she is interested exclusively in monetary income).

If it should turn out that bridge crossings are in great demand, so that Naomi's enterprising venture promises to be a

Annual net revenue from operation: $75.00

Scrap value of bridge: $1800.00

Earning rate at S and L: 5%

Annual loss from continued operation: $15.00

huge success, she should still ignore sunk costs in calculating her schedule of tolls. Sunk costs are of concern to historians, but not to economic decision makers. (In Chapter 9, we'll inquire more closely into the principles of price setting.)

Marginal Effects Guide Decisions

One of the economist's favorite words is *marginal*. It means in economics exactly what it means in everyday speech: situated on the border or edge. The concept is of fundamental importance in economic thinking, because economic decisions, like all effective decisions, always involve *marginal* comparisons. That is to say, they always have to do with movements at the border, with positive or negative *additions*. A synonym for marginal, in fact, is *additional*. What will be the *additional*, or *marginal*, cost that results from this decision? And how does it compare with the marginal cost of alternative decisions?

If you think about it for a moment, you will discover that opportunity costs are always marginal costs. The term *marginal cost* does no more than bring into strong relief an aspect of opportunity-cost thinking. That aspect is so important, however, that we shall want to make frequent use of the term. Later on we shall talk about marginal other things.

Marginal Does *Not* Mean Average

You will have no difficulty with the marginal concept if only you do not get it mixed up with the notion of *average*. You may have no intention of confusing marginal with average; if so, what follows may only plant in your head the seeds of a bad idea. Let's hope it doesn't. A simple production schedule of a hypothetical zerc manufacturer will illustrate the distinction.

Number of Zercs Produced	Total Cost of Producing Zercs
42	$4200
43	4257
44	4312
45	4365

A little long division reveals that 42 zercs can be produced at an average cost (total cost per unit) of $100; the average cost is $99 for 43 zercs, $98 for 44, and $97 for 45. A little subtraction reveals, however, that the cost of producing the 43d zerc is not $99 but $57. The incremental expenditure, or the extra cost, incurred by producing the 43d zerc, is its marginal cost. The marginal costs of the 44th and 45th zercs are $55 and $53, respectively. It is clear that marginal cost can be more or less than average cost and can even differ substantially from average cost. It should also be clear that for a zerc manufacturer trying to make production decisions, it is the marginal costs

$$\frac{\$4200}{42} = \$100 \qquad \frac{\$4257}{43} = \$99$$

$$\frac{\$4312}{44} = \$98 \qquad \frac{4365}{45} = \$97$$

$$\begin{array}{r} \$4257 \\ -4200 \\ \hline \$57 \end{array} \qquad \begin{array}{r} \$4312 \\ -4257 \\ \hline \$55 \end{array}$$

$$\begin{array}{r} \$4365 \\ -4312 \\ \hline \$53 \end{array}$$

that should guide him. Shall we produce more? Or less? Marginal cost is the consequence of action; it should therefore be the guide to action.

Are business people then not interested in average costs? Unless they receive sufficient revenue to cover all their costs they will sustain a loss. They won't willingly commit themselves to any course of action unless they anticipate being able to cover their total costs. They might therefore set up the problem in terms of anticipated production cost per unit against anticipated selling price per unit. But notice that the *anticipated* costs of any decision are really *marginal* costs. Marginal cost need not refer to the additional cost of a single unit of output. It could also refer to the additional cost of a batch of output, or the addition to cost expected from a decision regarding an entire process. Decisions are often made in this "lumpy" way. Naomi Ballistics, for example, would decide whether to keep the bridge in operation for another week or month, not for one more minute.

Similarly, no one plans to build a soda-bottling factory expecting to bottle only one case of soda. There are important economies of size in most business operations, so that unless business people see their way clear to producing a large number of units, they will not produce any. They won't enter the business. They won't build the bottling factory at all. The entire decision—build or don't build, build this size plant or that, build in this way or some other way—is a marginal decision at the time it is made. Remember that additions can be very large as well as very small.

Whether or not business people cast their thinking in terms of averages, it is marginal costs that guide their decisions. Averages can be looked at after the fact to see how well or poorly things went, and maybe even to learn something about the future if the future can be expected to resemble the past. But this is history again—admittedly an instructive study— while economic decisions are always made in the present with an eye to the future.

The Cost of Driving

The Hertz Corporation conducts an annual study of automobile operating costs to determine how much it costs the average motorist per mile to drive an intermediate size car. Hertz takes into account depreciation over the life of the car, license fees, insurance premiums, interest on the automobile loan, maintenance, and of course gas and oil. In 1978 they announced that the average driver of a 1977 car would pay 20.0 cents a mile to drive it, if it were driven 10,000 miles per year for the next 10 years.

Assuming that the data gathered were accurate, what does this tell us? Does it offer any guidance to someone who is trying to decide whether to drive or to take the bus to work each day? Or to someone weighing a commercial airplane against the family car for a vacation trip? Or suppose you have been asked by your college to drive your car to an intercollegiate student-government conference. You plan to attend the conference whether you drive your own car or not. The college offers you 15 cents a mile. Will it pay you to drive, or should you say no and hitch a ride with someone else? If you go about deciding by trying to calculate whether the cost to you of owning and operating a car is less than 15 cents a mile, you are being foolish. It makes no more sense to speak of the cost per mile of owning a car than to speak of the cost per mile of owning a house.

(For just the same reason it makes no sense to compute the cost per ton of owning a steel mill, or the cost per student of running a college library, or the cost per prescription of putting a cash register in the pharmacy. All such attempts suggest that someone is treating costs that cannot be affected by particular decisions as if they were relevant to the making of those decisions.)

Costs of purchase, license, insurance, borrowing, plus maintenance and depreciation not due to operation are all unrelated to your decision whether or not to drive. That is why they are irrelevant. The relevant cost is the marginal cost: How much extra will you be out of pocket if you drive? Be sure to include not only the cost of gas but the costs of oil, tire wear, and mileage-induced repairs. Insofar as cost can be expected to vary proportionally with mileage driven, it can properly be expressed as so many cents per mile. If it is less than 15 cents, as it probably would be, you make money by driving your car. As long as the marginal cost remains less than the price paid by the college, you gain from every additional mile "produced" and "sold."

Are the costs of purchase, license, insurance, borrowing, and time-related depreciation *completely* irrelevant? Shouldn't you be allowed to cover these costs, too? After all, you have to pay them even if they are not related to the trip you've been asked to undertake.

You are certainly free to ask the college for as high a mileage rate as you choose. And if you have no scruples, you are even free to trot out all your sunk costs and wave them righteously. There is ample precedent for such action. But the one person you don't want to confuse is yourself. Only marginal costs are relevant to your decision, whatever price the college finally agrees to pay you.

Perhaps you've begun to suspect that it's our example that

is irrelevant. We're interested, after all, in ordinary business decisions, and whatever may be true of the student driver as entrepreneur, businesses surely have to cover *all* their costs, not just marginal costs. It would seem so. But it isn't so. There is no more necessity to cover sunk costs in the business world than there is in our case study.

The plain fact is that each year many businesses fail to cover sunk costs. But most of them do not stop operating. We can illustrate the dilemma by supposing that you bought your car with the intention of driving it for the college. When you made up your mind to become a sort of taxi operator, you hoped to make enough money to pay your way through college. So you purchased a car, the license, and insurance. You probably would not have done so if you expected the college to pay only 15 cents a mile or realized how much the price of gasoline was going to go up. Maybe you had reason to believe they would pay you 25 cents. Your calculations in these circumstances might have run as follows:

> Purchase price: $5000.00
> License: 30.00
> Insurance: 250.00
> Gas and oil: .06 per mile
> Maintenance: .02 per mile
> Chauffeur service: 4.00 per hour

Your problem now is the familiar one of adding apples and oranges. Or even worse, adding apples and velocity. How can you add $5000 to 6 cents per mile and $4 per hour? Obviously you can't.

You could, however, turn all these figures into costs per year, much as Hertz does. The license and insurance are annual costs. The purchase price could be converted into an annual figure by estimating annual depreciation and adding the annual interest charge on your initial outlay of $5000. But you can't state the other costs on an annual basis without knowing how far and how long you'll be driving. You must anticipate. Remember what we said earlier: the significant costs and benefits in economics are *expected* costs and benefits. That means they are uncertain. But uncertainty is a fact of life, and if you want to be a student entrepreneur, you will have to live with it. So you estimate that you will obtain so many miles and so many hours of business per year. You can then plug in your estimate and obtain numbers for gas and oil, maintenance and chauffeur services per year.

Now you can do your addition and come up with a figure for the annual cost of doing business. You can then take your estimate of miles used in calculating gas and oil plus wear and tear charges, multiply by the rate you expect to be paid, and thereby calculate prospective revenue per year. If the anticipated annual revenue exceeds the anticipated annual cost, you take the plunge and buy a car. If it doesn't, you don't.

So sunk costs are relevant? Of course not. Until you take the plunge they aren't sunk. They are marginal. They are additions to cost which you are thinking about incurring. That's the essence of being marginal. And as long as they're marginal, they are relevant. But only that long! When you have yet to commit yourself in any way to a business operation, *all* your costs are marginal. Once you have committed yourself, the situation has obviously changed. If you want to maximize your profits (or minimize your losses, which comes to the same thing), you must produce and sell all those units of output whose anticipated marginal cost is less than the anticipated price to be set by the college.

Applications: The Rising Cost of Medical Care

Let's use this way of looking at costs and decisions to see if it can clarify the controversy over rising medical costs and how to contain them. We will focus on physicians' fees.

People often assert that physicians charge high prices in order to recover the cost of their education. Could this be true? The argument implies that dullards who take an extra year to finish medical school will set higher than average fees, while geniuses who breezed through in less than the normal time will set lower than average fees. We don't see that occurring. The argument also implies that physicians who went through college and medical school on full scholarships will establish lower fee schedules than will those who had to pay their own way. That implication is not confirmed by observation either. The assertion itself actually makes little sense. To a practicing physician, the cost of a medical education is entirely in the past and consequently irrelevant to current decisions.

Does the cost of acquiring a medical education have no effect, then, on physicians' fees? The answer is that it affects fees indirectly by influencing the supply of physicians' services. The prospect of many arduous years in preparation deters people from premedical programs. The necessity of forgoing income for all those years and of borrowing money to live and to pay tuition decreases the anticipated attractiveness of a physician's life. The expected future cost of going through medical school thus restricts the number that will eventually supply physicians' services. (This restriction is in addition to others, of course: not everyone who wants to graduate from medical school is able to.) All of this ultimately affects the prices physicians charge. But to see exactly how it does so, we must push our analysis further.

The fees that physicians charge for seeing patients are

indeed related to costs; but the relevant costs are *the costs of seeing patients*. What is the cost to Physician X of seeing Patient A? What opportunity does Physician X thereby sacrifice? In the common case today it will probably be an opportunity to care for Patient B. What determines the value to the physician of that opportunity? It will be the fee that Patient B is prepared to pay.

In other words, people bid for the scarce time of physicians on the basis of their demand for physician care. This demand interacts with the supply of physicians' services to determine the cost of a visit to the doctor, or the price that physicians will be able to charge. The more that Physician X can get from seeing other patients, the higher is the cost of tending Patient A. Note that this cost is not determined by the value of the time the physician spent in school, but by the value of the physician's time *to patients*. The point is a most important one. If the demand for physicians' services increases but there is no increase in the amount of such services supplied, demanders will simply raise the cost of medical care, essentially by trying to bid it away from other people. In short, we who call for appointments determine the cost of physicians' services.

Physicians are not required to raise their fees when demand increases faster than supply, and many do not. They can instead allow other elements of the cost to rise. "I can't get you in before next Thursday." "You can come into the office and wait, if you want to, but the doctor may not be able to see you." The less that fees rise in response to increased demand, the more will queuing costs tend to rise. As a result, those who were willing to pay more money will tend to surrender some portion of available medical services to those willing to sit for hours reading old magazines.

The reasons for the large increases in recent years in the demand for physicians' services are many. People are living longer, and older people have more ailments. Our expectations of what physicians are able to do have gone up, and so we consult them more often. And increasingly, the people who visit physicians are not required to pay the marginal cost of that visit. The last reason is an especially important one, because it contains a warning against a popular "solution" to the problem of rising medical costs that is really no solution at all.

Costs *to Whom?*

Any system of medical insurance that pays for physicians' services lowers the cost to patients of obtaining those services—and thereby increases the quantity demanded. It doesn't much matter for the present argument whether the insurance system is a public one financed wholly out of taxes or a private system under which the beneficiary pays all of the premiums. So long as Patient A's decision to visit the doctor has no discernible effect on the amount Patient A must pay, the relevant price is zero. It's true enough that if beneficiaries go to the doctor more often, premiums (or taxes) will have to be increased. But those additional payments will be made by the policyholders (or taxpayers) whether they decide to see their physicians or, alternatively, to stay at home, get plenty of rest, and drink lots of liquids. The additional payments are sunk costs, and so they cannot affect decisions.

Here is the catch in the insurance approach to the problem of medical costs. If we respond to higher costs by offering larger insurance benefits, we subsidize the use of these scarce services. But that increases the quantity demanded, bids up the cost, and necessitates yet another increase in benefits. It also makes people ask why we don't do something to keep medical costs down! We will certainly not keep them down as long as our response to the problem is one that pulls them up by increasing the demand for medical services faster than the supply is increasing.

Hospital Costs

The question of *who pays* is also important in the case of another, even more important, contributor to rising medical care costs—hospital services. The average cost of a hospital room increased more than 250 percent from 1967 to 1979. It is almost certain that this would not have happened if the people using the rooms had been the ones who paid the bills. But under a system in which payments for medical service are exactly the same whether patients enter the hospital or receive only out-patient care, patients are much more likely to enter the hospital. The care is usually better in the hospital than outside it, and physicians can more easily monitor the patient's progress in the hospital. On top of that, insurance often covers the full cost of hospital care, while paying only a part of out-patient care. That's a direct invitation to people to increase the demand for scarce hospital services, and it quite predictably produces a steadily mounting level of room charges.

Hospital administration also demonstrates that sunk costs do have their uses. Suppose a particular hospital adds a 200-bed wing and purchases a lot of sophisticated new laboratory equipment. Once these decisions have been taken, the costs associated with them are sunk costs. But that doesn't mean they cannot be useful to the hospital's administrators. If the government and private insurance companies have agreed to make payments to the hospital based on the hospital's cost

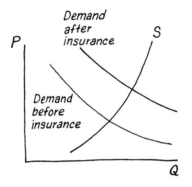

of providing service to patients, and if the hospital gets to decide what counts as cost, every dollar of those sunk costs will be used. The sunk costs will be "spread over" each patient, according to whatever formula enables the hospital to recover them as quickly as possible without unduly antagonizing those who must pay.

Cost *to whom*? Benefit *to whom*? That's always the way to pose the question of costs and benefits if you want to find out why some policy is being followed. If the benefits from a hospital's ownership of all the most modern equipment accrue largely to its medical staff, if the cost of not pleasing the medical staff falls primarily on the hospital's administrators, if the cost of acquiring that equipment is borne entirely and uncomplainingly by government, insurance companies, or philanthropists, then hospital administrators will purchase expensive equipment that is rarely used—and the cost of hospital care services will soar without restraint. That's just what happened until recently, when the people paying the bills suddenly stopped accepting as inevitable every increase in costs and started asking why average hospital cost per patient day had risen more than 1000 percent from 1950 to 1976.

Cost as Justification

The economic analysis of costs is an especially treacherous enterprise for the unwary, because costs often have an ethical and political as well as an economic dimension. Many people seem to believe that sellers have a right to cover their costs, have no right to any price that is significantly above their costs, and are almost surely pursuing some unfair advantage if they price below cost. This way of thinking, in which cost functions as *justification*, has even infiltrated our laws. Legislated price controls, for example, usually allow for price increases when costs go up but refuse to permit any price hikes that are not justified by higher costs. And foreign firms selling in the United States can be penalized for "dumping," if a government agency determines that they sold in this country at prices "below cost." In circumstances such as these, when costs become a rationalization rather than a genuine reason for decisions, all statements about costs must be inspected for evidence of special pleading.

Market-Determined Costs

Prices *ought* to be closely related to costs, in popular thought, because costs supposedly represent something real and unavoidable. The most enthusiastic advocates of rent control will agree, at least in principle, that landlords should be allowed to increase their rents when the cost of heating fuel goes up. They will never agree—if they did, they wouldn't advocate rent controls—that landlords should be allowed to raise rents merely because the demand for apartments has increased faster than the supply. That would be "gouging," "profiteering," or "rip-off," because it is unrelated to cost. But such a rental increase is just as surely related to cost as is an increase in response to higher heating bills. When the demand for rental apartments increases, tenants bid against one another for available space, thereby raising the cost to the landlord of renting to any particular tenant. What another tenant would be willing to pay for the third floor corner apartment in the Hillcrest Arms is the landlord's cost of continuing to rent to the present occupant. The case seems to be different with higher heating fuel prices but really is not. The cost of fuel oil is also determined ultimately by the bids of competing users in relationship to the offers of suppliers. Cost is always the product of demand and supply.

When you grumble to your butcher about the high price of hamburger, the butcher will deny all responsibility. "They keep raising the cost to me," he will say. If you were to investigate further to find out who "they" are and why "they" keep raising the butcher's cost, you would eventually discover that "they" are "we"—we who like hamburger and bid against one another for it. To see exactly how this works, imagine a sudden and unexpected increase in the demand for hamburger, occasioned perhaps by splendid summer weather and a surge of backyard cookouts. The first effect will be a depletion of butchers' hamburger inventories. When butchers find their hamburger inventories low and the demand continuing strong, they will increase their orders for beef suitable for grinding. With this happening all over the country, meat packers will in turn find their inventories of beef reduced and will try to buy more cattle. But the increased demand for cattle will encounter a relatively inelastic supply curve, and the price of cattle will rise. The packers who must consequently pay more for cattle will increase the price to the butcher, who can then honestly say "they raised the cost," without for a moment suspecting that "they" are in front of the checkout stand, not back at the wholesale meat market. The cost of hamburger in the supermarket is determined by the interactions of demanders and suppliers.

Price, Cost, and Suppliers' Responses

We can easily imagine circumstances under which such a surge in the demand for hamburger would *not* increase its cost to the butcher. Suppose that the increased demand for hamburger is accompanied by a *decreased* demand for round steak, chuck roast, and other beef cuts that can be used to make hamburger. The meat packers and the butchers may be able, under those circumstances, to produce the additional hamburger being demanded without increasing their demand for cattle. In that case, there would be no additional bidding for cattle to raise their price, create higher costs for the butcher, and hence produce a higher price for hamburger at the meat counter.

The passage of time can have a similar effect. Suppose the increased demand for hamburger is part of a general, widespread increase in the demand for beef. The demand for cattle will increase at the livestock market, the price per pound will rise, and consumers will end up paying more for beef.[1] The competitive bidding of consumers will have increased the price.

But that will trigger a new kind of competitive bidding, some of which will go on within the mind of single livestock growers. The higher price for cattle will make resources more valuable in cattle production than they were previously and will consequently "bid" some resources away from other uses—growing hogs, raising soybeans, feeding chickens, or working less at the business of feeding cattle. The more effective the higher price is in pulling additional resources into cattle growing, the less will the price of cattle (and hence the price of beef) increase as a result of the original increase in its demand. But the supply adjustments that we're now describing take time. That's why supply curves are typically more elastic—just as are demand curves—in the long than in the short run.

Let's summarize what we've been trying to say in this section. An increase in the demand for any good (hamburger, medical care, rental apartments) will bid up the cost of acquiring the good (its price) to the extent that it does *not* cause a larger quantity to be supplied. Or looked at from the other side, an increased demand for any good will *not* raise its price to the extent that suppliers respond by making larger quantities available. The responses of suppliers will depend on the marginal cost of transferring resources out of their current uses into the production of the good for which the demand has increased.

If resources can be shifted at marginal costs only slightly above those already prevailing, the increased demand will lead to a larger output rather than a higher price. But as the supply of such resources is used up, progressively higher prices will have to be offered to cover the rising marginal cost of shifting less suitable resources. Since resources are more mobile, or less

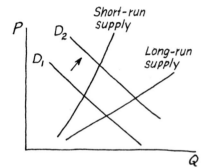

1. Don't forget that this higher price will also have the effect of decreasing the quantity demanded. Consumers will end up increasing their monthly beef consumption by less than they had originally intended—before their increased demand raised the price.

rigidly specialized to one use, in the long run than in the short run, the marginal cost of additional output will usually rise less when adequate time has been allowed for adjustments than when suppliers are restricted entirely to those responses that are immediately available to them.

Summaries tend to be both abstract and obscure. You can make the preceding paragraph more concrete and thus more comprehensible by testing each step of the argument against some real-life situation with which you're familiar. (The case of rental housing in the vicinity of your college might be an excellent example on which to practice.)

Another Note on Alternative Systems

All of this is just as applicable in a communist or socialist society as it is in a capitalist society. Resources will be differently allocated, and income and power differently distributed, depending on who owns the means of production. But the principles we have described are the general principles of economizing, applicable wherever resources are scarce. The central planners in a socialist state also operate within the constraints imposed by scarcity: the resources available to them have alternative uses; substitution possibilities are pervasive; one good can usually be achieved only by giving up some other good. The planners should therefore calculate the opportunity cost of contemplated actions, treating sunk costs as irrelevant and paying attention only to marginal costs.

Suppose that the minister of coal production in a socialist state is trying to decide how much coal should be mined this month. He can increase coal production by using more workers or employing them for longer hours, or by using more machinery or better machinery. The relevant cost to the society of doing so is the value of whatever is given up through his decision, or the marginal (opportunity) cost. If he obtains new machinery in order to increase coal output, society loses what could otherwise have been produced with the aid of that machinery, or what could have been produced with the resources employed in the construction of the new machinery. The real cost of increased coal production is therefore decreased production of locomotives, or cement, or farm tractors.

If the minister can expand coal production by using machinery already in place that would otherwise stand idle, the opportunity cost is much lower and may even be zero. The sunk cost of the equipment is irrelevant. Notice, though, that the marginal cost will be greater than zero if the machinery has any alternative use, including use as scrap metal.

We see the fundamental importance of evaluations in determining opportunity costs when we contemplate the costs, in such a situation, of expanding output by working the existing labor force longer hours. In a society where workers must be induced through monetary bribes (wages) to work in particular ways, the wage measures the opportunity cost to workers. The wage must be sufficient to attract them from their (subjectively) next best alternative. But if workers can be compelled to do what the state dictates, the wage need not bear any relation to the opportunity cost as determined by the workers. (We saw in Chapter 3 how that occurs under a military draft.) In moving from an eight- to a ten-hour day, the miners might be sacrificing two hours of leisure. Whether this is worthwhile would depend upon the *planners'* valuation of the extra coal produced in relation to the *planners'* valuation of the leisure forgone.

In any event, it would be clearly wrong to suppose that the cost of producing the extra coal can be determined from the *average* cost of coal production. This is worth mentioning because some socialists have argued in the past that marginal cost considerations were only relevant in an economy guided by the pursuit of private profit. It is true that in a capitalist society entrepreneurs will not choose to produce anything whose marginal cost of production to them exceeds its value to the consumer as measured by its price. But it is just as true that in a socialist society the central planners and enterprise directors should produce nothing whose marginal cost exceeds its value.

The major difference lies in the different social-political rules and procedures by means of which opportunity costs and prices are calculated: for workers, consumers, government officials, or any other resource managers. One of the distinct advantages of a system characterized by substantial private ownership and control of resources is its pricing mechanism. Under such a system, competitive offers to buy and sell resources interact to establish scarcity prices and opportunity costs expressed in monetary units. An enormous quantity of information summarizing a vast range of alternatives is distilled into the prices that in turn guide the choices of decision makers.

In no economic system past or present have prices ever summarized perfectly the available range of opportunities. And under certain circumstances, as we shall see later, they may do so in a fashion so inadequate as to be politically unacceptable. The relevance of all this for making a choice between alternative economic systems is a very complex issue that cannot be resolved exclusively by economic arguments.

In any economic system, however, the following general principles will be applicable:

Real costs are opportunity costs, the value of opportunities forgone.

Sunk costs are irrelevant, because they are costs that the decision cannot affect.

Opportunity costs are always additional or marginal costs, the costs entailed by the decision under consideration.

Some method of assigning indexes of value to alternative opportunities must be used in any economic system, or decision makers will be operating blindly.

Supply and demand, or the market process of competing bids and offers, creates indexes of value for decision makers by placing price tags on available resources.

If supply and demand are not allowed to set prices in a centrally planned economy, the planners will still want to know what prices supply and demand *would have set* if they hope to use the society's scarce resources efficiently.

Once Over Lightly

Supply curves reflect costs. All costs capable of influencing supply will have three interrelated characteristics that should be watched for: they will belong to actions, not to things; they will be opportunities forgone by particular decision makers; and they will be the expected, not-yet incurred consequences of decisions.

Past expenditures cannot be affected by present decisions: they are sunk costs and hence irrelevant to decision making.

Opportunity costs are necessarily marginal costs: they are the additional costs which a decision entails.

If costs per unit are to be used in making supply decisions, the units must be related to the decisions. The cost per mile of owning a car or the cost per bushel of owning a farm are both meaningless, because "owning" is not a decision that produces either miles or bushels (although it may be a precondition for such decisions).

Because economic decisions are based on future or expected consequences, they always entail some degree of uncertainty. The expectation that future revenue will cover future costs is often frustrated in experience.

The common notion that prices ought to be related to costs generates a substantial amount of confusing rhetoric among suppliers who want to justify (or others who want to condemn) a particular price.

Costs are not something independent of demand. The demand for goods is one factor that helps to determine the cost of supplying them.

Increases in demand for a good will result in higher prices, rather than additional output, to the extent that resources cannot be shifted into production of that good. To the extent that resources can be shifted with no significant rise in marginal cost, the increased demand will result in additional output rather than higher prices.

Because resources are more mobile in the long run than in

the short run, the output effect of a change in demand is likely to be greater and the price effect less the more time that elapses.

Under a system characterized by private ownership and control of resources, the forces of supply and demand will establish relative prices that function as indexes of scarcity. It will ordinarily be in the interest of private decision makers to be guided by these indexes in their decisions to demand or to supply.

In a social system not characterized by private ownership and control of resources, efficient resource use will still require that planners pay attention to the marginal costs of alternative decisions. In the absence of market-determined prices, these costs are extremely difficult to ascertain.

QUESTIONS FOR DISCUSSION

1. A news report from London stated that British doctors, while dissatisfied with some aspects of their country's National Health Service, generally appreciated the fact that they could treat patients under this system "without regard to cost." Correct those last four words.
2. a. What differences would you expect to observe in the fees set by three young physicians just setting up practice if one financed her education by borrowing and must now make payments of $4000 per year for 15 years, another had his entire education paid for by his parents, and the third went all the way through on government-provided scholarships and grants?
   b. Evaluate the argument, put forward in a *Newsweek* column of March 19, 1979, that the government could lower our doctor bills by paying for the entire education of physicians, thus making it unnecessary for physicians to recover the costs of their education (plus interest) by raising their fees.
   c. The author of the *Newsweek* article asserts that "you and I" will have to cover the cost of the doctors' loan repayments in our fees because these payments "are a legitimate cost of doing business." What difference does it make whether particular payments are or are not "a legitimate cost of doing business"? Suppose all physicians practicing in an area were required to pay $5000 a year to the local crime syndicate as protection money. Would these payments be "a legitimate cost of doing business"? Would they affect doctors' fees?
3. A study of the New York City housing situation revealed that many landlords are abandoning apartment buildings they own because, under rent controls, they cannot get enough revenue to cover their costs. What costs are relevant to such a decision?
4. An official of the National Association of Letter Carriers complained that postal service was deteriorating because "management has as its objective delivering mail at less expense." He argued that the postal system should not

be expected to break even because "it's a service for the people, not a profit-making organization." Can "service for the people" be provided at no cost to the people? Who should decide how much service the people deserve? Is Saturday delivery an essential service for the people? Does service for the people require that people pay the same cost to send a letter across town as across the country?

5. An airline is thinking about adding a daily flight from Denver to Billings. It has estimates of the number of passengers who would use the flight. What costs should and should not be considered in deciding whether the anticipated revenue is sufficient to make the flight profitable?

6. If you were the television dealer introduced in this chapter and you were trying to decide whether to display the sets in your showroom, how would you go about estimating the cost of the display space? Why would you *not* be interested in the cost per square foot of construction as you tried to decide? Under what circumstances would data on construction costs become relevant to your decision making?

7. The economist's rule, "sunk costs are irrelevant," is like a string around your finger. It reminds you to consider only marginal costs, but it cannot identify the marginal costs. That requires informed judgment. You could sharpen your judgment by trying to enumerate and assess the marginal costs of retaining or not retaining your college apartment over the summer vacation. Try to calculate the minimum rental from subleasing that would persuade you to retain it for fall reoccupancy.

8. Your boss tells you in an angry voice, "I don't care what you learned in economics. If you don't include all our sunk costs in your report and recommendation, I'll fire you." Are the sunk costs now irrelevant to your decision making?

9. Should the casualities already incurred in a war be taken into account by a government in deciding whether it is in the national interest to continue the war? This is obviously not a trivial question. And it is a much more difficult question than you might at first suppose, especially for a government dependent on popular support.

10. "Tuition covers only 43 percent of the cost of educating your son or daughter. We're counting on your annual gift to sustain operations that are fundamental to the kind of education for which our university is noted." Those sentences are from a letter sent to parents by a prestigious university whose tuition at the time was over $3500. Do you think that a student paying $3500 per year in tuition is paying only 43 percent of the education's cost? Would the university really save $4640 annually if the student dropped out?

11. In order to decide whether or not to drop intercollegiate football, your school undertakes a study of the program's cost. To what extent do you think the following budget items represent genuine costs?
    a. tuition scholarships to players
    b. payments on the stadium mortgage
    c. free tickets to all full-time students
    d. salaries of the athletic director, ticket manager, and trainer

12. What determines the cost to a university of providing parking spaces on campus for faculty, staff, and students? Why would it probably cost an urban

university more than it would cost a university located in a small town? If monthly parking fees are higher for students than for faculty, does this mean it costs the university more to provide parking for students?

13. The board chairman of the Tennessee Valley Authority complained in November 1974 that "prices charged for coal in today's market bear no reasonable relationship to the cost of producing it."

   a. What do you think he meant by cost of production?

   b. He also complained that TVA got no response when it asked for competitive bids from coal producers: "They don't need to compete because they can sell all the coal they want at their prices." If that's true, is the price of coal above its opportunity cost? What opportunities were determining the price TVA had to pay for coal?

   c. He also commented: "This country cannot afford to let something as vital to our well-being as coal be used to maximize profits." Do you think the prices charged for coal were harmful to the national well-being? What price structure for coal is most in the national interest?

   d. If the federal government, under these circumstances, had compelled coal mine operators to deliver to TVA the quantities of coal it wanted at the average cost per ton, what would have been the *real cost* of the coal burned in TVA generating stations?

14. In its 1973 annual report, Phelps Dodge Corporation said it would exhaust the copper in Lavender Pit (Arizona) by mid-1974 and close the mine at that time. But the June price of copper was 25 percent higher than the January price, and the mine kept on operating.

   a. Did the higher price put additional copper in the pit?

   b. What would a geologist mean by the statement, "I can't tell you how much ore is in that mountain until I know the price of copper"?

15. We don't often use the term *just price*. But we do frequently read or hear about prices that are "unfair" or "outrageous." Assuming that unfair or outrageous means "not just," how would you define a "just price"? Evaluate the hypothesis that a just price to most people is whatever price they've been accustomed to pay.

16. When the price of coffee quadrupled in 1977, many cafes and restaurants doubled the price they charged for a cup of coffee. Sometimes they accompanied the price increase with a statement to the effect that, while they were willing to absorb most of the price increase, harsh reality compelled them to pass along a portion of the increase to their valued customers. How many cents worth of ground coffee goes into a restaurant cupful? Why do restaurants and other businesses make such statements?

17. *Supply and demand* is a way of thinking about change and the effects to be expected from particular changes. You can develop your ability to use these concepts by working through the following set of exercises on the supply of and demand for taxicab service.

   Ask yourself first whether the change described will affect supply or demand. Then ask whether it will cause supply or demand to increase or decrease. Finally, ask yourself what effect it will have on taxicab rates and the quantity of the service exchanged. The objective is not to find *the* correct answer; good reasons are more important than a right answer. Long-run consequences may also differ from short-run consequences.

It might be a good idea to draw a simple straight-line supply curve and demand curve and to show the predicted shifts in the curves graphically.

Many city governments, as you probably know, regulate their taxicab industry. Rates are consequently fixed by ordinance and entry into the industry is restricted. In working through this exercise, assume that the industry is *not* regulated. Then, when you have finished, go through the exercise again and try to predict the results of each change that might be observed under a system of municipal regulation.

a. Convention business booms.
b. An airline strike occurs.
c. A major industry closes, throwing many people out of work.
d. Gasoline prices increase sharply.
e. The city cracks down hard on drunk drivers.
f. An increase occurs in the violent crime rate.
g. Parking fees increase sharply.
h. The city imposes a $500 annual license fee on all taxicabs.
i. The city imposes a 5 percent tax on the gross revenue of taxicabs.
j. A sleet storm ices the streets.
k. Nonindependent cab drivers strike successfully for higher wages.
l. A steady rain drenches the city.

18. Suppose that taxicabs raised their fares during rainstorms and lowered them again when the sun came out. How would these different prices be related to cost?

Efficiency, Exchange, and Comparative Advantage

Chapter 5 ended with the assertion that relative prices provide important information for anyone interested in using resources efficiently. But is efficiency an unmixed blessing? Voices have begun to appear in our society in recent years suggesting that we place too high a value on efficiency. Could this be true? We will try to persuade you in this chapter that most such criticisms are really aimed at some other target. To do that, we must begin by clarifying the concept of efficiency, another of the central concepts in the economic way of thinking.

Technological Efficiency?

Is a diesel locomotive more efficient than a steam locomotive? Most people would say yes. But what reasons would they give for their answer?

If efficiency is to have any precise meaning, it must be understood as a ratio of one thing to another. Engineers use a definition of efficiency that seems to satisfy this test. They define efficiency as the ratio of the work done by a machine to the energy supplied to it, and that ratio is usually expressed as a percentage. From the engineering standpoint, the diesel locomotive is therefore more efficient than the steam locomotive because, per unit of potential energy contained in its fuel, the diesel does more work.

This definition is somewhat unsatisfactory, however, when we think about it

$$\frac{Energy\ output}{Energy\ input} = One$$

$$\frac{Value\ of\ output}{Value\ of\ input} = ?$$

more critically. Efficiency cannot be simply the measure of energy output to energy input because, by the laws of thermo-dynamics, that ratio is always unity for any process. It is rather a measure of *work done* in relation to energy input. But what constitutes "work done"? Doesn't that depend on what is wanted? What qualifies as "work"? Engineers actually call a steam engine less efficient than a diesel because with a steam engine a higher percentage of the energy input is wasted. Strictly speaking, however, even wasted energy does work. It just doesn't do any *useful* work. That means it doesn't do work that anybody wants done. All of which implies that efficiency is not a purely objective or technological matter, but depends inevitably upon valuations.

The Meaning of Efficiency

Efficiency is inescapably an evaluative term. It always has to do with the ratio of the value of output to the value of input. Efficiency will always have an objective component, of course; our likes and dislikes don't determine the potential heat in a pound of fuel. But physical facts by themselves can never determine efficiency. It follows that the efficiency of any process can change with changes in valuations, and because everything depends upon everything else, any change at all in any subjective preference is in principle capable of altering the efficiency of any process.

Let's go back to the question of the relative efficiency of diesel and steam locomotives. Each can be put into operation only with the use of a large number of inputs: not only coal or oil and locomotive operators but also all the inputs used in manufacturing the locomotives, the inputs that went into the fabrication of these inputs, the inputs that went into the fabrication of the products that were inputs in the process of producing the products that were inputs in the manufacture of the locomotives, and so on, without any discernible limit. Anything that changes the value of anything that contributes to a locomotive's operation can in principle alter its efficiency.

We don't need any farfetched illustrations to make the essential point. An increase in the value of oil relative to coal, if it is large enough, can by itself transform their relative efficiencies so that a coal-fired steam locomotive becomes more efficient than a diesel. It follows that these relative efficiencies depend on the demand for and supply of oil and coal, and hence on such factors as the motoring habits of the general public, the political situation in oil-producing countries, and the value placed on the environmental effects of strip-mining coal. Perhaps it never occurred to you that the relative efficiency of the old steam locomotive was affected by the efforts of the United Mine Workers!

To test your grasp of the principle at work here, examine each of the statements below. Ask yourself what kind of change would be capable of creating or reversing the situation. The possibilities are limited only by your imagination.

1. Math can be taught more efficiently with programed textbooks than with teachers.
2. It is more efficient to cultivate corn with a tractor than by hand.
3. It is inefficient to use trained lawyers as court stenographers.
4. It is more efficient to cut down trees with a chain saw than with an ax.

If you thought through these statements, you should have noticed the possibility that changes in printing costs or teachers' salaries, tractor prices or farm labor wages, alternative opportunities available to people trained in law and shorthand, and even, in the fourth case, changes in attitudes toward noise in the forests are capable of altering relative efficiencies. (If you failed to notice these things and more, try again at the conclusion of this chapter.)

The Myth of Material Wealth

In emphasizing the essential role of valuations in any measure of efficiency, we are rejecting the common belief that economics has to do peculiarly with the "material": with material wealth, material well-being, or material pursuits. It just isn't so, and the word *material* actually makes no sense when attached to such words as *wealth* or *well-being*.

What does wealth consist of? What constitutes your own wealth? Many people have drifted into the habit of supposing that an economic system produces "material wealth," like cars, houses, basketballs, breakfast cereals, and ball-point pens. But none of these things is wealth unless it is available to someone who values it. Additional water is additional wealth to a farmer who wants to irrigate; it is not wealth to a farmer caught in a Mississippi River flood. A food freezer may be wealth to an American housewife but not to an Eskimo. The crate in which the freezer was delivered is trash to the housewife but a treasure to her small son, who sees it as a playhouse.

Economic growth consists not in increasing the production of *things* but in the production of *wealth*. And wealth is whatever people value. Material things can contribute to wealth, obviously, and are in some sense essential to the production of wealth. (Even such "nonmaterial" goods as love and peace of mind do, after all, have some material embodiment.) But there is no necessary relation between the growth of wealth and an increase in the volume or weight or quantity of material objects. The indefensible identification of wealth with material

Imagination creates wealth!

objects must be rejected at root. It makes no sense. And it blocks understanding of many aspects of economic life. Trade (or exchange) is the best example.

Trade Creates Wealth

Trading has long had an unsavory reputation in the Western world. This may reflect the enormous influence of Aristotle and his medieval followers, who thought there was something un-natural about exchange for monetary gain. But more likely it is the result of a deep-seated human conviction that nothing can *really* be gained through mere exchange. Agriculture and manufacturing are believed to be genuinely productive: they seem to create something genuinely new, something addition-al. But trade only exchanges one thing for another. It follows that the merchant, who profits from trading, must be imposing some kind of tax on the community. The wages or other profit of the farmer and artisan can be obtained from the alleged real product of their efforts, so that they are entitled in some sense to their income; they reap what they have sown. But merchants seem to reap without sowing; their activity does not appear to create anything and yet they are rewarded for their efforts. Trading, some have thought, is social waste, the epitome of inefficiency.

This line of argument strikes a deeply responsive chord in many people who still retain the old hostility toward the mer-chant in the form of a distrust of the "middleman." Everybody wants to bypass the middleman, who is pictured as a kind of legal bandit on the highways of trade, authorized to exact a percentage from everyone foolish or unlucky enough to come his way.

However ancient or deep-seated this conviction of the un-productiveness of trade, it is completely erroneous. There is no defensible sense of the word *productive* that can be applied to agriculture or manufacturing but not to trading. Exchange is productive! It is productive because it promotes greater efficiency in resource use.

Many have taken a fatal wrong turn at the very beginning in considering this question by assuming that exchange, unless it is fraudulent or coerced, is always the exchange of *equal values*. It just isn't so. The exact reverse is true: Exchange is never an exchange of equal values. *If it were, it would not occur.* In an informed and uncoerced exchange (and this is the kind we want to consider), both parties gain by giving up something of lesser for something of greater value. If Jack swaps his basketball for Jim's baseball glove, Jack values the glove more than the ball, and Jim values the ball more than the glove. Viewed from either side, the exchange was unequal. And that is precisely the source of its productivity. Jack now has greater wealth than he had before, and so does Jim. The exchange was productive because it increased the wealth of both parties involved.

"Not really," comes a voice from the rear. "There was no real increase in wealth. Jack and Jim feel better off, it's true; they may be happier and all that. But the exchange didn't really produce anything. There is still just one baseball glove and one basketball."

But the manufacturers of the baseball glove and the basketball didn't "really" produce anything either; they just rearranged materials into more valuable patterns. And isn't that essentially what occurs when people trade? Our suspicion of exchange is evidence of our materialist bias, a bias obviously shared by that small voice from the rear. Both Jack and Jim do have greater wealth after their exchange.

Recall what we concluded earlier about efficiency: it is measured by the ratio of one *value* to another, not by physical ratios of any sort. You can think of Jack and Jim's exchange as an act of production. Jack used the basketball as an input to obtain the output of a baseball glove. For Jim the glove was the input and the ball the output. The result of the productive process (the exchange) was an output value greater than input value for both parties. Nothing further is required to make an activity productive. The exchange expanded real output.

Efficiency and the Gains from Trade

The preliminary work has been done. We're ready now to introduce you to the principle of *comparative advantage*, a concept that sums up almost everything we've been talking about thus far. We'll allow Smith and Brown to make the introduction. They are suburban neighbors, each with a large lawn and a sizable flower garden. Every Saturday afternoon during the summer, Smith and Brown reluctantly go out to mow their lawns and weed their gardens.

(And you, patient reader, had better slow down your reading at this point, take out your pencil, and do the numerical calculations as you go. If you don't, Smith and Brown will be through with their Saturday chores, and you won't understand what happened. The argument from here to the end of the grain-textiles-radio case is not difficult. But you aren't likely to grasp it or retain it unless you *perform the calculations as you read*.)

Smith always finishes earlier, despite the fact that the lawns and gardens are identical in size. He is a strong and agile man who can mow his lawn in 40 minutes and weed his garden in 80 minutes. Brown takes two hours to mow his lawn and another two hours to weed his garden, so he is still toiling while Smith is sipping lemonade. You should have these data clearly before you as you proceed, so we'll summarize them in a little table:

	Smith		Brown
Lawn:	40 minutes	Lawn:	120 minutes
Garden:	80 minutes	Garden:	120 minutes

We're ready for the question: Is it possible for either or both to get to the lemonade sooner on Saturday by engaging in a little trade? (We shall assume that neither Smith nor Brown has a preference for one kind of chore over the other, and that the use of different tools is not a factor in the problem. Dropping these assumptions would add complexity without affecting the underlying principles.) We're all familiar with the advantages of specialization. If the mason builds the carpenter's chimney, and the carpenter builds the mason's garage, they each gain by taking advantage of their own and the other party's special skills. That's familiar enough.

But it doesn't seem to fit the case of Smith and Brown. For Brown appears to have no special skills, to be less efficient than Smith in both mowing and weeding. So it would appear, but appearances are misleading.

Suppose that Smith gave up all weeding and instead confined his yardwork to mowing first his own lawn, then Brown's. He could then finish his yard work in just 80 minutes, a gain of 40 minutes for Smith. If Brown meanwhile weeded both gardens, he would still be working 240 minutes, for no gain or loss. Smith has gained from trade with Brown without inflicting any loss on Brown.

Smith: 2 lawns – 80 minutes

Brown: 2 gardens – 240 minutes

The Principle of Comparative Advantage

What happened? Nothing very unusual. Smith just happens to be a more efficient mower than Brown and Brown a more efficient weeder than Smith. Like the mason and the carpenter. So each specialized in that activity in which he was more efficient; that is, each pursued his comparative advantage. It is a *comparative* advantage; each is more efficient in one activity than the other activity only *in comparison* with his neighbor. But that is what matters.

Whoa! The small voice from the rear is stirring again. "But Brown is *not* a more efficient weeder than Smith. The clumsy slob is less efficient than Smith in both activities." That small but helpful voice has erred again. It just is not true that Brown is less efficient than Smith in both activities. He really is more efficient than Smith in weeding.

Proof is provided by the arithmetic calculation which shows that Smith added to his wealth (his lemonade sipping

time) by specializing in mowing, and then trading with Brown.
And he did not do it at Brown's expense, for Brown's wealth
was not reduced. No such gain would be possible if Brown were
not more efficient than Smith in weeding—which implies, of
course, that Smith is less efficient than Brown in weeding.

Nonsense? No—just a momentary paradox. The paradox
disappears when we remember to wear the spectacles of opportunity cost. What is the cost to Smith of weeding a garden?
It is two lawns left unmowed. And the cost to Smith of mowing
a lawn is one-half a garden unweeded. The cost of anything is
the opportunity thereby forgone; the cost of weeding is therefore to be expressed in this case in terms of mowing, and the
cost of mowing in terms of weeding.

What about Brown? The cost to him of mowing a lawn is
one garden left unweeded, and the cost of weeding a garden is
consequently one lawn left unmowed. We can now determine
who is the more efficient or lower-cost producer of weeded
gardens by comparing relative costs.

The cost of a garden weeded by Smith is two lawns unmowed. For Brown it is one lawn unmowed. One is less than
two. Brown is therefore the lower-cost, or more efficient, producer of weeded gardens.

We aren't just playing with words, as is demonstrated by
the crucial fact that either or both can increase their wealth if
Brown specializes in weeding and the two engage in trade.
Common sense resists this conclusion only because Brown
takes *more time* to weed a garden than does Smith. Suppose,
someone objects, that we express the costs in man-hours. Then
Brown's cost will be one and one-half times as high as Smith's,
and common sense will be salvaged. But only at the expense of
everything we have argued for! Such an approach assumes that
the real measure and determinant of value is the labor embodied in a commodity. But the assumption fails completely to
explain relative prices. The cost of any commodity, in the
economist's way of thinking, is not what is embodied in it, but
what is given up in order to obtain it. It is the value of what is
sacrificed, or of the opportunities forgone.

But could we not take leisure, the third good in our problem, as the measure of cost? Let's examine this possibility.
Smith gives up 80 minutes of leisure to weed a garden, Brown
gives up 120. By this measure Smith is the more efficient producer of weeded gardens, and common sense is again salvaged.

You may take this route if nothing else will satisfy you. But
if you take it too far you will end up in confusion. Since leisure
or lemonade-sipping time is a valued opportunity, the cost of
mowing a lawn or weeding a garden can legitimately be expressed in terms of the leisure time given up. But the fact that
Smith sacrifices less leisure than Brown to do a job does not
prove that Smith is more efficient at the job in some absolute

The 80 minutes Smith spends weeding a garden could have been used to mow 2 lawns.

The 120 minutes Brown spends weeding a garden could have been used to mow 1 lawn.

So it costs Smith more in forgone goods to weed a garden.

sense. For Smith's leisure may be more valuable than Brown's! It makes sense to measure costs ultimately in terms of leisure only if we believe that leisure is "the ultimate good" *and* if we can assume that an hour of leisure is of equal value to everyone. This sort of absolutism does have a psychological appeal. There is a streak of egalitarianism in almost everyone which wants to assert that one person's leisure counts for exactly as much as any other's. And that conviction is remarkably resistant to all sorts of evidence suggesting that it just isn't so. Question 9 at the end of this chapter has been included for all those who have trouble freeing themselves from the presupposition that labor time or its opposite, leisure, is the proper ultimate measure of cost. And it's important to shake loose from that presupposition because opportunity cost thinking recognizes *no* absolute measures of value: the value of *every* good must finally be expressed in terms of other goods.

The Terms of Trade

We stated a few paragraphs back that Smith or Brown or both can gain from specialization and exchange. In the one case we worked through, Smith appropriated the entire gain. That was a result of the specific terms of trade: the relative prices at which mowing and weeding were exchanged. The terms of trade were one garden for one lawn. At that price, Smith appropriated the entire gain from trade.

Satisfy yourself that you understand what we're doing by calculating the terms of trade that would assign the entire gain to Brown. If Brown weeded his own garden plus only half of Smith's, Brown would be working 180 minutes altogether. Smith would be left with two lawns to mow (80 minutes) plus half of his garden to weed (40 minutes), so he would be no better or worse off. The terms of trade that assign the whole gain to Brown are thus

$$1L = \tfrac{1}{2}G \ \text{ or } \ 1G = 2L$$

The argument is consistent with what you know about relative prices. The people who gain from an increase in the price of a good relative to other goods are those who specialize in its production. Brown likes to see the price of a weeded garden rise from one mowed lawn to two for the same reason that any producer likes to see the price of his specialty increase.

Of course, at some intermediate price ratio they could share the gain from trade. If

$$1L = \tfrac{3}{4}G \ \text{ or } \ 1G = 1\tfrac{1}{3}L$$

Smith could gain 20 minutes and Brown 30 minutes from specialization and trade. (Don't conclude that Brown gains more!

That requires the doubtful assumption that leisure is equally valuable to both. Turn to question 9 for the antidote.)

Comparative Advantage in International Trade

Popular thinking hangs on tenaciously to the notion that some countries may be able to produce almost everything at a lower cost. If wages in Japan or Mexico or Italy are lower than in the United States, won't Japanese, Mexican, and Italian manufacturers be able to produce just about anything more cheaply than U.S. manufacturers can do it? How can the United States compete with countries that tolerate wage rates, even for skilled workers, below our legal minimum? In Japan, Mexico, and Italy, however, you could find workers arguing that they can't compete with America's low-cost techniques of mass production. And the suspicion would properly arise that something is wrong with the argument.

The basic flaw in such arguments is their neglect of opportunity cost. It is *logically* impossible for one country to be more efficient than another in the production of everything. And that becomes apparent as soon as you remember to calculate efficiency as a ratio between what is produced and what is consequently *not* produced. The real cost of producing anything is the value of what is given up in order to produce it. Calculations in dollars, yen, pesos, and francs (or working hours) all too easily obscure these real costs of production.

Suppose that Japan and the United States each produced only three goods: grain, textiles, and radios. Suppose further that competition had moved prices in both countries to levels that reflected the opportunity costs of each good, with these results:

PRICES PER UNIT OF GOOD
(identical quantity and quality)

	United States	Japan
Grain	30 dollars	9,000 yen
Textiles	20 dollars	4,500 yen
Radios	50 dollars	13,000 yen

Which country is the more efficient or lower-cost producer of these goods? Before we can answer we must find some way of comparing costs. What measure is available?

Dollars and yen clearly won't do. It's obviously absurd to suggest that the United States is more efficient in producing all three goods simply because the dollar prices are lower than the

In the U.S.: purchasing a radio (for $50) costs 1⅔ units of grain (at $30) or 2½ units of textiles (at $20).

yen prices. That would be true only if a yen had the same value as a dollar. We shall see in the later chapter on international exchange how the relative values of national currencies are established. It's enough for now to note that this is a blind alley because currency exchange rates only reflect, they do not determine, relative costs.

Some people might want to use the labor time invested in the production of these goods as the ultimate measure of their relative costs. To do that we would first have to find some common denominator for labor of different skill and effectiveness plus some way of translating such other inputs as machinery and land into units of labor time. And even if we could find a satisfactory way to do this, we would still be forced to adopt the arbitrary assumption that an hour of labor in Japan is as valuable as an hour of labor in the United States. But is it? Attitudes toward work and leisure are culturally determined, and there is no good reason to assume that an hour of working time is exactly as "costly" in one country as in another.

Then how can we decide which country is the lower-cost producer of these goods? The answer is: *There is no way at all to do so.* All we can do is determine that one country or the other is the more efficient producer of a particular good *relative to some other good or goods.* This is the meaning of comparative advantage.

Take radios, for example. The price ratios show that in the United States, a unit of radios costs either 1⅔ units of grain or 2½ units of textiles. It costs that much because that's what is given up in obtaining one unit of radios. In Japan, a unit of radios costs 1½ units of grain or 3 units of textiles. Those are the quantities of grain and textiles that are given up in Japan when additional radios are produced. It follows, then, that Japan is more efficient than the United States in producing radios *relative to grain,* but less efficient *relative to textiles.*

Which country is the more efficient textile producer? If you've gotten the idea by now, you will immediately ask: relative to what? A unit of textiles costs 2/3 unit of grain and 2/5 unit of radios in the United States, and 1/2 unit of grain and 1/3 unit of radios in Japan. So Japan is the more efficient (lower cost) producer of textiles relative to both grain and radios.

The United States in turn is the lower-cost producer of grain relative to textiles: 1-1/2 units of textiles are given up to produce a unit of grain, versus 2 units of textiles given up in Japan. The United States is also the lower cost producer of grain relative to radios: 3/5 unit of radios is the cost of a U.S. unit of grain; 2/3 unit of radios is the Japanese cost.

Don't lose the point in all the fractions. *A nation can become an inefficient producer of good X simply by becoming a fabulously prolific producer of good Y.* When you become extraordinarily good at one thing, it is costly for you to do anything else. If Japan starts to produce radios and TV sets at a lower cost than they can be produced in the United States, that does not imply that U.S. radio and TV manufacturers have failed in some fashion. It could just as well mean that U.S. productivity has been increasing rapidly in other industries.

The Pursuit of Comparative Advantage

No one except economists ever goes through these kinds of calculations, and even economists do it only in order to explain to students the logic of comparative advantage. In the real world people pursue comparative advantage, as distinct from merely talking about it, simply by choosing the option that seems most advantageous to them. The Smiths of the world mow lawns, the Browns tend gardens, American apparel makers buy Japanese textiles, and Japanese millers purchase grain from the United States because, in each case, they believe that is the best way to obtain what they want. In all of these decisions relative prices provide fundamental information. Given his various abilities and the price his work commands, Brown discovers that he can earn more income tending gardens than mowing lawns. Americans looking for textiles find Japanese products less expensive than domestically produced textiles of similar quality. Japanese farmers choose not to raise wheat because they know that they could not raise enough to earn a satisfactory living, given the fact that they could not sell it above the price at which U.S. grown wheat was available to Japanese millers. In short, they all behave as if the least costly way to achieve a given objective was the most efficient way.

This does not mean that they pay attention exclusively to prices, which would be an absurd and impossible way to behave. It means rather that relative prices guide their decisions when other things are equal. The other things that must be equal—or to be quite accurate, must be *thought* to be equal —include an enormous array of factors from the technological to the psychological. Consider a homeowner, for example, who wants to eliminate broadleafed weeds from a lawn. Would it be more efficient to dig them out with a handtool or spray them with a herbicide? The homeowner's decision will reflect a judgment on the effectiveness of each procedure in killing the root, on likely damage to ornamental shrubs, on the desirability of exercise, and on the joys of yard work and not just the relative prices of herbicide and hand tools.

Does Less Costly Mean More Efficient?

But will all this be enough to promote genuinely efficient decisions? More specifically, will the decision that seems most advantageous to the decision maker also be the decision that uses resources most efficiently from the long-run standpoint of the larger society? We can pose the same question in another way. Do relative prices take into account everything that ought to be taken into account? Can we legitimately substitute for the ratio of output value to input value the ratio of output price to input price?

Those who are currently answering that question with a vigorous *no* offer three principal arguments against reliance on the price system to secure efficiency.

Their first objection is that the process of competing bids and offers which creates relative prices completely ignores certain very important kinds of cost. Remember that decision makers tend to neglect costs that are not costs *to them*. In an industrialized, high-technology, heavily urbanized society, there are many such costs, and their systematic neglect entails an important failure from the standpoint of efficiency. An example in the case of the weed-hating lawn owner would be any failure to give appropriate weight to the broader environmental damage that may be done by herbicides draining off the yard or escaping into the atmosphere.

The weakness in this argument against the price system is that it suggests no alternative procedure for assigning appropriate values to such factors and persuading decision makers to pay attention to them. Telling people to "do better" is rarely enough. Efficient social cooperation requires that people receive correct information about relative costs, along with adequate incentives to take them fully into account. (We'll be returning to this important issue in Chapter 13.)

A second objection commonly made today against identifying *more efficient* with *less costly* is that current prices do not reflect the demand of future generations. It may be cheaper for someone to drive rather than take the bus, goes the argument, only because those not yet born have no way of registering their desire for the petroleum that we are currently burning up. If future generations could somehow enter their bids for oil, the price would supposedly rise beyond the aspirations of even OPEC, with the result that we would consume it far less rapidly and thereby leave more for the future.

This argument is formally similar to the first one and contains the same flaw: it does not indicate what institutional changes would yield *better* results than the current, admittedly imperfect system. Nor is it true that current prices completely neglect the demands of future generations. As we shall see in the next chapter, the expectation of future scarcity can itself produce higher current prices and thus more conservation for the future. What can and should be done beyond this, however, is by no means clear. Who has the right and obligation to represent the future? Since many government policies today actually encourage more rapid consumption of nonrenewable

Keeping down the prices of nonrenewable resources encourages consumption.

resources rather than increased conservation, it would seem doubtful that government can be relied upon to cast a responsible proxy for future generations.

The final objection that we want to consider to prices as criteria for efficient decision making is fallacious and not just inadequate. It asserts that many supposedly efficient processes that firms and individuals use are in reality inefficient because they use up more energy than would some alternative process. The process that is least costly in dollar terms is not, according to this argument, the most efficient unless it is also least costly in terms of joules, calories, or British thermal units. Firms that choose between alternative processes by comparing dollar costs may be wasting energy.

What we have here is a revival—in new dress—of the old contention that efficiency is ultimately an objective or technological phenomenon. In place of the old labor theory of value, we are being offered a new energy theory of value. But an energy theory of value makes no sense except to those who have somehow convinced themselves that only energy ultimately has value, and that all units of energy have the same value. If we follow this through to its logical consequences, we would have to disapprove of leisurely strolls and unite in one voice to condemn all mountain climbing. Crawling out of a sleeping bag to climb Mt. Rainier is an atrocious waste of energy, after all, for anyone who plans to crawl back into that sleeping bag in the evening and is looking for the shortest distance between those two points.

One application of this analysis, much favored by its adherents, is to agriculture. They argue that U.S. agriculture is inefficient, because the calories contained in the food produced are less than the calories contained in the fuel, fertilizer, and other inputs used to grow it. Notice that, by this definition, there is *no* efficient way to produce coffee or cotton, at least not for the uses to which people currently put them. Only if we burned coffee beans and cotton fiber to keep warm might we be able, from this perspective, to justify their production.

No one grows coffee beans or cotton for the sake of the calories they contain.

Disagreements on Values

But if efficiency is finally an evaluative concept, expressing the ratio of output value to input value, anything at all can be inefficient to a person who holds the appropriate values. There really are people to whom mountain climbing, as well as far less strenuous and dangerous exercise, is a total waste of energy. There are also people to whom a grassy knoll by the side of the road is a waste of space unless it displays a billboard. A person who neither visits wilderness areas nor derives satisfaction from knowing that they exist will correctly condemn as inefficient every legislative decision to create new wilderness preserves. Flying between cities rather than driving is a much more efficient travel arrangement for someone who gets carsick than for someone who enjoys the scenery. And someone somewhere may even believe that Rembrandt wasted time by not painting with a six-inch-wide brush.

We could multiply such examples indefinitely, but the point is surely clear by now. *What we value determines what we will consider efficient or inefficient.* It follows that disagreements in society about the relative efficiency of particular projects will often be disagreements about the relative value to be assigned to particular goods—or the relative disvalue of particular nongoods. Knowing this won't settle any controverted issue. But failing even to recognize what we're arguing about surely makes the resolution of controversy more difficult.

The best antidote to confusion is clarity about fundamentals:

1. Scarcity is a relationship between demand and supply.
2. Both demand and supply are responses to people's valuations of alternative opportunities.
3. There can be no satisfactory theory of value or definition of efficiency that is not grounded in evaluations.
4. Social cooperation in using resources efficiently would be impossible, except perhaps in extremely simple and primitive societies, in the absence of reliable indicators of relative scarcity.
5. Relative money prices function as such indicators in our society. They are not perfect indicators, for reasons that we have already noted and others that remain to be examined. But perfection is rare in social systems.

Comparative Advantage: The Economist's Umbrella

The term with which economists summarize almost everything we have been discussing in this chapter is *comparative advantage*. It might even be thought of as a term to summarize the entire collection of concepts presented thus far. To pursue comparative advantage means simply to sacrifice that which is less valuable for the sake of something more valuable.

Why do demand curves slope downward to the right? Because people pursue their comparative advantage. A rise in the price of any good means that its users will now be able to obtain the satisfaction it provides at a *relatively lower cost* by using some substitute.

How is the opportunity cost of any resource established? Through the pursuit of comparative advantage. People bid for a resource after estimating the potentiality of that resource *relative to other resources* for providing whatever they're after.

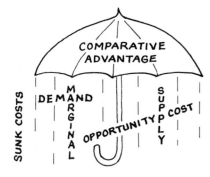

Why are only marginal costs and not sunk costs relevant to decision making? Because marginal costs reflect the *comparative advantages of alternative decisions*, while sunk costs can never do more than reflect the comparative advantages of past decisions. But no one makes decisions with the hope of affecting what happened yesterday.

It is comparative advantage—the advantage resources have over other resources in particular uses relative to other uses—that determines the most efficient way to employ a society's resources. And the pursuit of comparative advantage will lead decision makers to employ resources in the most efficient way if the relative costs decision makers must pay reflect opportunity costs.

The economic way of thinking may at root be nothing more than the ability to think consistently in terms of comparative advantage.

Once Over Lightly

Efficiency depends on valuations. While physical or technological facts are certainly relevant to the determination of efficiency, they can never by themselves determine the relative efficiency of alternative processes. Efficiency depends on the ratio of output *value* to input *value*.

Exchange creates wealth, because voluntary exchange always involves the sacrifice of what is less valued (input) for what is more valued (output). Exchange is as much a wealth-creating transformation as is manufacturing or agriculture.

People specialize in order to exchange and thereby increase their wealth. They specialize in activities in which they believe themselves to have a comparative advantage.

Comparative advantage is determined by opportunity costs. No person, no group, no nation can be more efficient than another in every activity, for even the most highly productive agents must have some activities in which they are less highly productive. If you're four times as intelligent, three times as strong, and twice as beautiful as another person, then that person has a comparative advantage in beauty—and you, handsome as you are, have a comparative disadvantage in beauty.

Relative prices help people decide where their comparative advantages lie insofar as relative prices reflect opportunity costs.

Relative prices also determine the distribution of income or the gains from specialization and trade.

Least expensive will also be most efficient to the degree that the relative prices of resources adequately reflect all evaluations of the alternative goods those resources could provide.

QUESTIONS FOR DISCUSSION

1. Is it more efficient to build dams with lots of direct labor and little machinery or with lots of machinery and little labor? Why might the answer vary from one country to another?

2. Which is more efficient: Japanese agriculture with its carefully terraced hillsides or American agriculture with its far more "wasteful" use of land? How have relative prices in the two countries brought about these different methods of farming? How have opportunity costs entered into the formation of these relative prices?

3. Attorney Fudd is the most highly sought-after lawyer in the state. He is also a phenomenal typist who can do 120 words per minute. Should Fudd do his own typing if the fastest secretary he can obtain does only 60 words per minute? Prove that Fudd is *not* twice as efficient as his secretary at typing, that he is in fact *less* efficient at typing, and that he should therefore retain a secretary.

4. The dean knows that Professor Svelte is the most capable administrator in his department, far more capable than Professor Klunk. Can you think of any reasons (related to efficiency rather than nepotism) for nonetheless appointing Klunk over Svelte as department chairman?

5. Have you ever noticed how few gasoline stations are found in the center of large cities? With such heavy traffic one ought to be able to do an excellent business. Why then are there so few?

6. The key to question 5 is the high price of land in the center of large cities. Would it make sense for the city government, which has the right of eminent domain, to take over some of this land in order to provide "vitally needed service stations"?

7. It has often been claimed that under a capitalist system business firms will sometimes continue to use obsolete equipment rather than the new, "most efficient" equipment because they have a lot of money tied up in the old equipment. Does this make sense? What is the relevance to such decisions of "money tied up"? Would an efficient enterprise manager want to behave differently under a socialist system?

8. You own and occupy a large brick house in an old residential neighborhood. The area is being rezoned to allow multiple-family occupancy and apartment buildings. How would you go about deciding whether to (a) continue to occupy the house as a single-family dwelling, (b) divide the house into several apartments, or (c) tear down the house and erect a new apartment complex? If you were to choose (b), could you be accused of retarding the economy by failing to adopt the most up-to-date equipment because of your vested interest in obsolete equipment? Does this differ from problem 7?

9. Here is a problem for those still infatuated with a labor-or-leisure theory of value. Suppose we want to verify the hypothesis that, since "a man's a man for a' that," one hour of Brown's leisure is equal in value to one hour of Smith's leisure. We gather the following evidence:
   a. We ask them. Brown says his leisure is worth more because he is fat and lazy. Smith agrees that Brown's leisure is worth more.

b. While Smith and Brown are sipping lemonade together, Jones across the street offers them $10 apiece to work for an hour cleaning his garage. Smith accepts with alacrity, but Brown says he won't do it for less than $20.

c. Smith often walks home from work because he has, as he says, "nothing better to do." Brown would take a cab if his car were in the shop because he is always eager to get home.

d. Smith daydreams while sipping lemonade. For Brown, this is a time for imaginative creativity; he thinks up all kinds of useful ideas for the employee suggestion box at the office.

If all this evidence is not sufficient to refute the hypothesis that Smith's leisure and Brown's leisure are of equal value, what possible evidence *could* refute it? If there is no way at all of refuting or confirming a hypothesis, does the hypothesis assert anything? If it asserts nothing, why retain it? You might still want to retain a hypothesis that can be neither proved nor disproved on the basis of existing data if it is useful in some way; we do speak of "useful hypotheses." But of what use is the hypothesis that every person's leisure is equal in value to every other person's leisure? It is seriously misleading for many purposes, and it contains implications that are contrary to a great deal of evidence.

10. Imagine a society with only two goods and three producers. We shall call the goods X and Y, and the producers Abe, Ben, and Cal. In a given period of time, each is capable of producing the following quantities of X and/or Y.

Abe: 8X or 4Y or any linear combination in between (6X and 1Y, 2X and 3Y, and so on)

Ben: 3X or 3Y or any linear combination in between

Cal: 1X or 2 Y or any linear combination in between

Is leisure a good in this society? Only if X or Y happens to be leisure! (We have craftily defined away that stumbling block.) Now answer the questions below.

a. What is each producer's cost of production for a single X and a single Y?

b. Who is the lowest-cost producer of X? of Y? Who is the highest-cost producer of X? of Y?

c. Who is the most efficient and the least efficient producer of X and of Y? If your answer does not agree with your answer to the preceding question, you have not accepted this chapter's explanation of efficiency.

d. If you were the commissar of production in this society and you decided you wanted only 2Y produced, plus as much X as possible, whom would you order to produce Y? What orders would you issue if you wanted 4Y, plus as much X as possible?

e. Explain to someone who is completely ignorant of economics exactly why you would not want to call Abe the most efficient producer of Y, even though he can produce more Y during a given time period than can either Ben or Cal.

11. The United States used wood as a fuel in metallurgy long after the British had changed to coal. Was this evidence of technological backwardness in the United States? If the United States was technologically backward, how would you explain the fact that all sorts of machines for woodworking were per-

fected in the United States in the first half of the nineteenth century? Fireplaces are often said to be inefficient ways to heat a room. Why then were they so widely used in the United States in the nineteenth century in preference to stoves? (Hint: larger logs can be used in fireplaces.) Why did stoves become more popular as wood prices increased?

12. When important supplies of natural rubber to the United States were cut off by World War II, scientists learned to make synthetic rubber products that eventually proved better than natural rubber products. Did the war increase the intelligence of chemists? Do you think that government price supports for cotton had anything to do with the discovery of synthetic textiles?

13. In 1977 the Environmental Protection Agency ordered eight Ohio utilities to meet federal sulfur-dioxide emission standards. The utilities could satisfy these standards either by installing "scrubbers" or by shifting to low-sulfur coal.

    a. They chose the second alternative because it was cheaper. Was it also the more efficient choice?

    b. Ohio coal mines produce high-sulfur coal that cannot be burned without exceeding EPA emissions standards unless expensive "scrubbers" are installed. The utilities therefore reduced their purchases of Ohio coal and began buying low-sulfur coals from Kentucky and West Virginia. This caused disruption and unemployment in Ohio coal fields. Does that fact change your answer to question a.?

    c. Special legislation enacted by Congress gave the EPA authority to *compel* utilities to buy "regionally available coal," when this was necessary to prevent significant disruption or unemployment in nearby coal fields— even though it would necessitate the installation of expensive scrubbers. Does this legislation compel inefficient decisions?

    d. Is it more efficient to relax EPA emissions standards for electrical utilities so they can burn high-sulfur coal, to permit strip-mining in order to obtain low-sulfur Western coal for electricity generation, to generate electricity by nuclear reaction, or to maintain clean air standards without strip-mining or an expansion of nuclear power by raising electricity prices so high that people cut their consumption to one-third of its previous level?

14. A small electrical generator that operates on either natural gas or gasoline and generates up to 5000 watts can be purchased for $3000. Under what circumstances might this be an efficient purchase for a homeowner, even though the cost of electricity so generated is much higher than the cost of purchasing it from the local utility?

15. A May 1979 letter to the editor of the *Wall Street Journal* wondered why, in view of the gasoline shortage, such "utterly wasteful uses of gasoline" as auto racing were still permitted. The writer also urged that such "obvious waste" be curtailed in the public interest. Is auto racing an utter and obvious waste of gasoline? Try to construct a clear and defensible definition of *waste* that would indict auto racing but exonerate other uses of automotive gasoline.

16. Grain farmers have many options when it comes to preparing the soil. They can plow and then thoroughly harrow a field before planting, they can practice minimum tillage, or they can go so far as to plant without preparing the ground at all. Heavy tilling buries and thus kills weeds and insects. No-till

farming requires careful and extensive use of herbicides and pesticides and also produces slightly lower yields. Explain how each of the following will affect the relative efficiency of maximum tillage and no-till farming:

    a. higher prices for diesel fuel

    b. improved herbicides and pesticides

    c. tougher government controls on stream and lake pollution caused by chemicals used in agriculture. (Note: untilled ground is more likely to retain the chemicals put into it.)

    d. farmers adopt the same attitude toward their fields that some suburban homeowners have toward their lawns: they find satisfaction in looking at a broad, well-tended expanse of land.

    e. higher prices for land.

17. Many people, including some economists, make a distinction between technological efficiency and economic efficiency. They either have not considered or else do not accept the contention of this chapter that every defensible notion of efficiency entails evaluative terms, either explicitly or implicitly. Can you construct a defensible definition of efficiency that does *not* depend at some point on subjective valuations? Can you assign a defensible meaning to the concept of *material wealth* as distinct from simple *wealth*?

18. Is it efficient to feed a family using large quantities of frozen "convenience" foods? Under what circumstances could these expensive grocery items provide the lowest cost inputs for producing the output of family dinner? What questionable premise is being used by someone who says that shoppers are wasting money by paying twice as much for convenience foods as they would have to pay for dinner items they prepare themselves?

19. If you saw a bumper sticker that said, "Eliminate Government Waste—At Any Cost," would you laugh, cry, or cheer?

20. Is it possible to assess the efficiency of the federal government's 55-mile-per-hour speed limit?

    a. What is the output or desired result whose value would go in the numeratator of the efficiency ratio? What is the input or cost or forgone opportunity whose value would go in the denominator? How would you choose appropriate values once you had decided on the appropriate output and input?

    b. Suppose we use fuel saved as the output of the 55-mph limit and time lost as the input. What might we use as appropriate value weights so that we can decide whether the value of the output is greater than the value of the input?

    c. If we include in the output not only fuel saved but also the lives saved, won't our assessment inevitably conclude that the 55-mph speed limit is efficient? How can we set a finite value on a human life?

    d. Far more lives would be saved if we required that all motorists be preceded by a person on foot carrying an orange flag. Would such an arrangement consequently be even more efficient than a 55-mph speed limit?

Information, Middlemen, and Speculators

The costs and benefits that affect decisions to demand or to supply are always *expected* costs and benefits. Producers decide to supply so many units of X because they expect to pay no more than a certain amount for the required resources and to receive at least some larger amount than that from selling X. Consumers decide to purchase a product because they expect to receive some benefit from its possession greater than what they expect to pay for it. But the future is uncertain. And so expectations are often frustrated by events. Decisions turn out to be mistaken. And mistakes are costly.

Because of all the interdependencies that characterize our highly specialized economic system, mistaken decisions will often have costly consequences for many more people than the ones who made the decision. If refiners don't build up adequate inventories of crude oil, motorists may have to wait in line for gasoline. If physicians don't anticipate the adverse side effects of a drug, a patient may die. And if manufacturers overestimate the demand for their product, employees who sacrificed other opportunities to work for those manufacturers may find themselves unemployed.

Since mistakes are costly, people try to avoid making them. Unfortunately, avoiding mistakes is costly too. The way to eliminate mistakes is to acquire more information before acting. But information is a scarce good with its own costs of acquisition. It may be less costly, as a result, to accept some mistakes than to acquire the information that could have prevented them. One mistake we can all avoid is the mistake of assuming that information is a free good. We shall see as we proceed through this chapter just how often that mistaken assumption does influence our attitudes and actions.

Real Estate Agents Are Information Producers

"How to save about $900 and lose $3000 . . . right on your own home."

That was the headline under which the National Association of Real Estate Boards ran an advertisement urging people to use the services of a realtor in selling their homes. The ad continued:

> Don't laugh. It could happen. For instance, suppose you decide to sell your house. Yourself. You decide it's worth $15,000, and you sell it for $15,000. Great. But how did you arrive at that price? By guesswork. It takes a lot more than that to determine a property's value. It takes a Realtor who knows houses and what they're worth. Suppose he said your house was worth $3000 more. A fair price to buyer and seller. It could happen. Of course, you'd save the Realtor's fee. But at quite a cost.
>
> So when you decide to sell a house, use your Realtor. He's not just anyone in real estate. He's the professional who is pledged to a strict code of ethics. That's good. Especially if you want to make the best sale you can. Or for that matter, the best buy.

That ad is eloquent testimony to something mentioned in Chapter 6: the public's deep-rooted suspicion of middlemen. The fact that the realtors association thought the ad worth running is strong evidence that such a suspicion exists, and the argument used in the ad is further evidence. For the ad seems designed to obscure the realtor's function while defending it, almost as if the truth is more than the public would tolerate.

Suppose, we might ask, that the realtor said your house was worth $3000 *less*: "A fair price to buyer and seller." Isn't it just as likely that homeowners selling their own houses will guess too high as too low? Or even more likely in view of the hopeful optimism typical of so many homeowners? Then the use of a realtor will cost the owner twice over. And just what constitutes a "fair price"? Moreover, if the realtors obtain higher prices for sellers, how can they simultaneously obtain better buys for purchasers, as the last paragraph asserts? Something is wrong with the argument.

Don't criticize the realtors association too harshly. The plight of middlemen forced to explain their function is not an easy one, because most people don't see that *information is a scarce good* or what this fact implies. If you want to sell your house for as much as you can get, the appropriate buyer is the one person in the world willing to pay the highest price. That seems obvious. What isn't obvious is how you find that person. You are presumably not omniscient, so you will never even discover the existence of many potential purchasers. It is almost a certainty, therefore, that when you finally do sell, you will not have found that one buyer willing to pay the very top price. Does this imply that you should keep searching indefinitely?

Information is a scarce good with its own costs of production, including all the costs of delaying action. It simply does not pay to go on acquiring information forever before acting. A rational seller will continue acquiring information, therefore, only so long as the anticipated marginal gain from doing so is greater than the anticipated marginal cost of acquiring information. A rational buyer will behave in the same way. The reason that both can gain from using the services of a realtor is that the realtor enables each to obtain additional information at low cost. When you think about it, this seems in fact to be the primary function of middlemen: they promote efficiency and hence increase wealth by acting as low-cost producers of valuble information. Realtors provide sellers and buyers with better opportunities than they would otherwise have, by putting them in possession of additional information. That is a valuable service. While it's true that only the seller actually "hires" the realtor, the fact that buyers go to them and make use of their multiple-listing services shows that realtors provide a service to buyers, too.

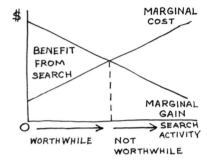

Reducing Search Costs

Suppose you own 10 shares of General Electric stock and want to sell. You could go around to your friends and try to peddle it or you could put an ad in the newspaper. But it is very likely that you would obtain a higher price by using the services of a middleman, in this case a stockbroker. No doubt if you advertised long enough you could find a buyer willing to pay the price the stockbroker obtained for you. But it is most improbable that the cost of your search would be less than the broker's fee.

"Getting it wholesale" is a popular pastime for many people who think that they're economizing. Perhaps they are. If they enjoy searching for bargains (and many people do), then they may well gain from their activities. But for most people, retailers are an important low-cost source of valuable information. The retailer's inventory reveals something of the range of opportunities available, information that is often difficult to obtain in any other fashion.

The same is true for job-placement agencies. Many people resent the fee charged by private agencies for finding them a job. But unless they felt that the information obtained through the agency was worth more than the fee, they would presumably not have used the agency's service. Employers are also willing to pay for such services, and for exactly the same reason.

A large part of the middleman's bad press stems from our habit of comparing actual situations with better but nonexistent ones. The exchanges we make are rarely as advantageous as the exchanges we could make if we were omniscient. So we conclude that the middleman takes advantage of our ignorance. But why look at it in that way? Using the same argument, one could say that doctors take advantage of your illnesses, and that they should receive no return for their services because they would be unable to obtain a return if you were always healthy. That is both true and irrelevant. We are neither always healthy nor omniscient. Physicians and middlemen are consequently producers of real wealth. Other prestigious persons performing similar services are lawyers, teachers, preachers, and corporation executives.

Markets Create Information

It is time to return to one of the continuing themes of this book. We have repeatedly asserted that supply and demand, or the market process of competing bids and offers, creates indexes of value for decision makers by placing price tags on available resources. The capacity of the market to generate high-quality information at low cost is one of its most important but least appreciated virtues. Middlemen are important participants in this process.

But what, you may ask, is "the market"? That's a good question and not an easy one to answer. The market is clearly not a place, though it may sometimes be closely identified with a particular place. Nor is it anything one can observe in the usual sense of observation. It is finally just a set of interrelationships, or what we have called a "process of competing bids and offers."

Markets are not peculiar to capitalism. They also exist in the most thoroughly socialist of societies. They aren't uniquely associated with business firms or the "private sector," either. Interrelationships characterized by competing bids and offers are also, as we shall see in Chapter 14, important characteristics of the political process and of government organizations. Nor must money change hands for markets to function, even though the use of money enormously facilitates their working. The commuters of Novato, California who were introduced in Chapter 4 exemplify a market. So do the rush-hour drivers who look for space, fill it up, and thereby continuously shift the relative value of the options that they all perceive. College students looking for courses to take and departments thinking of courses to offer are participating in a market.

Some markets, like stock markets and commodity markets, are "well organized," which means that the bids and offers of prospective buyers and sellers are rather comprehensively assembled, so that a single price for a fairly uniform good tends to be established for all transactions over a wide geographic area. Other markets, like the Commuter Connection market (or the market that even the least practiced eye can see operating in a singles bar), are much less well organized: the precise good to be exchanged and the terms of the exchange have to be negotiated for each separate transaction. The market for used furniture is relatively unorganized: transactions take place at prices that vary greatly, because buyers and sellers are not in extensive contact. The market for retail groceries, on the other hand, is far along toward the well-organized end of the spectrum, so that hamburger prices will vary much less over a given area than will used furniture prices.

It is sometimes said that stock markets and commodity markets are more nearly "perfect" than retail grocery markets and used-furniture markets. This is a misleading way to describe the difference, because it implies that the latter markets ought to be changed (perfection is better than imperfection). Such a recommendation makes sense, however, only if the costs of improving the markets are less than the gains from more efficient exchange made possible by the improvement. It is often the case, however, that we simply don't know of any way to improve a particular market except at costs too high to make it worthwhile. Commuter Connection will again serve to illustrate both what can be done along these lines and the obstacles that stand in the way of doing more.

But in every case the relationships between buyers and sellers, whether constant and extensive or sporadic and scattered, generate prices of some sort: terms of trade. Each such price is a piece of potentially valuable information to other people about available opportunities. The more such prices there are, the more clearly and precisely they are stated, and the more widely they are known, the greater will be the range of opportunities available to people in the society.

The range of available opportunities expands when restaurants post their menus outside.

Information and Wealth

Opportunity costs consequently decline *because markets exist*, which is really a way of saying that the range of opportunities available to decision makers expands. And that is a way of saying that wealth increases or that economic growth occurs. And is that not what we finally mean by an increase in wealth?

A wider range of available opportunities? The freedom and the power to do more of what one wants to do? Once again we would urge you not to confine your understanding and application of all this to what most people rather arbitrarily call "the economic area" of life. Information about what others are willing to do and under what circumstances is important in any area of life where social cooperation is desired. Clear and precise information does not guarantee effective cooperation, but it does make cooperation far easier to achieve. "I didn't realize that you were willing..." is the opening line in the often-repeated story of opportunities missed, a story that we would hear even more frequently were it not for the fact that we *never* find out about most of the opportunities that we lose through lack of information.

Summing up: information about available opportunities is valuable. Good information is often hard to come by. Markets generate vast quantities of clear and accurate information about available opportunities. Middlemen, brokers, and professional traders are specialists in the organization of markets and hence in the creation of valuable information. They presumably specialize in this way because they think they have a comparative advantage in information production. Whatever their motives, however, they provide services on which we all depend for our well-being far more than we realize.

That is one side of the coin. The other side is that we do not realize how important these functions are, largely because we have trouble seeing that information really is scarce. This blind spot frequently leads us to impose legal restrictions on traders whenever we don't like the information they are providing. It's a version of the old tale about the king who punishes the messengers who bring him unpleasant news. Kings who behave in this way deny themselves useful information. So do citizens who use the law to prohibit exchange or harass traders in ignorance of their functions.

What remedy would we prescribe for someone who has noticed that fire trucks are always present when buildings burn and therefore proposes to prevent fires by banning fire trucks from the streets? We would probably recommend a closer attention to cause and effect. Speculators are frequent victims of just this kind of public misunderstanding. We'll try to make the analysis of the preceding paragraphs more concrete by examining the functions of speculators in our society.

Varieties of Speculation

The dictionary defines speculation as "trading in the hope of profit from changes in the market price." That's good enough for our purposes. The most celebrated (or, more accurately, the most vilified) speculator is the "bear" of Wall Street, who "sells short"—that is, sells for future delivery shares of stock not actually owned at the time of sale. This speculator believes that the stock will go down in price, so that when the time comes for delivery of the shares, they can be purchased at a low price and sold at the previously agreed-upon higher price.

A more important speculator is probably the commodity speculator, who may trade in such items as wheat, soybeans, hogs, lumber, sugar, cocoa, or copper. This kind of speculator buys and sells "futures." These are agreements to deliver, at some specified date in the future, amounts of a commodity at a price determined now.

These are the spectacular speculators whose feats make the financial pages. A less publicized speculator is you yourself. You are buying education now, partly in the hope that it will increase the value of the labor services you'll be selling in the future. But the future price of your services could turn out to be too low to justify your present investment.

Another familiar speculator is the consumer who reads that the price of sugar is expected to rise and responds by loading the pantry with a two-year supply. If the price of sugar rises far enough, there is a gain. If it does not, there is a loss. The consumer's wealth has been tied up in sugar, cluttering the pantry shelves and blocking the opportunity to purchase more valuable assets—an interest-bearing savings account, for example.

The motorist who fills the gas tank at the sight of a sign advertising gasoline at two cents a gallon less than the usual price is speculating; the price may be four cents lower two blocks ahead. The motorist who drives on an almost empty tank in hope of lower prices up ahead is a notorious speculator. And the motorists who continually "top" their tanks when gasoline supplies are rumored to be short are surely speculators.

But many people overlook the fact that they themselves are speculators, heaping blame on the "profiteers" who allegedly "take advantage" of special situations and innocent people in pursuit of their own unprincipled profit. Is the speculator really the enemy of the people he is so often alleged to be?

Consequences of Speculation

It is often said that speculators exploit natural disasters by driving up prices before the disaster occurs. And sometimes the expected disaster never even materializes. That is true. But it is only one small and misleading part of the truth. Suppose evidence begins to accumulate in early summer that the fungus called corn leaf blight is spreading to major corn-producing areas of the Midwest. A significant percentage of the year's corn crop could be wiped out as a result. People who think this

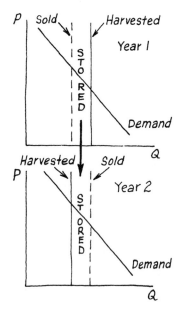

is likely to occur will consequently expect a higher price for corn next year. This expectation will induce some people to hold some corn out of current consumption in order to carry it over into the next crop period when, they believe, the price will be higher. That is speculation.

Notice how many different parties engage in such speculation: farmers who substitute other livestock feed for corn in order to maintain their corn stocks at a higher level, either to avoid having to buy corn next year at a higher price or to sell it then at the higher price; industrial users who increase their inventories now while the price is relatively low; and traders who might not know a bushel of corn from a peck of soybeans but who hope to make a profit from buying cheap now and selling dear later. There are well-organized commodity markets to facilitate this kind of transaction. The effect of all these activities is to reduce the current supply of corn; the price consequently rises. And just as the critic protested, it rises before the disaster occurs.

But that is only a part of the picture. These speculative activities cause corn to be transported *over time* from a period of relative abundance to one of greater scarcity. The price next year, when the blight is expected to have its effects, will therefore be lower than it otherwise would be. Speculators thus even out the flow of commodities into consumption and diminish price fluctuations over time. Since price fluctuations create risks for those who grow or use corn, speculators are actually reducing risk to others. More accurately, they are purchasing risk, in hope of a profit, from others less willing to take risk and willing to pay something in the form of reduced expected returns to avoid it.

Prophets and Losses

All this assumes, however, that the speculators are correct in their anticipations. What if the expected poor harvest fails to materialize? What if an unusually large crop appears instead? Then the speculators are transporting corn from a period of lesser to a period of greater abundance and thereby magnifying price fluctuations. This is clearly a misallocation of resources, involving as it does the giving up now of some high-priced corn for the sake of obtaining later an equal amount of low-priced corn. That is not socially profitable.

But neither is it profitable for the speculators! They will sustain losses where they had hoped for gains. We should not expect them, consequently, to behave in this fashion *except as a result of ignorance*. Are speculators likely to be ignorant?

No one is omniscient. And speculators make mistakes. (Why would they otherwise be called speculators?) But living as we do in an uncertain world, we have no option but to act in the presence of uncertainty. We cannot escape uncertainty and the consequences of ignorance by refusing to act or to think about the future. And if we think we know more than the speculators, we can counter them at a profit by betting against them. It is interesting and somewhat revealing to note that those who criticize speculators for misreading the future rarely give effective expression to their own supposedly greater insight by entering the market against them. Hindsight, of course, is always in copious supply—and the price is appropriately low.

As we have repeatedly tried to show, information is a scarce good. Better information means greater efficiency because it provides a wider range of opportunities and hence expanded scope for the exploitation of comparative advantage. Speculators provide information. Their offers to buy and sell express their judgments concerning the future in relation to the present. The prices generated by their activities are, like all prices, indexes of value: information for decision makers on present and future opportunity costs. This information is at least as important to conservatives as it is to gamblers. It is true that the information they provide is "bad" information whenever the speculators are wrong. But harping on this is again a case of comparing one situation with a better but unattainable situation. If we think we can read the future better then the speculators, we are free to express our convictions with money, profit from our insight, and benefit society in the process.

Meanwhile those whose ordinary business activities involve them in the use of commodities that are speculatively traded do make effective use of the information generated by the speculators. Farmers consult the prices predicted in the commodity exchanges and so do industrial users. And those who use goods not ordinarily thought of as speculative commodities also take advantage of the information generated by speculators. For we all use prices as information; and prices reflect competing bids and offers inevitably based to a large extent on a (speculative!) reading of the future.

A substantial part of the public's distrust and dislike of speculators is probably grounded in a suspicion that speculators take advantage of information from which they have no right to profit. The problems created by scarce information and consequent uncertainty are often complicated by this sort of disagreement about specific rights and obligations. What do buyers have a right to know? What do suppliers have an obligation to reveal? What constitutes an unfair advantage with respect to information? And who ought to be responsible for acquiring and disseminating important information about products? We can't begin to answer all these questions. But we may be able to clarify some of the issues and options by think-ing through a few specific problems created by the scarcity of information.

The Decline of *Caveat Emptor*

Let's look first at the decline of the *caveat emptor* doctrine and the rise of an increasingly comprehensive law of seller's liabil-ity. *Caveat emptor* means: let the buyer beware. It is a legal principle, once widely accepted by the courts, which holds that sellers can be held liable only for those qualities of a product that they specifically guarantee. Beyond that, the buyer must pay the consequences of a mistaken purchase. That doctrine has now been almost totally eclipsed by *caveat venditor*: let the seller beware. Buyers increasingly are receiving the legal right to demand compensation from sellers for any deficiency in the product, including deficiences of which the seller is not aware and even some deficiencies created by improper buyer use of the product. The buyer of a rotary lawnmower who cuts off a finger by pulling grass from the mower while it's running may be able to extract financial compensation from the manufac-turer by arguing that there wasn't an adequate warning, or that the mower should have been designed so that its user couldn't do such a foolish thing.

What consequences can we predict from an evolution of the law in this direction? People respond to the costs that they expect to bear. If sellers must pay for foolish actions by buyers, they will attempt to prevent foolish actions. How? By selling only foolproof products. Should we applaud? The trouble is that foolproof products will be very expensive products. When mattress manufacturers are only allowed to sell mattresses that cannot be ignited by a lit cigarette, everyone who buys a new mattress must pay for a quality that is only useful to that small minority which falls asleep while holding lighted cigarettes. Isn't that highly wasteful?

Sellers have a cost advantage in the generation of a great deal of information about products and in the creation of many product safeguards; but with other kinds of information and safeguards the comparative advantage will lie with buyers. If *caveat emptor* once compelled buyers to take high cost actions to protect themselves, *caveat venditor* is now compelling sellers to take some precautions for which buyers could undoubtedly find much less costly substitutes.

Physicians and Malpractice Suits

The furor over malpractice suits against physicians and the rise in the cost of malpractice insurance raises similar questions.

Malpractice once meant negligent or improper action by a physician that resulted in death or injury to the patient. Increasingly today it means making a mistake, any mistake at all that results in harm to the patient, even if the physician's diagnosis and treatment satisfied the highest standards of currently acceptable medical procedures. Where will this take us?

If physicians are held liable for malpractice whenever they make a mistake, they will try even harder to avoid making mistakes. Isn't that what we want? Not altogether. We actually *want* physicians to accept the risk of making mistakes when the cost of avoiding mistakes becomes greater than the cost of committing them. Forget about money costs, which tend to introduce irrelevant emotions into the discussion, and simply set pain against pain and death against death. How many tests should a physician perform before settling on a diagnosis? Each additional test reduces the probability of pain or death from a particular disease but also entails pain and risk of its own. Would you want to submit to a spinal tap to be certain you don't have an obscure but fatal disease never yet found outside the island of Madura in the Java Sea?

The common contention that even the smallest risk of death is too great to accept simply makes no sense. It might make sense if risk could always be avoided without incurring new risks. That isn't the case, however. It only appears to be the case to those who concentrate on just one risk at a time. The harsh-sounding truth is that some ways of saving life are not worth the cost. The apparent harshness of that statement disappears when we recall that resources used in one way to reduce the number of probable deaths are not available for use in other ways that could possibly save even more lives.

It also helps to remember that we're dealing with probabilities and uncertainty. If the highway department uses the rest of its budget to straighten out Deadman's Curve, where five people die each year, and consequently leaves uncorrected the Lake Road grade crossing where three people die each year, the department does *not* thereby "sentence three people to death." No particular persons must die because of the highway department's decision. And any driver who wants to get through that crossing safely has the option to stop, look, and listen. It may in fact be much more productive of "saved lives" in this case to take dollars out of highway improvements and put them into warning signs, thereby increasing the responsibility of buyers (drivers) for their own safety and reducing the responsibility of suppliers (highway builders).

We shall venture into one more issue to conclude this discussion of efficiency in the production of information: the question of advertising.

Resources used in one place are not available for use anywhere else.

Is Full Disclosure Possible?

Some advertising disseminates valuable information. Even the most fervent foe of advertising will concede that at least the Yellow Pages provide people with information that extends the range of their opportunities. Some advertising is a deliberate attempt to deceive and succeeds in its purpose. The most fervent fan of advertising will concede that there are a few bad apples in the barrel. But what about most advertising? Does it inform? Persuade? Manipulate? Misinform? Where does it fit on the continuum from informative (and therefore wealth-creating) to deceptive (and therefore wealth-reducing)?

A lot of people's lives would be simpler, although perhaps less interesting, if a thick, dark line could always be drawn between informative and deceptive advertising. One reason that such a line cannot be drawn is that information is not a simple matter of words. Telling people doesn't necessarily inform them. They can fail to understand, not believe, not be listening, not care, or not remember. In addressing any large group you will always find that some have forgotten what you said before others have understood, and that some still won't care enough to listen when others have stopped listening out of boredom. Moreover, what is valuable information to one person will often be mere noise to another, and if you try to tell everybody what they want to know, you may generate so much static that no one learns anything from your communication. If you try to avoid deceiving some, you will in the process fail to provide others with information they wanted to have.

"Full disclosure," consequently, is an illusion. It may be a useful ideal. On the other hand, it could be a dangerous delusion if it encourages us to believe that someone or some procedure can infallibly protect us from misinformation.

Once Over Lightly

An opportunity of which you're unaware is not a real opportunity. Information is therefore a valuable resource whose possession enables people to increase their wealth.

Information is a scarce good whose production usually entails costs. The efficient decision maker accumulates additional information only so long as the anticipated marginal benefit is greater than the marginal cost.

A great deal of economic activity is best understood as a response to the fact that information is a scarce good. The much abused "middleman" is in large part a specialist in information production. Just as the real estate broker enables prospective buyers and sellers to locate one another, so the typical retailer provides customers with knowledge of the goods sellers are offering and brings sellers into contact with those who want the sellers' offerings.

The common habit of viewing the middleman as an unproductive bandit on the highway of trade stems from the erroneous assumption that information is a free good.

Everyone who makes a decision in the absence of complete information about the future consequences of all available opportunities is a speculator. So everyone is a speculator.

People who think they know more than others about the relationship between present and future scarcities will want to buy in one time period for sale in the other. If they are correct, they make a profit on their superior insight and also transport goods through time from periods of lesser to greater scarcity. If they're wrong in their predictions, they perversely move goods from periods of greater to lesser scarcity and suffer the penalty of a personal loss on their transactions.

Because prices are summary indicators of scarcity, they are valuable information. Those whose buying and selling activities create prices are generating information that is useful to others.

The cost of producing information is not the same for everyone. People will specialize in the production of those kinds of information in which they have a comparative advantage.

A person who is able to shift the full cost of mistakes onto others has little incentive to gather information before acting. A person who is compelled to bear the full cost of mistakes committed by others will attempt to keep them from committing mistakes. Avoiding mistakes is also costly, but people will tend to slight the costs that they themselves don't have to bear.

QUESTIONS FOR DISCUSSION

1. Are you speculating when you buy fire insurance on your home? Could you save money by getting together with your friends to form an insurance cooperative, thereby eliminating the necessity of paying something to a middleman (the insurance company)? What kinds of useful information do insurance companies provide?
2. If you found that you could reduce your bills for new clothing 10 percent by buying exclusively from catalogs, would you do it? Why would some people be unwilling to take advantage of this "saving"?
3. Does advertising provide information? Before answering, think about the various kinds of advertising you're familiar with. What safe generalizations can one make about *all* advertising? Since advertisers sometimes deceive

customers, should advertising be put under government regulation to eliminate all deceptive claims? Would you include the claims of political candidates who buy time for advertising themselves on television?

4. A man approaches you in a busy airport terminal, shows you a handsome wrist-watch, which he says is worth $135, and offers to let you have it for $25. Would you buy it? Would you be more willing to buy it if you had better information? What do you "know" when you buy a watch from an established local jeweler that you do not know in this situation?

5. Evaluate the following paragraph from a newspaper article:

> One sure way to save money on groceries is to eliminate the middleman by buying directly from farmers and other suppliers. That is what a group of socially motivated and normally hungry people have decided to do by forming a grocery cooperative.

6. You find out in late December that you can probably make $1000 on a business deal if you can gain the goodwill of a client by getting him two tickets to the Super Bowl game. You manage to buy two well-located seats from a scalper for $250. Were you cheated by the scalper? Or are you glad that scalpers exist? Why do so many people dislike scalpers intensely?

7. In February 1972 the price of beef in grocery stores rose rapidly, contributing to an overall increase in the cost of groceries and pushing up the index of consumer prices at a time when the government had announced its determination to stop inflation. The president of the United States publicly blamed the middleman. Why?

8. A number of oil ministers from OPEC countries complained in mid-June of 1979 that some oil companies were "speculating" and "profiteering" with OPEC oil. What do you think they meant, and why did they make the accusation?

9. Students frequently complain about the low prices the campus bookstore pays for used texts. Why then do they sell to the bookstore? Is it true that they cannot find a buyer on their own? Or is it more true that they are unwilling to go to the trouble (incur the cost) of finding a buyer on their own? What useful service does the college bookstore perform in handling used texts? Can you be sure it's a genuine service and not just a "rip-off"?

10. Would you expect prices for goods of similar quality offered in garage sales to vary more than prices for goods offered in regular retail outlets? Why?

11. You decide in May that this summer's corn crop is going to be much larger than people expect. What buying or selling operations could you undertake to wager on your prediction? What kind of effect will your action have on prices? It obviously isn't possible to carry corn backward in time, to make the October harvest available in May. Nonetheless your action will have the effect of increasing May corn consumption and decreasing October consumption. How will this occur?

12. Walter Wriston, chairman of Citicorp, argued in an address to the American Society of Newspaper Editors that the government was suppressing information or censoring the news when it tried to prohibit firms from posting higher prices. He argued that firms don't so much raise prices as announce that prices have gone up. Evaluate this argument.

13. Nitrites have long been added to cured meats, such as bacon or sausage, to

prevent botulism, a kind of food poisoning that is often fatal. Evidence has recently been presented that nitrites can cause cancer. Is the risk of using nitrites or the risk of not using them too great to be acceptable?

14. A commissioner of the Food and Drug Administration said that, while he was willing to weigh health risks against health benefits in formulating commission rulings, he was absolutely opposed to weighing health risks against economic factors. Evaluate this statement.

15. Suppose that you are leaving tomorrow for a two-week combined business and vacation trip in a distant location. You'll be traveling by plane.
    a. In what way are you speculating as you pack your suitcase?
    b. On which side would you be more inclined to err—taking too many clothes and having to haul heavy suitcases around, or taking too few and finding yourself without an item you want?
    c. Would your answer to the previous question differ according to whether you were planning to be in a large city or a remote resort?
    d. Suppose you take only a single pair of dress shoes and accidentally spill ink on one of them just before an important business meeting. You dash out quickly and buy a new pair of shoes. Explain how the shoe seller's willingness to take a risk reduced your risk in taking only a single pair of dress shoes.

16. The June 18, 1979 issue of *Time* magazine contained an article on hoarding in the United States in which a number of social scientists were quoted. A sociologist said that gasoline hoarding was not rational but rather a result of Americans' emotional stake in their cars. An historian said hoarding was an absolutely typical American trait. Some attributed hoarding to a "shortage psychosis," and others spoke of "panic buying." Another sociologist said that strong leadership was required to jolt people out of such "competitive behavior."
    a. How could we decide whether hoarding is irrational, psychotic, a national character trait, a product of emotion and panic *or* an intelligent response to uncertainty?
    b. What is the difference between hoarding and maintaining an appropriate level of inventory?
    c. Why do both business firms and households maintain inventories? How do they decide upon the proper level of inventories for particular goods?

Chapter **8**

Price Setting and
the Question of Monopoly

The term *administered prices* was first introduced to public discussion in the 1930s in order to make a distinction between prices that were set by supply and demand and prices supposedly established by "administrative action." Since that time the term has been widely used, especially by critics of "big business." Some of these critics have accused professional economists of ignoring the dominant role of "administered prices" in the American economy, and of pretending that prices are all set by supply and demand. According to most of these critics, the American economy is today largely controlled by monopolists and oligopolists, who pay no attention to supply and demand, but instead use their market power to manipulate prices according to their own selfish and narrow interests.

It is impossible to evaluate any of these claims without first obtaining a clearer notion of what is meant by such terms as *administered prices* and *monopolist*. We have consciously steered around these issues as much as we could in the preceding chapters. The tactic that usually enabled us to do so was the implicit assumption that there were so many buyers and sellers in any market at which we were looking that none of them had any power to affect the price by his own individual action. It is now time to look more closely at issues that have been bypassed.

Who Qualifies as a Monopolist?

We begin with the word *monopoly*, the product of two Greek words meaning "sole seller." Are there any monopolists in that strict sense of the word? Try to think of something that is sold exclusively by one seller.

Telephone service is a favorite example. But is it an accurate example? There are many sellers of telephone service in the United States, as a matter of sometimes forgotten fact. Bell may have invented it, but neither regional companies with his name nor their parent, American Telephone and Telegraph, are the only ones who sell it. Still, that may be beside the point. For any given buyer there is typically only one seller, since telephone companies enjoy exclusive selling privileges in particular areas. On the other hand, a buyer doesn't have to live in a given area; he can move to another franchise area if he prefers the product there. Back comes a justifiably impatient snort: "That's irrelevant." But it's not completely irrelevant. Moving your residence may be a prohibitively expensive way to shift your telephone patronage, and it's hard to imagine anyone actually moving just because he resents the local phone company. But that *is* a way of obtaining a substitute product. And by its absurdity, our example calls attention to the crux of the problem: the availability of substitutes.

Suppose we redefine the commodity sold by telephone companies and call it "communication services." There would be nothing intrinsically misleading about that. After all, that is why anyone wants a telephone: to obtain communication services. But if this is the product being sold, the telephone company is clearly *not* a monopolist, but rather a seller in competition with Western Union, the post office, various messenger and delivery services, loud shouting, fast running, and coast-to-coast communication by computer. The point of all this is simply that, if we define the commodity broadly enough, not a single commodity in the country is sold by a monopolist.

Now let's look at the other side of the coin. Suppose we define the commodity very narrowly. If telegrams are not the same thing as telephone calls, neither is a gallon of milk at the little store next door the same thing as a gallon of milk three blocks away at the supermarket. If you have no car, are rocking a screaming baby who won't stop until he gets his bottle, and have no one to leave the baby with, the milk three blocks away is a vividly different commodity from the milk at the store next door. Ask any parent of a small baby. Thus we are forced to conclude that, when the commodity is defined narrowly enough, every seller is a monopolist, since no two sellers will ever be offering completely identical products.

We are trying to convince you that the word *monopoly* is extraordinarily ambiguous. For everyone or no one is a sole seller depending on how we define the commodity being sold.

Furthermore, there is no satisfactory way to decide in all cases just how broadly or narrowly the concept of a commodity ought to be defined. The Supreme Court of the United States has sometimes listened to persuasive arguments on both sides of a contested definition and then divided in its decision. Take cellophane, for example. Is it a separate commodity or should it be put in the category "flexible wrapping materials"? The answer given in cases such as this may determine whether a manufacturer is convicted under the antitrust laws.

Alternatives, Elasticity, and Market Power

So let's try another approach. What would be so bad about a sole seller if we found one? The telephone company hints at the answer when it advertises: "We may be the only phone company in town, but we try not to act like it." If we find a case where there really is a sole seller, the customer will have no alternatives. No one wants to be without alternatives. The poorer our alternatives, the weaker our position and the more easily we can be taken advantage of.

But we learned in Chapter 2 that there are always some alternatives. There is a substitute for anything, even the services of the local telephone company. After all, no one "needs" a telephone. On the other hand, a phone is a valued convenience for many families and business firms. The concept from economics that suggests itself is price elasticity of demand.

No seller is a monopolist in the strictest sense of the word because there is no such thing as a *perfectly* inelastic demand. No seller has any buyer totally over the barrel. On the other hand, very few sellers of anything face perfectly elastic demand curves. Anything less than complete elasticity means that sellers will retain some business when they raise their price, which in turn implies that sellers have at least a morsel of market power. Where is the line between a morsel and monopoly?

There is no clear line of demarcation unless we decide to draw one arbitrarily. Elasticities of demand reflect the availability of substitutes; other things remaining equal, the more good substitutes there are for anything, the more elastic will be the demand for it. Market power is thus seen to be a matter of degree, and to be inversely related to elasticity of demand. Defined in this way, the term *market power* has a meaning that we can talk about and use. But we have not yet found a useful definition for the word *monopoly*.

Privileges and Restrictions

Let's try another approach. In the early nineteenth century there was often no distinction made in the United States between a monopoly and a corporation. The reason was that

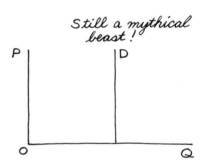

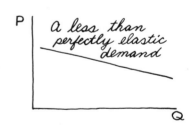

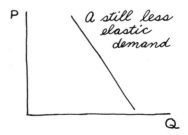

corporations had always been created by special governmental acts. They received, whether from Crown and Parliament prior to the Revolution or from state and national legislatures afterward, special "patents," as they were called: official documents granting rights and privileges not available to others. Corporate charters were therefore called "grants of monopoly," since they gave to one party a power that was withheld from others. The East India Company was such a "monopoly," and the special privilege of selling tea in the Colonies, given to it in 1773, helped bring on the American Revolution.

Here is another and quite different meaning of monopoly, one related to acts of the state. If the state allows some to engage in an activity but prosecutes others for doing so, or if it taxes or restricts some sellers but not others, or if it grants protection or assistance to some while compelling others to make their own way unaided, the state is creating exclusive privileges. This meaning for the word *monopoly* has contemporary relevance as well as historical significance.

Many business organizations operate with monopoly grants of this kind. In the name of all sorts of commendable-sounding goals—public safety, fair competition, stability, national security, efficiency—governments at all levels have imposed restrictions upon entry into various industries or trades. The beneficiaries of these restrictions always include the parties who can escape them. These parties will rarely agree that they enjoy a grant of monopoly power. But the effect of the restrictions nonetheless is to prevent some from competing who would otherwise do so.

We are not saying that restrictions on entry into a market are always to be condemned, or that the businesses which benefit necessarily behave badly afterward, or that society can never be better off as a consequence of restrictions on competition. We are only concerned that the restrictions be noted so that their consequences can be evaluated. They will often turn out to be different from what most people assume. We could, if we wished, use the word *monopolist* to describe any individual or organization operating with the advantage of special privileges granted by the government. The trouble is that most people no longer use the word in this way. By such a definition, the postal service is a monopolist, as are most public utilities, many liquor stores, morticians, and crop-dusters; the American Medical Association, state bar associations, and labor unions; farmers with acreage allotments, licensed barbers, and trucking firms. The list is long indeed.

And so we are going to take the heroic step of dropping the word *monopoly* from our working vocabulary. Its meanings are too many and too vague. " 'When I use a word,' Humpty Dumpty said in a rather scornful tone, 'it means just what I choose it to mean—neither more nor less.' " *Monopoly* is a

favorite word of contemporary Humpty Dumpties. And that's
why we are not going to employ it. We shall try to use alternate
terms that are more likely to communicate the precise situation
we have in mind.

Price Takers and Price Searchers

Let's go back now to the phrase with which this chapter
began: administered prices. Is there a distinction between
administered prices and prices that are set by supply and
demand?

It's a free country, as they say, and businesses are usually
free to set their own prices. The United States Steel Corporation
has substantial discretion when it prints up its price lists, and a
wheat farmer from Kansas can feel quite safe from the threat
of prosecution if he decides to offer his crop at $5.00 per bushel.
But there is obviously an important difference that helps to
explain why United States Steel keeps one eye on the government when deciding on its prices and wheat farmers do not.
The difference, we shall nonetheless insist, is a difference of
degree, not kind.

Take the case of the wheat farmer first. If he consults the
financial pages of his newspaper or tunes in for the noonday
market reports, he will find that number 2 ordinary hard Kansas City wheat opened at $3.34¾ a bushel. That news may
disappoint or delight him, but there is almost nothing he can do
to change it. If he decides that the price is an excellent one, and
sells his entire crop for immediate delivery, the market will feel
scarcely a ripple. Even if he is one of the biggest wheat farmers
in the state, he is still such a small part of the total number of
those offering to buy or sell wheat that he cannot affect the
price. The difference between what the closing price will be if
he sells all his crop, and what it will be if he sells only half of it,
will not be as much as ¼ cent.

Economists therefore call the wheat farmer a *price taker*.
He cannot affect the price by his own actions. The price at the
local grain elevator is determined by the actions of many
buyers and sellers all over the country. If the farmer exercises
his legal right to put a price tag on his wheat two cents higher
than the market decrees, he will sell no wheat. And since he can
sell all the wheat he has at the going price, he has no incentive
to offer to sell any wheat at less than the going price. Price
takers face perfectly elastic demand curves, or what for all
practical purposes amount to perfectly elastic demand curves.
The demand curves are horizontal at the going price.

Most sellers are not in this position. They can raise their
prices if they choose, without losing all their sales. And they
cannot, as can the farmer, always sell everything they're capable of producing without lowering their prices. At higher prices

THE DEMAND SCHEDULE
FACED BY A SINGLE
WHEAT FARMER:

PRICE	QUANTITY HE CAN SELL
$3.37	NONE
3.35	ALL HE HAS
3.33	ALL HE HAS

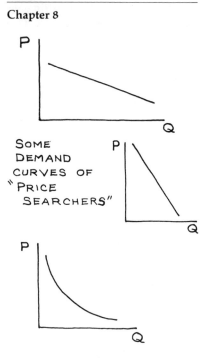

SOME
DEMAND
CURVES OF
"PRICE
SEARCHERS"

they will sell less, at lower prices they will be able to sell more. They must choose a price or set of prices. Economists therefore call them *price searchers*. Torn between the desire for higher prices and the desire for larger sales, they must search out the price or set of prices most advantageous to them.

Price searchers include United States Steel, the trustees of a private university weighing a tuition increase, the proprietor of a local grocery store, and the little boy selling lemonade on a hot afternoon. There is a long tradition in economics of referring to all price searchers as monopolists. But this is a technical use of the word *monopolist* that is confusing to everyone except professional economists. Since the little boy selling lemonade does not face a perfectly elastic demand curve, he is not a price taker but a price searcher. It seems silly to anyone not dipped in the history of economics to call him a monopolist. So we shall not do it. The term *price searcher* captures the situation in which we're interested. Price searchers all have some market power. But it is a matter of degree inversely related to the elasticity of the demand the seller faces.

Price Takers' Markets and Optimal Resource Allocation

Economists applied the disapproving term *monopolist* to what we shall call *price searcher* in large part because they wanted to emphasize the different consequences of these two types of price setting. Markets in which all buyers and sellers were price takers were graced with the approving term *competitive markets*. We want to point up the advantages they saw in price takers' markets without adopting the misleading monopolistic-competitive distinction, which erroneously implies that price searchers face no competition. To do so we shall use the graph of Figure 8A, which shows the demand and supply curves for house painters during a particular summer in the town of Pratte Falls.

The number of house-painting hours that will be demanded and supplied depends on the price per hour of house painters' services. Since people's skills in this area differ considerably, we shall simplify our exposition by assuming that each hour of service shown on the horizontal axis has been adjusted for quality. If Freddie Fumblefingers is only 40 percent as productive in an hour as the average Pratte Falls painter, he will take 2½ hours to supply "one hour" of the good shown on the graph. Betsy Brightbrush, who is three times as good as the average, supplies "one hour" of house painting every 20 minutes.

The first point to remember is that supply curves are marginal opportunity cost curves. The curve labeled *SS* in Figure 8A shows the value of all the opportunities given up as Pratte

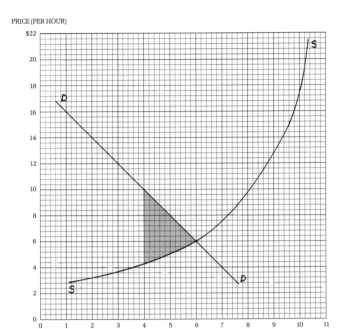

PRICE (PER HOUR)

THOUSANDS OF HOURS OF HOUSEPAINTING

Figure 8A Demand and supply curves for house painting in Pratte Falls

Fallers provide progressively larger amounts of house painting services. The people who contribute to the lower-left portions of the curve are people with large comparative advantages in house painting, because they are either extremely adept painters or because they are extraordinarily inept at everything else. The upper right-hand portion of the curve, including sections not even shown, depicts the supply responses of those who would have to give up a lucrative law practice to paint, who are subject to attacks of dizziness at heights above seven feet, or who for any other reason must sacrifice a highly valued opportunity in order to supply an hour of house painting. Keep in mind that the marginal cost curve of any single individual will also eventually slope upward to the right. The value of the opportunities forgone as one devotes more and more time to any particular activity is bound to increase as that activity crowds out alternative activities, simply because people sacrifice their least valued opportunities first and give up more highly valued opportunities only in response to a stronger inducement.[1]

---

1. This hypothetical example also illustrates the fundamental similarity of supply and demand. The people who are willing to pay up to $20 per hour to have someone else paint their houses, and who thereby create that portion of the demand curve below $20, may well be among the people who create the supply

If the price now settles down at $6 an hour, so that 6000 hours of the good are exchanged over the relevant time period, the heart of many economists will leap with a special kind of joy. Why? Because at the price of $6, given the demand and supply curves, no unit of the good is being produced whose marginal opportunity cost, as represented by the supply curve, exceeds its marginal benefit, as represented by the demand curve. Moreover, every unit of the good whose marginal benefit exceeds its marginal cost is being produced. And how could we do better than that? Economists have traditionally gone so far as to call such an arrangement an *optimal allocation of resources*. Optimal means best, which may be excessive praise; but it certainly looks better, given what we know, than any alternative arrangement. The condition of such an "optimal" allocation is that marginal cost (the marginal value of forgone production opportunities) be equal to price (the marginal value of forgone consumption opportunities). When production takes place at the level where marginal cost is neither less nor more than price, a full quart is being extracted from a quart pot.

While this concept of optimal resource allocation is somewhat abstract and ignores a number of potentially significant qualifications, it does provide a useful first approximation for evaluating the consequences of various market structures. Let's look more closely. Suppose that the people supplying those 6000 hours at $6 an hour decide that they deserve larger incomes, and somehow persuade the town council to pass a law setting $10 an hour as the minimum price for an hour of house painting services. We'll suppose further that the law is effectively enforced. What will happen? Only 4000 hours will now be demanded. And since that's all that can be sold, that's all that will *actually* be supplied, even though, as the graph shows, painters will *want* to supply over twice that amount at a price of $10.

Establishment and enforcement of the $10 price will make some people better off and others worse off. Note that some of those who are worse off may be former house painters forced into less desirable occupations by the legislated price increase. Economists have no satisfactory way of balancing one person's gain against another person's loss to decide whether net social well-being will go up or down as the result of such a change. But they can point out that the Pratte Falls law prevents mutually advantageous exchange and thereby creates a deadweight loss. The area under the demand curve between 4000 and 6000 hours represents the dollar value of what demanders

---

curve at prices above $20. Example: "I'll pay up to $20 per hour to get my house painted this summer. But if I have to pay more than that, I'll do it myself." Such a person, who stops demanding and starts supplying to himself at some high enough price may, at an even higher price, begin supplying also to others.

are willing to give up to obtain those units of the good. The area under the supply curve represents the dollar value of what suppliers are willing to give up to provide those units of service. The difference between the two areas, shaded in Figure 8A, is the deadweight loss imposed by the ordinance which prevents the price from moving to $6.

What does all this have to do with price takers' markets and their superiority, in traditional economic analysis, over price searchers' markets? It is simply this: production moves toward the optimal quantity when price approaches marginal cost, and price will move toward marginal cost in any price takers' market.

The crucial element in the situation is the large number of sellers who act independently. While some or all of them might be able to improve their position by acting collectively to reduce production, none has an incentive to do so individually. Each has a private incentive to carry production up to the point at which marginal cost approaches price. And so the outcome of their pursuit of private interests is, in a broad sense, the public interest. But that only occurs when suppliers produce and sell in price-takers' markets.

Insofar as sellers are price searchers with some power to restrict production and raise the price, the "optimal" allocation of resources will not be achieved. How serious that problem is and how high the costs of corrrecting it might be provides the fascinating question that runs through the next two chapters.

Administered Prices Once Again

It would seem then that price searchers set their own prices, whereas price takers accept what the market sets. Is this the distinction between administered prices and those prices which are set by supply and demand? Not if one thinks about it carefully. Every seller in the last analysis sets the final price, though some sellers can do so with little or no real searching, because they in effect accept the prevailing price (price takers). At the same time, price searchers are by no means free from the constraints imposed by supply and demand.

"Big oil" is a favorite target of those who decry administered prices, but whatever the faults or failings of corporations in the oil industry, their decisions are surely conditioned by supply and demand. Supply depends on cost, and cost is taken into account by every price searcher. Demand curves are never completely inelastic, so demand must also be taken into account if price searchers hope to find what they are looking for, which is presumably the most profitable price to set. Firms in the oil industry may have excessive market power. Whether or not they do, or which ones do and which ones do not, or how much market power any firm has—all these questions can best be investigated by looking at marginal cost curves and demand curves. We will discover nothing useful if we pretend that there are firms which "administer" prices *in total disregard of supply and demand.*

So we end up with no usable meaning for the term *administered prices*, either. *All* prices are administered and *all* prices are set by supply and demand. The term *administered prices* will consequently not be used in subsequent chapters. An examination of its history would reveal that it has more often been used as a polite "bad word" than as a concept to aid analysis or critical discussion. Economic problems are sufficiently complex without complicating them further by using terms that generate much heat and no light.

One other term appeared in the introductory paragraph: *oligopolist.* The dictionary suggests that an oligopolist is "one of a few sellers." The Big Three in automobiles and the major cigarette manufacturers are commonly cited as examples of oligopoly situations. But what about the daily newspapers in a large city? Or do they compete with other newspapers that can be trucked or flown in, with news magazines, billboards, television, the Yellow Pages? What is the commodity that allegedly has only a few sellers? Should it be broadly or narrowly defined? What about gasoline stations? Hardware stores? Automobile dealers? Shops that restring tennis rackets? How few is few? We don't have to multiply examples to discover that all the problems associated with defining a monopolist as a sole seller return to haunt us when we define an oligopolist as one of a few sellers.

There is a special market situation to which many economists have chosen to apply the term *oligopoly.* We'll examine and analyze that situation in Chapter 10. But we shall not use the word *oligopoly,* on the grounds that, like administered prices and monopoly, it creates confusion rather than clarity and understanding.

Once Over Lightly

The word *monopoly* means literally a sole seller. But whether any seller is the sole seller depends upon how narrowly or broadly we define the product. Under a sufficiently broad definition, there are innumerable sellers of every product. Under a sufficiently narrow definition, however, every seller's product differs from every other's and all sellers are monopolists. The word *monopoly* is therefore inherently ambiguous and will not be used in subsequent chapters.

The antisocial connotations of the word *monopoly* stem from the belief that the customers of a sole seller have no alternatives and are therefore at the mercy of the seller. Since there are in fact alternatives to every course of action and substitutes for every good, no seller ever has unlimited power over buyers. Market power is always a matter of degree.

The concept of price elasticity of demand provides a useful way of thinking and talking about the degree of market power. Demand elasticities, which can vary between zero and infinity, reflect the availability of substitutes. The more good alternatives buyers have, the more elastic are the demand curves sellers face and the more limited is the power of sellers to establish terms of sale strongly advantageous to themselves.

In the early years of the United States, a monopoly usually meant an organization to which the government had granted some exclusive privilege. The monopolist was thus the sole legal seller. While this meaning of the term is no longer common, it does have contemporary relevance since federal, state, and local governments are extensively involved in the granting of special privileges that reduce competition.

A useful distinction to make in trying to understand how prices are established is the distinction between *price takers* and *price searchers*. Price takers must accept the price decreed by the market. Buyers have such excellent substitutes for the product that any attempt to raise the price or otherwise shift the terms of sale will leave the seller with no customers at all. The price searcher, on the other hand, can sell different quantities at different prices and must therefore search for the most advantageous price.

Competition tends to push production in price takers' markets to the point where price and marginal cost are equal. This equality indicates that resources are being allocated in such a way as to obtain the largest possible *value* of output.

The concept of *administered prices* is misleading inasmuch as almost all prices are "administered" by sellers—within the constraints imposed by their situation. The important question is whether competition imposes adequate constraints in particular circumstances.

The word *oligopoly* is at least as ambiguous as *monopoly*; whether there are just a few or very many sellers depends upon how we choose to define the product. And so the word *oligopoly* will also be discarded in favor of terms that are more precisely descriptive.

QUESTIONS FOR DISCUSSION

1. List some commodities or services that are sold by only one seller. Then list some of the close substitutes for these goods. How much market power is possessed by the sole sellers whom you listed?

2. List some industries, trades, or professions in which government (federal, state, or local) has imposed legal restrictions on entry. Who benefits from these restrictions? Who is harmed by them?

3. There are approximately 11,000 newspapers currently being published in the United States, most of them weeklies. Only about 1800 newspapers publish daily. Of the dailies, there are only 13 published in South Dakota. Only one of these is a morning newspaper. Is a citizen of South Dakota who wants a morning newspaper carrying state and local news therefore at the mercy of a monopolist?

4. Adam Smith wrote the following in *The Wealth of Nations*: "The price of monopoly is upon every occasion the highest which can be got . . . the highest which can be squeezed out of the buyers, or which, it is supposed, they will consent to give." Does this assertion have any clear and defensible meaning, or must we conclude that even the founder of economics sometimes reasoned carelessly?

5. All the moorage space available for houseboats in the city of Seattle is currently in use. Some of those who pay rent to use the spaces asked the city to impose controls on the rents that owners charge for spaces on the grounds that, with the vacancy rate at zero, owners had acquired "a monopoly." One tenant maintained that this monopoly power allowed the owners to set a price as high as they pleased. Explain why this is an erroneous use of the world *monopoly*. (The moorage spaces are owned by many different people.) Why do you suppose the petitioners nonetheless used the word? Evaluate the claim that the owners can set prices as high as they please. What constrains the owners' power to raise the rents they charge for moorage spaces?

6. Is the college you're attending a price searcher? How much freedom does it have in setting the tuition rate you will pay? Might a just-enrolled freshman answer the above differently from an about-to-graduate senior? Does your college enjoy any special grants of legal privilege?

7. Electric utilities are usually given exclusive franchises by the government to sell electricity in a particular area. Are they in competition with sellers of anything else? Do they compete for sales in any way with electric-utility companies franchised to operate in other areas?

8. Can you think of any cases where price takers have persuaded the government to restrict entry by others into the markets where they sell?

9. Those who use the term *administered prices* do not include in this classification the prices charged by grocery stores. Nonetheless a grocer stamping prices on his products seems clearly to be "administering" his prices. Can you suggest criteria that would enable us to distinguish "administered" from "non-administered" prices?

10. The number of steel mills in the United States is about the same as the number of paper mills. Does this imply that paper users and steel users have about the same number of alternative supply sources from which to choose?

11. It has been argued that the development of the railroad in the middle of the nineteenth century substantially reduced the market power of many American manufacturing firms. Explain.

12. One often reads that there are "only three firms in the industry" (or five firms, or eight firms), and that this is too few for competition to be effective. How

would you define an industry? Do firms in different industries (however defined) compete with one another? Are all the firms within a single industry (however defined) in competition with one another?

13. In December 1978 the Secretary of Transportation predicted, during a televised interview, that gasoline prices would reach $1 a gallon in about two years. He attributed this to the "oligopoly that dominates the oil industry."

   a. Is the oil industry dominated by an "oligopoly," that is, a few sellers? Sellers of *what*? Crude petroleum? Refined products? Retail gasoline?

   b. About how many separate business firms in the United States produce crude petroleum? How many companies refine petroleum? How many independent gasoline retailers are there in the U.S.? (A good place to begin looking for information of this sort is the index of the most recent *Statistical Abstract of the United States*. Most librarians will allow you to consult the one they keep behind the counter.)

   c. The most concentrated of the three sectors mentioned above is petroleum refining. According to the Survey of Manufactures conducted by the U.S. Bureau of the Census, there were 152 companies engaged in the business of petroleum refining in the U.S. in 1972. Most of these were of modest size, but a few are among the largest corporations in the country. The table below shows the percentages of the total value of shipments sold respectively in 1972 by the 4 largest, 8 largest, 20 largest, and 50 largest companies in the petroleum refining business. For purposes of contrast and comparison, corresponding percentages are also shown for nine other industries.

	4 Largest	8 Largest	20 Largest	50 Largest
Petroleum refining	31%	56%	84%	95%
Bread, cake, and related products	29	39	50	62
Bottled and canned soft drinks	14	21	32	44
Malt beverages	52	70	91	99
Commercial printing, lithographic	4	8	15	24
Motor vehicles and car bodies	93	99	99 +	99 +
Tires and inner tubes	73	90	99	99 +
Toilet preparations	38	53	74	91
Photographic equipment and supplies	74	85	92	95
Newspapers	17	28	43	60

   d. Why will the degree of market power possessed by sellers in the industries mentioned above *not* be well correlated with the concentration ratios shown? What factors would make the degree of market power either more or less in particular industries than the concentration ratios alone might suggest? Think in terms of the number and quality of the options available to buyers. Remember that in some industries most sales are made locally, whereas in other industries firms sell nationwide and in competition with foreign sellers.

14. Do steel girders for bridge construction produced in Utah compete at all with girders produced in Maryland? (The phrase "at all" will usually make a statement true.) Can you think of ways in which wood products compete with steel girders?

15. Market power is not the only kind of power that business firms might have and exercise. Neither market power nor any of these other types of power is necessarily correlated closely with the size of business firms. You might want to think about the nature, sources, and consequences of some of the powers listed below and how they are linked (or not linked) with market power. Power:
    a. as capability, the ability to achieve desired results
    b. to influence the outcome of elections
    c. to influence legislation
    d. to influence regulatory agencies of government
    e. to manipulate people through advertising
    f. to pollute the environment; power to reduce pollution
    g. to pursue sexist and racist hiring policies; power to institute affirmative action programs
    h. to intervene in the affairs of other nations
    i. to shape the basic attitudes and beliefs of people
    j. What about the power that we sometimes assume others must have simply because we ourselves feel powerless? Is it true that someone always has power to cause or to prevent undesirable events?

Price Searching

How do price searchers find what they're looking for, and what happens when they find it? We're going to argue in this chapter that price searchers estimate marginal costs and marginal revenues and then try to set prices that will enable them to sell all those units of their product—and only those units—for which marginal revenue is expected to be greater than marginal cost. Does that sound complicated? It's just the logic of the process by which net revenue is maximized. But is it the procedure business firms actually use? It sounds much too theoretical, like something an economist might dream up, but which few real-world sellers would even recognize.

The Popular Theory of Price Setting

It certainly is not the way most people assume that prices get set. The everyday explanation is a simple cost-plus-markup theory: Business firms calculate their unit costs and add on a percentage markup. A large number of price searchers will themselves describe their price-setting practices in terms of the cost-plus-markup theory. Their testimony deserves to be taken seriously, but it isn't conclusive evidence. A lot of people cannot correctly describe a process in which they themselves regularly and successfully engage. Most people who ride bicycles, for example, don't know how they keep the bicycle balanced. And if asked to think about it, they'll conclude that they keep the bicycle from tipping by leaning or shifting their weight slightly each time the bicycle inclines in one direction. (Ask some of your friends what they do while riding a bicycle to keep it balanced. Chances are good that they will all give an incorrect answer unless they have been told how they do it.) If that were the way they actually balanced, they wouldn't make it to the end of the block. In reality they balance by steering, not leaning; they turn the front wheel imperceptibly and allow centrifugal force to counter any tendency to tip. The fact that they don't know what they're doing doesn't keep them from doing it. Although they can only balance successfully by winding along a series of curves whose precise curvature will be inversely proportional to the square of the speed at which they're proceeding, many mathematical illiterates are skillful cyclists.

There are excellent reasons for doubting the cost-plus-markup theory. One is that it tells us nothing about the size of the markup. Why choose a 25 rather than a 50 percent markup? Why do different firms mark up their prices by different percentages? Why will the same firm vary its percentage markup at different times, on different products, and even when selling to different people? Why do sellers sometimes set their prices *below* their average unit cost?

Moreover, if firms can always mark up their prices proportionately when their costs rise, why don't they raise their prices before their costs rise? Why are they satisfied with a smaller net revenue when they could be earning more? That doesn't square with the perennial complaints of many price setters that they aren't making adequate profits. We all know, too, that firms are sometimes forced out of business by rising costs. That couldn't happen if every firm were able to mark up its prices to cover any increase in costs.

The popular cost-plus-markup theory is obviously inadequate. It just doesn't explain the phenomena with which we're all familiar. We'll return to the question of why so many people, including price searchers themselves, nevertheless hold to the theory. But we can't do that until we've gone through the economist's explanation of the price-searching process.

Meet Mr. Artesian

Simple cases are best for illuminating basic principles. The complexities of actual experience can be introduced later. We shall be working for several chapters with the case of Mr. Artesian, who discovers in his front yard a flowing spring of mineral water. Many of his fellow townsmen believe that regular draughts of mineral water promote good health; they are willing to pay for the opportunity to drink from Artesian's spring.

(This is the most technical chapter in the book. But the argument is a simple one that can be easily grasped if you follow the calculations, examine the graphs, and check each conclusion.)

We assume to begin with that Artesian knows precisely the community's demand for his water (an assumption we shall want to relax later). Here it is:

Price per Cup	Cups Demanded per Day
$.40	1
.39	2
.38	3
.37	4
. . .	. . .
.03	38
.02	39
.01	40
.00	40

The demand curve is graphed in Figure 9A. The curve is stepped rather than smooth to enable us to read clearly certain values we'll be interested in.

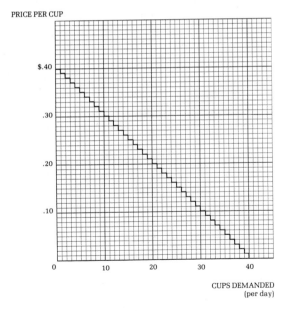

Figure 9A   Demand curve for mineral water

Artesian wants to sell the water and make as much money as possible. The spring produces more than 40 cups of water per day, but no more than that amount can be sold at any positive price. The remainder will be allowed to drain back into the ground. But before going into business Artesian must make an investment. He must acquire equipment to capture and dispense the water. While he could hire someone to do this, he estimates that the cost of hiring an attendant would be greater than the cost of renting an automated dispenser. (Don't forget that there would still be a cost for labor if Artesian tended the spring himself: the value of whatever Artesian was unable to do because he was tending the spring.)

So Artesian rents a coin-operated water dispenser for $200 per year plus 4 cents per cup dispensed. The company leasing the machine to him agrees to attach the machine, keep it serviced, provide the paper cups, and also provide an automatic changemaker for customers. Artesian doesn't have to do anything except write a check at the first of each year and hold out his hand each day for the receipts, minus 4 cents per cup of water sold.

What price should Artesian set? Let's follow him as he searches for the price that maximizes his return. He sees at a glance that some prices are too high. At 35 cents per cup, for example, he would sell 6 cups, collect $2.10, surrender 24 cents to the dispenser company, and be left with $1.86 per day. He can do better by cutting his price and increasing his volume.

But he must not cut the price too far. At 10 cents for example, he would gross $3.10 and net $1.86 again. He can do better at some price in between.

If you were to examine the demand curve for a while, you would discover that Artesian's net receipts reach a maximum of $3.42 at a price of either 23 cents or 22 cents and decline gradually as he moves the price either up or down from those values. This is because the marginal revenue equals the marginal cost as sales move from 18 (at 23 cents) to 19 (at 22 cents).

What in the world does that mean? And what is *marginal revenue* anyway? If you are already familiar with the concept of marginal cost, you should have no trouble with marginal revenue. *Marginal revenue is the additional revenue obtained from taking some action* under consideration, in this case selling additional cups of water. But if additional cups can be sold only by lowering the price on *all* sales, marginal revenue will be less than price. To see exactly why, and in what way marginal revenue is related to demand, we're going to abandon Artesian momentarily in favor of a digression on marginal revenue.

Revenue: 35¢ × 6 = $2.10
Cost: 4¢ × 6 =   .24
Net Revenue: $1.86

Revenue: 10¢ × 31 = $3.10
Cost: 4¢ × 31 = 1.24
Net Revenue: $1.86

23¢ × 18 = $4.14
 4¢ × 18 =   .72
                     $3.42
22¢ × 19 = $4.18
 4¢ × 19 =   .76
                     $3.42

Suppose you are a price taker. The demand curve you face is then, by definition, perfectly elastic at the prevailing price. You can sell all you want to at the going price. The additional revenue you obtain, therefore, from selling one more unit is always equal to the price per unit. *Marginal revenue equals price for all price takers.*

But suppose you are a price searcher. Your demand curve is now, by definition, less than perfectly elastic. You can sell additional units only by lowering the price. Each time you lower the price enough to sell one more unit, you gain an amount equal to the new price per unit *but you lose an amount equal to the price reduction multiplied by the number of units you could have sold at the higher price.* Gain something, lose something. Your marginal revenue is the first amount minus the second.

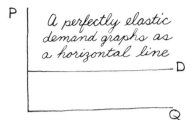

A perfectly elastic demand graphs as a horizontal line

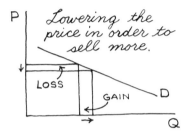

Lowering the price in order to sell more.

Price per Unit	Quantity Demanded	Total Revenue	Marginal Revenue
$6	0	0	
			5
5	1	5	
			3
4	2	8	
			1
3	3	9	
			−1
2	4	8	
			−3
1	5	5	

Marginal revenue is written in between the successive quantities because it's the change in revenue as we go from one quantity to another.

The logic is as simple as the arithmetic. The easiest way to grasp it is to do the calculations. When the price searcher whose situation is summarized in the above schedule reduces his price from $5 to $4, he sells one additional unit and so gains $4. But he loses $1 on the unit which he could have sold at $5 had he been willing to forgo selling the second unit. $4 minus $1 is $3, the marginal revenue associated with the second unit. We place it *in between* the first and the second unit in the schedule to indicate that $3 is the additional revenue gained *by moving from* the sale of one unit (at $5) to two units (at $4).

Similarly, cutting the price from $3 to $2 brings him an additional $2 from the extra unit sold at this price, but loses him $1 on each of the 3 units he could have sold at the higher price. $2 minus $3 is a marginal revenue of minus $1.

If you're still awake (it's the tedium that gets you, not the difficulty), you can observe this phenomenon on a graph. Figure 9B shows the same schedule drawn as a step curve built of lettered blocks. Cut the price from $5 to $4, and you gain the blocks C, E, H, and L, but lose block A. The marginal revenue is therefore three blocks or $3.

Cut the price from $3 to $2, and you gain blocks J and N, but sacrifice D, E, and F. The marginal revenue is minus one block.

PRICE PER UNIT

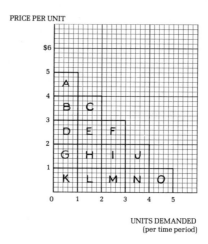

UNITS DEMANDED
(per time period)

Figure 9B   Step curve showing marginal revenue

Marginal revenue is *less* than price for this price searcher because, to put it in common language, he "spoils his market" by expanding his sales. He can expand his sales only by reducing his price. And we're assuming here that the reduced price must be offered to all customers, not just to the customers he attracted through the lower price. (He cannot engage in price discrimination.)

There are questions at the end of the chapter for additional practice on marginal revenue. Be sure you understand what the concept means or you will occasionally be confused by arguments in this and succeeding chapters. Once again: marginal revenue will be *equal* to the price for all price takers. It will be *less* than the price for price searchers who cannot confine a price reduction to the customers gained by that reduction, but must also offer the reduced price to previous customers. (It would be *more* than the price only for sellers facing upward-sloping demand curves. Upward-sloping demand curves are barred from this book, but figuring out why marginal revenue would be higher than price in such a weird circumstance might be a useful logical exercise.)

Back to Artesian

Let's return to Artesian's search for the most profitable price. We asserted that a price of either 23 cents or 22 cents maximizes Artesian's net receipts. This can be proved by anyone willing to calculate the consequences of all possible prices. Net receipts grow gradually as the price is lowered from 40 cents, reach a maximum at 23 cents or 22 cents, then decline gradually through successively lower prices.

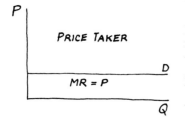

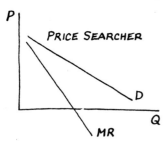

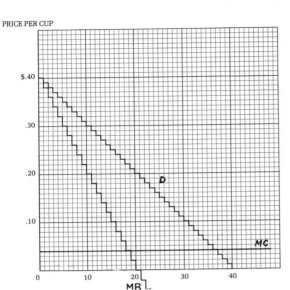

Figure 9C   Marginal revenue

We also asserted, and thereby launched ourselves on a long digression, that marginal revenue equals marginal cost as sales move from 18 units per day to 19 units, and gave this equality as a reason for maintaining that net receipts were maximized between the prices of 23 cents and 22 cents. Figure 9C shows the same information as Figure 9A, and adds the marginal-revenue curve derived from the demand curve on the assumption that the same price will be charged for each sale.

The marginal revenue is 40 cents from the first unit, 38 cents from the second unit, 4 cents for the nineteenth unit, zero for the twenty-first unit, becoming negative and progressively more negative after the twenty-first unit. You should be able to see now why net receipts are maximized at a price of either 23 cents or 22 cents.

Marginal revenue is the addition to Artesian's receipts as his sales expand. Marginal cost is the addition to his costs as his sales expand. He maximizes his net receipts by selling *every* unit whose marginal revenue exceeds its marginal cost, and selling *no* unit whose marginal revenue is less than its marginal cost. Artesian stops selling, therefore, when marginal revenue equals marginal cost.

Don't allow yourself to be hypnotized by the *equality* between marginal revenue and marginal cost. Obsession with this equality has lost many a beginning economics student a good night's rest. The equality is significant only inasmuch as it demonstrates the absence of an inequality! Think in terms of *inequalities* and you'll rest easily tonight.

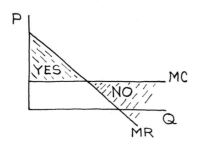

Any unit that adds more to revenue (marginal revenue) than it adds to cost (marginal cost) is a profitable unit to sell, no matter whether it adds a lot or a little.

Suppose that Artesian is selling 17 units. Should he cut his price in order to sell 18? Is the 18th unit a profitable one to sell? The marginal cost is 4 cents; the marginal revenue is 6 cents. Sell it, and add 2 cents to the daily profit.

Suppose he is selling 20. Is this a profitable policy? He may well be making a profit, but the question is whether he is maximizing his profit. The marginal cost of the 20th unit is 4 cents. The marginal revenue is 2 cents. Do *not* sell it, and add 2 cents to the daily profit by avoiding a reduction of 2 cents from the daily profit. The principle we're using is common sense itself. Any action that yields more revenue than cost is a profitable action, and should be taken; any action that yields more cost than revenue is an unprofitable action, and should not be taken.

Doing Well and Doing Better

How does Artesian fare? Is he better off as a result of his newly discovered spring? He nets $3.42 per day as a consequence of his price searching, or $1248.30 per year. After writing the check for $200 to cover his remaining annual costs he is left with an increase of $1048.30 in his annual income. Artesian is happy.

But could he possibly fare still better? Artesian consults the demand curve (which he came to know miraculously, you recall) and notices that some cups could be sold at prices higher than 23 cents. There is even one devotee of mineral water in the community who would pay 40 cents to obtain his daily draught. Moreover, water is going to waste in a frustrating fashion. There are people willing to pay more than the marginal cost of 4 cents who are excluded from purchasing by Artesian's price of 23 cents. Wouldn't it be lovely, Artesian muses, if he could sell each cup for the maximum amount the customers are willing to pay. But how?

Artesian decides to place a sign by the fountain: "Please pay whatever the water is worth to you." He sets the machine to dispense a cup of water at 5 cents or more, in order to exclude those who would only be willing to pay the marginal cost or less. If the customers followed instructions, Artesian would sell 36 cups per day at prices ranging from 40 cents to 5 cents, with these results:

Daily gross receipts	$ 8.10
Daily net receipts	6.66
Annual net receipts	2430.90
Annual net income	2230.90

There are stories about price searchers who try such tactics. A justice of the peace might ask each groom after the wedding to pay "whatever it's worth to you," hoping that the presence of the bride and the general awe of the occasion will prompt the groom into exuberant generosity. Charitable organizations sometimes conduct sales on this principle, hoping that philanthropic impulses will overcome each purchaser's understandable reluctance to reveal the full value of an item to him. And there exist complicated auction techniques that would accomplish a similar result. But Artesian's customers are not starry-eyed, they do not regard Artesian as a charitable enterprise, and Artesian himself is unwilling to incur the costs of running a complicated auction. So his sign is a dismal failure. His first day's receipts came to only $1.80. Each customer paid the minimum price of 5 cents, and he sold 36 cups.

$$36¢ \times 5 = \$1.80 \ (receipts)$$
$$- \ \underline{1.44} \ (cost)$$
$$\$ \ .36 \ Net \ Receipts$$

The College as Price Searcher

We'll come back to Artesian in Chapter 10. The time has arrived for applying some of what we've learned.

College administrators often talk about the high costs of providing an education and the need for charitable contributions to make up that 50 percent or so of the cost not covered by tuition. Have you ever wondered why it is, then, that privately owned colleges grant tuition scholarships to needy students? If colleges are so poor that they must ask for charity, why do they simultaneously *dispense* charity? The answer is that they probably don't. Tuition scholarships for needy students may be a partially successful attempt to do what Artesian failed to do.

Figure 9D is the demand for admission to Ivy College as estimated by the college administration. We shall assume that the marginal cost of enrolling another student is zero. That isn't accurate, but it's realistic enough for our purposes and it doesn't affect the logic of the argument in any event. Ivy College wants to find the tuition rate that will maximize its receipts.

If Ivy restricts itself to a uniform price for all, it will set the tuition at $1000 per year, enroll 2000 students (the enrollment at which marginal revenue equals marginal cost), and gross $2,000,000. But some students whom it would be profitable to enroll are excluded by this tuition rate; and some students who would have been willing to pay more are admitted for only $1000. Ivy's administrators wish they could charge each student what he's willing to pay. If they could find out the maximum each student or his parents would pay rather than be denied admission to Ivy, they could set the annual tuition at $2000 and then give scholarships (price rebates) to each student. The scholarship would equal the difference between $2000 and the maximum each student is willing to pay.

The problem is how to get information on willingness to

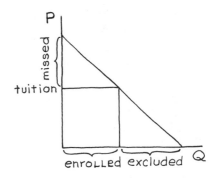

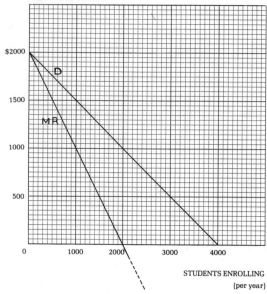

ANNUAL TUITION PER STUDENT

STUDENTS ENROLLING
(per year)

Note: There is a simple gimmick you can use to obtain quickly the marginal-revenue curve corresponding to any straight-line demand curve. Draw perpendiculars to the price axis from the demand curve; bisect the perpendiculars; extend a straight line through these midpoints. The marginal revenue corresponding to any point on the demand curve will then be the point on this line (the marginal-revenue curve) directly below the point on the demand curve in which you're interested. Thus in Figure 9D, the marginal revenue is zero when the price is $1000.

Figure 9D　Demand curve for Ivy College

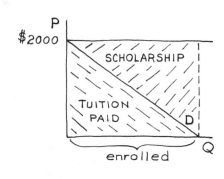

pay. Students or their parents will not reveal the full value of Ivy to them if they know that candor will cause them to pay a higher price. But if willingness to pay is correlated with wealth, a solution lies at hand. Ivy announces that scholarships are available to needy students. Need must be established by filling out a statement on family wealth and income. Families will complete the forms in order to qualify for scholarship aid and will thereby provide the college with information it can use to discriminate. If the correlation were perfect between income and willingness to pay, and if families filled out the forms honestly, Ivy could discriminate with precision and increase its gross receipts to $4,000,000 (the area under the entire demand curve). Marginal revenue would be equal to price despite the fact that Ivy is a price searcher.

Be careful about condemning Ivy College! Notice some of the consequences of this discriminatory pricing policy. First of all, Ivy earns more income. If you approve of Ivy, why begrudge it a larger income from tuition? Is it better for philanthropists and taxpayers to cover Ivy's annual deficit than for students (or their parents) to do so through being charged the

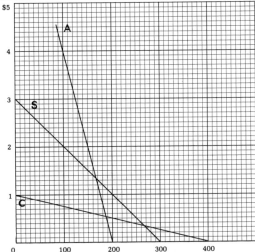

Figure 9E Demand curves for theater tickets

maximum they're willing to pay? Notice, too, that under a perfectly discriminating system of tuition charges, 2000 students who would otherwise be turned away are enabled to enroll at Ivy. They aren't complaining.

Setting Movie Prices

If we assume, as seems reasonable, that price searchers would like to charge customers the most they will pay, we should expect to observe many instances of price discrimination in our society.

The local movie theater charges $4 for adults, $1.50 for students, and 50 cents for children under 12. Is this because the theater owner likes kids or because it costs her less to show a movie to kids? It is more probable that the theater owner is acting like a discriminating price searcher.

Let the demand curves shown in Figure 9E represent the demands of adults, students, and children for tickets to the local movie theater. Children won't come at all if the price is above $1, but will come in droves as the price goes down below $1. Students start attending at prices below $3. Adults attend movies less, but will pay higher prices to do so.

Let the marginal cost of another patron be zero for the theater owner. (Why is this fairly realistic in light of what you know about sunk costs and marginal costs?) If the owner sets one price for everyone, her profit-maximizing price is $2. (The

$\$4 \times 100 = \$400$
$1.50 \times 150 = 225$
$.50 \times 200 = \underline{100}$
$\$725$

proof is a bit complicated. You could figure it out on the basis of what you know; but the marginal benefit from your efforts is likely to be less than the marginal cost of finding the solution.) She will sell 100 tickets to students and 150 to adults for a total weekly revenue of $500.

By discriminating among these three classes of customers, however, the owner can do better. She should charge $4 for adults, $1.50 for students, and 50 cents for children and raise her weekly receipts to $725. With this policy she sets marginal revenue equal to marginal cost *for each separate class of potential customers*. In effect, she is cutting the price to gain additional customers without offering equal price reductions to all customers. She is bringing her marginal-revenue curve closer to her demand curve. As a result, fewer adults will go to the movies. But maybe they'll be happier with the teenagers and the little kids out of the house more often. A total evaluation of the discriminatory pricing policy poses a much more complex problem, of course.

Perhaps you've noticed in passing an important prerequisite for successful discrimination of the kind we've been describing. It must not be easy for low-price customers to resell to high-price customers. And that explains why discrimination is usually observed only in situations where sellers have some effective way of identifying purchasers, and where they can make sure that the consumer of their product is the original purchaser.

Another Type of Price Discrimination

Before leaving the topic of the price searcher as a discriminating seller, we want to consider one more possibility. Additional sales are obtained through reduced prices not only by attracting new customers but also by inducing present customers to purchase more.

Horty Kulcher just built a new house and wants to landscape his lot. He loves roses. But his demand curve is downward-sloping. Let us assume he has this schedule:

Price per Bush	Quantity Demanded
$8	1
5	2
3	3
2	4
1	5

Assume that the owner of the garden shop pays $1.25 to obtain rose bushes from his nursery. He would like to sell 4 to Horty. On the other hand, he can only sell 4 if he offers Horty a price of $2, and it's obvious that $2 is not a profit-maximizing price for his transactions with Horty. Marginal revenue falls from $8 to $2 to *minus* $1 as the owner adjusts his price to sell alternatively 1, 2, and 3 bushes. On any sale beyond 2, marginal cost exceeds marginal revenue. Will the owner therefore settle on a price to Horty of $5?

Not if he knows Horty's demand and he's searching for the profit-maximizing set of prices! A better option is the following price schedule:

$8 per rose bush
2 for $13
3 for $16
4 for $18

It would now be consistent with Horty's demand schedule for him to purchase 4 rose bushes even though the price is in a sense $4.50 a bush. Horty is caught by the fact that he can only obtain a price that low *if* he buys at least 4 rose bushes. The garden-shop owner is thereby attempting to extract the full value to Horty of each successive rose bush. In other words, he is trying to keep his marginal revenue from falling below the price.

Pity Horty if you wish. On the other hand, you might remember that Horty is paying for nothing he does not want, and that his front yard will be more beautiful as a result of the garden-shop owner's "exploitation."

The 1st rose bush is worth $8 to Horty, the 2nd is worth $5, the third worth $3, the 4th worth $2, and the 5th is worth only $1____ less than marginal cost.

Cost-Plus-Markup Reconsidered

So how do price searchers find what they're looking for? By (1) estimating the marginal cost and marginal revenue, (2) determining the level of output that will enable them to sell all those units of output and only those units for which marginal revenue is greater than marginal cost, and (3) setting this price or prices so that they can just manage to sell the output produced. That sounds complicated, and it is. The logic is simple enough. But the estimates of marginal cost and especially the estimates of demand and marginal revenue are hard to make accurately. That's why price searchers are called "searchers." And why they could sometimes be called price "gropers."

The complexity and uncertainty of the price searcher's task helps explain the popularity of the cost-plus-markup theory. Every search has to begin somewhere. Why not begin with the wholesale cost of an item plus a percentage markup adequate to cover overhead costs and yield a reasonable profit? If costs increase, why not assume that competitors' costs have also increased and try passing the higher cost on to customers? Why not begin with the assumption that the future will be like the past and that the procedures which have previously yielded good results will continue to do so? In that case one would try to increase prices roughly in proportion to any cost increases experienced, and one would expect eventually to be forced by competition to lower one's prices roughly in proportion to any lowering of costs.

The cost-plus-markup procedure is in general a rule of thumb for price searchers, offering a place from which to begin looking, a first approximation in the continuing search for an elusive and shifting target. But price searchers only engage in cost-plus-markup pricing as a search technique and only until they discover they are making a mistake. The marginal cost-marginal revenue analysis of this chapter explains how price searchers recognize mistakes and what criteria they use in moving from rules of thumb and first approximations toward the most profitable pricing policy.

Selling below Cost?

Do you agree with the following paragraph?

"In order to preserve our competitive economic system, we need laws that prohibit unfair practices such as sales below cost. Large firms can often afford to sell products below cost until their rivals are driven out of business. If they are not restrained by law, we could easily wind up with an economy dominated by just a few huge corporations."

Most Americans apparently accept this argument. For our laws, at the federal, state, and local level, abound with provisions designed to prevent or inhibit price cutting. Until recently many states enforced resale price maintenance laws, laws that permitted (and in fact assisted) manufacturers and retailers to work together to establish minimum prices and to prosecute retailers who sold below these prices. A special federal law passed in 1937 to exempt such practices from prosecution under the Sherman Act was finally repealed in 1976. But many states still have statutes prohibiting sales below cost, statutes that usually go by some such name as Unfair Practices Act. And regulatory commissions, ostensibly created to hold down the prices that may be charged by public utilities, often wind up enforcing minimum rather than maximum rates. This is true, for example, of the grandfather of all such commissions in the United States, the Interstate Commerce Commission (created by Congress in 1887).

It's fairly obvious why some business firms would approve that kind of legislation: they want protection against competition. But why do consumers and the general public go along? The public seems to have accepted the argument that price cutting can create "monopolies" by driving competitors out of business. And monopolies, of course, are Bad Things.

The paragraph with which this section began states the essential argument. How valid is it? Is it possible to construct a defensible case for laws that prohibit "sales below cost"? A lot of questions should immediately arise in your mind.

What Is the Appropriate Cost?

What is the cost below which prices should not be set? Does anyone actually sell below cost? Why would anyone interested in increasing his wealth ever want to?

Case: Matilda Mudge, proprietor of the Thrifty Supermarket, orders 1000 pounds of ripe bananas. She gets them for 5 cents a pound, because the produce distributor is eager to move them before they become too ripe. Mudge advertises a weekend special on bananas: 10 cents a pound. But Monday morning finds her with 500 pounds of bananas, now beginning to turn brown. How low can Mudge cut her price without selling below cost? The answer is *not* 5 cents a pound. That is sunk cost and hence no cost at all. If Mudge will have to pay someone to haul the unsold bananas away on Tuesday morning, her cost on Monday could be less than zero. In that case it might be to her advantage to give the bananas away. If a zero price is to her advantage, how can it be "below cost"? (By the way, did Mudge *buy* the bananas below cost?)

Or suppose Mudge bought a truckload of coffee: 1000 one-pound cans for $750. It was an unknown brand on which a local distributor offered her an attractive price. But it turns out that her customers aren't interested. She cuts the price down to 80 cents a pound, but still can't move it successfully. Four weeks after her purchase she still has 987 cans of coffee cluttering her shelves and storage room. If she now cuts the price below 75 cents, is she selling below cost? She is not. She has no intention of replacing the cans she sells, so that each sale is that many additional cents in the till and one less can in the way. The relevant cost of a pound of coffee could well be zero. The relevant cost is, of course, the marginal cost.

Let's try a different kind of example and then return to Matilda Mudge. It might make sense to estimate the cost of producing a steer, but does it make any sense to estimate separately the cost of producing hindquarters and forequarters? Should the price of steaks, which come from the hindquarter of a beef carcass, cover the cost of producing the hindquarter, leaving it to pot-roast prices to cover the cost of the forequarters from which they derive? The question is nonsensical. Unless it is possible to produce hindquarters separately from forequarters, one cannot speak of the cost of producing one and the cost of producing the other. Hindquarters and forequarters, or steaks and pot roasts, are joint products with joint costs. There is no way to determine the specific costs of joint products or to allocate joint costs "correctly."[1]

Back to Matilda Mudge. Can we legitimately segregate the costs of each item sold in her grocery store? Think of her frozen-food items, for example. How much of the cost of owning and operating the freezer case should be allocated to vegetables, how much to Chinese dinners, and how much to orange juice? It's true that she could not carry frozen cauliflower without a freezer case. But if she finds it profitable to own and operate a freezer case just for the sake of the frozen juices she can sell, and if she then has some extra room in which she decides to display boxes of frozen cauliflower, it might make sense for her to assign none of the freezer cost to the cauliflower.

A successful businesswoman (or businessman) is not concerned with questions of cost allocation that have no relevance to decision making. She knows that production—and a merchant is a producer just as certainly as is a manufacturer—is usually a process with joint products and joint costs. The businesswoman is interested in the additional costs associated with a decision and the additional revenue to be expected from it, not in such meaningless problems as the allocation of joint costs to particular items for sale. If there is room for a magazine rack near the check-out counter, the question is: How much will its installation *add* to total costs and how much will it *add* to total revenue? If the latter is larger, the rack makes sense; and the magazines sold need not have a price that covers utilities, rent, depreciation on cash registers, *or even the wholesale prices of the magazines.*

Is free carryout service a service sold at less than cost?

Mark well the italicized phrase. It may be profitable to sell a magazine for 5 cents even if it costs 10 cents to obtain it from the distributor. Why? Because the magazine display may bring in new customers who add to net revenue through their purchases of other items. Matilda Mudge is not interested in her net revenue on any one item she sells but in the difference between total revenue and total costs. Retailers have often carried cigarettes not for the sake of the profit they make on the sale of cigarettes but for the sake of the profitable sales of other items that are made possible by carrying cigarettes. Similarly, hardware stores that sell odd-lot bolts, screws, and nuts

---

1. If there are techniques for growing steers with relatively larger hindquarters than forequarters, or vice versa, then it may be possible partially to distinguish the costs under appropriate circumstances. Hindquarters can be enlarged at the cost of smaller forequarters, and livestock breeders and feeders do calculate such costs. More advanced economic analysis provides techniques for making these calculations.

lose money on each sale but (or so their owners hope) more
than make it up through the goodwill they thereby create.

"Predators" and Competition

There would be little point in stressing all this were it not for the
popular mythology of "selling below cost." Our argument
suggests that many allegations of sales below cost are based on
an arbitrary assignment of sunk costs or joint costs. Business
firms often complain about below-cost sales, of course; but
that is because they dislike competition and want government
to protect them from its rigors by prohibiting price cutting.

But aren't there dangers to competition in allowing firms
to cut prices as low as they wish? It is odd, but not really
surprising, how often people identify the protection of competitors with the protection of competition. In reality they are
more like opposites. Competitors are usually protected by laws
inhibiting competition, laws that benefit privileged producers
by restricting consumers and nonprivileged producers. The
hobgoblin hauled out to justify this is "predatory price cutting"
backed up by a "long purse."

Predatory price cutting means reducing prices below cost
in order to drive a rival out of business or prevent new rivals
from emerging *with the intention of raising prices afterward to
recoup all losses*. It is supposedly a favorite tactic of larger firms
who can stand prolonged losses, or temporary losses on some
lines, because of their larger financial resources—the so-called
"long purse." Economic theory does not deny the possibility of
predatory price cutting. But it does raise a long list of skeptical
questions, headed by all the questions we have been discussing
regarding the proper definition of an item's cost.

How long will it take for such a policy to accomplish its
end? The longer it takes, the larger will be the short-run losses
accepted by the predator firm and, consequently, the larger
must be the long-term benefits if the policy is to justify itself.

What will happen to the physical assets and human resources of the firms forced out of business? That's an important
question, because if those assets remain in existence, what is to
prevent someone from bringing them back into production
when the predator firm raises its prices to reap the rewards of
its villainy? And if this occurs, how can the firm hope to benefit
from its predatory policy? On the other hand, the human resources may scatter into alternative employments and be
costly to reassemble.

Is it likely that the predator firm will be able to destroy
enough of its rivals to secure the degree of market power that it
must have to make the long-run profits justify the short-run
losses? Charges of predatory pricing have most frequently been

leveled against large discount houses, drug chains, and grocery supermarkets. But these sellers are not pitted exclusively against small independent competitors: they must tangle with other large discount houses, other drug chains, and other supermarkets. Perhaps A&P could cut its prices far enough and long enough to drive Matilda Mudge out of business; but that wouldn't work on Safeway. And it's Safeway, not Matilda Mudge, that keeps A&P executives awake at night.

We are not denying the possibility of predatory pricing in business. Well-documented examples are hard to find, but it is surely possible. Minimum-price laws, however, offer the *certainty* of higher prices in order to eliminate the *possibility* of higher prices: a case of accepting a known and certain evil as a way of avoiding an uncertain evil of unknown dimensions. That may or may not be a good social bargain. But since it is so often advocated by business firms that clearly stand to gain from it, we should at least approach their arguments skeptically.

Once Over Lightly

Price searchers are looking for pricing structures that will enable them to sell all units for which marginal revenue exceeds marginal cost.

The popularity of the cost-plus-markup theory of pricing rests upon its usefulness as a search technique and the fact that people often cannot correctly explain processes in which they regularly and successfully engage.

A crucial factor for the price searcher is the ability or inability to discriminate: to charge high prices for units that are in high demand and low prices for units that would not otherwise be purchased, without allowing the sales at lower prices to "spoil the market" for high-price sales.

A rule for successful price searching often quoted by economists is: set marginal revenue equal to marginal cost. This means: continue selling as long as the additional revenue from a sale exceeds the additional cost. Skillful price searchers are people who know this rule (even when they don't fully realize they're using it) and who also have a knack for distinguishing the relevant marginal possibilities. The possibilities are endless, which helps to make price theory a fascinating exploration for people with a penchant for puzzle-solving.

Firms often charge that their competitors, whether domestic or foreign, are "selling below cost" and call for the government to prevent such "predatory" practices. Most such charges only make sense if they include some expenses in per-unit cost that are irrelevant to the particular decisions under attack. They make a different kind of sense when we remember that sellers characteristically prefer less competition.

QUESTIONS FOR DISCUSSION

1. If you're still uncertain about the meaning of marginal revenue, here is some additional practice.

Price per Unit	Quantity Demanded
$12	1
11	2
10	3
9	4

   a. Assume that all sales take place at a single price. What is the *addition to total revenue* from selling the second unit, the third, the fourth? Why is marginal revenue less than price?
   b. What set of prices could make marginal revenue *equal* to price as shown by this schedule? (Check the case of Horty and the rose bushes.)

2. "A price searcher should set marginal revenue as far above marginal cost as possible." Explain why this statement is wrong. What is being erroneously assumed by someone who thinks that net receipts will be zero at an output where marginal revenue equals marginal cost?

3. Locate the most profitable uniform price for sellers to set in each of the situations graphed below and the quantity they will want to produce and sell. Then shade the area that represents the net income from that pricing policy. What will happen to net income in each case if the price is raised? If it's lowered? (Caution: What happens if a seller whose marginal revenue curve is the same as the demand curve raises the price?)

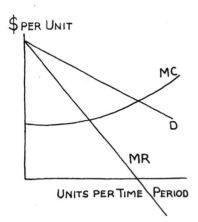

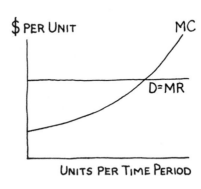

4. You want to sell at auction an antique dining-room suite. There are three people who want it, and they're willing to pay $8000, $6000, and $4000, respectively. Your reservation price (the price above which the bidding must go before you'll sell) is $5000. No one in the room has any information about the value of the suite to anyone else.
   a. At about what price will the suite be sold?
   b. Suppose you run a Dutch auction. The auctioneer announces a price well

above what anyone would be willing to pay and then gradually lowers the price until a bid is received. At about what price will the suite be sold?

5. A privately owned university in the Southwest wants to increase the percentage of Mexican-Americans in its student body. Very few of them are willing to pay the university's high tuition rates, however, and the university is reluctant to spend money for scholarships. Outline a system for granting scholarships to Mexican-Americans that would not reduce the university's net income. (You will have to figure out a way of estimating the relevant marginal costs.)

6. List some cases of discriminatory pricing similar to the cases of the college and the movie theater. How do the sellers identify particular customers with the appropriate class of demanders? How do they prevent reselling?

7. You and your fiancée are shopping for wedding rings. After showing you a sample of his wares, the jeweler asks, "About what price did you have in mind?"
   a. Why does he ask this question?
   b. If you tell him you don't plan to spend more than $100 on each ring, are you helping him find the rings to sell you or the price to charge for the rings you prefer?
   c. What might be a good technique for finding out the lowest price at which the jeweler is willing to sell the rings you like?

8. How should Artesian take into account the price he paid for the land on which the spring was discovered in deciding what price to charge for his water?

9. Grocery stores often run newspaper advertisements containing coupons that entitle customers to price discounts. What is the rationale for such a policy? (Hint: Price searchers would like to use lower prices to attract additional customers without being compelled to offer the lower price to customers already secured.)

10. One store sells Wilson Championship extra-duty felt optic yellow tennis balls at $3.49 for a can of three. Another store in the same shopping center sells Wilson Championship extra-duty felt optic yellow tennis balls at $2.89 for a can of three. How is this possible? Why would anyone buy balls from the first store? Why do you think we repeated the long description in the second sentence instead of just saying "identical tennis balls"?

11. If a surgeon charges $1500 to remove the gall bladder of a wealthy patient and $500 to remove another patient's gall bladder, is she exploiting the first patient or giving a discount to the second? How does she prevent the second patient from buying several operations at the lower price and reselling them for a profit to wealthy patients?

12. Many firms use a technique called "target pricing" in trying to decide what prices to set for new products they're introducing. The target price is a price that enables the firm to recover a certain percentage of the product's development and production costs. What, in addition to costs, must the seller know in order to calculate the return a particular price will yield? If earnings from the sale of the product turn out to fall short of the target, should the firm raise the price? If earnings exceed the firm's expectations, should it lower the price?

13. If it's true that big supermarkets almost always have lower unit costs than small grocery stores, why does anyone ever build a small grocery store?

14. Information is a scarce good and its acquisition has a cost. How does this fact explain the frequent willingness of small firms to charge whatever prices are set by much larger firms?

15. Which of the following products are being sold below cost? With what other products are they competing? Is the competition "unfair"?
    a. Coffee offered by a bank to its customers without charge
    b. As many cups of coffee after dinner as the diner in an expensive restaurant requests, at no extra charge
    c. Commercial television programs
    d. Soft drinks on an airline flight
    e. A roll of film given to each adult customer during the pizza shop's first week of operation

16. There are three elements that must all be present for a firm to be engaged in predatory pricing: pricing (1) below cost, (2) in order to eliminate rivals, and (3) with the intention of raising prices afterward to recoup. What factors would make the last step of the process difficult to complete? Under what kinds of circumstances would it be relatively easy? Can you cite any actual examples?

17. If the railroads, barge lines, and trucking firms of this country were allowed to set their rates free from government regulation, what do you think would follow: "gouging of customers" (higher prices) or "ruinous price cutting" (lower prices)? Does this happen in other areas of the economy where prices are not regulated by commissions, for example, in the grocery or automobile industries?

18. The marginal cost curves of the Anchorage Aardvark Breeding Company and the Houston Aardvark Breeding Company are identical; but the demand curves they face differ, as shown in the graph below.

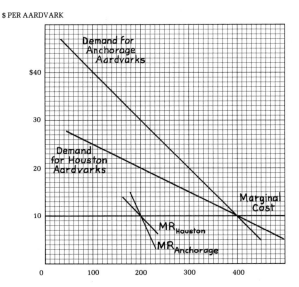

a. What price will each firm want to set?

b. What are their respective percentage markups?

c. Suppose something happens to raise marginal cost for each firm to $20 while nothing else changes. What price will each now set? What will be their new percentage markups?

d. What is the relationship between elasticity of demand and the profit maximizing percentage markup?

19. How should the British and French manufacturers of the Concorde supersonic commercial airliner take account of the plane's development costs in determing the prices to charge airline companies? Should they suspend production if they can't obtain a price that will cover development costs?

20. Can hog growers raise the prices at which they sell when their feed costs go up? (Hog growers are typically price takers.) If feed costs are expected to remain at this higher level, what will happen after a time to the number of hogs reaching the market? How will this affect the price of hogs?

21. When California voters passed Proposition 13 in 1978—substantially reducing property taxes—many of them expected landlords who had benefited from the tax reduction to pass some of their savings along to tenants in the form of rent decreases. When this did not happen, some people were outraged, and the Los Angeles city council responded by imposing rent controls.

a. Use the analysis of this chapter to show why a change in property tax rates, whether up or down, has *no effect* in the short run on the rental rates landlords will want to set.

b. How will changes in property tax rates lead in the long run to changes in rental rates?

22. When the university's athletic director announces that football ticket prices are being raised for next year, he is likely to say this unfortunate step has been made necessary by rising costs—perhaps the rising cost of the women's sports program. How does the cost of the women's sports program affect the marginal cost of selling a football ticket? If you are unable to think of any answer to that question, ask yourself how the prospect of a winning season affects the cost of selling a football ticket. Which plays a larger role in determining the most profitable price at which to sell football tickets: the athletic department's budget for women's sports or an excellent team?

23. Have you ever wondered why otherwise identical books usually sell for so much more in hardcover than in softcover editions?

a. Is it because publishers must pay so much more to produce books with hard covers?

b. Some potential buyers will have a strong preference for a hardcover edition. They include libraries, purchasers who intend to use the book intensively, and people looking for gift items. Would you expect the price elasticity of demand at any particular price to be greater or less for the hardcover than for the softcover edition?

c. The graph on the facing page shows the marginal cost to a publisher of producing and selling hardcover and softcover editions of a particular book and the demand curve for each edition. What prices will the publisher want to set? How much of this reflects cost differences?

$ PER BOOK

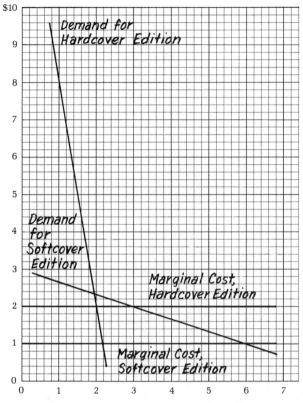

THOUSANDS OF COPIES (per Edition)

177

Chapter **10**

Competition and
Government Policy

Will economic competition disappear unless the government has an active program to preserve it? Or does competition preserve itself, sometimes in the face of diligent efforts by the government to restrict it?

Is the government promoting competition when it prevents larger, more efficient, or more unscrupulous firms from driving other firms out of business? Or does the protection of competitors entail the suppression of competition?

When the government prohibits mergers, is it preventing competitors from eliminating rivals? Or is it barring the development of more competitive and efficient organizational forms?

What do we mean by competition and how are we to decide whether the economy or some sector of it is adequately competitive? Is competition in an industry to be measured by the number of competitors, by the practices in which they engage, or by the behavior of prices, costs, and profits and the industry's record with respect to innovation?

Those questions will not be conclusively answered in this chapter. But we hope that when you've finished thinking through the sources and consequences of competition as well as the origins and effects of government policies you will have a better sense of what the issues are.

Competition Appears

When we last saw Artesian the price searcher, he was ruefully contemplating the consequences of an attempt to extract from his customers the full value to them of a cup of mineral water. As we rejoin him now, he has returned to the price of 23 cents. He is selling 18 cups of water a day and enjoying a daily income of $3.42 from his mineral spring.

Artesian's demand curve reflects the tastes and preferences of people in the community, their income, and the availability of substitutes for Artesian's mineral water. Let's see what might happen if better substitutes became available.

A good substitute for Artesian's mineral water is the mineral water of other suppliers. Perhaps there are no other springs in the community; but mineral water can be bottled and shipped from neighboring towns. Moreover, Artesian's annual income from his spring, if it becomes known, will act as information and incentive to others. The owner of a local grocery store might decide to stock bottled mineral water in the hope of appropriating for himself some of the gains now going to Artesian. Let's assume this occurs.

The grocer can purchase bottled mineral water for $1.40 a gallon. That comes to about 10 cents per cupful of the size which Artesian is selling for 23 cents. The grocer thinks he can undersell Artesian and capture the bulk of his trade. What would be the best price to set?

If we knew the demand curve faced by the grocer, we could use the information we have on marginal cost to determine the profit-maximizing price for which he is searching. We assumed that Artesian knew his demand miraculously, and we could, if we wished, make the same heroic assumption for the grocer. But the assumption would now be considerably more heroic; a larger miracle would be required. For now we would have to know (a) the relative valuations placed on bottled versus fresh water; (b) the proximity of customers to Artesian and to the competing grocery and the costs of patronizing one rather than the other; (c) the customers' evaluations of the advantages and disadvantages of buying two weeks' supply at one time; (d) the extent to which information is available to customers regarding these alternative supplies; and other similar factors. Moreover a fundamental uncertainty of a more radical sort is introduced by the probability that the demand facing each supplier is partially dependent on the pricing policy of the other.

Notice what this implies. The price set by Artesian will affect the grocer's demand and hence the most profitable price for the grocer to set. But the price set by the grocer will in turn affect Artesian's demand and thus alter the data with which

Artesian determined his original price. What it comes to is that the best price for either one to set depends in part on the price which he himself decides to set. The neat little world of Chapter 9, with its clearly defined curves, becomes blurry. Unfortunately from an analytic standpoint, but perhaps fortunately from an esthetic one, the real world is not as neatly outlined as the pictures in a coloring book.

Perhaps you recall from Chapter 8 the word *oligopoly*, meaning "few sellers." We decided there that the concept of a few sellers shared all the ambiguities of the concept of a sole seller, ambiguities inherent in the problem of deciding just how broadly or narrowly to define the commodity being sold. Some economists have retained the slippery word *oligopoly* and have assigned it a very special meaning: a situation in which the demand curve of one seller depends on the reactions of identifiable other sellers, sometimes called rivals. Whether or not we choose to call this oligopoly—the usage is certainly misleading—situations of that sort, where the demand curves of different sellers are significantly interdependent, are obviously both common and important. As a result, price searchers must often plan their course of action in the manner of chess or poker players.

Effects of Competition

What can we expect to occur in such a situation? Precise predictions are impossible to make, but a number of possibilities suggest themselves:

1. Sellers will try to make their products more attractive in the hope of capturing and retaining customers. Artesian may install a bench under the shade tree by his dispenser. The grocer may offer to carry the gallon bottle to the customer's car. There are many other ways to differentiate the product, too many even to begin listing them. These actions raise the cost of doing business, but they may also increase the value to the customer of what he obtains for his money.

2. Sellers will try to disseminate information concerning the special virtues of their products. This is usually called advertising, and it has a poor reputation among many observers of the capitalist economic system. It is allegedly a very wasteful activity. Remember, however, that information is a good, a scarce good whose possession enables people to increase their wealth by discovering more profitable exchange opportunities. Much advertising is no doubt wasteful, in the sense that its total cost exceeds the sum of the benefits it provides in the form of better information. But it is not easy to decide just where the line should be

drawn. Artesian and the grocer will want to spend more on advertising as long as the anticipated marginal revenue from advertising exceeds the anticipated marginal cost. It would be a lot easier to decide whether this results in an optimal or an excessive amount of advertising if we had a clearer notion of what constitutes an optimal amount of information. Meanwhile, we are left with the admittedly unsatisfactory conclusion that advertising sometimes promotes efficiency and sometimes does not.

As long as the marginal revenue to each seller exceeds the marginal cost, the seller will want to expand sales. This is a very significant prediction, because it sheds important light on a third possibility.

3. Artesian and the grocer may meet for lunch and agree to work together. "Why compete," Artesian asks rhetorically, "when all we're doing is wiping out one another's profits? I'll keep my price at 23 cents per cupful, you set a corresponding price of $3.22 per gallon, and we'll just share the market." The grocer agrees and they shake hands. They don't put their agreement in a written contract, because such agreements between competing sellers to maintain prices and share markets are usually unenforceable in court and are, moreover, illegal under the laws of many states and under federal law where it is applicable. In addition, as we shall see, it might be very difficult to write a contract that would cover all the possibilities, and even more difficult to police it. So Artesian and the grocer content themselves with a "gentleman's agreement."

What might happen now? Suppose that geography, consumer tastes, and other factors are such that exactly half of Artesian's customers switch over to the grocer. Artesian will find his annual profits more than cut in half. He will sell 9 cups daily and net $1.71, or $624.15 annually. After payment of $200 to the dispenser company he is left with only $424.15 (as against $1048.30 previously). Artesian mourns the day the grocer decided to enter the mineral water business.

Competition Reappears

But agreements of this sort are notoriously unstable. The incentives to change are so persistent that soon one or the other party will seek to circumvent the terms of the agreement. Let's see why.

Fundamentally, the explanation has to do with the inequality of marginal revenue and marginal cost. Artesian would incur only 4 cents in additional costs if he could attract just one of the grocer's customers. And he would add 23 cents to his daily revenue. That is 19 cents worth of inducement to violate the agreement (in a gentlemanly way, of course). Artesian would be willing to pay *up* to 19 cents to attract another customer, if he thought he could do so without inviting retaliation from the grocer or being forced to reduce prices to his existing customers.

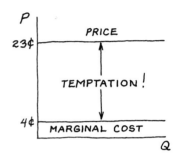

He might advertise more, add vitamin C to his water, provide selective delivery service, give trading stamps, or maybe even offer secret price rebates. Meanwhile the grocer's marginal revenue is also well above his marginal cost, and the grocer is contemplating similar actions to "build volume" on mineral water. Maybe the grocer offers a special low price on paper cups to customers who buy a gallon of mineral water, thereby escaping the charge that he has violated the agreement not to reduce the price of mineral water.

Even if the gentlemen were to resist all these temptations, their agreement might still be undermined. For what is to keep some other grocer or the local druggist from doing exactly what the first grocer did? If Artesian and the grocer do not take these new competitors into their cartel,[1] the price of 23 cents will be undercut. If they do take them in, profits on the mineral water business will shrink further. And the new and larger agreement would be still harder to enforce effectively, since it now involves more parties and presumably more ways to honor the letter while violating the spirit of the agreement.

The recurring lesson under this third possibility is that a downward-sloping demand curve is insufficient to guarantee continuing profits. Competition (and every seller faces competition; remember that there is no such thing as a perfectly inelastic demand curve) tends to bring down the price, raise the quality of the product sold, and whittle away the price searcher's net income. That is why price searchers and even price takers yearn so ardently for legal restrictions on competition. Let's turn to this possibility.

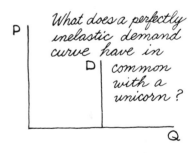

Enlisting the Government

Artesian had a good thing going until the grocer found out what a good thing it was. "If people would only be loyal to their local mineral water," Artesian muses one evening, "I'd still be earning over $1000 a year from my spring." The wish becomes father to a thought and the thought inspires a course of action.

---

1. A cartel is an agreement among a group of sellers to regulate prices or output. There are also buyers' cartels, such as the owners of professional basketball teams mentioned in Chapter 3 who want a single league to keep down the cost of hiring players.

Artesian drafts a memorandum to the town council setting forth the following points:

1. Water is a basic necessity of life. Adequate local supplies of high-quality water must therefore be assured.
2. Mineral water is even more basic than regular water, containing as it does vital nutrients.
3. Unrestricted competition, especially from outside the town, can lead to irresponsible price cutting and the destruction of local mineral water suppliers, thus depriving the town of an important industry, citizens of regular income, and consumers of assured domestic supplies of mineral water.
4. Unrestricted competition will lead to cost-cutting procedures that may threaten the purity of the mineral water supply and hence the health and safety of the whole community. No price is too high if it guarantees pure water!
5. The town council should therefore pass an ordinance stipulating that every seller of mineral water within the town limits be licensed; that a license be granted only after careful scrutiny by a board of knowledgeable people in the mineral-water industry of the applicant's qualifications and ability to satisfy minimum health and safety standards; and that the board be empowered to revoke the license of any seller who engages in conduct that is unethical or inconsistent with the public interest.

Since legislative bodies at the federal, state, and local level have often adopted just such licensing laws on the basis of very similar arguments, we shall assume that the town fathers grant Artesian's request. Market entry is now restricted and Artesian is in a more fortunate position. If he is doubly fortunate, Artesian will even be appointed chairman of the licensing board. Why not? He is, after all, the local mineral water expert.

The board will now set high standards of purity and excellence. It will probably not be so crude as to deny licenses outright. It will rather decree that bottled mineral water must be sold only in containers that have been sterilized by being boiled for 24 hours at 120 degrees centigrade (fresh water sold in cups is exempt); that stores selling mineral water must do so in separate areas so that the water does not stand closer than 25 feet to any other food or beverage by which it might be contaminated (businesses selling only mineral water are exempt); and perhaps that a tax of $2 per gallon be levied on all water sold to defray the costs of the inspection and licensing services (mineral water sold from private residences is exempt).

Entry into a market can be prevented without going so far as to prohibit it flatly. Anything that increases the costs of suppliers will restrict their supply, and the imposition of sufficiently large costs will restrict it completely. Licensing can be used to do exactly this, and often is. The prevention of competition is never given, of course, as the reason for licensing. It is always "the public interest" for which sellers profess a fervent concern when they seek to have the government impose controls on potential competitors.

Restricting Competitors

Here are some actual newspaper items with names changed to protect the guilty. Who stands to gain and who to lose in each case?

"Government officials are demanding that hospitals provide registered nurses 24 hours a day or lose their Medicare certifications."

"All plumbers must spend a minimum of 140 hours a year for five years learning higher mathematics, physics, hydraulics, and isometric drawing."

"Woolen makers are arguing that, since woolen worsted fabric is essential to national defense, the government should impose quotas on imports from abroad."

"The prominent owner of a local television sales and service center said today that he welcomed the state's investigation of the television repair business and he demanded regulation of the industry. 'We must eliminate janitors, fire fighters, messengers, and similar amateurs who defraud the public by providing poor quality repair service at cut-rate prices,' he argued."

"Automobile dealers are vigorously protesting Sears' application to enter the car financing business, and are demanding that the state corporations commissioner reject the application."

"The Senate Public Health Committee yesterday rejected a bill to allow use of multiple offices and trade names in the diagnosis of eye problems and fitting of glasses. Single-office optometrists contend that optometrists who have private offices are in effect employed by their patients. If optometrists work under a trade name, their boss is their company."

"The owner of the Piney Woods Nursing Home and secretary of the State Association of Licensed Nursing Homes accused the state health department last night of approving new nursing home construction without proper investigation of the need for additional facilities or the qualifications of the applicants. 'Unqualified people, including speculators from other parts of the country, are hoping to reap big profits,' he said. 'A great surplus of beds will bring about cutthroat competition, which means nursing homes will have to curtail many needed services, resulting in lower standards detrimental to patients and the community.' "

And once again, the plumbers, who aren't any worse than many others but seem to draw better press coverage:

"Changes proposed in the plumbing section of the city building code would require that a plumber serve as an apprentice for five years, instead of the present three, before becoming a journeyman. In addition, apprentices would have to register annually with the city and could not become apprentices after reaching the age of 25. For a plumber to become a master plumber, that is, one contracting plumbing work, an examination would be required. The code now requires only that a plumber seeking master plumber status furnish bond."

The Ambivalence of Government Policies

An old proverb wisely asserts that the wolf should not be sent to guard the sheep. Should the government be relied upon to preserve competition in the economy? The history of government intervention in economic life reveals a pattern of concern for the special interests of competitors at least as strong as concern for competition. And the two are not identical, even though our rhetoric so often and easily uses them interchangeably.

The real and hypothetical cases described in this chapter show government acting at several levels and in a variety of ways to prevent potential sellers from offering more favorable terms or more attractive opportunities to buyers. They constitute restrictions on competition, regardless of the arguments used to defend such actions. The ultimate effect of a particular restriction on competition may be to preserve competition, by protecting a substantial number of competitors who would otherwise be forced out of business. But whether or not that is the long term effect in certain cases, it is important to begin any evaluation of government policy toward competition by acknowledging one principle: *A law that restricts competitors restricts competition.*

We shall see in Chapter 14 why it is that governments so often intervene in ways that harm consumers by *reducing* competition, despite the fact that consumers and competition always win easily in the rhetorical battles. But local and state governments and especially the federal government also have adopted specific policies to *promote* competition, policies that are ordinarily justified on the ground that competition is an effective coordinator of economic activity but requires some government maintenance if it is to be adequately preserved. The assessment of these laws, their applications, and their consequences forms an interesting study in history and judicial interpretation as well as economic analysis. All we shall try to do here, however, is raise a few fundamental questions.

The most important such law is the Sherman Act, often called the Sherman Antitrust Act, enacted by Congress with almost no debate or opposition in 1890. (The name reflects the attempts of nineteenth century businessmen to use legal trusteeships as a device to prevent competition.) Its sweeping language has caused some to call it the constitution of the competitive system. It forbids all contracts, combinations, or conspiracies in restraint of interstate trade and all attempts to monopolize any part of interstate trade. The language is so sweeping, in fact, that it was bound to be qualified in its application. After all, any two partners entering into business together could be deemed to have combined with the intention of making trade more difficult for their competitors and thus gaining an ever larger share of trade for themselves. The federal courts consequently came to hold that combinations or other attempts to monopolize had to be "unreasonable" or major threats to public welfare before they could be prohibited under the Sherman Act.

Interpretations and Applications

To help the courts out in their efforts to apply the policies of the Sherman Act, Congress has passed additional legislation such as the Clayton Act and the Federal Trade Commission Act, both of which became law in 1914. The latter act created the Federal Trade Commission as a supposedly expert body and authorized it to promote competition by prohibiting a wide range of "unfair" practices. A principal provision of the Clayton Act (and subsequent amendments) aims specifically at the question of mergers, prohibiting all mergers that might "substantially" lessen competition. But difficult and important questions remain unresolved.

When does a merger substantially lessen competition? And do mergers ever increase competition? Suppose two steel firms want to merge. This is usually referred to as a *horizontal merger*. At first glance we would be inclined to say that the merger will substantially lessen competition in an industry already made up of a relatively few very large firms. But suppose they sell in different geographic areas? Suppose they each specialize in a different line of steel products? Suppose each is on the edge of failure and that the merger will lead to certain economies which may enable both to survive?

A great deal of dispute has arisen in recent years regarding so-called *conglomerate mergers:* mergers between firms producing widely divergent goods. Does the acquisition of a car-rental firm by an electrical machinery manufacturer enable the rental firm to compete more effectively against Hertz and Avis?

1

Does it lead to special arrangements between the machinery manufacturer, its suppliers, and the rental firm that tie up a portion of the car-rental business and thus reduce competition? Do conglomerate mergers lead to concentrations of financial power that are dangerous and undesirable regardless of their effects on competition?

What about *vertical mergers*, mergers between firms that previously existed in a supplier-buyer relationship, as when a supermarket chain acquires a food processor? Is this more likely to increase efficiency or to reduce competition by depriving other food processors of opportunities to sell?

What constitutes an illegally unfair trade practice? Is it unfair for a large firm to demand discounts from its suppliers? Is it unfair for suppliers to offer discounts to some purchasers but not to others? What about the whole question of advertising? Do large firms have unfair advantages in advertising, advantages that advertising increases? Must advertising be truthful in order to be fair? Of course it must, almost by definition. But what is the truth, the whole truth, and nothing but the truth? Anyone who thinks about this issue seriously or for very long is forced to admit that the regulation of "deceptive" advertising by the Federal Trade Commission inevitably involves the Commission in complex questions of purpose and effect and in a large number of judgments that appear quite arbitrary.

And always we return to the root problem: restrictions on competitors will reduce their ability to compete. Competition is essentially the offering of additional opportunities, and additional opportunities mean a wider range of choices and hence greater wealth. But the manner in which a firm expands the set of opportunities it offers may diminish, over a short or a longer period, the set of opportunities other firms are able to offer. Under what circumstances do we want the government to restrict one firm's competitive efforts for the sake of the larger or long-run competitive situation? It is important to remember that many of the most effective pressures on government policies stem not from consumer but from producer interests. And those policies will too often be shaped by the desire of producers to protect themselves against the rigors of the competitive life. Many arguments in the name of the public interest are about as honest as Mr. Artesian's moving petition to the town council.

The Range of Opinion

Is the whole body of "antitrust" law perhaps more of a hindrance than a help to competition? There are some who come to that conclusion. There are others, heavily concentrated, it often seems, in the economics profession, who would retain the Sherman Act and the antimerger provisions of the Clayton Act and junk the rest. Some of these defenders claim that the Sherman and Clayton Acts have made important contributions to the maintenance of a competitive economy. Others claim that they could make a much larger contribution if they were seriously enforced. But still others view them at best as harmless rhetoric, at worst as weapons which, in the hands of ignorant political appointees, may do a lot of damage to the economy.

The author is firmly convinced that he doesn't know who is right. "Antitrust" policy is certainly full of contradictions, of cases where the right hand is doing what the left hand is undoing. State laws rarely promote competition; more often they promote the interests of the competitor-protectors rather than the competition-protectors. Federal enforcement of the Sherman Act and the antimerger provisions of the Clayton Act often seems to strain at gnats while swallowing camels. On the other hand, the existence of the Sherman Act, with its ringing denunciation of price fixing conspiracies, may have retarded the development in this country of the cartel arrangements that have so often appeared in Western Europe and Japan. The economist George Stigler once suggested that "the ghost of Senator Sherman is an ex officio member of the board of directors of every large company." That statement will never meet the minimum criteria for empirical scientific truths; but good history is still a long way from being a pure science.

Toward Evaluation

The conclusions that we shall offer at the end are far more modest than the questions with which we began.

The principal observation to be made is that price searchers' markets tend to result in reduced output. To avoid spoiling the market, price searchers forgo some sales that could be made at prices above marginal cost. They look at marginal revenue, not at price; and so they sell less and at a higher price than they would if they were price takers. We introduced the other half of this argument at the end of Chapter 8, when we tried to show the sense in which price takers' markets led to an "optimal" allocation of resources. The argument, admittedly somewhat formal and abstract, is an important argument to understand if you want to evaluate the effects of market power. In short: price searchers refrain from providing goods that could be provided at a cost below what people are willing to pay. This constitutes an inefficient use of resources.

Some further observations and words of caution can now be added.

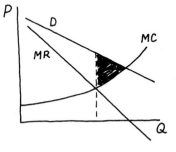

First of all, price discrimination is capable of reducing this inefficiency. If the price-searching widget producer can find a way to do what Artesian attempted unsuccessfully with his you-set-the-price policy, and what Ivy College did more successfully through tuition scholarships, he improves the allocation of resources. Of course, he also increases his own net income, a fact that will prompt him toward more astute price searching.

Second, the burden of such inefficiency diminishes as price searchers' demand curves become more elastic. Since elasticity depends crucially on the availability of substitutes, legal restrictions on entry will tend to aggravate inefficiency. Restrictions on potential competitors reduce the range and diminish the availability of substitute goods, and allow the price searcher more room to increase his own wealth by allocating resources inefficiently.

Third, competition is a process, not a state of affairs. To put it another way, competition can only be recognized in motion pictures, not in still photographs. The fact, for example, that the price of some good is exactly the same, no matter from which seller you buy, establishes absolutely nothing about whether the industry producing that good is adequately competitive. The important question is how those prices all came to be identical. It happens with surprising frequency that even public figures, who ought to know better, will infer an absence of competition from the uniformity of prices. The quickest antidote to this error is the recollection that wheat farmers all charge the same price.

Finally, for policy purposes an inefficient situation must be compared with more efficient situations that are actually attainable. We objected earlier to the frequent error of contrasting a less than ideal situation with an ideal but unattainable situation. There are costs involved in changing market structures, such as the cost of an investigation, prosecution, court order, and compliance under antitrust statutes. Only if these marginal costs are less than the marginal benefits can one maintain that efficiency would be increased by legal action aimed at reducing the market power of price searchers.

Once Over Lightly

A gap between the price of a good and the marginal cost of making it available is a source of potential advantage to someone. Competition occurs in the economy as people locate such differentials and try to exploit them by filling that gap with additional goods.

Competition can take more forms than we can list and

usually more forms than a price searcher can anticipate and head off.

Because competiton tends to transfer the gains from providing a good to purchasers and other suppliers, firms frequently try to obtain government assistance in excluding competitors, often displaying remarkable ingenuity and stunning sophistry.

The notion that government is the Defender of Competition against Rapacious Monopolists is probably more a hope than a reality. Federal, state, and local governments have created and preserved numerous positions of special privilege whose effect is to restrict competition and reduce the options available to consumers.

An adequate and balanced evaluation of that substantial body of statutes, commission decrees, and judicial holdings which makes up federal antitrust policy has not yet been published.

Competition is a process in which competitors engage. We obviously cannot have competition without competitors. It does not seem as obvious to people that we also cannot have competition if we prohibit competitors from taking actions intended to increase their share of the market.

While price searchers' markets entail a misallocation of resources when compared with price takers' markets, the significance of that misallocation and the cost of correcting it are difficult to determine.

QUESTIONS FOR DISCUSSION

1. How would you account for the fact that while some observers claim competition is declining in the American economy, every business firm insists that it faces strenuous competition?
2. Consult the technical definition of *oligopoly* presented in the text. Are the manufacturers of cigarettes oligopolists by that definition? Are the owners of the gasoline stations in a small town oligopolists? Name some other sellers who are and are not oligopolists by that definition.
3. The attempt by sellers to make their product more attractive to consumers is sometimes called *product differentiation.*
   a. Is product differentiation a wasteful process, imposing costs on sellers that are greater than the benefits conferred on buyers? Think of cases where it probably is wasteful in this sense and other cases where it is not.
   b. Evaluate the following argument: "New practices initiated by sellers to differentiate their products are liable to be wasteful from the social point of view because they are liable to entail high marginal costs and low marginal benefits. But this only means that producers have already made

use of the low cost-high benefit techniques of product differentiation; it does not show that the whole process of product differentiation is wasteful."

4. Why must an effective price-fixing agreement between sellers include such restrictions on sales as output limitations or geographic divisions of sales territory?

5. Some states have established legal minimum prices for liquor sold at retail. Do you think this eliminates competition among retail liquor stores? Why do you think retailers in such states often lend glassware without charge to customers planning parties?

6. All the real estate brokers in an area will generally charge the same fee for selling a house, a certain percentage of the sales price established by some association and adhered to by all real estate agents as a matter of "ethical practice."

   a. Why would it be unethical if a broker offered to accept 5 rather than 6 percent for selling your house? Toward whom would it be unethical?

   b. How do real estate agents compete with one another?

   c. Is an industry likely to become overcrowded if it's successful in fixing a high minimum price for its product? Is the real estate profession overcrowded in your judgment? What evidence might be used to answer this question?

7. A survey reported in the *Harvard Business Review* asked businessmen to describe the unethical practices in their own industry that they would most like to see eliminated. Of those responding 62 percent mentioned "unfair pricing," "dishonest advertising," "unfair competitive practices," or "cheating customers." How would you interpret these responses? How would you define the practices they condemn?

8. Examine the paragraph in the text (page 185) recounting the complaint of the nursing-home operator. How many wrong or misleading assertions can you locate in that paragraph?

9. The legislature of a large state recently considered a bill that would require all grocery stores and drug stores selling package liquor to provide separate entrances to their liquor departments. It was maintained by supporters of the bill that this was necessary to prevent minors from entering the liquor department. Who do you think lobbied for this bill? Why?

10. A study several years ago pointed out that 73 percent of the professions licensed by a populous Midwestern state required entrants to have "good character." Why? How can good character be determined? Who is best able to determine whether a mortician's character is sufficiently blameless to entitle him to a license?

11. Is the patent granted to an inventor a grant of special privilege? Would you favor abolition of the patent privilege? Why or why not?

12. How might laws prohibiting collusion on pricing encourage mergers? (Hint: Can a firm collude with itself?)

13. What is the difference between reducing prices to attract more customers and reducing prices in order to monopolize?

14. It is often argued that large corporations have undue political influence. It is

also argued by some that large corporations are convenient political scapegoats. Which argument is closer to the truth?

15. How important is free entry in promoting efficiency, low prices, and innovation in an industry? What are some of the barriers to free entry in addition to legal restrictions?

16. Think about this assertion put forward by the economist M. A. Adelman: "A useful if not very precise index of the strength of competition . . . is the resentment of unsuccessful competitors." How would you evaluate the argument by other firms in their industries that General Motors and International Business Machines ought to be broken up into several separate companies?

17. Which of the options below more adequately states the opinion of U.S. citizens as to the proper and primary purpose of the Interstate Commerce Commission and the Civil Aeronautics Board?

    a. To protect shippers and travelers against unreasonably high prices that might be charged by shipping companies or airlines.

    b. To eliminate the pressure that would be exerted on shipping companies and airlines to reduce their prices and improve their services if entry into these industries and indiscriminate price cutting were not controlled.

    Which of the above more accurately describes the policies actually followed during most of the lifetime of the ICC and the CAB?

Chapter **11**

Profit

"Perhaps no term or concept in economic discussion is used with a more bewildering variety of well-established meanings than *profit*." That sentence was written about 50 years ago by Frank Knight, a distinguished student of the subject, to introduce an encyclopedia article on profit. The situation has not changed greatly since then. A few years ago the *Wall Street Journal* ran a feature article entitled "Some Plain Truth about Profit." The author listed no fewer than seven distinct definitions of the word *profit* that have been employed by "economic experts," decided none of them was very helpful, and then offered his own. A month later the *Journal* published seven letters of response from its readers; their verdicts on the new definition and accompanying exposition ran from excellent through misleading to ridiculous.

So what shall we do? We shall take the coward's course and assert that *there is no correct definition of profit*. The meaning of any word depends, after all, on the way people use it; and it is an incontrovertible fact that people (including economists) use *profit* in many different senses. We certainly don't want to quibble about mere definitions. But attitudes toward profit and such closely related concepts as cost of production and interest affect economic legislation, and those attitudes depend in large part on what people have in mind when they use the terms. So we're going to expend an unusual amount of effort in this chapter trying to decide what things ought to be called, but only insofar as we must do so to avoid both misleading distinctions and misleading identifications. We do not want to ignore important realities. But neither do we want to be misled by language into seeing things that don't exist.

Profit as "Total Revenue Minus Total Cost"

The most common definition of profit is simply *total revenue minus total cost*. That's almost everyone's intuitive definition of the term and that's how we have used it until now. When a business firm has paid all of its costs, what it has left over is profit. But before we can agree on the size of profits, defined in this way, we must agree on what is to be counted as costs.

What Should Be Included in Costs?

Monetary outlays are not the same as costs from the opportunity-cost perspective. This is clear in the case of an owner-operated business: part of the cost of doing business is the owner's own labor, even though owners may not figure their salaries as part of their regular costs and write no weekly payroll check to themselves. If owners pay rent for the building they use, they will count the rental payments as part of their costs; but they may fail to do so if they themselves own the building. They ought to do so, however, because they are losing the amount that could be obtained from renting the building to someone else. From the standpoint of society, too, there is a genuine cost in having the building not available for alternative uses.

Business proprietors may also be using equipment that they bought and now own. If they bought the equipment with a bank loan, they will include the interest on their bank payments in their costs. But suppose they bought the equipment out of previously accumulated savings? Then they gave up income that they could have obtained from letting someone else use their savings, and this is certainly part of the opportunity cost of doing business. But they may or may not decide to include this forgone income in their costs. The point is that they should. The income forgone represents a genuine cost.

Let's next consider the accounting procedures of corporations. Corporate profits have a legal definition because corporations must pay taxes on their profits. But the legal definition is unsatisfactory from an opportunity-cost point of view. It begins with the commonsense definition of profit as revenue minus costs. But it excludes from cost the dividend payments made to stockholders of the corporation while including the interest payments made to bondholders. Are these payments that different? Both are payments for the use of borrowed funds or the resources that the corporation was able to purchase with those funds. The principal difference is that payments to bond-holders are a contractual obligation of a fixed amount, whereas the dividends paid to stockholders are a kind of residual that may vary from year to year or quarter to quarter. Still, the funds loaned by the stockholders are funds not earning income somewhere else, and the resources purchased by the corporation with these funds are pulled away from alternative opportunities. Surely some portion of the dividends paid by corporations represent genuine opportunity costs, no matter how they are regarded for purposes of taxation.

The total cost of operating an enterprise is the value of all the opportunities given up in order to be able to operate it.

Profit versus Interest

A persistent difficulty in the measurement of profits is the difficulty of deciding just how much interest a business firm is paying. The legal definition of interest isn't adequate, for payments to banks and bondholders often will not differ functionally from the payments made to shareholders in dividends or even as increases in the market price of their shares attributable to reinvestment of earnings. What we are after in trying to measure the true interest costs of a business firm is the amount the firm must pay in order to obtain the capital it uses.

Capital means produced goods used to produce future goods: like cash registers in retail stores, typewriters in an office, drill presses in a sheetmetal fabricating shop, or reading skills that are used to produce knowledge. In later chapters we'll take a closer look at the concept of capital and some of the ambiguities associated with its definition. But the simple definition given above is enough to get us into the puzzling phenomenon of interest.

Why Is Interest Paid?

Usury and interest were originally synonyms. Today the word *usurious* carries connotations of overreaching and grasping greed—evidence in our language of popular hostility toward the taking of interest. The hostility seems to be largely rooted in misunderstanding. Interest is not the price of using money, although that is sometimes a convenient way of expressing it. *Interest is the difference in value between present and future goods, the premium paid to obtain current command of resources rather than wait.* Once you understand why present goods are more valuable than goods in the future, you realize that interest is not something peculiar to capitalist economies, or a consequence of the avarice and monopoly power of bankers and other moneylenders, or something that could be eliminated just by making more money available. Interest rates

People are willing to pay interest to borrow money because money borrowed confers power to act at the present time rather than later.

are generally talked about as if they were the cost of borrowing money, because money is the usual means by which people acquire possession of present goods. But interest would exist in an economy that used no money at all, since it is fundamentally the difference in value between present and future goods.

Why are present goods more highly valued than goods in the future? This is a question that has intrigued a number of the most distinguished minds in the history of economics, and the higher subtleties of the problem still arouse controversy in some quarters. There are, however, two aspects of the question whose significance can be readily grasped.

Time Preference

In the first place individuals have, on the average, *a positive rate of time preference.* That is to say, people tend to place a higher subjective value on consumption in the near future than on consumption in the more distant future. Some have interpreted this as evidence of shortsightedness, or of inability to imagine the distant future with as much vividness and force as one contemplates the immediate future, or of an innate human tendency to view the future through rose-tinted glasses. Each of these interpretations casts suspicion on the ultimate "rationality" of time preference. On the other hand, given the facts of human mortality and all the contingencies of life, it is not necessarily irrational or shortsighted to prefer a bird in the hand to two in the bush. Moreover, if people have reason to believe that their income will increase over time, they could very logically conclude that giving up something now entails a larger subjective sacrifice than giving up quite a bit more of the same thing at a future date when one's income is expected to be larger. Whatever the explanation or explanations, however, there can be no doubt that people do display positive rates of time preference. To obtain 100 strawberries today, a person may be willing to give in exchange 115 strawberries one year from now. Conversely, such an individual could be persuaded to give up 100 strawberries now only by the promise of 115 strawberries or more one year hence. This person displays a 15 percent rate of time preference. While these subjective rates of time preference seem to vary widely from individual to individual and from one culture to another, they are, on the average, positive in every known society. This by itself would be sufficient to create a premium on present goods over future goods and thus a positive rate of interest.

It may be instructive to consider a case of apparent *negative* time preference. This should help you grasp the principle at work. Consider a man who receives, as a gift, 100 quarts of strawberries. He loves strawberries and vastly prefers one quart now to one quart a month from now. But he does not want to eat more than one or two quarts a day, for fairly obvious reasons, so that many of these 100 quarts are without any value to him. They will spoil before he wants to eat them.

Such a man would be willing to give up strawberries now to obtain *fewer* strawberries in the future! He might go down the block offering each of 45 neighbors two quarts of strawberries apiece in return for one quart at a later date when he will be able to eat them. By this act, which seems to reveal a negative time preference, he clearly increases the value to himself of the gift he received.

Surpluses of this kind are not uncommon. How much pressure do they exert to reduce the average premium on present over future goods, or the rate of interest? Probably very little in an economy with a well organized system for extensive exchange. If the recipient of the 100 quarts of strawberries can easily sell them (for money), and then use the money (which will not spoil after a few days) to buy strawberries as he wants them, his present surplus will not cause him to reveal a negative rate of time preference. Opportunities to exchange at low cost, which are enlarged by such institutions as money and commodity speculators, keep the rate of interest from falling.

The Productivity of Capital

The second main factor making for positive interest rates in a society—though perhaps it is only another aspect of the factor already discussed—is *the potential productivity of goods*. Suppose that Robinson Crusoe, a familiar figure in economists' arguments, can keep himself alive from day to day only by digging for clams. Five clams a day will barely enable him to keep body and soul together. And five clams a day is the most he can obtain by digging with his hands during every working hour. If he had a shovel, however, he could increase his daily output to ten clams. But a week's work is required to manufacture a suitable shovel. Since Robinson would starve if he took a week off to make the shovel, he cannot attain this higher income level.

It is clear in such a case that Robinson would be eager to obtain 35 extra clams, and willing to give in return more than 35 clams in the future, for the opportunity to increase his productivity by first making a shovel. The shovel is capital for Robinson. And it is the shovel's value as capital, that is, its potential as a producer of future goods, that causes Robinson to want it and makes him willing to pay a premium to obtain it.

35 clams now are worth 5 additional clams per day in the future.

The Risk Factor in Interest Rates

The rates charged by banks to corporate borrowers, by department stores to customers with revolving charge accounts, or by individuals lending to savings and loan institutions, all reflect the society's rates of time preference and the potential productivities of goods. But they also include risk premiums of various sizes plus differences in the cost of negotiating loans. It will ordinarily cost you more per dollar to borrow from a commercial bank than it will cost a large and successful corporation.[1] This does not really mean that you are paying a higher rate of interest, however. You are paying for the costs incurred by the bank in investigating your credit standing and doing the bookkeeping entailed by your loan, as well as a kind of insurance premium that the bank collects from each borrower in anticipation of losses through costs of collection and defaults. If the bank could not charge this premium, it would not find it advantageous to make loans to customers in higher risk categories. So when legislators impose ceilings on the "annual interest" that may legally be charged by lenders, they do not reduce interest rates so much as they exclude certain categories of borrowers from contracting for loans. Since the borrowers would not contract for the loans unless they deemed them advantageous, it is difficult to discover in what way maximum interest rate laws benefit borrowers.

This is an important point, and not only because it corrects certain popular but mistaken notions about interest rate legislation. The return that any lender will demand as a condition of lending depends on what the lender could obtain by loaning to a different borrower *plus* the risk assigned to that particular loan. Commercial lenders aren't unique in that respect. Imagine the bonds of two corporations, one of them General Motors and the other a shaky corporation teetering on the edge of bankruptcy. Both sets of bonds have a maturity value of $1000 and are scheduled to mature one year from now. At what prices will these bonds be bought and sold on the market?

Suppose the General Motors issue sells at $952. Nine hundred and fifty-two dollars now is worth $1000 at maturity (in one year) at a 5 percent rate of interest. The $952 price would mean, in effect, that people are willing to hold General Motors bonds for a 5 percent annual return, because $952 times 1.05, the principal plus the interest, is $1000.

$48 is 5% of $952

But the bonds of the shaky corporation would sell for far less even if they were bought by the same people who purchased the General Motors bonds. The probability of default is so much higher in the second case that buyers could only be persuaded to take the risk if they were offered the possibility of a very high return. If the second issue sold for $714, buyers

---

1. When the prime rate rose above 12 percent in 1974 and again in 1979, it exceeded the maximum legal rate that may be charged in some states for consumer loans. Some banks nonetheless made small consumer loans to their own depositors, below the rate they could get on less risky loans, in order to retain the goodwill and continued patronage of established customers.

would be demanding the possibility of a 40 percent annual return.

If all works out well, they will receive $238 more than they would have earned from holding a General Motors bond. But that outcome is highly uncertain, and there is also the possibility they will lose most or all of the principal. The higher "interest rate" on the latter bonds should therefore be interpreted as a risk premium, rather than as pure interest. Perhaps when legislators contemplate interest rate ceilings, they should ask themselves whether they have ever purchased bonds at a heavy discount.

$286 is 40% of $714

The Opportunity Cost of Obtaining Capital

Before moving on into the important problems raised by uncertainty, let's pause to underline the point that launched us into this discussion of interest. Part of the cost of producing goods is the interest that must be paid in order to obtain command of the required capital. This is as fully a cost of production as are the wages that must be paid to attract workers from their next most valued opportunity, or the rent that must be paid to a building owner to bid the building away from others who want to use it. If a firm purchases capital out of current earnings and consequently doesn't have to borrow, it does not really avoid interest costs. It pays, in the form of income forgone, what it could have earned by investing those earnings in something else, including even the stock of an entirely separate corporation in a completely unrelated industry.

Consequences of Uncertainty

When we began to think about the different rates of return that lenders demand on risky and relatively riskless loans, we came back to the one fact that does more than anything else to complicate economic reality and the lives of economic analysts. *Decisions are based on expected outcomes, but what actually happens is seldom exactly what anyone expected to happen and is sometimes dramatically different.*

What term shall we use to refer to the differences that arise between expected and realized outcomes? We want a special term, because these differences are extremely important. They make some people wealthy and throw others into bankruptcy. They turn some firms into Cinderellas and end the lives of other firms. They cannot be avoided, because uncertainty cannot be eliminated. The hope for a positive difference and the fear of a negative one provides significant incentives in every known economic system. The consequences to which they lead will differ from one economic system to another, depending largely on how the society handles them. Does it, for example, compensate people who make unfortunate decisions, perhaps by appropriating the proceeds of highly fortunate decisions for common use? Or does the society refrain from confiscating the proceeds of fortunate decisions and simultaneously expect individuals to bear the consequences of their own mistakes? The truth is that every known society comes down somewhere in between. But precisely where it comes down or exactly how it attempts to deal with the consequences of uncertainty will make a huge difference in the way the members of that society behave.

"Windfall" Profits and Losses

One term that is widely used to describe these differences between expected and realized outcomes is *windfalls*. Because the differences can be positive or negative, we would thus speak of *windfall profits* and *windfall losses*. We don't often encounter the term *windfall losses*, however, and it is worthwhile to think about why we don't. The word *windfall* originally referred to fruit that was blown down from a tree. The fruit was not earned through the effort of climbing and picking but was a gift of the wind, which blows unpredictably and beyond anyone's control. The term *windfall profit* implies an origin in luck rather than merit. Windfall profits are thus undeserved profits, because no one *deserves* good luck.

Of course, no one deserves bad luck either. So why don't we speak of windfall losses? The reason would appear to be that people do not go about claiming a *right* to losses, or insisting that society is violating their rights in compensating them for losses sustained. The adjective *windfall* is only attached to *profit* because only in the case of profit do people wish frequently to counter the claim that the recipient earned or otherwise deserved what happened.

When we talk about what people do or do not deserve, we're talking about ethics rather than economics. Ethics is such a difficult subject that we would much prefer to go around it. But economists are once again beginning to discover (Adam Smith was fully aware of it two centuries ago!) that supply curves and demand curves—the most basic building blocks of economic analysis—depend on convictions and commitments that are fundamentally ethical in nature. This fact will be dogging our steps throughout this and the next three chapters. We had better turn now and face it squarely.

Property Rights: An Introduction to the Concept

The heart of the matter from the standpoint of the economic analyst is that the decisions which people make in any economic system depend in a crucial way upon the property rights that are established and accepted in that society. The term *property rights*—as we are now using it and will continue to use it in subsequent chapters—has a much broader connotation than what is usually conjured up in people's minds. Perhaps when you hear the term you picture a rancher with a shotgun saying, "Git off my land," or someone indignantly announcing, "It belongs to me and I can do what I want with it!" We must enlarge the concept far beyond those pictures if it is to help us understand how economic systems function, how income is distributed, why pollution occurs, or what we can reasonably expect from government. When economists speak of *property rights*, they mean the entire set of *people's expectations about what they can and may do*.

Perhaps the best way to explain is to illustrate, and the best illustrations at this point will be ones that illuminate the issue of windfall profits and losses.

your rights are what you expect to be able to do.

How Shall We Treat "Windfalls"?

Oil refiners maintain sizable inventories of crude oil in order to assure a smooth and continuous operation of the refinery. If forces beyond their control increase the demand for or reduce the supply of crude petroleum, its price will rise. The value of the refiners' inventories will therefore rise, too. An increase in the value of a firm's inventories is an addition to its wealth, and additions to wealth are what we call income. Any income of business firms in excess of costs we call profit. So oil refiners, in this case, receive a profit from the occurrence of events beyond their control. Almost everyone will (and did) call that a windfall profit. Some go further and argue that it ought to be taxed away, because the refiners have no right to receive windfall profits. They belong by right to . . . whom?

This case illustrates the importance of decision makers' expectations about what they can and may do, as well as the significance of ethical convictions—notions about what is right or fair—in the shaping of those expectations. The managers of a refinery accumulate inventories in the first place because they expect to be able to use them when and how they please. (That's not quite accurate; the managers know that they would not be allowed to use the inventories as they pleased if it pleased them to pump some onto the city's sidewalks for the fun of seeing pedestrians slip and slide. But they did expect to be allowed to use the inventories for accepted business purposes.) This expectation is a property right. In the absence of that property right or expectation, the managers of the refinery might have chosen to accumulate less inventory or even none at all. They would have chosen to accumulate very little if, according to the accepted rules of the society, anyone who wants some crude is entitled to draw freely on the inventories of anyone else who happens to have some in stock. The refinery managers would also have chosen to carry smaller levels of inventory had they thought that the taxing authorities would appropriate any increase in inventory value due to price increases, without compensating the firm for losses due to price declines and a fall in the value of inventory. People do not normally accept wagers of the form, "Heads I break even, tails I lose."

Expectations and Actions

We're focusing on property rights related to the oil inventories of refiners. But you should notice that everything else associated with the operation of the refineries, including the actions of employees, stockholders, motorists, or legislators, can also be viewed as a response to prevailing property rights. People act as they do because of their expectations about exactly what they can and may do. Employees show up for work because they confidently expect to be able to claim a paycheck on Friday. Stockholders purchase and retain shares because they expect to be cut in, as a matter of legal right, for a percentage of the firm's earnings, proportionate to the number of shares they own. Motorists buy automobiles because they expect to be able to obtain suitable fuel at acceptable prices. And legislators draft laws that may alter the expectations of everyone else because they themselves expect to be able to win reelection by doing so.

Expectations are always much more complex than any of the capsule summaries above suggest. Oil refiners do not accumulate inventories exclusively in order to smooth the flow of production or fulfill their contracts with customers. They also look ahead, try to anticipate changes in supply or demand, add to inventories if they predict higher prices in the future, and reduce inventories to some minimum level if they expect prices to fall. To some degree, in short, the inventory managers of an oil refinery function like the speculators described in Chapter 7. *They cannot choose not to speculate*, since both holding and not holding large inventories are speculative decisions, either of which could lead to a substantial gain or loss. Which of these eventually appears will depend on the relationship between what the managers expect to happen and what actually happens.

Have we come full circle? The difference between expected and realized outcomes is what we tentatively agreed to call windfalls. But the windfalls that result from the inventory decisions of oil refinery managers turn out now to be not altogether windfalls after all. Windfalls are, by definition, the product of pure luck. It follows that managers who obtain them for their firms by predicting the future a little bit or a whole lot better than others are not really obtaining windfalls. They *are* obtaining increased profits—of that much we can be sure. The source of these profits is the fact that the managers' decisions predicted the future more accurately than did the predictions of others. That's also clear. Were the profits deserved? That is not as clear. It is at least in part an ethical question, and one on which opinions differ sharply.

While economic analysis cannot by itself resolve such ethical issues, it can perhaps contribute to a resolution of the debate by clarifying the consequences of alternative answers. If people expect to have the profits from correct decisions taken away from them on the grounds that such profits are undeserved and also expect that the losses that accrue from incorrect decisions will not be fully subsidized, they will attempt to minimize risk. Decisions will converge toward the average. Only short-range projects will be undertaken. Fewer resources will be invested in research. Innovative projects will be explored less often. Problems that could have been avoided through better foresight will more frequently be encountered.

If both the profits and the losses that arise from the inescapable necessity of making decisions in the presence of uncertainty are removed from those who made the decisions and shared by everyone in society, less care will be invested in the making of decisions. Taking care is costly whenever it means, as it usually does, the forgoing of valuable opportunities. That is why people behave "care-lessly" when they themselves have nothing to gain or lose. It is also why students usually read more "care-fully" in a course taken for grade credit than one in which they are only auditing. And it explains why people without theft insurance on their automobiles more often take the trouble to roll up all the windows and lock the doors.

The significance of these consequences can, of course, be debated. To what extent do progress, achievement, creativity, wealth, harmony, happiness or any other of these hard-to-define social goods depend on the willingness to take risks or to take care? But the consequences themselves could be denied only by someone who was prepared to argue that superior knowledge of a legitimate kind does not exist, that everyone is equally well informed or equally ignorant—except insofar as some have unfair advantages. That, too, could probably be argued. All advantages become unfair advantages if one begins with the assumption that no one *ought* to have any kind of advantage over another. But does anyone seriously maintain this? Are we prepared to restrict the game of basketball to people who are 5 feet, 9 inches tall and require Van Cliburn to wear mittens while playing the piano? The issue of merit, of what people deserve, does without question influence our con-

People's expectations direct their decisions.

victions about the rights that people ought to have. But the rights that people believe themselves to have also entail consequences. In order to secure certain consequences that we want, we may be required to concede rights to people without regard to their personal merit. If rewards to criminal informants, for example, can be justified by the benefits they produce for the rest of us, then probably such rewards ought to be paid, even though the informants obviously do not deserve them in any moral sense.

Windfall Profit or Simply Profit?

The term *windfall profit* is dangerous, because it suggests that such profits ought to be taxed or otherwise taken away. The difficulty with this is that no one knows how to distinguish the profits that are produced by astute forecasting from those profits that are purely the product of luck. Moreover, the potential of profit is an important, perhaps indispensable stimulus to action. The potential of a profit prompts people to search for more efficient ways of combining resources, new products for which there may be a demand, and organizational innovations that promise to increase effectiveness. The potential of profit often persuades people to take pains when they would otherwise prefer not to and to take chances in which the possible benefits to society are associated with the possibility of substantial losses for the one taking the chance. The potential of profit persuades some people (the unusually courageous, or foolhardy, or adventurous, or greedy, or perceptive, or knowledgeable, or public-spirited—who among us is competent to judge?) to increase the security of others by accepting risks themselves.

If it is misleading to use the term *windfall* to describe *the difference between the outcome generally anticipated when a decision was made and the outcome actually realized*, what other term might we use? One possibility is just the word *profit* itself, without the qualifying adjective. *Profit* would then mean *the income or addition to wealth that arises from predicting more correctly than others*. This seems at first to be quite different from the definition with which we began the chapter: total revenue minus total cost. But is it really all that different?

Uncertainty as the Source of Profit

Total cost is opportunity cost, and so it includes not only a firm's payments to others for commodities and services used, but also the implicit value of any goods—labor, land, capital—that the firm itself supplies. Interest payments are part of the firm's costs, including that portion of its dividends which is about equal to the interest return its shareholders could have received by loaning their money elsewhere. When we include all these opportunity costs in our calculations of total costs, there seems to be no reason why any firm would have to earn revenues in excess of costs. Firms could make zero profits and continue in business. They could even be considered successful firms and be able to borrow new funds for expansion—so long as their revenues were adequate to cover all their costs.

In fact, if there were some way for a firm to get into a line of business that guaranteed more in revenue than it entailed in cost, wouldn't so many people move into that line of business that competition would reduce the difference between revenue and cost to zero? Remember that cost means all costs, including an actual or implicit payment for getting the business organized and keeping it in operation. The certainty of a return greater than this would surely attract new business firms. Their entry would increase output, reduce the price of the product consistently with the law of demand, and thus reduce the gap between total revenue and total cost. The gap might simultaneously be reduced from the other direction as the new entrants increased the demand and raised the cost for the inputs used in turning out the product. Only when the gap between total revenue and total cost had disappeared, or when profits had been reduced to zero, would there no longer be any incentive for new firms to enter.

In the actual, continually changing, and always uncertain world, it doesn't work that way. People see profits being made in particular lines of business but they aren't sure how to go about cutting themselves in on the profits. In a world of scarce information, the existence of such profits might not even be widely known. And so *profits do exist and continue to exist* without being reduced to zero by competition. But this happens *because of uncertainty*, in the absence of which everything relevant to profit making would be generally known, all opportunities for profit making fully exploited, and profits everywhere consequently equal to zero. Defining *profit*, therefore, as the income that arises from predicting more correctly than others is not a rejection of the earlier definition—total revenue minus total cost. It is rather an explanation of the fact that total revenue so often diverges from total cost.

Investors' Search for Profit

The same analysis applies to the case of individual investors looking for a profit. Suppose you read an advertisement urging you to invest in Florida real estate because its value increases by 30 percent each year. A 30 percent annual return is far more than you can expect to receive from alternative investments, so you sink $30,000 into an undeveloped lot near Orlando. You plan to sell it in a year for $39,000. But you will probably be disappointed.

If Florida real estate really can be expected to increase in value by 30 percent per year, many people will be eager to buy Florida lots. Their eagerness to purchase will bid up the price of the lots, until the lots are no longer better buys than other available investment opportunities. If there happen to be many investors who uncritically accept the claims of the advertisement, their eagerness to benefit from the promised appreciation in real estate prices could even bid the present price of lots so high that price decreases—rather than increases—will subsequently occur. The key point is this: *The price of any marketable asset reflects the present value of generally expected future earnings.*[2]

No one can make a profit by putting money into an asset or an operation that is generally expected to return more than the going rate of interest. For that would be a "good deal." And the demand for a "good deal" bids up the cost of getting in on it, until it's no longer a better deal than other assets or opportunities.

Every investor knows this. The time to buy Xerox or Polaroid was before the word got around. Those who bought stock in these companies after it became widely known that they were going to earn large net revenues from their new products received no profits. About the best they could hope for was the going rate of interest as a return on their investment. The market price of Xerox and Polaroid stock was bid up by people eager to share in those companies' future earnings, until the earnings relative to what had to be paid to share in them were not that greatly more attractive than earnings generally available in the market.

The common notion that one can accumulate wealth by investing in profitable companies is therefore seriously misleading. General Motors is rightly regarded as a highly profitable corporation, because it has consistently earned large returns for many years on its original investment in plant, machinery, and other assets.[3] But the market value of General Motors stock long ago increased to take full account of its expected high future earnings. Consequently, General Motors

The widespread belief that a corporation is going to develop a profitable product will cause the price of its stock to rise even __before__ the product has been developed.

---

2. An appendix to this chapter explains the process of determining the present value of future earnings and provides tables to make the calculations easier.

3. Profit comparisons mean little unless they are stated as a percentage return on investment. United States Steel earned a net income in 1978 of $242 million; Avon Products earned $228 million. Were they equally profitable? U.S. Steel employed assets with an estimated value of $10.5 billion to generate that income, whereas Avon Products generated almost the same income with $1.2 billion of assets. Avon products was by far the more profitable firm in 1978. Remember, though,

stock is not necessarily a better buy than the stock of many companies with dismal earning records. (In fact, it may have been a very poor buy in recent years as stockholders failed to anticipate the effect of higher gasoline prices on the earnings of automobile manufacturers.)

The way to accumulate a fortune is to invest in companies that are going to make large earnings that no one else currently knows about. And there's the rub. You must know more than others—or be able to read the uncertain future more accurately—if you hope to make large profits. Or else you rely solely on luck. But if you rely on luck, you have an equal probability of being unlucky and sustaining a large loss. The significant thing about pure luck is that it's pure. Any investors who consistently make profits, defined as net income *beyond the common rate of return from readily available investment opportunities*, must be predicting the uncertain future more successfully than others.

We have omitted one very important qualification or addition to the preceding argument. Before taking it up, however, we ought to pause a moment to clear the concept of profit (and loss) from the narrow connotations that it may have acquired in the course of this discussion. Profits and losses appear everywhere, for everyone, and not just for business firms or those who invest in financial assets.

Everyone Is Doing It

Consider the sad case of Giuseppe Vibrato who attends a music conservatory for three years, planning for a career in opera. At about the time of Vibrato's graduation, the public abandons all interest in opera. So Vibrato sustains a loss. We mustn't exaggerate the loss, for Vibrato may receive a generous return on his educational investment in the form of many years of listening to himself sing Verdi and Wagner. (Education can prepare people to enjoy life as well as provide them with marketable skills.) But to the extent that Vibrato paid tuition and sacrificed earnings for three years in order to earn an income in opera, the unexpected change in public tastes caused him to sustain a loss.

In the same way aerospace engineers suffer losses when the federal government cuts back on the space program and cancels the SST (supersonic transport), college professors receive profits when the federal government decides to spend huge sums on higher education, authors make a profit when

---

that current investors are not interested in the historical question of how many dollars are being earned for every $100 originally invested in the firm. They want to know how many dollars *will* be earned for every $100 invested *now*.

they hit on a book that captivates the public, and highly trained astrologers took a loss when people abandoned the belief that the stars shape individual destiny. (But note also that in the last case some of their intellectual descendants have recently made profits from an unexpected return to older persuasions.)

All these examples involve monetary income. But profits and losses don't have to entail changes in monetary wealth. The skier who goes to the slopes and finds rain incurs a loss. If he heads for the lodge to drown his sorrows and there meets his future wife, he makes a profit. If she turns out after several years of marriage to be even more pleasant and intelligent than he had thought, his profit increases. And the windfall profit from that rain-drenched ski trip becomes almost exorbitant if they jointly produce a cherubic child who fills their days with cheer. These examples may be frivolous. However, they serve to remind us that undeserved profits occur in all aspects of life, and—equally important—that they also depend most of the time on the exercise of some discretion.

Profit as the Consequence of Restricted Competition

Let's return now to the important possibility we have neglected. What if some profit makers, even in a world without uncertainty, were able to prevent others from entering their line of business and competing away their profits? Then total revenue could exceed total cost and continue to exceed it indefinitely.

We must therefore add a second explanation or cause of profit, something in addition to uncertainty and quite separate from it: *Profit can also arise from restrictions on the ablity to compete.*

Such restrictions arise primarily from two sources and can therefore usefully be divided into two kinds: (1) restrictions imposed by the natural scarcity of particular resources; and (2) restrictions imposed by social or political actions. We can see both kinds at work in the case of Mr. Artesian.

One Source of Artesian's Profits: Uncertainty

Recall that Artesian was earning about $1000 per year over and above his total costs when he first got his mineral-water spring into operation. This was clearly a profit by our general definition: total revenue minus total cost. But what was its cause or source?

In the first instance the source of Artesian's profit was uncertainty. If it had been generally known at the time Artesian purchased the property that there was a valuable mineral-water spring on the premises, a spring that could net its owner more than $1000 per year, then Artesian would have had to pay more than he actually did for the land. An asset that can be confidently expected to yield its owner $1000 per year has the same value as $20,000 in a savings account earning 5 percent interest. So if the property had a value, let us say, of $10,000 apart from the spring, its value might be as much as $30,000 with the spring taken into account. Artesian obtained the land for $10,000 rather than $30,000 only because no one knew about the existence of the spring. The difference between the outcome that was generally anticipated when Artesian bought the lot and the outcome actually realized, our first explanation of profit, was $1000 of extra income per year to the owner of the lot. If Artesian had incurred some costs in finding out about the spring, that would have to be subtracted from his profit.

Suppose Artesian decided to sell his land and move to Alaska. He would find people willing to bid the price up well above his own purchase price of $10,000 because they would want to obtain ownership of that $1000 per year stream of income. Of course, they aren't likely to bid the price as high as $30,000 because $1000 of net income from a mineral-water spring will be regarded as a less certain prospect than $1000 in bank interest on a $20,000 savings account. Only if that $1000 could be expected with the same certainty as the bank interest would the sale price approach $30,000. Suppose Artesian is able to sell his land for $22,500. If the spring then earns its new owner $1000 in every subsequent year, the new owner also makes a profit. But his profit is only $375. Do you see why?

We're assuming $10,000 of the purchase price to be the value of the land—for living on, raising radishes, or whatever. This was the value generally anticipated when Artesian made his purchase, and we're assuming it remains unchanged. (It wouldn't have to. The value of the land for residential purposes could go down because the owner's privacy is destroyed by all the customers of the spring.) So we just ignore $10,000 of the purchase price and all the benefits of ownership not related to the mineral-water spring. We're left with $12,500 paid to obtain the income from the spring. But now $625 of that income has to be considered a cost of doing business ($625 is the annual interest at 5 percent on $12,500, the amount the new owner is giving up by putting his $12,500 into ownership of the land). So if the spring continues to yield him $1000 per year, his profit —total revenue minus total cost—is only $375. On the other hand, if competition appears, as it did in Chapter 10, so that his net revenue falls to $400, the new owner sustains annual losses. For $400 is only 3.2 percent of $12,500, and that's 1.8 percent less than the opportunity cost of owning the spring.

a $400 annual return on a $12,500 investment is actually a loss – the consequence of a mistaken decision.

Another Source of Profits:
Restrictions on the Ability of Others to Compete

But will competition necessarily appear? We can see both kinds of restriction at work in the mineral-water case. There may be in the area only one spring whose water has all the invigorating qualities so valued by Artesian's customers. Other sources may be so far away that the water can only be transported into Artesian's market area at a prohibitive cost. In such a situation Artesian could continue indefinitely to earn his $1048.30 annual profit, even though there is no longer any uncertainty about revenues and costs, because he is the owner of a naturally rare resource. Others would like to cut themselves in on Artesian's profit; but they cannot do so without access to mineral water and Artesian has control of the only available supply.

There are many types of unique productive resources. One important type that we might tend to overlook is human skills. Very often firms will continue to earn profits year after year, despite the best efforts of their competitors, because the firms are managed with exceptional skill. Other kinds of rare resources that may restrict the ability of others to diminish a firm's profits are location, reputation, and experience.

But the restrictions imposed on competition by the natural scarcity of resources are seldom enough to satisfy firms that find themselves making profits. For one thing, there are just too many alternative ways of doing things. Even if there is no other mineral water within an economical distance, competitors could sell tomato juice fortified with vitamins and minerals, and claim that it's more healthful and better tasting than Artesian's water. Moreover, unless the profit-earning firm owns the scarce resources that give it a permanent advantage, potential competitors can try to hire those resources away. They can bid for the choice location when the current tenant's lease expires; and even if they don't manage to bid it away, they may force the firm to pay a higher rent to maintain control of the advantageous location. That would erode the firm's profits by raising its costs. If the natural scarcity that is responsible for persistent profits happens to be managerial skills, potential competitors can try to hire away those managers. Again, even if they don't succeed, they may raise the firm's costs by forcing it to pay higher salaries to key employees. So it isn't hard to understand why profit-making firms turn regularly to the government for help in imposing restrictions on competition.

Patents granted to inventors are one important type of political restriction. The purpose of a patent is precisely this: to help the patent owner earn profits over an extended period of time by prohibiting others from making use of the process that is the source of those profits. This can be justified on the grounds that new and more efficient processes would not be developed as often if the developers could not count on earning profits from their innovative efforts. The patent privilege is thus a temporary grant of privilege from the government designed to raise the wealth of successful innovators with the long run aim of raising the wealth of society.

Other forms of government restrictions on competition are usually harder to defend. We discussed this question in Chapter 10 and won't repeat what we said there. All that we're looking for in this chapter is an understanding of the sources and functions of profit. And we're ready now to put it all together.

The Big Picture View

Profit is total revenue minus total cost. That's an acceptable definition from the economist's point of view if cost is calculated as opportunity cost. Some of what is commonly called "business profits" ought to be regarded, from a functional point of view, as implicit payments to factors of production. A substantial portion of corporate profits and especially of the net income of unincorporated enterprises, including professional income, is actually a payment for the use of capital or the labor and other resources of proprietors and ought therefore to be designated as cost.

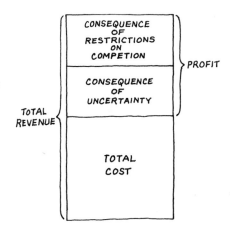

What, then, is the source of pure profits? There are two sources, we have argued. One is uncertainty. Because the future cannot be accurately predicted, actual outcomes will often differ from what is generally anticipated at the time decisions are made and hostages are given to fortune. But uncertainty creates losses as well as profits, a very important point to remember in assessing the size and social importance of profits.

The other source of profits is restrictions on competition. These may be due to scarcities maintained by nature or to social and political restrictions of many kinds.

That's the big picture view. If the road toward it was unusually long and tortuous, it's largely because the concept of profit is used in so many different ways and often without much thought. But the perspective one acquires by thinking carefully about the functions of profit makes the trip worth the effort. At least we hope it does.

AN APPENDIX: DISCOUNTING AND PRESENT VALUES

If the prevailing annual interest rate reflects the greater value that people assign to goods now over goods one year from now, it follows that the value of goods expected to be received a year from now must be discounted by the rate of interest to determine their *present value*. The process of discounting to determine the present value of future goods plays a large part in economic decision making. Mastering this process will equip you better to understand the analysis of subsequent chapters and will acquaint you with procedures widely employed in the business and financial world.[4]

Suppose that Ivy College, that well-managed institution of higher learning introduced in Chapter 9, offers the parents of entering students a Tuition Stabilization Plan. Tuition is almost sure to rise each year, they point out, because of continuing inflation. Ivy even announces in advance its intention to increase the annual tuition charge by $200 in each of the next three years. But parents who subscribe to the TSP receive a special deal. They pay $8000 in September of the first year and nothing thereafter. In effect, says Ivy's multicolored brochure, parents who sign up for TSP save $1200 on the cost of their child's education. Ivy may go so far as to call it a 15 percent saving.

But is $8000 paid now really less than $2000 now plus $2200 one year from now, $2400 two years from now, and $2600 three years from now? The last three amounts are amounts due in the future, and future dollars, like any other future goods, must be discounted if we want to assess their present value. What interest rate should we use? The best answer is provided by the opportunity cost to the parents of lending money to Ivy College, since that is in effect what they are doing. They are lending Ivy money by paying the tuition before it is due. $2000 of the sophomore year tuition is lent for one year, $2000 of the junior year tuition is lent for two years, and $2000 of the senior year tuition is lent for three years. What is the alternative opportunity for those amounts?

What a Present Amount Grows To

Suppose the parents sell stock to obtain the money, and their stock investments ordinarily earn an annual return, in dividends plus increased market price, of 12 percent a year. Then the opportunity cost of lending $2000 to Ivy College for one year is $240. That's $240 expended to avoid $200 in increased tuition, not an attractive arrangement. The junior year loan is an even poorer investment. $2000 grows in two years, at 12 percent per year, to $2000 × 1.12 × 1.12 or $2508.80. The phenomenon of compound interest is at work, and it makes the three-year loan still less appealing. To avoid the $600 in addi-

---

4. It's all quite simple to grasp if you're willing to do the calculations as you read.

tional tuition due for the senior year, the parents give up $809.86 that they might otherwise have earned from the ownership of stock, since 2000×1.12^3 is $2809.86.

Present Value of Future Amounts

We have assessed Ivy's proposal by calculating what a dollar now will grow to, at the appropriate rate of return, in one year, two years, and three years, and comparing those amounts with the tuition that would ordinarily be due in one year, in two years, and in three years. We can reach the same conclusions by working in the other direction. What is the *present value* of the $2200 that will be due in one year? That amounts to asking: What present sum would grow to exactly $2200 in one year if invested at 12 percent? The answer is $2200 divided by 1.12, or $1964.29, which means that in prepaying the sophomore year tuition the parents give up $2000 now to save $36 less than that in present value. The $2400 that would be due in two years has a present value of $2400 divided by (1.12 × 1.12), or $1913.27, which is $87 less than what the parents actually pay. The $2600, when divided by 1.12,^{3} turns out to have a present value of only $1850.63.

People who make these computations in the course of their everyday business decisions use tables that enable them to calculate quickly the sum to which a present amount will grow or the present value of future amounts. Three such tables are provided on the succeeding pages. You can use the first two, Tables 11A and 11B, to check the conclusions just presented, which is a subtle way of suggesting that you practice with the tables until you are able to obtain the above results. One more problem will be presented to introduce you to the third table, Table 11C.

Present Value of Annuities

What should a buyer be willing to pay for Artesian's spring if its ownership brings in an annual income of $1048.30? We already pointed out that the confidence with which this income can be expected makes a large difference in the answer. But so do the number of years that the income can be expected to continue. In the text above we assumed that the income would continue indefinitely. But that wouldn't have to be the case. Perhaps the buyer has good reason to believe that the spring will dry up after 20 years. Or Artesian may want to sell the rights for only 20 years, so that he can leave it to his grandchildren. What is the present value of $1048.30 for each of the next 20 years if we assume that the sums are received at the end of each year?

First we have to choose an interest rate at which to discount these future values. Let's pick 12 percent again, on the

TABLE 11A AMOUNT TO WHICH $1 WILL GROW IN THE DESIGNATED NUMBER OF YEARS WHEN COMPOUNDED ANNUALLY AT VARIOUS INTEREST RATES

Year	0.01	0.02	0.04	0.06	0.09	0.12	0.18	0.24
1	1.0100	1.0200	1.0400	1.0600	1.0900	1.1200	1.1800	1.2400
2	1.0201	1.0404	1.0816	1.1236	1.1881	1.2544	1.3924	1.5376
3	1.0303	1.0612	1.1249	1.1910	1.2950	1.4049	1.6430	1.9066
4	1.0406	1.0824	1.1699	1.2625	1.4116	1.5735	1.9388	2.3642
5	1.0510	1.1041	1.2167	1.3382	1.5386	1.7623	2.2878	2.9316
6	1.0615	1.1262	1.2653	1.4185	1.6771	1.9738	2.6996	3.6352
7	1.0721	1.1487	1.3159	1.5036	1.8280	2.2107	3.1855	4.5077
8	1.0829	1.1717	1.3686	1.5938	1.9926	2.4760	3.7589	5.5895
9	1.0937	1.1951	1.4233	1.6895	2.1719	2.7731	4.4355	6.9310
10	1.1046	1.2190	1.4802	1.7908	2.3674	3.1059	5.2338	8.5944
11	1.1157	1.2434	1.5395	1.8983	2.5804	3.4786	6.1759	10.6571
12	1.1268	1.2682	1.6010	2.0122	2.8127	3.8960	7.2876	13.2148
13	1.1381	1.2936	1.6651	2.1329	3.0658	4.3635	8.5994	16.3863
14	1.1495	1.3195	1.7317	2.2609	3.3417	4.8871	10.1473	20.3191
15	1.1610	1.3459	1.8009	2.3966	3.6425	5.4736	11.9738	25.1956
16	1.1726	1.3728	1.8730	2.5403	3.9703	6.1304	14.1290	31.2426
17	1.1843	1.4002	1.9479	2.6928	4.3276	6.8661	16.6723	38.7408
18	1.1961	1.4282	2.0258	2.8543	4.7171	7.6900	19.6733	48.0386
19	1.2081	1.4568	2.1068	3.0256	5.1417	8.6128	23.2145	59.5679
20	1.2202	1.4859	2.1911	3.2071	5.6044	9.6463	27.3931	73.8642
21	1.2324	1.5157	2.2788	3.3996	6.1088	10.8039	32.3238	91.5916
22	1.2447	1.5460	2.3699	3.6035	6.6586	12.1003	38.1421	113.5735
23	1.2572	1.5769	2.4647	3.8197	7.2579	13.5524	45.0077	140.8312
24	1.2697	1.6084	2.5633	4.0489	7.9111	15.1787	53.1091	174.6307
25	1.2824	1.6406	2.6658	4.2919	8.6231	17.0001	62.6688	216.5421
26	1.2953	1.6734	2.7725	4.5494	9.3991	19.0401	73.9491	268.5121
27	1.3082	1.7069	2.8834	4.8223	10.2451	21.3249	87.2600	332.9551
28	1.3213	1.7410	2.9987	5.1117	11.1671	23.8839	102.9668	412.8643
29	1.3345	1.7758	3.1186	5.4184	12.1722	26.7500	121.5008	511.9517
30	1.3478	1.8114	3.2434	5.7435	13.2677	29.9600	143.3710	634.8201
31	1.3613	1.8476	3.3731	6.0881	14.4617	33.5552	169.1777	787.1770
32	1.3749	1.8845	3.5081	6.4534	15.7633	37.5818	199.6298	976.0994
33	1.3887	1.9222	3.6484	6.8406	17.1820	42.0917	235.5631	1210.3633
34	1.4026	1.9607	3.7943	7.2510	18.7284	47.1427	277.9645	1500.8503
35	1.4166	1.9999	3.9461	7.6861	20.4139	52.7998	327.9982	1861.0544
36	1.4308	2.0399	4.1039	8.1472	22.2512	59.1358	387.0378	2307.7075
37	1.4451	2.0807	4.2681	8.6361	24.2538	66.2321	456.7048	2861.5576
38	1.4595	2.1223	4.4388	9.1542	26.4366	74.1799	538.9116	3548.3315
39	1.4741	2.1647	4.6164	9.7035	28.8159	83.0815	635.9156	4399.9316
40	1.4889	2.2080	4.8010	10.2857	31.4094	93.0513	750.3806	5455.9140
41	1.5038	2.2522	4.9931	10.9028	34.2362	104.2175	885.4492	6765.3339
42	1.5188	2.2972	5.1928	11.5570	37.3175	116.7326	1044.8303	8389.0155
43	1.5340	2.3432	5.4005	12.2504	40.6760	130.7304	1232.8996	10402.3788
44	1.5493	2.3901	5.6165	12.9854	44.3369	146.4181	1454.8218	12898.9491
45	1.5648	2.4379	5.8412	13.7645	48.3272	163.9883	1716.6899	15994.6971
46	1.5805	2.4866	6.0748	14.5904	52.6766	183.6669	2025.6941	19833.4217
47	1.5963	2.5363	6.3178	15.4658	57.4175	205.7069	2390.3188	24593.4490
48	1.6122	2.5871	6.5705	16.3938	62.5851	230.3918	2820.5766	30495.8707
49	1.6283	2.6388	6.8333	17.3774	68.2177	258.0388	3328.2807	37814.8746
50	1.6446	2.6916	7.1067	18.4201	74.3573	289.0035	3927.3720	46890.4526

TABLE 11B PRESENT VALUE OF $1 AT THE END OF THE
DESIGNATED NUMBER OF YEARS WHEN DISCOUNTED
AT VARIOUS INTEREST RATES

Year	0.01	0.02	0.04	0.06	0.09	0.12	0.18	0.24
1	0.9901	0.9804	0.9615	0.9434	0.9174	0.8929	0.8475	0.8065
2	0.9803	0.9612	0.9246	0.8900	0.8417	0.7972	0.7182	0.6504
3	0.9706	0.9423	0.8890	0.8396	0.7722	0.7118	0.6086	0.5245
4	0.9610	0.9238	0.8548	0.7921	0.7084	0.6355	0.5158	0.4230
5	0.9515	0.9057	0.8219	0.7473	0.6499	0.5674	0.4371	0.3411
6	0.9420	0.8880	0.7903	0.7050	0.5963	0.5066	0.3704	0.2751
7	0.9327	0.8706	0.7599	0.6651	0.5470	0.4523	0.3139	0.2218
8	0.9235	0.8535	0.7307	0.6274	0.5019	0.4039	0.2660	0.1789
9	0.9143	0.8368	0.7026	0.5919	0.4604	0.3606	0.2255	0.1443
10	0.9053	0.8203	0.6756	0.5584	0.4224	0.3220	0.1911	0.1164
11	0.8963	0.8043	0.6496	0.5268	0.3875	0.2875	0.1619	0.0938
12	0.8874	0.7885	0.6246	0.4970	0.3555	0.2567	0.1372	0.0757
13	0.8787	0.7730	0.6006	0.4688	0.3262	0.2292	0.1163	0.0610
14	0.8700	0.7579	0.5775	0.4423	0.2992	0.2046	0.0985	0.0492
15	0.8613	0.7430	0.5553	0.4173	0.2745	0.1827	0.0835	0.0397
16	0.8528	0.7284	0.5339	0.3936	0.2519	0.1631	0.0708	0.0320
17	0.8444	0.7142	0.5134	0.3714	0.2311	0.1456	0.0600	0.0258
18	0.8360	0.7002	0.4936	0.3503	0.2120	0.1300	0.0508	0.0208
19	0.8277	0.6864	0.4746	0.3305	0.1945	0.1161	0.0431	0.0168
20	0.8195	0.6730	0.4564	0.3118	0.1784	0.1037	0.0365	0.0135
21	0.8114	0.6598	0.4388	0.2942	0.1637	0.0926	0.0309	0.0109
22	0.8034	0.6468	0.4220	0.2775	0.1502	0.0826	0.0262	0.0088
23	0.7954	0.6342	0.4057	0.2618	0.1378	0.0738	0.0222	0.0071
24	0.7876	0.6217	0.3901	0.2470	0.1264	0.0659	0.0188	0.0057
25	0.7798	0.6095	0.3751	0.2330	0.1160	0.0588	0.0160	0.0046
26	0.7720	0.5976	0.3607	0.2198	0.1064	0.0525	0.0135	0.0037
27	0.7644	0.5859	0.3468	0.2074	0.0976	0.0469	0.0115	0.0030
28	0.7568	0.5744	0.3335	0.1956	0.0895	0.0419	0.0097	0.0024
29	0.7493	0.5631	0.3207	0.1846	0.0822	0.0374	0.0082	0.0020
30	0.7419	0.5521	0.3083	0.1741	0.0754	0.0334	0.0070	0.0016
31	0.7346	0.5412	0.2965	0.1643	0.0691	0.0298	0.0059	0.0013
32	0.7273	0.5306	0.2851	0.1550	0.0634	0.0266	0.0050	0.0010
33	0.7201	0.5202	0.2741	0.1462	0.0582	0.0238	0.0042	0.0008
34	0.7130	0.5100	0.2636	0.1379	0.0534	0.0212	0.0036	0.0007
35	0.7059	0.5000	0.2534	0.1301	0.0490	0.0189	0.0030	0.0005
36	0.6989	0.4902	0.2437	0.1227	0.0449	0.0169	0.0026	0.0004
37	0.6920	0.4806	0.2343	0.1158	0.0412	0.0151	0.0022	0.0003
38	0.6852	0.4712	0.2253	0.1092	0.0378	0.0135	0.0019	0.0003
39	0.6784	0.4619	0.2166	0.1031	0.0347	0.0120	0.0016	0.0002
40	0.6717	0.4529	0.2083	0.0972	0.0318	0.0107	0.0013	0.0002
41	0.6650	0.4440	0.2003	0.0917	0.0292	0.0096	0.0011	0.0001
42	0.6584	0.4353	0.1926	0.0865	0.0268	0.0086	0.0010	0.0001
43	0.6519	0.4268	0.1852	0.0816	0.0246	0.0076	0.0008	0.0001
44	0.6454	0.4184	0.1780	0.0770	0.0226	0.0068	0.0007	0.0001
45	0.6391	0.4102	0.1712	0.0727	0.0207	0.0061	0.0006	0.0001
46	0.6327	0.4022	0.1646	0.0685	0.0190	0.0054	0.0005	0.0001
47	0.6265	0.3943	0.1583	0.0647	0.0174	0.0049	0.0004	0.0000
48	0.6203	0.3865	0.1522	0.0610	0.0160	0.0043	0.0004	0.0000
49	0.6141	0.3790	0.1463	0.0575	0.0147	0.0039	0.0003	0.0000
50	0.6080	0.3715	0.1407	0.0543	0.0134	0.0035	0.0003	0.0000

assumption that 12 percent is the rate of return which the prospective buyer anticipates from alternative investments of comparable risk. Table 11C is an *annuity* table. An annuity is an annual amount. The table shows the present value of a $1 annuity, received for anywhere from one to 50 years, at various rates of discount. Thus $1 received at the end of each of the next 20 years has a present value, when discounted at 12 percent, of $7.4694. Under all the circumstances described, Artesian's spring therefore has a value of $1048.30 times 7.4694, or $7830.17.

Perpetual ownership of the spring when it is expected to flow on indefinitely isn't worth much more than that: only $8735.83, the sum that would yield $1048.30 per year indefinitely if invested at 12 percent. ($1048.30 divided by .12 = $8735.83). If you're surprised to discover that 20 years is almost as good as forever, you have forgotten that anything more than 20 years in the future has little present value when discounted at 12 percent.

Once Over Lightly

Profit is a term with many meanings. The meanings must be sorted out if we want to understand the way in which economic systems function.

Profit can be usefully defined as total revenue minus total cost if we include all opportunity costs in our calculation of total cost.

Insofar as interest represents an opportunity cost, it must be distinguished from profit.

Interest is the difference in value between present and future goods. It is usually attached to money simply because money represents general command over present or future goods.

The rate of interest in a society is typically positive because present goods are more valuable than future goods. This reflects positive rates of time preference and the fact that capital is productive (in other words, goods now can often be employed to create more goods later).

The decisions that people make and which create demand and supply curves are based on their expectations of what they can and may do. The entire set of such expectations among the members of a society comprises the currently accepted property rights in that society.

Because economic decisions are always made *in anticipation of future costs and benefits*, they are often mistaken. The difference between generally expected and actual outcomes, due to uncertainty, is one source of profit (and loss).

TABLE 11C PRESENT VALUE OF $1 RECEIVED AT THE END OF
EACH YEAR FOR THE DESIGNATED NUMBER OF YEARS
WHEN DISCOUNTED AT VARIOUS INTEREST RATES

Year	0.01	0.02	0.04	0.06	0.09	0.12	0.18	0.24
1	0.9901	0.9804	0.9615	0.9434	0.9174	0.8929	0.8475	0.8065
2	1.9704	1.9416	1.8861	1.8334	1.7591	1.6901	1.5656	1.4568
3	2.9410	2.8839	2.7751	2.6730	2.5313	2.4018	2.1743	1.9813
4	3.9020	3.8077	3.6299	3.4651	3.2397	3.0374	2.6901	2.4043
5	4.8534	4.7135	4.4518	4.2124	3.8896	3.6048	3.1272	2.7454
6	5.7955	5.6014	5.2421	4.9173	4.4859	4.1114	3.4976	3.0205
7	6.7282	6.4720	6.0021	5.5824	5.0329	4.5638	3.8115	3.2423
8	7.6517	7.3255	6.7327	6.2098	5.5348	4.9676	4.0776	3.4212
9	8.5660	8.1622	7.4353	6.8017	5.9952	5.3283	4.3030	3.5655
10	9.4713	8.9826	8.1109	7.3601	6.4177	5.6502	4.4941	3.6819
11	10.3676	9.7869	8.7605	7.8869	6.8052	5.9377	4.6560	3.7757
12	11.2550	10.5754	9.3851	8.3838	7.1607	6.1944	4.7932	3.8514
13	12.1337	11.3484	9.9856	8.8527	7.4869	6.4236	4.9095	3.9124
14	13.0037	12.1063	10.5631	9.2950	7.7861	6.6282	5.0081	3.9616
15	13.8650	12.8493	11.1184	9.7122	8.0607	6.8109	5.0916	4.0013
16	14.7178	13.5777	11.6523	10.1059	8.3126	6.9740	5.1624	4.0333
17	15.5622	14.2919	12.1657	10.4772	8.5436	7.1196	5.2223	4.0591
18	16.3982	14.9921	12.6593	10.8276	8.7556	7.2497	5.2732	4.0799
19	17.2260	15.6785	13.1339	11.1581	8.9501	7.3658	5.3162	4.0967
20	18.0455	16.3515	13.5903	11.4699	9.1285	7.4694	5.3527	4.1103
21	18.8569	17.0112	14.0292	11.7641	9.2922	7.5620	5.3837	4.1212
22	19.6603	17.6581	14.4511	12.0416	9.4424	7.6446	5.4099	4.1300
23	20.4558	18.2922	14.8568	12.3034	9.5802	7.7184	5.4321	4.1371
24	21.2433	18.9140	15.2470	12.5503	9.7066	7.7843	5.4509	4.1428
25	22.0231	19.5235	15.6221	12.7833	9.8226	7.8431	5.4669	4.1474
26	22.7951	20.1211	15.9828	13.0032	9.9290	7.8957	5.4804	4.1511
27	23.5595	20.7069	16.3296	13.2105	10.0266	7.9426	5.4919	4.1542
28	24.3164	21.2813	16.6631	13.4062	10.1161	7.9844	5.5016	4.1566
29	25.0657	21.8444	16.9837	13.5907	10.1983	8.0218	5.5098	4.1585
30	25.8076	22.3965	17.2920	13.7648	10.2737	8.0552	5.5168	4.1601
31	26.5422	22.9377	17.5885	13.9291	10.3428	8.0850	5.5227	4.1614
32	27.2695	23.4684	17.8736	14.0840	10.4062	8.1116	5.5277	4.1624
33	27.9896	23.9886	18.1476	14.2302	10.4644	8.1354	5.5320	4.1632
34	28.7026	24.4986	18.4112	14.3681	10.5178	8.1566	5.5356	4.1639
35	29.4085	24.9986	18.6646	14.4982	10.5668	8.1755	5.5386	4.1644
36	30.1074	25.4889	18.9083	14.6210	10.6118	8.1924	5.5412	4.1649
37	30.7994	25.9695	19.1426	14.7368	10.6530	8.2075	5.5434	4.1652
38	31.4846	26.4407	19.3679	14.8460	10.6908	8.2210	5.5452	4.1655
39	32.1629	26.9026	19.5845	14.9491	10.7255	8.2330	5.5468	4.1657
40	32.8346	27.3555	19.7928	15.0463	10.7574	8.2438	5.5482	4.1659
41	33.4996	27.7995	19.9930	15.1380	10.7866	8.2534	5.5493	4.1661
42	34.1580	28.2348	20.1856	15.2245	10.8134	8.2619	5.5502	4.1662
43	34.8099	28.6616	20.3708	15.3062	10.8379	8.2696	5.5510	4.1663
44	35.4554	29.0800	20.5488	15.3832	10.8605	8.2764	5.5517	4.1663
45	36.0944	29.4902	20.7200	15.4558	10.8812	8.2825	5.5523	4.1664
46	36.7271	29.8923	20.8847	15.5244	10.9002	8.2880	5.5528	4.1665
47	37.3536	30.2866	21.0429	15.5890	10.9176	8.2928	5.5532	4.1665
48	37.9739	30.6732	21.1951	15.6500	10.9336	8.2972	5.5536	4.1665
49	38.5880	31.0521	21.3415	15.7076	10.9482	8.3010	5.5539	4.1666
50	39.1960	31.4236	21.4822	15.7619	10.9617	8.3045	5.5541	4.1666

The possibility of a profit encourages risk-taking, innovation, and special effort on the part of those who expect to appropriate the difference between generally anticipated and actual outcomes. The particular property rights that govern profits and losses when they appear will affect people's behavior in ways that are partly predictable.

In the absence of uncertainty, any differences between total revenue and total opportunity cost would be competed away and profits would become zero—except insofar as restrictions exist on the ability to compete successfully.

Opportunities to compete are restricted by the limited availability of particular resources, which may in turn be due to nature or to social and political contrivance. Such competition-restricting scarcities are an additional source or cause of profit.

Before we decide that any particular profits are excessive or inadequate, it is important that we know what we mean by profit, how it arose, what function it performed, and the consequences of adding to or subtracting from it.

QUESTIONS FOR DISCUSSION

1. You ask your college for permission to set up a lemonade stand at the annual spring commencement, and the college grants permission. After paying your bills for materials (lemons, sugar, cups, and so forth), you clear $250 for an afternoon's work.
   a. Did you make a $250 profit?
   b. Are you likely to be given the lemonade concession again next year? What difference does it make whether or not word gets around how much you cleared?
   c. If the college next year auctions off the franchise, how much would you be willing to bid? Who will then get the profit from the lemonade stand?
2. If a district-court judge enters a $300-million judgment against a corporation for violation of antitrust statutes, do the owners of that corporation sustain a loss? What form will it take? If you believe that the judge was in error and that his decision will eventually be reversed on appeal, how could you profit from your knowledge?
3. You buy shares of common stock in two corporations. Over the next six months, the price of one falls and the price of the other rises. Which was a better buy? Which would be the better one to sell if you want cash?
4. Evaluate the following argument: "General Motors has taken advantage of its dominant position in the automobile industry and made huge profits year after year. It would be perfectly just, therefore, to impose a special tax on General Motors as a way of recovering for society some of the exorbitant profits earned in the past." Who would pay that tax?
5. Oil producers immediately objected when President Carter proposed in 1979

that the decontrol of oil prices be accompanied by a "windfall-profits" tax.

a. The oil producers claimed that the tax would reduce companies' incentives for new exploration and drilling. The press secretary for Henry Jackson, Chairman of the Senate Energy Committee, denied this claim in the following words: "As far as increased production is concerned, the oil companies have an enormous cash flow right now. The incentives are already there." Do profits earned in the past (or current cash flow) provide incentives to explore and drill for oil?

b. The reported net income after taxes in 1978 of 94 leading companies in the petroleum production and refining industry was $14,971 million. Is $15 billion dollars enough money to finance extensive exploration and drilling for new oil? Were those $15 billion dollars an incentive to explore and drill?

c. The 9 largest manufacturers of tobacco products in the U.S. earned a net income after taxes of $1,313 million in 1978. Would $1.3 billion pay for much oil exploration? Under what circumstances might the profits earned in the tobacco industry be used to explore for oil?

d. Much of the exploration and drilling for oil that occurred in the U.S. in the past was financed by borrowing, not out of the net income from previous production or refining. Under what circumstances can money be borrowed to finance the search for new oil?

e. Why would any firm in the business of producing or refining oil choose to invest some of its profits in shopping center development (or anything else) rather than in exploration for oil?

f. Does the news that the 94 largest firms in the petroleum production and refining industry earned $15 billion in 1978 make *you* eager to (a) explore and drill for oil, or (b) buy stock in oil companies?

g. What difference would it make to your answers in the preceding part of this question to know any of the following (which all happen to be true)? (a) Oil industry profits rose 12 percent from 1977 to 1978. (b) The average return on stockholders' equity in the oil industry in 1978 was 14.3 percent compared with 14.0 percent in 1977. (c) The average percentage return of leading manufacturing corporations in 1978 was 15.9 percent; it was 14.9 percent in 1977.

h. Suppose the government imposes a windfall-profits tax on all net income received from the sale of oil already discovered and flowing, but exempts from the tax all oil that is found after the tax is imposed. Will this maintain incentives to explore and drill for oil?

i. Why do critics of the oil industry rarely distinguish between producers (who bring oil out of the ground) and refiners (who turn it into useful products)?

j. Senator Jackson popularized the term "obscene profits" in discussing the profits of the oil industry during and immediately after the original OPEC price increases of 1973–74. Assuming that he intended *obscene* to mean repulsive or disgusting, rather than lewd or sexually exciting, explain the circumstances under which one might reasonably describe profits as obscene.

6. In June 1979 the provincial legislature of Quebec gave final approval to legislation authorizing the expropriation of Asbestos Corporation, a mining concern with headquarters in Montreal. Asbestos Corporation was at the time a 55 percent-owned subsidiary of General Dynamics Corporation.

   a. General Dynamics had repeatedly insisted that it did not want to sell to the province of Quebec. What do the officers of a corporation usually mean when they say they do not want to sell a subsidiary?

   b. In a voluntary sale the price is set by mutual agreement. In a forced sale some other method must be used to determine the price or compensation to be received for the expropriated property. A study commissioned by the province put the value of Asbestos Corporation at about $42 a share. A valuation done for General Dynamics set the value at almost $100 a share. If you were the arbitrator asked to decide upon the *true value*, what data would you consult to find the answer?

   c. Suppose someone suggests that the fair value of the corporation be determined by the going market price of Asbestos Corporation stock. If the stock were widely held by the public, investors would determine the value of a share by what they were willing to pay to own it or had to be paid to surrender ownership. What is the flaw in this proposal? What determines the price of a corporation's stock when that corporation faces imminent nationalization?

   d. Could General Dynamics benefit from nationalization if the compensation received was less than the sum of what was originally paid to purchase the assets of Asbestos Corporation, plus the cost of all subsequent additions and improvements to those assets?

   e. Why might it not be in the interest of Quebec to compel the sale at its own low valuation even if the province has the legal and political power to do so?

7. Marxists often used to argue that the owners of capital were not entitled to any income from that ownership because labor produced all value. Today they are more likely to admit that capital contributes to the production of value, but they still deny the right of capitalists to receive a profit on the grounds that the *ownership* of capital is not productive.

   a. Would you be willing to argue that those who own capital *have a right* to whatever income they can obtain from that capital? Is this the same as arguing that they *deserve* the income? Is it the same as saying that they *ought to be allowed* to receive the income?

   b. Does the productivity of resources depend at all on who manages those resources, or are all individuals and all organizations equally good at managing resources efficiently? Does the ownership of resources have anything to do with who manages those resources? Is it true that the ownership of capital is not productive?

8. You purchase for $950 a $1000 government bond maturing one year from the date of purchase. Will you make a profit if you hold the bond to maturity? Will you make a profit if there is a sharp, general increase in prevailing interest rates a week after your purchase? What effect will this have on the price you can obtain from selling your bond in the market?

9. Humbert and Ambler are very different personalities. Humbert likes to eat,

drink, be merry, and let the future care for itself. He suspects that the world is going to disintegrate in a few years anyway. Ambler is only 21 but is already planning conscientiously for his retirement years. What would you predict about their respective rates of time preference? How do people of Humbert's type benefit from the existence of people like Ambler, and vice versa?

10. What effect would you expect the rate of technological innovation in a society to have on the level of interest rates? Why?

11. "When lenders extend credit to high-risk borrowers, they must raise the interest rates they charge low-risk borrowers in order to cover their losses from defaults." Do you agree?

12. What arguments can you offer to support the establishment of legal ceilings on interest rates?

13. Suppose that Congress imposes a 6 percent ceiling on the interest rate that may be charged for federally guaranteed mortgages. Lending institutions, meanwhile, find themselves able to obtain all the mortgage business they want at 8 percent interest. Will they lend at 6 percent? How might the interest ceiling be circumvented? If you wanted to purchase a house and were eligible for a federally guaranteed mortgage, would you want Congress to set an interest-rate ceiling on such loans?

14. "A wealthy society has little difficulty paying interest. But in a poor country with almost no capital, economic planners cannot afford to take interest charges into account in their calculations." What's wrong with that argument?

15. Why would an agricultural economist conclude that the benefits of a government price-subsidy plus acreage-restriction program accrue largely to the owners of the land *at the time the program was started*?

16. In the spring of 1963 Fidel Castro announced a sugar-production goal for 1970 of 10 million tons. As the target date approached, and it began to appear that this much publicized target might not be attained, the Cuban government transferred labor and other resources in large amounts from the production of alternative goods into the production of sugar. The goal was still missed by a large margin. How do you suppose the consequent loss was distributed? How would the profit have been distributed had this decision turned out better than anticipated?

17 Why do corporate officers sometimes make illegal election contributions? Are those contributions "investments" subject to profit or loss?

18. When the government takes over privately owned land for a highway and pays compensation to the owners, should that compensation be based on its value in its present use, on its value in the use to which the government will put it, or on the value of the adjoining land that will increase (or decrease) in value because of the highway? What is unfair about each option?

19. Does ownership of gold or silver enable a person to protect himself against the hazards of uncertainty?

20. It has been proposed that state and local governments abolish property taxes for homeowners and turn to sales or income taxes for revenue. What effects on home prices would you predict from such a step? Who would be most likely to benefit?

21. In June 1972 the National Coalition for Land Reform asked the Secretary of

the Interior to reclaim land given to the Southern Pacific Railroad in the nineteenth century. The Coalition claims the railroad was supposed to sell this land for family-sized plots at $2.50 an acre or less, or forfeit the land. What do you think would happen if the federal government now required that all such land be sold within the next year in family-sized plots and at prices not to exceed $2.50 an acre? Who would lose and who would gain?

22. The Corps of Engineers estimates that a canal between Tussle and Big Stone would save shippers $500,000 per year. The canal would cost $20 million to construct and $200,000 per year to maintain.

   a. Is it correct to say that the canal is a good investment in the long run because it will save society a net $300,000 per year and eventually that will come to more than the $20 million construction cost?

   b. About how low would the interest rate have to be to make the canal a profitable investment? (The canal would not be profitable if the interest payments plus maintenance costs ate up the saving to shippers.)

   c. "The advantage of having the government build the canal is that government can do things that are in the public interest while private enterprise is constrained by narrow considerations of profitability." Evaluate that argument.

23. Are the profits of U.S. corporations currently earned more through coercion or through persuasion? (Definitions of terms: *Coercion:* inducing people to cooperate by reducing their options. *Persuasion:* inducing people to cooperate by expanding their options.) If you don't know how to answer the question, try thinking about the adequacy in this context of the proposed definitions for coercion and persuasion.

24. What is the present value of each of the following when discounted at interest rates of 4 percent and of 18 percent?

   a. A $10,000 prize in a limerick-writing contest, to be received one year from now.

   b. A $10,000 cash legacy from your Aunt Mehitabel, to be received when you reach your 25th birthday. (If you have already passed it, choose some other birthday.)

   c. $10,000 per year for each of the next 10 years, beginning one year from now, as first prize for telling in 25 words or less why you like a detergent.

   d. Ownership of an office building from which you expect to receive an annual net income of $10,000 per year for each of the next 30 years, at the end of which time you expect to sell the building and land for $100,000. Assume the annual amounts are all received at the end of each year.

   e. $10,000 in additional income per year from age 25 to age 65 if you are willing to go to school for an extra 5 years when you reach the age of 20.

25. If a gallon of gasoline currently costs $1, and if the price increases in future years at exactly the rate of inflation, what will be the price of gasoline 5 years, 10 years, and 20 years from now if inflation occurs at an annual rate of 2 percent? If it occurs at a 6 percent annual rate? If it occurs at a 12 percent annual rate?

224

Chapter 12

The Distribution of Income

Most of us know far less than we think we do about the distribution of income in the United States. We are like the typical witness to a crime or an accident who "saw it all" but cannot, when questioned, describe any of it accurately. We know there are rich people and poor people. We know there are lots of people somewhere in the middle. And we know where we ourselves stand. Or do we even know that? Most people have a fairly accurate notion of their annual income, because they have to reveal it every year on their tax forms. But it is only their *taxable* income with which they're familiar, and that's far from the total income of even the most scrupulously honest and law-abiding citizen.

Money Income and Real Wealth

Income really means additions to wealth, and everything that contributes to our welfare adds to our wealth. If we compare people's incomes but look only at their money incomes, we're going to be ignoring some very important differences. Consider two individuals of the same age who live in the same city and receive each year identical amounts of money income. Would you want to insist that their incomes are equal if the first is in excellent health and the second is chronically ill? If the first lives in a house that she owns free of any mortgage and the second must pay rent? If the first lives near her parents and siblings, whose companionship she thoroughly enjoys, while the second also lives near her parents and siblings, but they are all chemically addicted, violent, and ill-tempered freeloaders? Moreover, people extract well-being from a dollar of money income at vastly different rates. One person will obtain as much satisfaction from a robin's song as another person can get only from an expensive concert. If we really were determined to evaluate the existing distribution of income from the standpoint of human welfare, we would somehow have to take account of such facts as these.

There is much more we don't know. While we may know our own monetary incomes with some precision, we probably have a very inaccurate idea of where we stand relative to everyone else. Many who believe that the federal government should ease the tax burden on middle income groups and raise the rates paid by the rich are unaware that, by their own definition, they themselves are rich. A common way of distinguishing the rich is to call all those rich whose family incomes place them in the top 5 percent of income receivers or even in the top 20 percent. But how much income would a family have had to receive in 1977 to make it into the top 20 percent? Are you surprised to discover that $26,000 per year was enough to do it? Or that $40,500 was enough in 1977 to put a family in the top 5 percent? Many people who encounter these statistics cannot believe them, because they had always thought of the top 5 percent as those with butlers and colonnaded homes overlooking the golf course.

What Is Revealed by the Data?

We would like to say that we chose the year 1977 just now for illustrative purposes because it was the first year of America's third century. The truth is that we chose 1977 because that was the most recent year for which reliable data were readily available at the time of writing in mid-1979. This points up a further source of our ignorance about the distribution of income. We are dependent for our data on surveys and samples that can never tell us where we are but only where we were a year or more ago. That can matter quite a bit when the distribution of income happens to be changing rapidly.

A much more serious problem with these data, however, is that they must necessarily conceal more than they reveal. If we were able to gather and publish—within a reasonable time period and at an acceptable cost—accurate data on the monetary income of each of the approximately 220 million people living in the United States, we would learn very little from the results. It would take most of a lifetime just to read the data. By the time we had finished reading, most of the people would be dead, the data would all be hopelessly obsolete, and we would have forgotten completely what we had read at the beginning. You cannot find your way through unfamiliar country with the aid of a map that is drawn to the same scale as the country itself! Maps are helpful only because they leave out most of the detail. Similarly, data describing the distribution of income among citizens of the United States are useful only when they drastically suppress detail, giving us only broad summaries and averages for large groups.

The necessity to suppress such details rarely poses a problem for mapmakers, because those who use maps are interested only in the same limited facets of reality. All they want to know is the number of miles from Moab to Missoula and which highways most directly connect them. They do not want to know each hill and curve to be traversed, the number and color of the houses on each route, or the crops that will be growing in the fields on the way. But in the case of a "map" designed to acquaint us with the facts of income distribution, we must know such details and the interrelationships among them just to decide what the data mean.

A few quick examples will serve to illustrate. The mean after-tax income of Americans per capita in 1977 was $6009.[1] You cannot conclude from this that the average child with three brothers and sisters lived in a family that received $36,000 in after-tax income in 1977. Larger families have, on average, lower incomes per capita. Perhaps that's obvious. But is the next example equally obvious?

The median income of two-parent families in 1977 was $17,616. This does not mean that the median salary of men living with their families was $17,616, because many families contain more than one earner and not all family income stems from earnings.

One more example. The mean income accruing to families headed by women was $7182 in 1977 if the woman was separated from her husband and $10,311 if she was divorced. Does this mean that women who are separated can raise their incomes 44 percent by obtaining a divorce? Or does the $12,052 mean income of widows imply a 68 percent increase in income for women who are separated if their husbands die? The suppressed but essential details in these cases have

---

1. The *mean* or, more accurately, the *arithmetic mean*, is the total divided by the number contributing to the total, or what people commonly have in mind when they say "average." Another useful average or measure of central tendency is the *median*, which is the value associated with the unit exactly in the middle of the range. If the annual incomes of your five friends are $1000, $2000, $4000, $8000, and $20,000, their mean income is $7000 and the median is $4000.

TABLE 12A   MONEY INCOME OF FAMILIES—PERCENT
OF AGGREGATE INCOME RECEIVED BY EACH FIFTH
AND THE HIGHEST 5 PERCENT

	1950	1960	1970	1977
Lowest fifth	4.5	4.8	5.4	5.2
Second fifth	12.0	12.2	12.2	11.6
Middle fifth	17.4	17.8	17.6	17.5
Fourth fifth	23.4	24.0	23.8	24.2
Highest fifth	42.7	41.3	40.9	41.5
Highest 5 percent	17.3	15.9	15.6	15.7

SOURCE: U.S. Bureau of the Census, *Current Population Reports*, series P-60.

to do with the greater initial income of couples that choose divorce, rather than separation, and the greater average age and hence higher average incomes of widows.

Family Incomes Since World War II

There are many ways to summarize and present the data on income distribution that the Bureau of the Census gathers. The most common is the quintile (by fifths) distribution of family income. The Census Bureau counted 57,215,000 families in the United States in 1977. This includes everyone except individuals living alone or living with persons to whom they were not related by kinship or marriage.[2] Table 12A shows the percentage of total family income received in selected years by the 20 percent of these families with the lowest incomes, by the second-lowest fifth, and so on up to the 20 percent who received the highest incomes. If family income were equally distributed, each fifth would receive 20 percent of the total. That obviously isn't the case. The percentage received by the highest 5 percent is also shown in the table.

People who encounter these data for the first time are usually quite surprised. The figures seem to indicate that the distribution of income in the United States has not changed significantly since World War II, despite progressive income taxes and vastly expanded government programs for transferring income to low-income families and individuals. The data don't agree with "what everyone knows."

In this case, however, "what everyone knows" may be more accurate than what the percentages seem to show. To begin with, these percentages refer to income before the payment of personal taxes. Second, the data take no account of

---

2. Here is another measurement problem. A married couple is treated as a family. Two friends sharing a house or apartment are treated as individuals. But if those two individuals share their incomes, shouldn't they be treated the same as a family?

TABLE 12B PERCENTAGE OF AGGREGATE FAMILY
MONEY INCOME RECEIVED BY EACH FIFTH OF
FAMILIES, ADJUSTED TO REFLECT PERSONAL TAXES
AND IN-KIND TRANSFERS AND CALCULATED ON
A PER CAPITA BASIS

	1952	1962	1972
Lowest fifth	8.1	8.8	11.7
Second fifth	14.2	14.4	15.0
Middle fifth	17.8	18.2	18.2
Fourth fifth	23.2	23.1	22.3
Highest fifth	36.7	35.4	32.8

SOURCE: Edgar K. Browning, "The Trend Toward Equality in the Distribution of Net
Income," *Southern Economic Journal* (July 1976).

in-kind transfers. They do reflect *money transfers*; that is, money *payments to people that are not compensation for services currently being rendered*. Thus they include income from private pensions, veteran's benefits, social security benefits, the program of Aid to Families with Dependent Children (AFDC), and all other welfare assistance—*when paid in money*. But they do not include the value of such in-kind transfers as medical assistance, rent subsidies, or food stamps—all of which are income even though they don't involve the exchange of money. Third, these data are not adjusted to take account of differing family sizes. When these three adjustments are made, the percentages going to each quintile change over time in precisely the direction we would expect. The share of lower-income groups rises, and that of upper-income groups falls.[3] One careful attempt to make these adjustments produced the results shown in Table 12B—results that are far more consistent with common sense than are the unadjusted data of Table 12A.

A Spurious Rigidity

A more fundamental difficulty with data of this sort is that they don't actually mean what they seem to say. Even the adjusted data of Table 12B give a misleading picture of the actual inequality and rigidity of the U.S. family-income distribution since World War II. We are inclined to assume without thinking about it that the families in the second or fourth fifth in a current year are the same families (or an earlier generation of

---

3. Even the adjustment for family size helps to reduce the measured inequality. Contrary to popular belief ("the rich get richer and the poor get children"), the average number of persons in families *increases as family income increases*. A better way to put it, and one that makes the assertion more plausible, is that family income increases as the number of persons in the family increases. One reason for this is that the number of earners in a family is positively correlated with family income, as we would expect.

the same families) who occupied those fifths in some preceding year. This is not necessarily the case. In fact, it is quite unlikely to be the case for one simple reason: The relative income position of a family depends very much on the age of the family's principal earner.

The data of Table 12C illustrate what we're talking about. They show the mean income of all families in 1977 by the age of the family head. (The Bureau is embarrassed by its use of the term *head* and is looking for a substitute. The alternative, *principal earner*, is not adequate, either, where two family members earn approximately equal amounts or where a substantial portion of family income comes from investments or transfer payments.) The table shows unmistakably that a substantial amount of the inequality that shows up in a still picture would disappear if we were able to take a moving picture—that is, to compare the incomes of families over the lifetimes of their heads.

When we compare the data of Table 12C with the upper limits of the various family income quintiles in 1977, we find that "an average family" would move in its lifetime from the second fifth through the middle fifth into the fourth fifth and descend again into the second fifth upon retirement of the head.[4]

Constraint and Choice

We have said almost nothing so far about the processes through which income is distributed. But if we are interested in the patterns of income distribution because we are concerned about their implications for human welfare, we cannot separate those patterns from the human decisions that shape them. The distribution of income among families is not an objectve fact—something determined by "outside" events independently of the opportunities people perceive and the responses they make, analogous to the distribution of heights and weights. A better analogy would be the distribution of residential locations. Families do not choose where they want to live without any constraints, but they obviously do exercise some choice. Shall it be Iowa or California, city or suburb, close in or farther out? The constraints may be so severe in the case of some families that we will be willing to say (never altogether accurately) that they "have no choice of where to live." But we also know it would be absurd to pretend that the population growth in California since World War II, the suburbanization of

---

4. The upper limits of the lowest through the fourth fifth in 1977 were, respectively, $7,903, $13,273, $18,800, and $26,000.

TABLE 12C
FAMILY INCOMES IN 1977

Age of Head	Mean Income
14 to 24 years	$10,970
25 to 34 years	16,661
35 to 44 years	20,631
45 to 54 years	23,049
55 to 64 years	20,170
65 years and over	12,482

SOURCE: U.S. Bureau of the Census, *Current Population Reports*, series P-60.

America over the same period, or the movement of higher-income people back into the cities in the late 1970s were in no way a result of people's preferences.

The relevant preferences in the case of residential location are not exclusively the preferences of families deciding where to live. The preferences of private employers, housing developers, government officials, and many others interact with the preferences of families to make particular alternatives more or less attractive. The distribution of residential locations is thus the outcome of millions of interrelated decisions.

Supply and Demand Once Again

This is also the way in which the distribution of income is ultimately determined. Economic theory views that distribution as the outcome of interacting decisions, decisions that both affect and are affected by changing expectations of relative benefits and costs. To put it more briefly, economic theory views the distribution of money income as the product of supply and demand. You probably aren't the least surprised to hear that, since supply and demand are the two major categories into which economists seek to group all the variegated facts and events of the economic system. But supply of what? Demand for what? The answer is: the supply of and demand for *productive services*. Money income—and we'll be focusing now on money income despite its limitations as a measure of well-being—arises from the supply of productive services to those who are willing to pay for them.

This is a procedure for organizing the question and not a moral endorsement of all the ways in which people obtain money income. The word *productive* means no more than "demanded," so that an activity is productive for our purposes if it enables people to obtain something for which they are willing to pay. All sorts of thoroughly disreputable persons (you may provide your own list) are thus suppliers of productive services. Nor does the word *service* necessarily mean that effort is being put forth. A person who lives entirely on the dividends from inherited common stock is supplying a productive service, in our sense of the term, by giving up some command over current resources. No one would dream of commending him for *effort*, since he makes none. But a playboy heir who lives off dividends still contributes to current production by the activity of *not consuming* his capital. The relevant fact for economic analysis is not the merit of the playboy but the product of the resources whose ownership provides him with regular income.

The Law of Demand and Productive Services

The demand for the services of productive resources is like all other demand curves, in that it slopes downward to the right. Other things remaining equal, a larger quantity will be demanded at lower prices and a smaller quantity at higher prices. In the case of productive resources, this relationship may be so well disguised that people won't see it or will refuse to believe it. But the relationship will hold whether it is recognized or not.

The best example is probably the case of labor services demanded by an employer. Employers purchase labor services after estimating the probable contribution those services will make toward the creation of income. They will hire only when they expect the additional revenue from a hiring decision to be greater than the additional cost which that decision entails. They use the simple rule of Chapter 9: take those actions and only those actions whose expected marginal revenue is greater than their expected marginal cost. The higher the wage rate, the higher the marginal cost of purchasing labor services. Other things remaining equal, therefore, a smaller quantity of labor services will be demanded as the price that must be paid to obtain them goes up.

Why is this so widely and frequently denied? It is denied, for example, by those who insist that opposition to legal minimum wages is evidence of indifference toward the plight of the poor. But do poor people really benefit from legislated increases in the minimum wage? If the legal minimum is no higher than what employers are already paying, it has no effect. It will have an impact only if some covered employers are paying less than the legal minimum. But won't those employers lay some workers off if they are compelled to pay a higher wage?

"They wouldn't have to" is not a good answer. It's a common answer, because so many people believe that employers pay wages "out of profits" and can therefore refrain from lay-

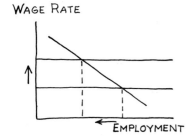

WAGE RATE

EMPLOYMENT

ing workers off when wage rates rise, so long as profits are adequate to cover the increased wages. This seems to imply that the quantity of labor services demanded is a constant, dictated perhaps by technology, so that the only options before employers are either to pay the higher wage rates or close down the operation. But the demand for labor services is not perfectly inelastic and will at times be highly elastic, because employers can almost always find substitutes, within some range, for labor services of a particular type.

People or Machines?

The strange notion that the demand for labor services of any type is completely inelastic with respect to the wage rate also seems to underlie the widespread belief (or fear) that machines "destroy" jobs because they are so much more productive than people. But what could it mean to say that machines are "more productive" than people? Employers aren't interested in mere physical or technical capabilities; they're interested in the relation between marginal revenues and marginal costs. A machine is more efficient than a person, and hence will be substituted for a person, only if the marginal revenue from the machine's use *relative to its marginal cost* is greater than the same ratio for a person. That implies, among other things, that wage rates play an important part in shaping the speed and direction of technological change in the economy.

It would be a mistake to suppose that automatic elevators replaced elevator operators in the United States over the last two decades merely because of improvements in technology. Time, money, and energy were spent to develop automatic elevators—and building owners subsequently installed them—because of benefit-cost estimates they made, not because automatic elevators were new and shiny. In some other society where the wage rates (opportunity costs) of elevator operators are quite low, elevators run by trained operators could still be more efficient than automatic elevators.

The fear that our society or any society may run out of jobs is an odd kind of fear. A job, after all, represents an obstacle to be overcome. A society that has run out of jobs for people to do has come very close to overcoming scarcity; and that would be something to cheer, not fear. We are not in any such fortunate situation. Technological innovations release labor resources from some employments to make them available for others. The automatic or self-service elevator made it possible for people who were formerly employed in transporting passengers up and down to do something else, to make some other and additional contribution to our total output of commodities and services.

The reallocation of labor in response to changed circumstances, even though it increases the total value of society's output, does lead to a loss of wealth for some people. A rising demand for labor attracted some elevator operators into more remunerative employments and pulled up the wages of the rest; automatic elevators were in part a response to this situation. But as they were introduced, some elevator operators found themselves pushed rather than pulled: deprived of their present jobs and compelled to accept less desirable alternatives, rather than attracted away from their present positions by better opportunities. Such people suffered, at least temporarily, a loss of wealth. They were forced to incur the cost of searching for new employment, and they were not guaranteed that the new job would be better than the old. Resistance to technological change and the fear of automation is therefore quite understandable. Even college professors have been known to speak harshly about the introduction of such technological innovations as videotaped lectures and teaching machines.

The Derived Demand for Productive Services

Another factor that may help to conceal the downward sloping character of the demand curve for productive services is the derived nature of that demand. The demand for productive services is derived, of course, from the demand for the goods they produce. When firms announce that they are expanding their hiring or laying some workers off, they almost never attribute the decision to a change in wage rates. They will rather credit (or blame) the market for their product: "Sales have increased beyond our expectations" or "Inventories of finished goods have grown to unacceptable levels because of disappointing sales." Thus the quantity of services demanded at any time from carpenters or automobile assemblers will seem to depend on conditions in the housing or automobile market, rather than upon the wages of carpenters or automobile assemblers.

But they actually depend on both. The point to be noted is that the prices of houses and of automobiles and the way they are produced have been influenced by the wage rates that had to be paid to obtain the services of carpenters and of automobile assemblers. In the case of carpenters, fewer new houses are purchased, and hence fewer carpenters are employed, insofar as the cost of obtaining carpenters' services has raised the price of new construction. Moreover, houses are increasingly constructed in ways that economize on carpenters' services, with less elaborate woodwork, for example, and with factory-built cabinets.

Demand Creates Income

Our discussion of the demand for productive services has until now emphasized the demand as a constraint. The income that owners of productive resources can obtain by supplying the services of the resources they own is limited by the demand for those services. We must not leave this topic without pointing out the corollary: The income that resource owners can receive is also *created* by the demand for the services of those resources. Any sheik who owns an oil well provides a vivid illustration.

Whether a country like Kuwait, which each year produces about 1500 barrels of oil per inhabitant, is fabulously wealthy or almost desperately poor depends on the demand for the services of a thick and flammable liquid hydrocarbon that seemed both ugly and useless when it was first discovered. In the absence of that demand, the Organization of Petroleum Exporting Countries would today have less influence over world affairs than the Audubon Society. But given the enormous demand that has developed in this century for the services of petroleum, OPEC became a household word.

Who Competes Against Whom?

When owners of productive resources form organizations like OPEC in an effort to increase their incomes, they often argue that their association will enable them to compete more effectively against the buyers of whatever service they are supplying. Whether we call this argument confused or devious depends on how we want to assess the motives of those who make it. The plain fact is that buyers do not compete against sellers. Buyers compete against one another to obtain what sellers are supplying. Sellers compete against sellers to obtain the custom of buyers. The competition that OPEC was designed to eliminate was competition among the petroleum exporting countries. It succeeded because it was able to restrict production.

Buyers prefer that sellers have 12 players on the field rather than 11 — because sellers don't compete against buyers.

Buyers may try to play the same game. We can refer at this point to an example used earlier: the agreement among owners of professional sports teams not to compete for the services of athletes. To make this agreement effective they had to assign the exclusive right to each athlete's services to a single owner. This is the purpose of the "draft," as developed by owners' associations in major professional sports. When buyers present this kind of unified position, organization on the part of sellers may be an effective way of countering their power. But the objective of the sellers' association in such circumstances would be to *reactivate competition* among the buyers or to *reduce competition* among the sellers, and could not be correctly described as an attempt to compete more effectively against the buyers.

Unions and Competition

In the case of labor unions, the basic federal statute regulating union organization and collective bargaining makes the mistake of asserting in its preamble that unorganized workers need unions to help them compete against corporations. But workers compete against workers, corporate employers against corporate employers. And this is the competition that affects wage rates.

Employers cannot pay their workers whatever wage their callous hearts suggest for the same reason that Exxon was never able to buy oil from Saudi Arabia for whatever price it chose. Workers have alternative opportunities in the form of other employers, and Saudi Arabia always had alternative opportunities in the form of other refiners. The services of workers are valuable to employers, and so they are willing to bid for them, even though that may raise the going wage. The services of crude oil are valuable to refiners, and so they too are willing to bid, raising its price above $3 a barrel in 1972, before OPEC learned how to restrict production, and above $30 a barrel for some oil in 1979, when OPEC had learned very well.

Similarly, workers cannot successfully insist on the wage they think they deserve if other workers are willing to supply very similar services at lower wage rates. Workers compete against other workers, and unions are in part attempts to control *this* competition. The implication is that unions improve the position of the members they represent by finding ways to restrict competition from those who are not members of the union. They may do this directly, for example, by securing contracts with employers that make union membership a prior condition of employment and then limiting membership. Or they may do it indirectly. Just as a legal minimum wage excludes some people from employment opportunities, so a high wage secured by union contract (perhaps under the threat of a strike, or total withdrawal of labor services) excludes those who would be willing to work for less.

The belief that unions arose in the United States to counter the power of large corporations is unsupported by history. Unions first became powerful in this country in industries characterized by small scale firms: construction, printing, textiles, mining. The railroads are an exception that supports the rule: it was special legislation that enabled unions to become powerful in the railroad industry. The unions that today bargain with the large corporations in steel, automobiles, and electrical machinery were originally missionary projects of the unions that bargained mostly with small employers.

WAGE RATE

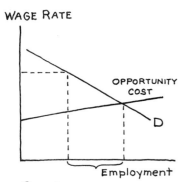

Employment opportunities are eliminated by enforcement of high wage.

The demand for productive services will generate no income for a person who owns no resources capable of supplying those services. The distribution of income among individuals or families depends fundamentally, therefore, on the ownership of productive resources.

Sometimes this is expressed by saying that the distribution of income depends on the prior distribution of wealth. That is an acceptable restatement, as long as we don't define wealth too narrowly. The trouble is that most empirical studies of personal wealthholdings, as well as the ordinary connotation of the word, restrict wealth to such assets as cash, stocks, bonds, and real estate. However, most of the income that Americans receive annually does not derive from ownership of wealth in these forms but rather from the ownership of *human capital*.

Capital and Human Resources

We defined the term *capital* in Chapter 11. As economists use the word, it means *produced means of production*, or *goods that can be used to produce future goods*. Machinery is capital, as are industrial and commercial buildings.[5] But so are the knowledge and skills that people accumulate through education, training, or experience and that enable them to supply valuable productive services to others. Only when we include human capital in our definition of wealth is it at all adequate to say that the distribution of income depends on the distribution of wealth.

In support of this assertion, we can simply cite data from recent years on national income, as calculated by the Bureau of Economic Analysis in the Department of Commerce. The specific concept of *national income* refers to the *total net income earned from production in a given year*. It comprises employee compensation, the net income of unincorporated businesses, corporate profits, net interest, and the rental income of persons. Corporate profits after the payment of corporate profits taxes, interest, rental income, and some portion of the net income of unincorporated enterprises represent income from the ownership of nonhuman resources (stocks, bonds, real es-

---

5. The word *capital* is like the word *cost*, in that confusion may arise if we fail to make clear *to whom* something is capital or cost. Calling a good *capital* implies that the person who owns it intends to use it to produce goods in the future. An ordinary bed is capital to a motel owner, but to a patron of the motel it is a consumer good. The critical reader may object that the bed is also capital to the motel patron who intends to use it to produce a restful night's sleep and a profitable day tomorrow. This objection correctly points out that no sharp line of distinction can be drawn between capital goods and consumer goods. But it remains true that capital is only capital to some person with the appropriate intentions. The motel bed would not be capital to a patron who only rented the room in order to use the swimming pool.

tate, cash, and so forth.) Employee compensation plus the rest of the net income of unincorporated enterprises represent income from the ownership of human resources. What is the relative size of each?

If we leave out the net income of unincorporated businesses on the grounds that any allocation of it would be arbitrary, we find that 85 percent of the national income from 1975 through 1977 was income arising from the ownership of human resources. Contrary to popular belief, inequality in the distribution of income in the United States today arises primarily from unequal abilities to supply valuable human services. A moment ago we insisted on including human capital in our definition of wealth, because most income is earned by supplying the services of human resources.

Human Capital and Investment

It may be misleading, though, to refer to these resources as *capital*. Capital means *produced resources*. To what extent are the abilities that enable people to command high incomes *produced*, rather than inherited or just stumbled upon? It seems impossible to generalize safely or usefully in response to this question. Perhaps the word *capabilities* would therefore be a more neutral and consequently more satisfactory term.

On the other hand, the implication that these capabilities are *produced* does call attention to a fact of some importance. People can and do choose to acquire additional capabilities in the expectation of earning additional income. They invest in themselves by going to school, acquiring special job training, practicing certain skills, or otherwise adding to the value of the services they can supply to others. It makes sense to refer to such investments in oneself as the acquisition of human capital.

We must once again beware of confusing the question of function with the question of merit, a confusion to which we referred earlier in discussing profits—and which seems to crop up in conjunction with any issue of income distribution. The value of a tax accountant's services does not depend on the extent to which his or her skills were acquired rather than inherited. But they do depend on the level of those skills, and that level can usually be raised through diligent effort. The expectation of an increased income from the sale of their services induces tax accountants to pore over tedious tax-court rulings, when they would rather be playing golf. Pride and a sense of craftsmanship may also be at work. But the prospect of a greater income exercises a constant and steady pressure on people to acquire capabilities that will permit them to supply more valuable services to others. That is a useful social function, even if we decide that all differences between people are ultimately matters of good or evil fortune, so that no one is ever authorized to say that he *deserves* the income he receives.

Property Rights and Income

Who then owns productive resources? They are owned by many different people, individually and jointly, through partnerships, corporations, and informal arrangements. The owners acquired these resources by many different means, most of which we can never hope to untangle in retrospect. The resources themselves have an enormous variety of forms, running all the way from ideas and skills to turret lathes and fertile fields. In every case, however, *the owners of the resources will be those who can sell the services of the resources.*

We have not italicized the obvious. We have rather proposed a definition of the word *ownership*. Recall from the preceding chapter how economists employ the concept of *property rights*. The concept refers to *people's expectations about what they can and may do.* Since expectations govern the processes of both supplying and demanding, the property rights that prevail in a society will determine how that society's economic system functions, how resources are allocated, and how income is distributed. All this is merely a review of Chapter 11. What we are now asserting is that property rights in this sense are best described by observing what actually occurs. The people who own productive resources are not necessarily the people who have the title deed in their safe deposit box. The effective property rights belong to those who can expect to appropriate whatever income is generated by selling the services of the resources.

If no service can be sold, even to oneself, no productive resource exists. Suppose you "own" your driveway but are unable to prevent people from parking on the street in a way that blocks your entrance. Since you cannot expect to park in it yourself or to receive income from renting the space to others, you do not have an effective property right and consequently don't own a parking space. (Perhaps you own a shuffleboard court.)

Consider the case of a woman who has been expertly trained as a physician but cannot obtain a license to practice because she was educated in a foreign country. She owns a human resource of limited value; the only services she can supply will be to her own family and friends.

The owner of an apartment building under rent controls may be unable to set rents high enough to cover taxes and maintenance. In that case, he does not actually own the units. The services that the units provide are appropriated by the tenants occupying the apartments, who are thus the effective owners. The proof of the nominal owner's actual nonownership

Those who can expect to benefit from use of the resource are in actuality the owners of the resource.

will be his inability to sell the units at any price and his willingness simply to abandon them by surrendering legal ownership to the taxing authorities.

Federal law says that the airwaves belong to the public. But the Federal Communications Commission allows the owners of television stations to use assigned channels at no charge. Since the owners of the stations can appropriate the income from supplying television services, they are the actual owners of the channels. A proof of this will be their ability to sell the physical plant and facilities at a price many times greater than the cost of the facilities' reproduction—*if* the purchaser can expect to obtain, along with the station, the right to use the assigned channel.

The mayor of a city does not legally own any of the city's facilities. But if she can expect to enjoy the benefits supplied by a spacious office, a large staff, motorcycle escorts for her limousine, and a place at the head table for just about any banquet she chooses to attend, her wealth is much greater than it seems. She cannot sell these property rights, it is true; so they are limited in that respect. But *all* property rights are limited to one's expectations of what can and may be done with the resources in question.

Expectations and Investment

Every decision about the use of resources is based finally on the expectations of the decision maker. Families and individuals decide whether to consume or to invest their income by assessing the relative values of the benefits they expect to receive from each option. And they choose among alternative investments by considering not only the expected rates of return, but also the confidence with which those returns can be expected. People who fear confiscation of their investments will opt for investments that are difficult to confiscate, even though they promise a lower return than more vulnerable investment projects. Dictators who suspect their control is slipping shift into Swiss bank accounts, and ethnic minorities encountering native hostility invest in jewelry or other readily portable wealth. The most readily portable form of wealth is human capital, which may explain why prospering ethnic minorities have so often obtained unusually high levels of education. Of course, even human capital *can* be confiscated; people who are barred from practicing a profession for which they were trained have been effectively deprived of the human resource which that training created.

When you reflect upon the fact that the returns from investment decisions are *future* returns, you realize that a person's rate of time preference also affects consumption or investment decisions. Someone who discounts future events at a high rate will be present-oriented, will prefer consumption to investment, and will thereby choose in effect to receive a lower income in future years. On the other hand, people who discount at a low rate of interest will be more willing to give up present consumption for the sake of greater consumption in the future and will consequently invest more heavily while they are young, thereby securing for themselves a higher expected income in later years. The interesting implication of all this is that people choose, to some extent, their lifetime income profiles.

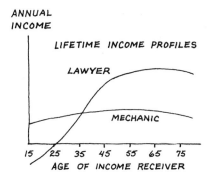

A further implication is that we cannot always tell from a simple comparison of two people's current incomes which of them has the higher income. A promising student in the last year of medical school probably has a large *negative* income. But would we really want to say that he or she is poorer than someone the same age who is earning $10,000 a year from a semiskilled job? The relevant comparison is *lifetime* incomes. That was the comparison relevant to the medical student's decision to become a physician, and it is probably the more relevant comparison for anyone who wants to evaluate the equity of a particular income distribution.

Data on lifetime incomes are not available, of course. That is why we continue to exaggerate the poverty of many people who are students and the wealth of many who were students long ago. The two errors don't necessarily cancel out, however. If public policy responds to these opposite exaggerations by transferring income from the older to the younger group, it lowers the expected rate of return and, presumably, the amount of investment that will occur during people's younger years.

Change, Stability, and Coordination

Public policies that alter the distribution of income necessarily entail a change in property rights, with consequences not always foreseen by those who only wanted a more equal distribution of income. U.S. energy policy in the seventies provides a most vivid example. Increased scarcity of energy resources threatened to create higher relative prices for fossil fuels and thus to transfer income from consumers to producers of those fuels. It was largely in an effort to prevent this outcome that the federal government continued obstinately to suppress the prices of natural gas, crude petroleum, and gasoline in the 1970s.

Many supporters of these price controls undoubtedly believed that their only effect would be to keep producers from becoming wealthier at the expense of consumers. It didn't work out that way. The controls altered the property rights of (among others) oil and gas producers, refiners, retailers and distributors, independent truck drivers, farmers, fishing boat owners, managers of electrical utilities, ordinary motorists, homeowners wondering how to heat their houses, and the governors of states to which the federal allocation system assigned less fuel than the citizens of that state expected and thought they deserved. Any sudden and extensive alteration of property rights will tend to produce chaos, because people do not passively accept changes in their expectations. They adjust their behavior to take account of the new expectations.

Gasoline-station owners, for example, when denied an opportunity to increase their wealth by raising prices, increased their wealth by staying open for fewer hours. This in turn produced a sudden change in the property rights of motorists who had always expected to obtain gasoline whenever they wanted it and without waiting in line. Motorists' adjustments included tank topping, leaving earlier for work and arriving late more often, and bitterly complaining. The complaints of motorists altered the property rights of politicians, who suddenly found that they could not expect to remain in office unless they demonstrated their dedication to the public interest by finding some villains to chastise. But threatening to punish alleged villains prompts them to adjust their behavior in ways that will minimize the impact of political retaliation. There is no predictable end once the basis of prediction, which is stable expectations, has been eliminated.

Social cooperation becomes much more difficult in a society subjected to sudden, extensive, and unpredictable changes in "the rules of the game." That is no trivial consequence in a society whose members are all dependent on the finely adjusted cooperation of millions of other people.

Once Over Lightly

Real income is whatever increases the wealth or well-being of people. Money income is an important contributor to real income but not an adequate measure of it.

Data on the distribution of money income must be simplified if they are to be useful; but even the most elementary simplifications begin to conceal the numerous additional factors that are associated with and determine the welfare significance of a particular money income.

Census Bureau data on the distribution of family money incomes exaggerate the inequality of income in the United States by neglecting in-kind transfers, personal taxes, and differences in family size. They also give an erroneous impression of rigidity by ignoring the extensive circulation of individual families throughout the overall distribution.

The distribution of income is the result of the supply of and demand for productive services.

The demand for productive services of any kind will not be

perfectly inelastic. A greater quantity will be demanded at lower prices and a lesser quantity at higher prices, because there are substitutes for any productive service.

Potential users of productive services decide on the amount they will demand by comparing the marginal-benefit-to-marginal-cost ratios of alternative procedures for achieving their purposes.

The demand for productive services and hence their price is partly dependent on the demand for the goods they produce. But the price of productive services also reacts back upon the cost and price of producing particular goods and thus upon the quantity that will be produced and sold.

Suppliers of productive services do not compete against buyers of those services. Suppliers compete against other suppliers, buyers against other buyers. The quest for higher incomes produces attempts to suppress competition, because what a seller can obtain and what a buyer must pay will depend on the alternative opportunities that competitors are providing.

The production of productive resources is investment, or the creation of capital. One important form of capital is human capital, or productive capabilities embodied in human beings. The distribution of human capital is an important consideration, because monetary income is primarily earned in the United States, even by the wealthy, by supplying the services of human resources.

The amount and nature of the investment that will occur in a society depends on prevailing property rights, defined as people's beliefs about what they may expect from the actions that are open to them.

From the standpoint of economic theory, ownership of a resource means the ability to appropriate the benefits accruing from use of the resource. Changing the distribution of these benefits will alter people's consumption and investment decisions.

Lower rates of time preference encourage investment over consumption. Greater uncertainty about future returns from investment will prompt the discounting of future income at higher rates and consequently will lead to less investment.

Social cooperation on any extensive scale requires relatively stable expectations.

QUESTIONS FOR DISCUSSION

1. The following details from the Census Bureau's *Current Population Reports* for 1977 provide a small indication of how much is omitted from the usual summary statistics on income distribution. They may also be used to test your ingenuity. What kinds of plausible supply or demand decisions might

have produced these results? Is racial or sexual discrimination something altogether different from, or something that influences, supply and demand?

   a. The median income of all black families in the U.S. in 1977 was only 57 percent of the median income of all white families.
   b. The median income of black families containing two earners was 79 percent of the median income of white families containing two earners.
   c. The median income of white families containing four or more earners was 97 percent higher than the median income of white families containing only one earner. In the case of black families, the median income was 166 percent higher for families with four or more earners than for families with only one earner.
   d. The median income of black families in which the family head was 25 years old and over was 59 percent of the median income of white families whose heads were 25 years old or more. When we compare only those families, however, in which the head has completed 4 years or more of college, the ratio of black-to-white median family incomes rises to 84 percent.
   e. In families with incomes above $50,000 per year, the median number of school years completed by the family head was 16.5 years in 1977. It was 13.2 years for the heads of families with incomes between $25,000 and $50,000, and less than 12 years in the case of families with incomes below $10,000.
   f. The median age of white males in the U.S. in 1975 was 28.4 years. The median age of black males was 22.2 years.

2. Teachers began encountering serious job shortages in the early 1970s after many years of rising demand for their services. An intensified interest in unionization has been observed. What can unionization accomplish for teachers in a highly unfavorable job market? Who is likely to benefit? Who will it harm?

3. "Farmers complaining that they can't get field hands now that the bracero program has been curtailed aren't sincere," said an official of the United Packinghouse Workers Union. "About one-third of the unemployed in Los Angeles are former farm workers, and the farmers could get them back if they'd make wages and working conditions attractive enough." Do you think farmers are insincere? Could they get enough workers if they tried harder? Explain.

4. In 1940, according to the Bureau of Labor Statistics, there were 9,540,000 persons employed in agriculture. The population of the United States in 1940 was 132,122,000. In 1970 the corresponding figures were 3,462,000 farmers in a population of 205,395,000. Thus in 1940 it took one farmer to provide agricultural produce for every 14 Americans. Thirty years later one farmer could take care of almost 60 people.

   a. What made this dramatic change possible?
   b. What happened to the "excess" farmers? Where did they go?
   c. What factors induced people to move out of agricultural employment?

5. Under a closed-shop arrangement, employers may hire only workers who are already union members. Under a union-shop arrangement, employers may hire whomever they please but the employees must then join the union. What

different effects would you expect these alternative arrangements to have on wages? On employment? On discrimination by the union against members of minority races? Why?

6. College professors in the United States have never had an effective union. Then why did their average wage rise spectacularly in the 1960s? How might college professors have used unionization to obtain even larger salary increases over this period? Why might some professors be interested in a law that prohibited anyone without an earned doctorate from teaching in colleges? What consequences would you predict if a few states passed such a law?

7. Do high wage rates in such strongly unionized industries as steel and automobiles pull up the general level of wages in nonunionized, lower-wage industries? If you think they do, what is the process by which this occurs? If contracts that call for high wages reduce employment opportunities in the industries that must pay these wages, where do the excluded workers find employment?

8. How would each of the following groups be affected by a large increase in the legal minimum wage?
   a. Unionized workers
   b. Teenagers
   c. Unskilled workers

9. A plumbers local in Fort Lauderdale, Florida voluntarily lowered the hourly rate for union workers on low-rise construction projects from $10.70 to $6.90 an hour (in June 1972). The $10.70 rate continued to apply to high-rise construction. The business manager of the union said this was being done to curb inflation and help homeowners. Do you think it might also have been done because nonunion plumbers were available in the area at $4.50 to $5 an hour? Why do you suppose the union did not lower the rate on high-rise construction work?

10. The five states with the highest median family incomes in 1975 were Alaska, Hawaii, Maryland, New Jersey, and Connecticut, in that order.
   a. How would you explain this?
   b. The median family income in Alaska in 1975 was $22,432. The other four states ranged from $17,770 to $16,244. Are people in Alaska as wealthy as these figures might suggest?
   c. The lowest median family incomes, ranging from $9,999 up to $11,785, were in the states of Mississippi, Arkansas, Kentucky, Tennessee, and Alabama. How would you account for the low average incomes in these states?

11. Do the relative salaries of humanities professors and football coaches at major state universities reflect the relative value of football and humanities? Do they reflect the number of years that professors and coaches must spend acquiring an education? The number of hours they work? The difficulty or unpleasantness of their work? Why do the football coaches usually receive salaries that are so much higher?

12. Why does the National Collegiate Athletic Association (NCAA) set limits to the value of inducements that colleges can offer prospective athletes in an effort to attract them? Why does it penalize schools that exceed these limits?

Isn't it true, after all, that the school itself is hurt if it spends more on recruiting an athlete? Is the NCAA protecting its member schools against the costly consequences of their own generosity?

13. A television station whose physical facilities could be replaced for $2 million is sold for $22 million. For what was the extra $20 million a payment? What happens when the Federal Communications Commission revokes a license of a station and awards it to another ownership group?

14. If you know that a license to operate a taxicab in New York City can be purchased from an existing license holder for $80,000, what could you infer about the profitability of operating a taxicab in New York City? What actions by the city could raise or lower the market value of a license?

15. Alpha and Beta are identical twins. Alpha takes a job right after high school, because she thinks four years of college would be an eternity and she wants a sporty car. Beta believes her sister is foolish; she intends to go to college, take an additional two years to earn an MBA, and make far more money than Alpha will ever see.

   a. Why does the fact that Beta's income will be far larger than Alpha's after six years not necessarily mean that Alpha made a foolish decision from the standpoint of monetary income?

   b. Use the tables of Chapter 11 to compare (1) the present value at age 17 of $10,000 per year to age 65, with (2) the present value of $20,000 per year to age 65 when the latter income doesn't start until age 23. Compare these amounts at discount rates of 18 percent and again at discount rates of 6 percent.

   c. Would it be irrational for Alpha to discount future income at a rate of 18 percent? For Beta to discount at 6 percent?

16. In each of the cases described below, an increase in the family's monetary income puts all members of the original family into families with lower incomes. Explain how this occurs. Does it imply that the individuals involved are worse off? What important questions does it raise about the interpretation of family income data?

   a. An elderly couple living with their married son receives an increase in social security benefits that permits the couple to obtain their own apartment.

   b. Two married people who fight constantly and stay together only because they can't afford to maintain two homes separate with great relief when both receive promotions and raises, each taking one of the children.

   c. The husband of an orthopedic surgeon quits his job to stay home, tend the house, and give the children better care when his wife's practice begins to earn a very large income.

17. The claim is often made—and also often ridiculed—that taxes on income reduce people's incentives to earn income.

   a. If you were required to pay the government 50 percent of all money income you earn during the summer, would you choose to work more or fewer hours than if your income was not subject to tax? Would you look for ways to raise your income without raising your money income or taxable income?

   b. How does a 50 percent marginal tax rate (additional taxes divided by additional income) affect the cost to a physician of building his own home rather than hiring a contractor?

c. An unmarried woman with three preschool children has no earned income but is receiving $200 a month in cash welfare assistance, plus food stamps worth $100 a month and government-financed medical care worth $50 a month. She is offered a job that will pay $500 a month. If she takes the job, she will no longer be eligible for any of the cash or in-kind assistance. What is the marginal tax rate to which her earnings are subject? Would you take the job in her situation?

18. A substantial number of government programs are specifically intended to improve the relative position of lower income groups. In addition, government economic policies in other areas are often formulated in ways designed to avoid harming lower income groups. Such policies are usually defended on the grounds that they promote greater justice in the distribution of income.

a. Can you defend the assertion that the distribution of income which emerges from the interactions of demand and supply is just? Can you defend the assertion that it is unjust?

b. How would you define a just distribution (or an unjust distribution) of income?

c. If the preceding question is too difficult, perhaps you can define a *more* just (or less unjust) distribution of income.

d. Two common but very different ways to define justice are in terms of *rules* and in terms of *results*. We usually define a just (or fair) game of any sort in terms of rules: were the rules clearly stated, known and accepted in advance, and impartially enforced? We do not use the game's final score as a test of its fairness. On the other hand, we are likely to assess the justice with which food, clothing, and other goods are distributed among children in a family in terms of results: does each child receive an equal share except insofar as differences among the children clearly call for unequal shares? Few would want to define a just distribution of income among children in terms of impartial rules regarding competition for goods.

Which of these provides better criteria for assessing the justice or injustice of the income distribution in a society such as the United States?

Chapter **13**

Pollution and Conflicting Rights

Many people have concluded in recent years that the growing problem of pollution demonstrates the inadequacy of a purely economic point of view. That position is vigorously rejected in this chapter. Ecology and economics are very closely related, as a matter of fact, and in more than the common Greek stem of the words. Ecology in the narrow sense is a branch of biology that deals with the interrelations between organisms and their environment. In the broader meaning of the word, it is a point of view, an informing conviction that everything ultimately depends upon everything else. Actions prompt reactions; the reactions set the stage for all future actions. And that is also the point of view of economic theory. Economics and ecology are allies, not competitors or antagonists.

The economist maintains that, if pollution is a growing problem in our society, it is because we have allowed or even encouraged people to neglect certain important costs. The problem requires for its solution that we find ways to correct this neglect. If, like Stephen Leacock's Lord Ronald, we fling ourselves upon a horse and ride madly off in all directions, we are not likely to find acceptable solutions.

Pollution Is a Cost

A good way to begin is by noticing that pollution is a cost. It is a cost created during the production of goods, and in that respect it is not essentially different from any other cost. Pollution, like all costs, represents opportunities forgone: opportunities to breathe clean air, fish or swim in sparkling streams, enjoy pleasant vistas, find solace in solitude, listen to birds sing, or eat fish without fear of mercury poisoning. All these activities are goods. They are valued opportunities that many must now forgo because they have been sacrificed for the sake of other goods.

To think about pollution in this way recalls us from Utopia to the real world where there are many goods, almost all of them scarce, desired with different intensities by different people, with varying marginal costs of production. Pollution cannot be eliminated simply by banning all activities that damage the environment. The opportunity costs of doing that would be far too high to make it politically feasible, or even acceptable to anyone at all who really thought about it. What we actually want is *the optimal amount of environmental damage.* No more. But no less either. We want to reduce such damage as long as the marginal social benefit of doing so exceeds the marginal social cost. And we want to *expand* it—heresy!—whenever the marginal social benefit of doing that exceeds the marginal social cost.

No one lobbies for more environmental damage, of course. But people do want a lot of goods whose production or use entails exactly that. Perhaps they should not want these goods, or would not want them if they fully knew the consequences. Those are difficult and debatable assertions. The economist makes a somewhat different assertion with considerable confidence: People *will* want less of such goods if they are themselves forced to pay more of the unpleasant consequences of having or using them.

It's just our old friend the law of demand in another set of clothes. The quantity of anything demanded decreases as its price increases. "Not so," comes that voice from the rear, which has been silent through several chapters. "We are right now paying a heavy price for pollution in the form of ugliness, discomfort, destruction, and disease. But people go right on polluting in disregard of the consequences."

The voice from the rear has made a point and missed the point. The law of demand does not predict that Rod will drive his car less because Tom, Dick, and Harry must now pay more to let him do so. Rod responds to *his own costs and benefits as he perceives them.* Whether or not we decide that this is selfish and inconsiderate on the part of Rod, we had better not decide

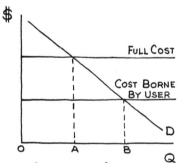

Only OA rather than OB would be demanded if user had to pay the full cost.

to pretend that Rod will behave otherwise or to put all our eggs in the basket of moral restraint.

Internalizing Costs

The core of the pollution problem is what the economist calls *externalities*. These are *spillover costs or benefits*: consequences of action that are not taken into account by the actor and which therefore do not influence his decisions.

Individuals engage in activities for the sake of the benefits they expect to receive, after taking into account the associated costs they expect to bear. But the full costs and benefits of activities are never confined entirely to the actor. They may be spread out over many other people. In some instances they cannot even be traced to the activities of the people who created them. When people make decisions solely on the basis of the costs they themselves bear and the benefits they incur, but those decisions entail substantial additional costs or benefits to others, a serious misallocation of resources may result.

The spillover effects of people's choices tend to become larger, more significant, and more difficult to predict, measure, or control as a society becomes increasingly industrialized and urbanized. This suggests that we should now give more careful attention to ways of *assigning responsibility to people for the consequences of their actions, persuading them to internalize more externalities* (to use the barbarous terminology of economic theory). That brings us back once again to the concept of property rights.

What Is *Private* Property?

Do you believe in the importance of private property? Think carefully before you answer. There seems to be little that is private about much of what we call "private" property, and a surprising amount of private rights are connected with what we call "public" property. What exactly do we mean by *private* property?

Property comes from the Latin *proprius*, meaning "one's own." When is something one's own, and when is it not? We have already seen in Chapter 12 that *legal* ownership may not carry with it the expectations that we usually associate with ownership, and that *the person who expects to appropriate the benefits* from using a resource might better be regarded as the owner of that resource. When we look at ownership in this way, we see clearly that *private* property is inevitably a matter of degree.

If you are the legal owner of an automobile in our society, what can you realistically expect from that fact? You can probably expect to drive the car when you please and to grant or withhold permisson for others to drive it. You can also expect to see dirty oil on the dipstick and bald tires on the wheels until you do something to replace them. Underline that last sentence. Ownership isn't merely an assignment of privileges—it is also an assignment of responsibilities. People take good care of cars or other property when they believe that the flow of benefits to themselves depends on such care. That simple principle goes a long way toward explaining why the same people will sometimes "leave it to George" and at other times will prefer to "do it themselves."

But the expectations you may reasonably hold as the owner of the car are much more complex than this. You may not expect to drive it north very far on a southbound one-way street. You will not be able to prosecute successfully other drivers who splash mud on your automobile. And under certain circumstances, you will be prosecuted yourself if you transport people for hire. Moreover, your right to drive your car when you please will be largely fictitious if the police can't prevent theft of tires, spark plugs, or the entire automobile. And of what value is your right to drive when you please if there are no roads, or the streets that you want to travel are choked with other vehicles, or there are so many drunk and reckless drivers in the community that the probability of returning alive from the supermarket is only 80 percent?

The property rights of an automobile owner are the complete set of actions the owner expects to be able to take with that automobile. In a society, *any* society, those actions just won't be possible without the cooperation of other people. Some of the cooperation will be active, and some of it will be passive. Owners expect active cooperation when they pull into a gas station and offer to trade money for gasoline. They expect passive cooperation from drivers on the intersecting street when the traffic signal gives them a green light. You don't have a real right to buy gasoline if no one accepts an obligation to provide it to you. You don't actually have the right of way on a green light if the crossing drivers don't accept the obligation to stop on red. Rights for some always imply corresponding obligations for others. We would have a much better understandng of the way the social world works if we began to appreciate the extent of our dependence on the cooperation of others.

Clear Rights rather than Private Rights

Private property consequently cannot entail an absolute and unlimited right to do as one pleases, because doing as one pleases must at some point interfere with the ability of others to do as they please. The important question about property is not the question of *private* rights; the very phrase is a contradiction in terms, if rights for anyone always entail obligations for someone else. The important question is the *clarity* with which rights are defined, the *stability* of the expectations that constitute rights, and the *confidence* with which people can predict exactly what they will be able to do.

Let's go back to our initial definition of pollution. Pollution, we said, is a cost created in producing goods. But which costs qualify as pollution? Only those costs are pollution that are inflicted on other people *without their consent*. The problem of pollution is the problem of negative externalities, which simply means costs imposed on others who have not consented to bear those costs. This implies that pollution always involves a disagreement about property rights: a disagreement about which set of conflicting expectations ought to be satisfied. Pollution is eliminated *not* by eliminating environmental damage, which is an impossibility anyway, but by resolving disagreements over property rights.

An Analysis of Airport Noise

Does this make sense? Let's try it out. Commercial jets make a lot of noise. Is the noise pollution? It is not pollution to airport baggage handlers, because they consent to be subjected to the noise. Their consent is secured by the payment of a wage. Is the noise pollution to families who live near the airport? It is if they bought their house before the airport was contemplated. The noise of the jets deprives them of peace and quiet without their consent.

Now change the situation. Suppose the airport authorities buy all the adjacent land at prices that reflect the land's value before the planning of the airport. Then, after the airport is finished, the airport authorities resell the land for whatever price buyers consent to pay. Those who build or buy homes on this land will hear the noise of the jets, but the noise will not be pollution, because they have consented to bear it. They knew about the noise when they bought, but presumably decided that the lower price for the land was adequate compensation for the noise of the jets.

Let's introduce a further change in the situation. The people who bought their houses after the airport had been constructed, fully knowing about the noise, may now decide to lobby the city council for noise abatement restrictions. If they succeed and the airlines are required to eliminate all flights before 7 A.M. and after 10 P.M., the airlines then become, in an important sense, the victims of pollution. The new noise abatement rules deprive the airlines of valuable opportunities. The restrictions impose costs on the airlines without securing their consent.

Conflicting Rights

But should those costs be called pollution? There is little point in arguing about what we're going to call something. It is important, however, that we clearly see what is happening, and that we not suppose we have solved a problem when we have only created a new one to take its place. The characteristic of jet noise that we must not overlook is its association with valuable opportunities. Jet noise is not created around airports in order to bedevil the neighbors but is a by-product in the production of the valuable service of rapid transportation. We could without doubt eliminate jet noise by eliminating jet airplanes. But would the gain in peace and quiet be enough to outweigh the loss to all those who want to travel quickly between distant points? That is the question.

We pointed out way back in Chapter 2 that the demand is never completely inelastic for *any* good, not even for the good of clean air. With clean air, as with peace and quiet, we must decide exactly how much we want—in view of the fact that more can be obtained only by giving up increasing amounts of other goods that we also want. It would all be so much simpler if we had to choose only between the wicked polluters and the virtuous citizens. This kind of choice is so easy and appealing, in fact, that we often succumb to the temptation of defining the problem in exclusively moral terms. *Industry* and *corporations* and *vested interests* want to foul our streams, darken our air, cut down our forests, strip-mine our land, and destroy our heritage for the sake of "their" profits. Who would hesitate a moment in deciding between the conflicting claims of greedy exploiters and "the American people"? But those who pose the issues in this way are either engaging in propaganda or deceiving themselves. Our actual choices are almost always choices between the legitimate expectations of some and the legitimate expectations of others.

Moreover, we have confused the issue for ourselves by identifying pollution with environmental damage. The flaw in this identification is that it fails to indicate when and why pollution is a problem. Everything, including the simple act of breathing, damages the environment, whereas many polluting acts do not damage the biological environment in any accepted sense of that term. Actions that alter the environment do not become problems until they infringe on someone's expectations. The infallible sign of pollution is the statement, "You have no right to do that, because it interferes with my right to do this." Pollution exists when people's expectations about what they can and may do come into conflict. Pollution is eliminated when disagreements about property rights are resolved—when those who formerly protested the actions of others consent to those actions.

An Impossible Goal

"That's absurd," says the voice from the rear in an unmistakable tone of disgust. "People's expectations will always conflict to some extent. People in a large society like ours are bound to disagree about who has which rights. We can't expect everybody to consent to absolutely everything that other people want to do. With your definition of pollution, pollution would be impossible to get rid of."

Precisely. There may be no more important lesson for us to learn about pollution than that pollution so thoroughly permeates our society that we cannot realistically hope to eliminate it. Pollution exists when teenagers play their transistor radios and thereby infringe on the right of other bus passengers to enjoy peace and quiet; pollution still exists, though in a changed form, when the other bus passengers infringe on the teenagers' right to hear music by enforcing their own desire for peace and quiet. Pollution exists when a rose lover cultivates his bushes and thereby infringes on the right of rose-fever victims to breathe easily; the pollution does not disappear but only changes its form when the rose-fever sufferers infringe on the right of the rose lover to enjoy those blooms.

Traffic on a residential street imposes costs on the homeowners which they would like to eliminate. But sealing off one end of the street imposes costs on the drivers who are now compelled to take a less satisfactory route. A coal-burning utility pumping sulphur dioxide into the air is imposing costs on people in the vicinity of the plant. But if those people compel the utility to burn more expensive low-sulfur coal, they are imposing costs on consumers of the utility's electricity. Pollution means that rights are in conflict and poses the question: Whose rights ought to prevail?

Reducing Pollution: The First Steps

We want to turn our attention in the rest of this chapter to four procedures for reducing pollution or maintaining it within acceptable bounds. The first is the cultivation of the civic virtues of empathy, courtesy, humility, and tolerance among the members of a society. Civilization will simply be impossible among a people who do not possess substantial amounts of these virtues. If people insist on obtaining absolutely everything to which they think they have a right, civilization will give way to warfare. But how to cultivate or renew these virtues where they have withered—that is a question far beyond the scope of this book. We would do well to remember, however, that the other procedures for controlling pollution that we shall now examine—negotiation, adjudication, and legislation—presuppose these virtues to some extent, because they presuppose an established society, and they work more effectively the more widely these virtues are practiced.

Reducing Pollution by Negotiation

Our everyday garden-variety procedure for minimizing pollution is *negotiation*. We strike bargains with one another. People consent to bear the costs associated with the production of particular goods because other people who want those goods offer compensation that makes it worth their while. That is why baggage handlers don't complain about jet noise, why the grease on the clothes of an automobile mechanic is not pollution, and why the owner of a dog kennel will cheerfully let other people's dogs perform the same task that arouses an urban lawn fancier to fury.

"Work it out for yourselves" is sound advice. Because people differ so widely in their tastes, talents, and other circumstances, they will often be able to negotiate an exchange of costs that makes everyone involved better off than before. Moreover, the necessity of working it out for themselves encourages cooperation among those who are in the best position to know the possibilities. When people are not required to negotiate, they often adopt positions that are costly to others. For example, they demand legislation that would prohibit smoking in restaurants, rather than ask for a table where no smoke will blow. And they point indignantly to minute traces of tobacco smoke in the air, while ignoring the dangerous emissions that they themselves put in the atmosphere by driving to the restaurant.

Negotiation produces accommodation, or mutual gains from exchange.

We would probably have a much greater respect for negotiation as a social procedure for reducing pollution if we learned to recognize the myriad of ways in which we actually use it. People who hate the noise and dirt of the city move to outlying areas. People who detest the culture of suburbia live in small towns. People who despise the isolation of rural life choose to live in the city. The hard-of-hearing get residential real estate bargains under airport approach lanes. Surfboard riders seek out companions and thereby voluntarily segregate themselves from swimmers who hate to dodge surfboards. The afternoon naptaker pays $1.59 for a box of wax earstoppers and thereafter lives in peace with the neighboring teen-ager's mufflerless motorcycle. Not everyone is perfectly happy even in the best of all possible worlds. But voluntary exchange does reduce the total of costs imposed on reluctant bystanders. It's far from the worst of all possible worlds.

Negotiation cannot be effective, however, unless property rights are clearly defined. Voluntary exchange of any sort works well only when all involved parties agree on who owns what. In some cases, a clarification of property rights may be all that stands in the way of a mutually satisfactory agreement.

Suppose, for example, that Smith and Brown disagree by two feet on the location of the boundary line dividing their properties. It wouldn't matter much, since both want to plant flowers in the disputed strip, except for the fact that Smith wants to plant marigolds and zinnias—while Brown has his heart set on pansies and petunias. Until the question of who has a right to do what is settled, neither one will plant flowers, and both will be living with the distinctly inferior alternative of dandelions and crab grass.

If they then hire a surveyor who proves that Smith in fact owns the disputed strip, flowers can finally bloom. Nor will the flowers necessarily be marigolds and zinnias! Once it is clearly established that Smith is the owner and hence has the right to decide what will grow in the boundary strip, Brown may be able to purchase that right. Brown's passion for pansies and petunias could be so powerful that he offers Smith $25 a year for the right to grow them between their lots. And if Smith prefers pansies and petunias *with $25* to marigolds and zinnias without $25, the flowers that bloom will be pansies and petunias.

Reducing Pollution by Adjudication

In introducing the boundary surveyor, we introduced another important social procedure for reducing pollution: *adjudication,* by which we mean a process for deciding who actually has which rights. People will not be able to improve their positions through the exchange of rights if they aren't sure what rights anyone has to begin with. Clearly defined property rights are not a sufficient condition for successful negotiations, but they do seem to be a necessary condition.

It is important at this point to recall the economist's definition of property rights; namely, the expectations of the owner about what he or she can and may do with the resource in question. Property rights that might once have been clearly and adequately defined can become vague and uncertain when surrounding circumstances change, for the simple reason that what one person is able to do will often depend on what other people are able to do.

Clearly established property rights facilitate negotiation.

Adjudication clarifies property rights.

The development of low-cost photocopying techniques, to take one example, created an enormous amount of uncertainty about what copyright holders could realistically expect to sell in view of the new capability that photocopy machines gave to every possessor of a book. When evolving circumstances make previously compatible property rights incompatible, adjudication is one way of settling the conflict.

We are using the term *adjudication* to refer specifically to the kind of resolution that the surveyor provided: a resolution that *discovers* who has which rights. The surveyor answered the question, Who owns the boundary strip? by investigating, not by choosing. If Smith and Brown had agreed to flip a coin, they would have relied on a procedure that does not discover but rather *creates* property rights. The distinction between the discovery and the creation of property rights is an important one, because *discovery or adjudication aims at maintaining the continuity of expectations*. At the end of Chapter 12 we emphasized the importance of stable expectations in securing effective cooperation among the members of a society. When expectations change radically, supply and demand decisions also change radically. That, in turn, alters in unpredicted ways the relative costs and benefits of all kinds of actions and so induces additional changes in supply and demand. In short, if no one knows what to expect, no one knows what to do or what others will do. The result is chaos. Stable expectations are another of those realities whose importance we have not learned to recognize, because we don't notice how society is working whenever it's working well.

The Case of the Complaining Homeowner

We can use the airport example once more to bring out the importance of adjudication, or the discovery rather than creation of rights, in resolving disputes over property rights. Bill Hinks, who owns a house 10 miles from a major airport but directly under the principal approach route, may decide one morning—when his sleep has been interrupted by commerical jets—that he deserves compensation. The airport or the airlines ought to pay him something, he decides, for depriving him of the opportunity to use his bedroom as a place of rest and renewal. He is the victim of pollution, of costs imposed upon him without his consent. So he files suit demanding compensation.

Ought he to get it? Is he likely to get it? Assume that Bill bought the house before the airport was even thought about, so that no one can say he knew the situation when he bought and has already received his compensation in the form of a lower purchase price. He is consequently, by our definition, the victim of pollution. The noise pollution to which he is subject could be eliminated if he were paid the amount by which the airport reduces the market price of his house. But *should* he be compensated?

The trouble is that there are thousands of homeowners with equally valid claims. If one receives compensation, all ought to receive compensation. But if all receive compensation, a heavy cost will be imposed on the airport and the airlines, who will pass that cost along to airline passengers in the form of higher ticket prices.

At first glance that might seem fair enough. The higher prices will compel airline passengers to pay the costs of the noise that is created as a by-product of their travel. We will have internalized an externality by requiring the payment of compensation. But now a new problem forces itself upon our attention. Externalities run throughout society. Shall we internalize them all? Shall homeowners receive compensation for the automobile traffic that goes past, the dandelions that their neighbors let go to seed, the passing gifts of dog-walkers and their pets, the noise of the neighborhood children, the sound of power mowers, the spreading chestnut tree next door that blocks their view, as well as the loss of the shade if their neighbor cuts down the spreading chestnut tree because it blocks *his* view? When we are through with homeowners, we can start ordering the compensation of pedestrians, many of whom suffer from the same externalities that afflict homeowners. Perhaps we could, in the final stages of our effort to internalize all externalities, impose fines on especially dull people in order to compensate those whom they bore.

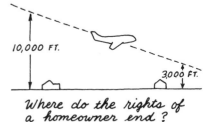

Where do the rights of a homeowner end?

We just can't do that. There are too many externalities; the appropriate compensations would be too difficult to determine. Even the direction in which compensation ought to be paid won't always be clear. Wouldn't it be just as much in order, for example, to levy fines on inattentive people to compensate the bores whose sensitivities they offend? Who says bores are worse than boors?

The Importance of Precedents

We are ready for the question: *Should* the homeowner 10 miles from the airport be compensated by airline passengers for the inconvenience he suffers as a result of the flights from which they benefit? Our answer: It would be extraordinarily difficult and probably impossible to do so in a way that was both practical and fair.

We originally asked *two* questions, however. The second question asked whether homeowners in such circumstances were *likely to receive compensation*. The answer to this question is almost certainly *no*. The courts would attempt to decide the issue by *discovering* what rights the contending parties have, and homeowners would end up with very little to show on their behalf. The ruling consideration would almost surely be this: that homeowners and those in the business of providing airline transportation have proceeded for a long time on the expectation that no such compensation must be paid. *These expectations are the respective property rights of homeowners and airlines.*

We could prove that homeowners 10 miles from the airport do not have a right to be compensated for the noise, simply by showing that the market price of homes under the approach route would jump sharply if the court decision held in favor of the homeowner. This would be an *unexpected event* that would create windfall profits for homeowners and windfall losses for holders of airline stock. The appearance of these windfalls would be conclusive evidence that the affected parties did not believe such compensation was owed, and that the court decision had consequently *created* property rights that had not existed previously.

There is a qualification to this conclusion that further establishes the point we are making. If a judge held for the homeowner in such a case, the price of affected houses might rise very little, because prospective home buyers would probably be advised that the judge had erred and was likely to be reversed on appeal. The concept of error is instructive. There can be no error when the decision *creates* the rights. Error is possible only when the decision seeks to *discover* what the rights are that actually prevail and therefore ought to govern the outcome of the case.

Adjudication, or the attempt to resolve conflicting claims by seeking to discover existing rights, always tries to avoid unexpected decisions or outcomes. It tries to settle disagreements over property rights by supporting and reinforcing *the expectations that are most widely and confidently held.* Adjudication is thus an effort to maintain the continuity of expectations in the presence of changing circumstances. And stable expectations, we remind you once more, are the foundation of effective cooperation in any large, complex society.

The Problem of Radical Change

Adjudication is an evolutionary approach to the problem of pollution. But sometimes changes don't occur at an evolutionary pace. When we're overtaken by events so novel that established principles and practices don't furnish any guidance in dealing with them, adjudication cannot work. Technological innovations often force rapid changes upon us in a wide variety of situations. Snowmobiles, pesticides, radar-assisted whaling ships, antibiotics, and nuclear reactors are just a few of the many examples that could be cited from recent years. When technological innovation radically expands our capacity to inflict costs upon others without obtaining their consent, new rules may be required to maintain the level of pollution within tolerable limits.

The demand for new definitions of property rights has also been created by rising incomes. Not too many years ago Americans seemed to have had a working consensus that the social advantages from allowing the atmosphere to be used as an industrial dump were greater than the disadvantages. Our laws and customs decreed that the atmosphere belonged to everyone and therefore to no one, so that factory owners were free to use it as a receptacle for industrial wastes. People could move away from factories, or purchase residential space near the factories at a low price if they preferred that saving to the delights of clean air. Meanwhile factories held their costs down by discharging wastes into the atmosphere, and this meant a greater availability of the goods that factories produced. But the situation has changed. The goods that factories produce are now available in much larger quantities, and many people have begun to place a lower relative valuation on them. When we begin to place a higher relative value on blue skies and clean air, we start to think of them as our *right*. We start to claim a property right in these environmental goods and demand that others stop putting them to uses that are incompatible with our ability to enjoy them. That requires new rules, not just an application of the old rules to new situations.

Reducing Pollution by Legislation

We call the creation of new rules *legislation*. The line between adjudication and legislation is not as clear in practice as all this pretends. But the distinction is important in principle, because legislation creates changes in prevailing property rights, and changing the "rules of the game" always raises the question of fairness and often compels major adjustments in behavior. The challenge for a society that wants to reduce pollution is to legislate in ways that avoid gross injustices and that minimize the cost of achieving the objectives. We shall focus on the second of those criteria, not because it is more important, but only because economic theory has more to say about inefficiency than about injustice.

Physical Restrictions on Polluters

The legislation of uniform physical restrictions is a popular approach to the problem of pollution. After some date, no one is allowed to discharge more than so many particles of this or that into the air or the water system. This approach will usually fail to minimize the cost per unit of pollution reduction. It ignores the variety of ways in which a given objective can usually be achieved, and therefore offers no incentives to people to search for and implement the least costly alternative. We're going to use a very simplified example to illustrate some principles of pollution control that deserve to be better understood and more widely appreciated.

Suppose that everything which fouls the air over the city of Springfield comes from three sources: automobiles, utilities, and factories. The table below shows the quantities of polluting material put into the air of Springfield monthly by each source. It also shows the cost to each polluter of eliminating the objectionable emissions. (You will notice that the analysis treats each of the three sources as a *single decision-making unit*, to keep the analysis simple enough to be useful.)

	Units of Obnoxious Material Emitted Monthly	Cost of Eliminating Emissions, per Unit
Automobiles	20,000	$ 5
Utilities	30,000	10
Factories	40,000	20

Now let us suppose that the Environmental Protection Agency (EPA) decides to improve the air quality over Springfield by securing a reduction of monthly emissions from the present total of 90,000 to a tolerable total of 60,000. (We'll pass by the question for now of how the EPA decides that 60,000 is the tolerable level.) There are many ways to reach that objective. The EPA could set 20,000 as the maximum allowable emissions from each source, or require each source to reduce its emissions by 10,000, or order a one-third reduction in emissions by each source. Let's compare the costs of each approach.

Setting a 20,000 unit ceiling on each source would achieve the goal at a total cost of $500,000. Utilities would pay $10 for each of the 10,000 units by which they reduce their emissions, factories would pay $20 for each of the 20,000 units by which they reduce their emissions, and automobiles would escape all costs, because they're already at the target level.

Requiring each source to reduce emissions by 10,000 units would achieve the goal at a total cost of $350,000. Automobiles would pay $50,000, utilities $100,000, and factories $200,000. This is clearly a less costly way to reach the goal.

Ordering a one-third reduction by all sources would result in total costs of $400,000: $33,333 to the automobiles, $100,000 to the utilities, and $266,667 to the factories. From the standpoint of cost minimization, that's better than the first solution but not as good as the second.

There is an even less costly way to go, however. The EPA would minimize the cost of achieving its objective if it ordered a 20,000 unit reduction by automobiles and a 10,000 unit reduction by utilities and left the factories alone. The total cost of getting pollution down from 90,000 to 60,000 units by this method would be $200,000: $100,000 paid by the automobiles and $100,000 paid by the utilities. Would the EPA be likely to choose this approach?

Another Approach: Taxing Emissions

Let's defer that question and examine the problem further. Suppose that the EPA does not actually know how much it will cost per unit to reduce pollution from each source. That's much more plausible than our original assumption, for several reasons. The polluters themselves will be in the best position to know the actual costs, but they will also have an incentive to exaggerate their costs in pleadings before the EPA or the public. Moreover, exaggeration will not be wholly dishonest, because one never knows for certain the costs of something that hasn't yet been tried, and it's just ordinary prudence to estimate them high, especially if higher estimates mean the costs are less likely to be imposed. Finally, though costs can usually be reduced through research and experiment, no one can predict the results that research and experiment will produce. What is the least-cost solution when the EPA is faced with this kind of information scarcity?

The EPA would gain the applause of many economists if it responded to this situation by imposing a tax per unit of pollution and then allowed each polluter to respond as it thought best. If you're willing to grant that pollution is a negative externality, a cost not borne by its producer, placing a tax on polluting activities makes good sense. If the tax per unit of pollutant can somehow be set equal to the spillover cost per unit, the externality is fully internalized. The creator and presumed beneficiary of the costs is made to bear them.

If that makes the polluting activity too costly to continue, it will cease, as it should if its costs are greater than its benefits. If the benefits still outweigh the costs when the tax is being paid, then the polluting activity will continue, though at a lesser rate because it is now more costly. But in that case the tax revenue will be available to compensate—to buy the consent of—those upon whom the spillover costs are falling.

In the Springfield case, any tax rate between $5 and $10

will reduce pollution by 20,000 units per month. It will induce the automobiles to avoid the tax by choosing the lesser cost alternative of eliminating their obnoxious emissions. Utilities will choose to avoid the tax when it rises above $10 per unit of pollution, so that a tax rate of $11 would reduce pollution by 50 thousand units per month, while simultaneously garnering $440,000 in revenue with which to compensate the suffering citizens of Springfield for the continuing pollution from the factories.

As we have set up the problem, there is no tax rate that achieves a reduction to exactly 60,000 units: $9.99 would lower pollution to only 70,000 units, while $10.01 would lower it all the way to 40,000 units. In the real world, costs would not be the same for all levels of pollution reduction, but would be relatively low for small percentage reductions from each source and extremely high as we approached 100 percent. The pursuit of perfection is almost always prohibitively expensive.

But the inability of *any* tax rate to achieve some particular physical target is not so much a criticism of the tax approach to pollution control as a criticism of physical targets. Why aim at 60,000 units? *Every* unit is a bad, so why not eliminate them all? The answer, as you know by this time, is that there are costs of eliminating those costs which we call pollution. The task for the EPA is to compare the marginal costs of reducing pollution with the marginal costs that are avoided by reducing pollution, or the marginal benefits. The use of taxes enables the EPA to acquire informaton about these costs and benefits by observing what happens when variously estimated pollution costs are assessed against the polluters. It's an approach that lends itself to learning by experimentation. And obtaining reliable information about costs and benefits is essential to any program of environmental protection that is concerned with human well-being.

The Issue of Fairness

Let's go back now to a question that we asked but deferred answering. After comparing the costs of four different ways of reducing Springfield air pollution to 60,000 units per month, we asked whether the EPA was likely in such a situation to choose the least costly approach. We put off answering in order to argue that physical directives of any sort were generally inferior to taxes as a way of controlling pollution. But the tax approach is not popular with the public for a reason that would also make it difficult for the EPA to issue the least costly set of physical directives. *It doesn't seem fair.* Taxes on pollution have acquired the derogatory label, "licenses to pollute," and they are widely rejected because they supposedly place the whole burden of reducing pollution on the poor, while allowing the rich to go right on fouling the environment. Choosing the people who must reduce their pollution on the basis of the cost to them of doing so, which is required by the least-cost solution, also seems arbitrary and unjust to many people.

The "license to pollute" argument, however, is confused from the outset. If pollution is a cost inflicted on others without their consent, people who secure consent by paying the cost are no longer polluting. It's true enough that they will still be imposing costs on others. But there's nothing at all wrong with that as long as they compensate others for the opportunities forgone. If people object that the tax they pay isn't enough to make up for the costs they create, they are really saying that the tax rate should be increased, not that such taxes are a "license to pollute."

Exchange and Efficiency in Pollution Control

The best reply to those who raise the fairness issue, however, is to show that the *efficient* solution can be achieved while settling the *fairness* issue in different ways. In other words, we do not necessarily commit ourselves to place the costs on any particular parties when we select the most efficient solution. The Springfield case can again provide our illustration.

Suppose that the EPA wants to impose the entire cost of pollution reduction on the factories, whether because the factories can best afford it or because they have long been the heaviest polluters or because everyone in Springfield dislikes them. All the EPA need do is tell the factories that they will have to pay a tax of $10.05 for each unit of pollution emitted monthly in excess of 60,000, regardless of the pollution's source. The factories will then look for the least costly way to deal with this situation. If they have all the information that we have, they will offer the automobiles $100,000 to eliminate all their pollution and offer the utilities $100,000 to reduce their pollution by 10,000 units.

The factories will thus reduce the level of pollution in Springfield to 60,000 units. They will do so to avoid a tax of $303,000. But rather than reduce their own emissions by 30,000 units, which would cost the factories $600,000, they will pay the most efficient pollution-reducers in the city $200,000 to do the job for them.

Pollution reduction is a lot like any other useful activity in that some are more efficient at it than others. Just as we gain from having our food, toys, and cosmetics produced by those with a comparative advantage in their production, so we gain by having additional clean air produced by those with the greatest comparative advantage at the job. But comparative advantages are exploited through exchange. That is why the tax approach to pollution reduction is in general superior to an approach that assigns physical restrictions to particular firms. The tax approach tries to correct relative money costs so that they more accurately reflect actual costs to the members of society. But it then leaves all parties free to trade on the basis of their own comparative advantages and to secure the new social goals in the most efficient manner.

Progress and Regress at the EPA

In December 1978 the Environmental Protection Agency took a step in the direction suggested by this analysis when it proposed new regulations that would permit more trade-offs among pollution sources. Rather than set rigid limits on allowable emissions from particular production processes, enforcement agencies would permit firms to exceed the limits in one process if they could compensate by reducing emissions from another process. Under this policy, firms could lower the cost of achieving a target level of environmental quality by allowing emissions to rise where their control is most costly and reducing them where reductions are possible at the least cost. Some EPA officials have also suggested that firms be allowed to buy and sell rights to pollute the air, a proposal that neatly incorporates the principles outlined in this chapter. This has already been done, in effect, where companies desiring to build plants in an area have satisfied air-quality standards by paying other companies to reduce their emissions. It makes good sense. Why should an oil company pay $150 million for pollution control equipment in a refinery it wants to build if it can obtain the same results in air quality by building the refinery without the pollution control equipment and purchasing $75 million of pollution control equipment for a neighboring power plant?

EPA reports unfortunately don't always show the firm grasp of economic principles demonstrated by the above proposals to encourage trade-offs and exchange in pollution control programs. In March 1979 the EPA released a report which claimed to show that the total economic benefits of cleaning up air pollution from factory smokestacks outweigh the total cost. The report was a response to complaints, coming even from other government officials and agencies, that the EPA often issued regulations without paying sufficient attention to their cost.

But the nature of the EPA's response showed that the point had been missed. We learn nothing of significance if we discover that the cost of controlling air pollution from plants in 1977 was $6.7 billion, and that the subsequent benefits in higher productivity and lower medical bills were worth $10 billion. It is *marginal* costs and *marginal* benefits that matter, the additional costs and additional benefits *expected to be associated with a specific regulatory decision*. A new EPA decision that added $3 billion to costs and $1 billion to benefits would be a wrong decision, even though it left total benefits higher than total costs, just as a decision would be worthwhile if it added three times as much to benefits as to costs, regardless of the previously existing level of total benefits and total costs. Totals and averages are simply irrelevant to economic decisions. A person with sunburn should get out of the sun, even if benefit-cost studies show that the benefits of sunshine to human beings far exceed its costs.

Once Over Lightly

Pollution is a cost created in the process of producing goods but paid by people who have not consented to do so. It is thus a cost external to the decision making of its creator, or what the economist calls a negative externality. Externalities are internalized when their full consequences enter into the calculations of decision makers.

The first condition for the reduction of pollution is that people understand clearly who has which rights. The existence of pollution entails disagreement over property rights, and disagreements must be clarified before they can be resolved.

Pollution can be entirely eliminated only if everyone consents freely to everything that others want to do. Perfection is consequently impossible. But the degree to which it can be approached in any society will depend crucially on the extent to which very traditional civic virtues are honored and practiced.

Negotiation is the standard procedure used by members of a society to secure the cooperation and consent of others and thereby achieve their purposes while holding down the level of pollution. Negotiation is easier and more effective when property rights are more clearly specified.

Conflicting claims of right can often be resolved by examining established principles and practices. Adjudication in this manner preserves the continuity of people's expectations. Unexpected changes in effective property rights are in general not desirable, because they arbitrarily transfer wealth from one party to another and also make social coordination more difficult by making it harder for anyone to plan with confidence.

Rapid or radical social change may make it so difficult to resolve conflicting claims through adjudication that legislation is called for. Legislation means the creation of new rules to establish and define what people can and may expect to do with the resources at their command.

New rules are more likely to produce efficient solutions to pollution problems if they make it easier rather than more difficult for parties to employ their comparative advantages by exchanging rights and obligations.

Rules that place taxes on undesired emissions are usually more effective than detailed physical regulations in reducing pollution, because they make greater use of people's detailed knowledge of relevant differences.

Fairness and efficiency can often be partially reconciled in the creation of new rules by allowing those to whom the costs of change are assigned to negotiate an exchange with others who can realize the same objectives at a lower cost.

QUESTIONS FOR DISCUSSION

1. Why do people disturb others by talking during movies? How do such disturbances illustrate the text's definition of pollution and of negative externalities? What are some of the ways in which these externalities can be internalized?

2. Does an extremely bright student create any externalities for other students in her classes? Can you mention some specific external costs? Some external benefits? How could such a student be persuaded to internalize those externalities? What would that imply?

3. How many instances of significant externalities can you find on your campus? Why do they arise? How might the people who create them be induced to internalize them?

4. What are some of the obligations or responsibilities that go along with owning a house? What will happen if the owner does not acknowledge and accept these obligations? Who accepts and acknowledges these obligations in the case of a fraternity house, a sorority house, or a house that is jointly owned by the members of a commune? Would you be willing to make any predictions about the usual quality of maintenance that will be observed in a house owned by one person, by a commune, by a fraternity, and by a sorority?

5. You have the right to live in a house and do everything with it and to it that owners usually can do *except sell it*. Is it your property? Are your actions with respect to that house likely to be different from what they would be if your ownership included the right to sell the house? In what ways?

6. You own a car and live in lower Manhattan. In what ways are your property rights in the car limited? What consequences are these limitations likely to have for the decisions Manhattanites make with respect to cars?

7. "I know I ought to buy an umbrella. But I always lose them within two months." In what sense does this person have an unclear property right? How is that affecting his decisions? Would you expect to find more or fewer umbrellas in use in a society where umbrellas are regularly stolen or mislaid than in one where they are rarely lost? Why?

8. No one "owned" the bison that roamed the Great Plains in the nineteenth century. How did this fact contribute to their near extinction?

9. Each additional vehicle that enters the freeway during the morning rush hour slows all the other automobiles using the freeway. What are the private costs considered by each motorist as he decides whether or not to use the freeway? What are the costs created for others by his decision? How does the divergence between private and social costs lead to a misallocation of resources in this case? How could this divergence be narrowed?

10. Show that the allocation of resources might be improved by making the freeway into a tollway. Why might you, as a regular user of the expressway, prefer a toll during the rush hour to not paying any toll? When is it more efficient for a limited-access highway to be a freeway, and when is it more efficient for it to be a tollway?

11. If a tax on downtown parking is used to subsidize and improve the city's bus system, are drivers being taxed to provide benefits that accrue only to nondrivers? If you commuted to work each day in your own car because you had to use the car in your work, why might you want to vote in favor of an increased tax on downtown parking?

12. The text asserts that rights for anyone always imply corresponding obligations for someone else. Who must be induced to accept which obligations in order for you to have each of the following rights? The right to:
   a. attend college
   b. vote
   c. work
   d. sing in the church choir
   e. smoke cigarettes
   f. obtain medical care

13. "Human rights must take precedence over property rights." Do you agree? Can you name one property right that is not the right of some humans? Can you name any human rights that are not property rights, as the term is defined and used in this chapter?

14. All these questions involve some degree of incompatibility between alternative goods. How are such conflicts of interest to be resolved?
   a. Do owners of motorcycles have the right to improve the operation of their vehicles by removing the mufflers?
   b. Do zoning laws infringe on property rights or protect property rights?
   c. Do commercial airlines have the right to interfere with your television reception by flying over your house? Should they be compelled to compensate you for the violation of your air space? What would happen if a way were found to compel commercial airlines to compensate everyone adversely affected by their operation?
   d. What would you expect to occur if motorists were required to pay a tax per mile driven approximately equal to the costs their driving imposes upon all others in the society? (Assume we somehow obtained the necessary information on these costs.) Would you favor such a tax? Why or why not?
   e. A large mulberry tree in your neighbor's yard provides you with welcome shade but gives her only a lot of inedible and messy mulberries. She wants

to cut the tree down. Does she have the legal right to do so? Does her action affect the value of your property? Is it better from a social point of view that the tree be felled or remain standing? How might an answer be found and the better result obtained?

    f. Do the owners of land along the highways have a right to erect billboards on their own private property? Who owns the view from the highway?

    g. Do owners of recreational vehicles have a right to park them in front of their houses whenever they don't have them out on the road?

    h. Should people have the right to use city buses if they never bathe? Should they have the right to stroll in public parks if they never brush or comb their hair?

15. Does it make sense to define pollution as "damage to the environment"?

    a. Sunshine changes the environment, and the changes are sometimes damaging or even fatal to various living organisms, including human beings. Is sunshine therefore pollution?

    b. If you are unwilling to think of sunshine as pollution, *why* do you reject the designation? Is it because sunshine cannot be controlled by humans? (It can.) Is it because sunshine occurs naturally? (Do you, I, or the manufacturers of aerosol sprays occur *un*naturally?)

    c. Why do some people try to acquire dark suntans every summer, despite evidence that extensive exposure to sunshine often causes sunburn, sunstroke, and skin cancer?

    d. If you love sunshine, are the clouds that cover the sun pollution? Is a new high-rise building pollution if it casts a shadow on your home and yard?

16. Two children are quarreling about who gets to choose the program that will be watched on the family's single television set. This is a case of conflicting property rights.

    a. Should the parents tell them, "Work it out for yourselves"? Under what circumstances is this more likely to produce a satisfactory resolution of the conflict?

    b. How do poorly defined property rights make it more difficult in such a case to achieve a satisfactory resolution through negotiation?

    c. Show how the parents might contribute to a resolution of the conflict that would be both efficient and fair by offering what the text calls adjudication or by offering legislation.

17. "I'd pay almost anything if I could get all my classes scheduled before 11:30 so that I can take this great job I've got lined up for the afternoons." Why will it be difficult for the speaker to get what he wants despite his willingness to pay a high price for it?

18. You and your family enjoy camping in the national parks. Therefore, in February you urge your congressional representative to oppose a bill that would increase the fees for such camping during July and August. The following August you enter Teton National Park at 4:00 P.M. on a weekday and find that all the campsites are occupied.

    a. Would you now like to see a higher schedule of camping fees? Why or why not?

    b. Why are fees for the use of privately owned resources more likely to rise when demand increases than are fees for the use of government-owned resources?

   c. How do varying ownership systems affect resource allocation? Why?

19. When you bought your house, only 5 commercial planes passed over it daily, on the average. That number has grown slowly and almost imperceptibly over the intervening years and now numbers 150. Is the change from 5 to 150 a drastic or radical change? Is your situation with 150 planes flying over your house each day more tolerable because the number increased slowly and imperceptibly? Would you be more likely to receive compensation of some sort if the changes had occurred over a very short period of time? Does the fact that we can't tell which straw broke the camel's back mean that the addition of more straw to the camel's burden was not the cause of its broken back?

20. The industrialized nations of Europe and North America have been eager in recent years to secure international agreements to restrict industrial practices that threaten to cause deterioration in the quality of the environment. The less industrialized countries of the world have been far less eager for such agreements. How would you explain this? Why are people more likely to become concerned about the quality of the environment as their incomes rise?

21. The second annual report of the President's Council on Environmental Quality recommended the use of charges to industry based on the type and amount of pollutants discharged into waterways. How would the adoption of such a system constitute a redefinition of property rights? Is it correct to call this a system of "licenses to pollute"? Why might such a system move us closer to what the text calls an optimal amount of environmental damage?

22. Trace out the sequence of probable consequences from the imposition of taxes on the pollutants that steel mills emit into the atmosphere. How might such taxes affect the distribution of wealth and the allocation of resources?

23. "Taxes can't control pollution. They'll just drive the little firms out of business while the big firms, who can afford to pay, go right on polluting." Do you agree?

24. What's the difference between a tax on noise emitted by cars without mufflers and a fine for not having a proper muffler?

25. Milk trucks traveling from the dairy farms of Pushpin to the bottling plants in Poetrie must travel an additional 18 miles each day because the bridge is out over the Bentham River. The county road commissioners ask you to do a benefit-cost study to determine whether a new bridge should be built.

   a. What would you want to include in benefits and in costs?

   b. Would you want to know the total benefits from milk drinking in the county or the total cost of driving milk trucks?

   c. How is this related to comparisons of the total benefits and total costs of pollution-control programs?

   d. If appendectomies have saved far more lives than they have cost over the years, should you have your healthy appendix removed by a welder? (The point of this absurd question is that the net benefits from appendectomies do not justify removing *every* appendix by *any* means.)

26. A political cartoon shows a man in a gas mask wheezing and gasping his way to the bank to deposit a sack of money. The caption reads: "News item: The Environmental Protection Agency has decided federal smog standards are too costly for cities and industry."

   a. How does the use of the money sack in the cartoon misrepresent the issue? What are some of the *real* costs of strict smog standards?

   b. Why does the assertion that current smog standards are too costly *not* necessarily mean that smog should be allowed to increase? (Hint: There are many different ways to improve air quality. Current standards actually require specific actions; they do not simply establish a target in terms of air quality.)

Chapter **14**

Markets and Government

What should we leave to the market, and what are appropriate tasks for government? It will be difficult to answer that question unless we know what we mean by *the market* and by *government*. What are the differences, the similarities, and the mutual dependencies that exist between markets and government? We cannot choose intelligently until we know what the options are, and the choice between market and government is by no means as clear as our public policy debates often make it seem.

Private versus Public?

Most of the standard contrasts between the market system and government don't hold up very well under close examination. To begin with, the market is usually characterized as the *private* sector, with government agencies and officials occupying the *public* sector. But what can this possibly mean? It surely does not mean that consumers and the managers of business firms pursue private interests, while everyone who works for government pursues the public interest. The Senator who claims that "the public interest" guides all his decisions is in fact guided by a private interpretation of the public interest, filtered through all sorts of private or personal interests: reelection, influence with colleagues, relations with the press, popular image, or place in the history books.

Senators *may* be less interested than business executives in maximizing their private monetary income, but they are probably more interested on average in acquiring prestige and power.

The same analysis applies to any employee of a government agency, whether it's a high appointed official on a regulatory commission or someone just starting a job at the lowest civil service rank. However lofty, noble, or impartial the stated objectives of a government agency, its day-to-day activities will be the consequence of decisions made by ordinary mortals, subject to the pull and push of incentives remarkably similar to those that operate in the private sector. Moreover, in recent years a special devotion to "the public interest" has been claimed for themselves by many executives in leading private corporations. Many owners and managers are eager to persuade us that the ultimate touchstone for their policies is not the maximization of net revenue but the fulfillment of their social responsibilities. We would be well-advised to discount *all* the rhetoric about public versus private interests, and to look for the incentives that actually shape the decisions that people make.

Competition and Individualism

Other contrasts between the market and the government also grow more indistinct the longer we look at them. The market sector is sometimes called the competitive sector. But there is competition in government, too, as every election year demonstrates. Within any government agency, competition for promotion exists among employees. Competition also occurs between government agencies vying for a larger share of appropriations. The two major political parties are continually competing. The executive branch competes with the legislative, members of Congress compete for committee assignments, even district judges compete with one another in the hope of an eventual appointment to a higher court. Do Supreme Court justices, holding appointments for life at the pinnacle of their profession, compete for reputation among editorial writers and law-school professors?

Sometimes we are told that *individualism* is the distinguishing characteristic of the market sector. But what constitutes "individualism"? Many of those who enter the market sector go to work for large corporations right after leaving school and continue as employees until retirement. Is there any significant difference between working in Baltimore as an employee of the Social Security Administration Division of Health, Education, and Welfare and working in Flint as an employee of the Buick division of General Motors? When Britain experimented after World War II with nationalizing, de-nationalizing, and renationalizing its steel industry, most of the employees (and lots of other people, too) had trouble discerning any difference. Some of the characters who frequent the halls of Congress seem far more individualistic (or at least more idiosyncratic) than the people who pass through the corridors of business.

Economic Theory and Government Action

Economic theory attempts to explain the workings of society on the assumption that all participants want to advance their own interests and try to do so in a rational way. The marginal cost-marginal revenue rule that we introduced explicitly in Chapter 9 but have in fact been using throughout the book, is merely a formal expression of these assumptions: The way to advance one's interests is to expand each activity whose marginal revenue exceeds its marginal cost and to contract any activity whose marginal cost is greater than its marginal revenue. The economist does not assume, as we have pointed out before, that money or material goods are the only costs and revenues (or benefits) that consumers and producers care about, or that the interests people pursue are narrow and selfish ones. Economic theory can throw light on the social consequences of every kind of human interest.[1] Why shouldn't that apply to the human purposes and the social processes that control the course of government activities?

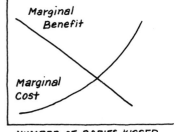

RE-ELECTION PROSPECTS

Marginal Benefit

Marginal Cost

NUMBER OF BABIES KISSED

Our answer is that it *does* apply. The principles of social interaction that guide production of *Time* or *Newsweek* are not as different from those that guide production of the *Federal Reserve Bulletin* as people commonly suppose. Governments as well as privately owned firms produce commodities and services. Governments, too, can only do that by obtaining productive resources whose opportunity cost is the value of what they would have produced in their next most valuable employment. Governments as well as privately owned firms must therefore bid for the resources they want and offer the owners of those resources adequate incentives. You'll want to note (we'll come back to it) that the government can use negative as well as positive incentives: the threat of imprisonment, for example, may be a major incentive as some people decide what portion of their income to offer the Internal Revenue Service each spring. Governments even face the problem of marketing

---

1. An interest in chaos might be the one exception. In a society where people did not value rationality, but celebrated instead the rule of caprice, accident, and purposeless action, economic theory would have almost no predictive power. Its predictive power is correspondingly greatest in those areas of social life most marked by foresight and premeditated action.

their output and of price searching, though monetary prices do play a much smaller role in the distribution of government products. But there can be no doubt that demand curves exist for government goods and that, since these goods are characteristically scarce, they must be rationed by means of some discriminatory criteria. And the people with a demand for government goods will consequently compete to satisfy those criteria, to pay the established price.

The main advantage of looking at government in this way is that it counters the tendency to think of government as a deus ex machina: a heaven-sent power that can resolve difficulties as magically as a playwright does in the final act of every farce. It makes our expectations of government more realistic. It encourages us to ask about the conditions that enable government to act effectively in any given circumstance and not just to suppose that government always gets what it wants or catches what it chases. This way of looking at government also reminds us that the immediately preceding sentence was misleading in its suggestion that government is an "it"; for government is *many different people interacting on the basis of prevailing property rights.*

If you're wondering what property rights can possibly have to do with the behavior of government, you may have forgotten momentarily how economists use the concept. Every participant in the processes of government, from voters through civil service employees to the president, has certain expectations about what voters or civil servants or the president can and may do. Those expectations we call property rights. Maybe it would help if we substituted for *property rights* the phrase *what people think they can get away with.* That has connotations of conniving and unethical behavior that we don't intend at all. But the phrase does convey the force of the property rights concept: The actions that people take will depend on their expectations about the consequences of those actions, upon the anticipated marginal benefits and marginal costs to themselves of the decisions they're weighing. That is as true in the Senate Office Building as it is on the floor of the New York Stock Exchange. The key to understanding each of those worlds is a grasp of the very different property rights of senators and of stockbrokers.

The Right to Use Coercion

There is one significant difference between government and nongovernment that does not grow indistinct or disappear as we inspect it more carefully. *Government possesses a generally conceded and exclusive right to coerce adults.* The right is *generally* conceded, but not universally; thoroughgoing anarchists don't grant it, and neither do those who accept government in principle but reject as illegitimate the authority of the particular government under which they live. It is an *exclusive* right, because, as we say, "people don't have the right to take the law into their own hands"; everyone is supposed to appeal to officers of government (police, judges, legislators) when coercion seems called for. It is the right to coerce *adults* that uniquely distinguishes government, because parents are generally conceded the right to coerce children under certain circumstances.

What does it mean to coerce? We introduced our definition of coercion in a discussion question at the end of Chapter 11. *To coerce means to induce cooperation by withdrawing or otherwise reducing people's options.* Coercion should be contrasted with the other way of obtaining cooperation from people, which is persuasion. *To persuade means to induce cooperation by offering people additional options.*

In a few cases we may not be able to agree whether particular actions are coercion or persuasion. These cases will usually turn out to involve real or alleged deception, so that our disagreement will turn on the issue of what people actually thought their options were when they were induced by others to cooperate. But this definition will usually allow us to distinguish coercive from noncoercive efforts to influence the behavior of others. It is only to government that we grant the right to secure cooperation by withdrawing options.

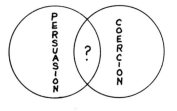

Coercion has a bad reputation, because most of us believe (or think we believe) that people should generally be allowed to do what they want to do. In addition, coercion implies authority, and many of us react with automatic hostility to claims of authority. But the traffic laws that tell us we must drive on the right and stop when the light turns red simultaneously coerce us *and* expand our freedom. The reason they expand our freedom is that they also coerce others. We all get where we're going faster and more safely, because we accept the coercion of traffic laws. This is the traditional defense of government and its right to coerce, that we may all be able to achieve greater freedom (expanded options) if we all accept limitations on our freedom (reduced options).

Is Government Necessary?

But do we have to use coercion? Couldn't we get equally good results by relying on voluntary cooperation? We have seen throughout this book that voluntary exchange is the principal mechanism of coordination in our society. Why couldn't voluntary exchange become the *only* means through which we induce cooperation? By asking this question seriously and pushing for an answer, we can gain some important insights into the capabilities and limitations of the various ways in which we try to get things done.

One way to get at the issue is to ask what would happen if there were no government at all in our society. What problems would arise? Would important tasks cease to be performed? Couldn't people resolve those problems and accomplish those tasks either through individual action or by forming voluntary associations? A good example with which to sort out the issues is the case of police protection. Would there be no police if there were no government? That can't be the case, since private police forces exist at the present time. But these forces supplement a basic, given level of government police protection, providing additional protection for those who want it and are willing to pay for it. Could we obtain that *basic* protection in the absence of government?

Transaction Costs

Why couldn't the people living on one block or the business firms in a particular area get together and agree to contribute toward their own police force? They could, of course. But they would encounter significant costs. Think of all the block meetings, the long discussions, the arguments over the quantity and quality of protection desired, the nuisance of collecting contributions regularly, the negotiations with police-service suppliers. Every block would have to do that. The more that blocks combined in an effort to spread these costs over a larger number of people, the more difficult would be the task of getting the voluntary association started.

Think for a moment how long it would take you just to contact all the people in an eight-block-square area, going back time after time to find those who never seem to be at home; then to explain your proposal to each household and persuade them all to attend an organizational meeting on an evening that doesn't conflict with plans that some would have made already; then to conduct that meeting, allowing the floor to all those who want to speak but without boring, irritating, offending or otherwise losing those who want particular speakers to shut up and sit down; then forming the planning committees, contacting those who missed the meeting, catching the new people who move in, pacifying those who don't like the direction in which you're going. And we haven't even mentioned the issues of substance yet, such as the precise quality and quantity of police protection your neighborhood association will want to purchase.

We have encountered the problem of *transaction costs*.

This is the economist's term for *all the costs that are incurred in the process of carrying through an exchange.* Transaction costs arise in connection with every voluntary exchange. Buyers and sellers will inevitably "pay" something in addition to the money or other goods that they turn over to the other party. These costs—of searching, advertising, inspecting, bargaining, and so on—reduce the amount of exchange that occurs because they are *deadweight costs.* Like the costs of standing in line to buy a good whose money price is below the market clearing price, they are *costs to one party in the transaction that do not become benefits for the other.* They therefore diminish one party's desire to carry through the exchange without increasing the eagerness of the other party. That is how transaction costs reduce the amount of exchange that will occur.

Look again at the case of "Commuter Connection" in Novato, California, discussed at the beginning of Chapter 4. We now have a concept with which to summarize the peculiar difficulties that were anticipated by the originators of "Commuter Connection." The founders created the organization in order to reduce the transaction costs of completing satisfactory exchanges among Novato commuters. And they were apprehensive about the success of the program, because they knew that the transaction costs that still remained would be considerable. High transaction costs reduce the effectiveness of voluntary exchange as a way of obtaining cooperation among people in using what they have to satisfy their wants. Transaction costs may have proved too high in Novato. They would almost surely be too high in the case of our imaginary effort to secure police protection through voluntary association.

The Problem of Free Riders

We can make that pessimistic prediction with considerable confidence because of an important asymmetry in the costs and benefits of providing private police protection. Even if the total benefits that the neighborhood will receive from this police protection exceed the total costs of organizing to secure it, the protection would probably *not* be supplied in the end. The reason is that the benefits will be received by all residents in the neighborhood, regardless of their contribution toward covering the costs. Everyone will therefore have an incentive to become a *free rider: one who accepts the benefits without paying the costs.* But if no one has an incentive to pay the costs, the good will not be obtained, and no one will receive the benefits either.

The free-rider concept describes one of the most frustrating problems in the study of social organization. It frustrates those who do not understand why the problem exists and who therefore keep insisting that it *ought* to go away:

> "We can lick the energy problem if each of us will only . . ."
> "There would be no litter on our highways if each of us would only . . ."
> "If each of us studies the issues and goes to the polls on election day . . ."
> "If every nation would only renounce forever the use of force as a means of resolving international disagreements . . ."

Those who plead so plaintively in all of these and dozens of similar cases recognize correctly that we could all gain "if each of us would only." They are frustrated by the persistent failure of people to do what would clearly and by everyone's admission make them all better off.

The free rider problem frustrates economists, too, because economists encounter so much resistance when they try to persuade people that *each will not do what is in the interest of all unless it is in the interest of each.* People's actions are guided by the costs they expect to bear and the benefits they expect to receive *as a result of those actions.* If the benefits accruing to Jane Blow will be for all practical purposes exactly the same whether or not she takes a particular action—but she will incur significant costs by taking it—she will not take the action.

If Jane is noble and generous, she will derive a great deal of benefit from helping others, while thinking lightly of the sacrifices she makes to do so. Consequently she will take some actions that others will not take. That must be stressed, because the free-rider concept definitely does not assert that people are completely selfish or that altruism plays no part in social life. Quite to the contrary, no society could continue to exist in which people were *completely* selfish. We asserted in Chapter 13—and will remind you again here—that some amount of genuine concern for the well-being of others is essential if any social cooperation at all is to occur. Neither markets nor governments could exist among people with no ability to empathize, to internalize at least some of what others experience.

Positive Externalities and Free Riders

In stressing the significance of the free-rider concept, the economist is insisting only that people have *limited* concepts of self-interest, that they do not by and large entertain the inner feelings of others, especially more distant others, with as much vividness and force as they experience costs and benefits that impinge on them more directly. The economist who calls attention to the free-rider problem is saying that positive externalities exist as well as negative ones, and that these externalities encourage people to behave as free riders. *Positive externalities* are *benefits that accrue to people other than those who created the benefits*. They raise this question: Will anyone have an adequate incentive to create them, or will everyone wait to receive them as a spillover benefit from the actions of others?

The free-rider problem would probably prove fatal to our projected voluntary association for the creation of a police force. Who would be willing and able to pay the enormous transaction costs that would be preliminary to the negotiaton of such a neighborhood agreement? If you are tempted to answer that everyone could chip in something to pay the organizer, you have not yet grasped the full significance of the free-rider problem. People won't want to contribute to the organizer's salary, because they know that their contribution is a cost that will make no difference to the benefits they finally receive. They cannot be compelled to pay their share, of course, because we are trying to organize a police force without using coercion. No "government" exists in our hypothetical community to levy such a compulsory contribution or "tax."

But suppose the neighborhood did have one individual with such vast reserves of leisure, patience, ingenuity, and devotion to the community that she was able to obtain unanimous consent among all the people in the neighborhood to a specific arrangement for hiring and deploying a police force. A crucial difficulty would still remain. How will all the people who have agreed to contribute X dollars per month be induced to make their contribution and get it in on time? If you don't think this will be a problem, you are very young indeed. In any eight-block-square area of any city there will be several dozen people who do not send in their contributions on time. *All* will have what they think are legitimate excuses: they forgot, they had unusual expenses this month, they aren't getting the benefits they were promised, they lost their jobs, their assigned contributions are too high relative to someone else's, they just joined a group that is opposed to police on theological grounds, they won't pay unless their nephew is appointed to the force, they won't pay until somebody else's nephew is dismissed from the force, etc., etc.

People are more liable to behave in this uncooperative way when the benefit for which they are supposed to pay is going to come to them whether they pay or not. Notice that a mere tendency to behave in this way will be sufficient to create an initial problem. But the initial problem will tend to grow into a larger problem. When payments are not received in a timely fashion, expenses cannot be met on time. If service quality starts to decline as a result, more neighbors will acquire addi-

If all wheat farmers reduced their planting by 50 percent, all would earn a larger net revenue.

But ...

If all *other* wheat farmers reduce their planting by 50 percent, any *one* wheat farmer could make a fortune by increasing his planting by 50 percent.

What would you predict?

tional incentive to withhold all or part of their contributions. As the word gets out that some are not paying and are getting away with it, reluctance to contribute will increase. And all this will occur in an association that has no effective means to *compel* payment.

Public Goods

It is the character of the good itself that creates a free-rider problem now. Police protection is a good of an unusual kind, to which economic theory applies a somewhat misleading name. It is an instance of a *public good*, which specifically means *a good that cannot be supplied exclusively to those who agree to pay for it.* The act of providing it to those who pay makes it available also to some who do not pay. Police protection is a public good, because security officers patrolling the block to protect the homes of contributors provide a significant amount of protection also, as a spillover benefit, to those on the block who have not paid for the service. When people can obtain at least some of a good without paying, their incentive to pay obviously declines.

Why and to what extent is a Fourth of July fireworks display in the city park a public good?

What could the neighborhood association do to maintain its revenue in the face of the public-good character of police protection? Perhaps it could meet this dilemma by exerting pressure on the free riders. Community disapproval, openly expressed, might bring them in. And if that didn't work, there are other ways to exert pressure. In fact, why not just take a vote and decide that anyone who refuses to cooperate with the association has to move from the neighborhood? Antisocial families could then be moved out by force if necessary. Wouldn't coercion be justified under such circumstances?

Perhaps it would. But then the neighborhood would have created a government! The distinguishing characteristic of government is precisely its power to secure cooperation through coercion. And this is why societies resort to coercion. Coercion is a way of obtaining goods which are not likely to be supplied in adequate amounts when their supply is left entirely to voluntary efforts. Coercion may be able to increase the supply of such goods by reducing transaction costs and by overcoming free-rider problems that arise in conjunction with positive externalities and public goods.

Some Traditional Functions of Government

How much of what government does in our society can be explained with the concepts of transaction costs, positive externalities, public goods, and free riders? Does this way of thinking help us to predict where coercion will be used to supplement persuasion and with what consequences? Let's try it out.

National Defense

National defense is a very traditional function of government, and it provides the classic example of a public good. There is no way to provide military protection to those inhabitants who are willing to pay for it, without providing it also to those who don't pay. Because free-rider problems would make it practically impossible to rely on voluntary contributions to finance a system of national defense, societies resort to coercion, collecting the funds through involuntary contributions called taxes.

Note carefully, however, because the point is easily overlooked, that government does not have to rely entirely on coercion to produce the good called national defense. And no government does. The taxes used to finance a military force are coercive levies. But when the funds are used to hire people for the armed forces and to purchase equipment from suppliers, government is relying on persuasion and voluntary cooperation to create a system for national defense. This raises an interesting question. Why will a government sometimes use coercion to achieve its objectives when it would appear that persuasion would work just as well or even better? Why will a government choose to draft people into the armed forces (and onto juries) rather than rely on volunteers? Most people who work for government are persuaded, not compelled to do so. Why are some coerced? The dangers to which military personnel are subject cannot be the whole answer, since people are attracted into far more dangerous occupations without conscription. We'll suggest an explanation a little further on.

Law and Order

It is also generally assumed that government should be responsible for maintaining "law and order" within society. We have just seen how transaction costs and positive externalities would make it extremely difficult for citizens to organize a community police force entirely by persuasion. A judicial system for resolving disputes that arise between citizens could perhaps be created through voluntary efforts somewhat more easily than a police force, as is suggested by the existence of numerous arbitration systems financed by voluntary efforts. But everyone benefits when the people occupying a common territory are all subject to the same system of laws and judicial rulings. Uniform and consistently enforced rules that are binding upon all, whether or not they consent, make it much easier for everyone to plan with confidence. And the ability to plan confidently is what distinguishes a cooperating society from a chaotic mob. Since a system of laws and courts confers substantial benefits upon people whether or not they choose to help pay for it and to be bound by it, societies use coercion to create and operate systems of justice. Are there any other duties that are as universally assigned to government as are the duties of providing for national defense and domestic order?

Roads and Schools

What about roads? Would we enjoy an adequate system of streets and highways if we did not use coercion to finance them? Be careful; an adequate system doesn't necessarily mean the quantity and quality we now have. Roads are *over*supplied if the benefits from particular additions are less than the costs of making those additions, and that can surely occur. But is there any reason to expect a systematic *under*supply of streets and highways if their provision is left entirely to voluntary efforts? The transaction costs could be rather staggering if all streets and highways were owned and operated by people who had to rely entirely upon tolls for the collection of revenue. The benefits, moreover, don't accrue exclusively to those who drive. People who live along a dusty gravel road receive benefits from the paving of that road even if they never drive. The experience of those who have built roads in remote areas or in private developments without using coercion suggests both that it can be done and that the costs of securing cooperation by exclusively voluntary means can be quite high.

What is the case for using coercion to finance education? The argument here is that people will acquire education only up to the point at which the marginal cost to themselves equals the marginal benefit to themselves. But education supposedly generates substantial externalities, benefits that accrue to people other than the person acquiring the education. Thus everyone in a democracy benefits when citizens learn to read and to think. Because we don't take account of the benefits to others in deciding how much education to obtain, we obtain less than the optimal amount. By using taxes to subsidize education, the government lowers its cost to potential students and induces them to acquire more than they otherwise would. The question arises, as it does with roads, whether the use of coercion to prevent undersupply does not lead in practice to oversupply. We'll return to that question.

Income Redistribution

Another important category of government action is the provision of special benefits—money grants, food stamps, medical care, housing subsidies, and a variety of social services—to impoverished or disabled people. Why does this kind of activity require the use of coercion? Why don't we leave it to voluntary philanthropy, rather than compel people to contribute through the tax system? One part of the answer is that charity is subject to the free-rider problem. Assume that all citizens are charitably disposed and want to see more income made available to especially poor and unfortunate people. While some citizens derive satisfaction from contributing to a charitable cause, most would prefer that problems be solved and suffering relieved at a minimum cost to themselves. They want to see poor people helped, but they also want to see others do the helping. And so they will tend to behave like free riders. They will hold back somewhat on their contributions in the hope that others will contribute enough to take care of the problem. But with everyone waiting for others to contribute, contributions fall short of the amount that everyone would prefer to see raised. Taxation under such circumstances can make people want to contribute more by assuring them that others are also doing their share.

The Regulation of Voluntary Exchange

What about the extensive list of government activities that fall under the category of regulation? Why do federal, state, and local governments regulate so many of the activities of citizens, using coercion to control the terms on which people may engage in voluntary exchange? Putting it in just that way—using coercion to control voluntary exchange—may prompt us to think a little harder and longer about all the things that government does in the name of regulation.

Transaction costs provide part of the answer. It would be very costly for all of us to carry our own scales to check the accuracy of the ones that butchers use and our own gallon cans to be sure the gasoline pumps aren't cheating us. When physicians must be licensed and new drugs approved by the Food and Drug Administration before they can be marketed, buyers are spared the cost of evaluating goods whose quality most of them would be unable to assess for themselves—except at prohibitive costs. By compelling sellers to obtain certification, government agencies can enable us all to make satisfactory exchanges at lower cost. A substantial amount of government regulation can be viewed as coercion designed to reduce the cost of acquiring information.

The glaring flaw in this defense of regulation, however, is that it fails to account for the enthusiasm with which sellers so often support regulation. Those who have studied the matter know very well that the demand for government regulation of sellers more often originates with the sellers than with their customers. We saw in Chapter 10 why this occurs; sellers are eager to restrict competition, and government regulation in the name of consumer protection is a technique of proved effectiveness for eliminating competition. But why do the victims cooperate? Why does government employ coercion to promote special interests when it is the responsibility of government to promote the public interest?

Government and the Public Interest

The basic answer suggested by economic theory brings us back in a surprising way to the problem with which we began this chapter. The coercive actions taken by government to compensate for the limitations inherent in purely voluntary cooperation are themselves subject to the same limitations. The reason for this is that coercion itself depends on voluntary cooperation. Persuasion always precedes coercion, because government will not act until particular people have been persuaded to act. Government is not the genie in Aladdin's lamp. Government is people interacting, paying attention to the expected costs and benefits of the alternatives that they perceive. The disconcerting part of all this is that the problems created by transaction costs, positive externalities, and free riders are particularly acute in the political life of democracies.

A surprising number of people assume without thinking about it that "government acts in the public interest." But does it really? Does it always do so? Why do we think so? Do citizens become more virtuous when they move from the line in the supermarket to the line at the polling place? Do people's characters change when they give up a post in industry or academia to take a position with the government? Here is our formal definition of the public interest: *The public interest is what everyone would want if everyone was adequately informed and impartial.* Does economic theory have anything useful to say about the likelihood that government actions will proceed from adequate information and an impartial viewpoint?

Those whose decisions make up the sum of government actions will pay attenton to the information actually available to them and the incentives that actually confront them. Economic theory predicts that this information and these incentives will tend to be both limited and biased.

Information and Democratic Governments

We can begin with citizen voters. None of us knows enough to cast an adequately intelligent vote. To persuade yourself that this is so, conduct a little mental experiment. Suppose you know that your vote, whether on a candidate or a ballot proposition, would determine the outcome of the election; your vote and your vote alone will decide the question. How much information would you gather before casting that crucial vote? A lot would depend, of course, on the importance of the office or the issue. But you would surely invest far more time and energy in acquiring information than you do when you're just one voter among 50 thousand or 50 million. As it is, most citizens, including intelligent, well-read, and public spirited citizens, step into the polling place on election day equipped only with a lot of prejudices, a few hunches, some poorly tested bits of information, and vast areas of total ignorance. We do this because it's rational to do so! Given the actual importance of our one vote in 50 thousand or 50 million, it would be an almost unconscionable waste of time for us to learn enough to cast an adequately informed vote. The issue is not simply one of selfishness or lack of dedication to the well-being of society. A voter who wanted to make a personal sacrifice for the good of the commonwealth could do far more per hour, per dollar, or per calorie in social service volunteer work than by gathering enough information to cast an adequately informed vote.

"But if everybody thought that way," goes the standard objection, "democracy wouldn't work." This objection is another instance of *the argument that the free-rider phenomenon does not exist because the world would be a more satisfactory place if it did not exist.* Those who are committed to democracy had better concern themselves with ways to make it work when citizen voters are uninformed and misinformed, and not pretend that voters have knowledge they obviously do not have.

Some defenders of democracy are not overly discouraged by the incompetence of citizen voters. They rely on elected representatives to acquire the information that must be available if decisions are to be made in the public interest. Their confidence has a reasonable foundation in reality. Because the vote of each legislator has a far greater probability of affecting the outcome, because legislators can use the information they acquire to influence others in significant ways, because legislators are provided with staff and other information gathering resources, because many people will have a strong interest in making relevant information available to legislators, because legislators' votes are monitored and must be defended—for all these reasons and more, elected representatives are far more likely to be adequately informed about the issues on which they vote than are ordinary citizens.

The Interests of Elected Officials

But even if we can assume that legislators' votes are adequately informed, are we entitled to assume that they will be votes in

Is a $1000 benefit today worth a $1200 cost one year from now? To anyone who discounts future events at a rate higher than 20 percent, it is.

the public interest? Are elected representatives impartial? Another way of asking the same question is to ask whether they will always vote in the way that the information available to them tells them they ought to vote. Economic theory assumes that people act in their own interest, not that they act in the public interest. Sometimes it will be in a legislator's interest to pursue the public interest. But finding ways to produce such harmony is the major issue in the design of political institutions; we cannot simply *assume* this advantageous concord without asking whether the institutions under which we live are likely to produce it. Because an interest in reelection is a common and healthy interest among most elected officials, we'll focus our analysis on this one particular private interest. Is an interest in being reelected likely to lead elected officials to vote and act in the public interest?

Let's begin by noticing how it limits their planning horizons. Elected officials cannot afford to look too far ahead. Results must be available by the next election or the incumbent could be replaced by someone who offers better promises. We shall see in the last part of this book how an emphasis on the short run makes it difficult for governments to deal effectively with recessions and inflations. But the same will be true for any policy that requires current sacrifices for the sake of future benefits. Elected officials will tend to discount heavily the value of all future benefits that aren't expected until after the election. Their interest in reelection will thus keep them from fully using their own superior knowledge about the consequences of particular policies.

In listing some of the reasons why legislators are likely to be well informed, we mentioned two that also explain why legislators will not always vote in the way that their information tells them they ought to vote. These were the last two reasons cited: Many people have a strong interest in making relevant information available to legislators, and legislators' votes are monitored and must be defended. The problem is that the interest in providing information (or lobbying) and in holding legislators accountable for their actions is concentrated in special-interest groups. The positive externalities associated with the political process make this almost inevitable.

The controversy over deregulation of the trucking industry nicely illustrates the problem. Regulation by the Interstate Commerce Commission over the years has produced wasteful practices and higher prices to shippers that ultimately show up as higher prices for just about everything we buy. But there are people who benefit from all this. By restricting competition, regulation has created privileged positions for the trucking firms that own operating rights and for members of the Teamsters Union. These groups expect deregulation to reduce their wealth substantially. They have therefore been extremely active in lobbying members of Congress, in making campaign contributions, and in threatening retaliation against elected officials who vote to "throw the trucking industry open to the chaos of competition."

The benefits to the rest of us from lower transportation costs would almost surely be greater in the aggregate than the losses that the trucking firms and the drivers expect to suffer from deregulation. Nonetheless we don't see any significant amount of lobbying effort, campaign contributions, or demonstrations directed at getting Congress to vote *for* deregulation. The individual interest that each of us has in deregulation is simply not great enough to induce any of us to involve ourselves actively in the fight. As all of us, opponents and proponents of deregulation, consult our own personal marginal benefits and marginal costs, here is what occurs.

The few opponents who have much to lose invest vast resources in trying to influence the legislature. The many proponents with more to gain in total—but less to gain individually—invest nothing. Legislatures respond to this sort of pressure, because a substantial number of them find that doing so serves their interest in being reelected. It seems rather futile to fault them for this; an ex-legislator with untarnished principles is not always a more effective public servant than a legislator who has bent a few principles to survive and fight another day. The fault lies with the externalities that prompt most of us to behave like free riders, hoping that someone else will assume the costs of lobbying for the measures from which we would all benefit.

Positive Externalities and Government Policies

Our conclusion should come as no surprise. Government policies will tend to be dominated by special interests. Government will lean toward actions that harm many people just a little bit, rather than actions that displease a few people very much. Government policies will be guided not so much by the public interest as by an endless succession of extremely partial interests. This is why consumer interests win the oratorical contests, but producer interests control policy. The interests of producers are simply more concentrated, more sharply focused. Producers know that their action or inaction can make a significant difference to their own welfare, and so it is in their interest to act. But no individual consumer can expect more than a small benefit from political action, so none of them has an incentive to accept the costs.

Is this why the use of coercion to prevent an undersupply

of roads often leads to an oversupply? The taxpayers' general interest in economy does not fare well when it goes head to head with a small group's intense interest in having a road or building a road. The same analysis applies to schooling. Those who produce schooling (the author's own vested interest, let it be noted) can make life difficult for legislators who try to save taxpayers money by reducing expenditures on education or research. Here is an explanation for the otherwise puzzling behavior of legislatures that approve larger and larger expenditures—even when every member favors reduced expenditures. There is no way to cut a budget without cutting specific projects. With every special interest organized to make certain that the cuts occur in someone else's project, expenditures cannot be reduced.

Why did we long have a military draft in this country, and what is the probability that Congress will restore it? Military conscription, as we noted earlier, extends the use of coercion into areas where persuasion is quite capable of securing the cooperation we want (at least in peacetime). The draft probably persisted as long as it did because the military establishment had a strong and sharply focused interest in maintaining a ready flow of personnel for the armed forces, whereas most of those who were adversely affected by the draft had a stronger incentive to find a personal escape route than to attack the whole system. It is interesting to note how many current advocates of reinstating the draft are now talking about *universal* conscription of young people for short-term service of some kind. Will this tactic (assuming that it is a tactic) increase the number of those who are opposed to the draft? Or will it reduce the expected cost to each draftee below that critical point at which he or she would be willing to do political battle to prevent reestablishment of the draft?

What can we say about government actions to relieve poverty? We can predict that legislators will be slow to replace in-kind transfers with money transfers. Farmers benefit from the food-stamp program, the building trades benefit from housing subsidies, the medical-care industry expands with health-care assistance, teachers benefit from educational subsidies for the poor, and social workers know that giving money to the poor will never be as advantageous as hiring more members of the "helping professions." The political influence of these groups makes it easier for legislatures to support in-kind transfers to the poor than to support money transfers. There may be other and better grounds for rejecting money transfers; but this alternative would get more respectful attention in Congress if money were produced and sold by a money industry.

None of this implies that farmers, hospital administrators, or social workers have *no* regard for the public interest. It implies only that they all have *some* regard for their own interests. And even those who work for government agencies charged specifically to protect the public interest define it with reference to their own special interests.

Consider, for example, a member of the Food and Drug Administration, responsible for preventing the introduction of new drugs without adequate testing. What is adequate testing? It's testing that makes sure we know all the side effects of a new drug before we allow it on the market. But we can *never* be sure. All we can do is acquire additional information and thus reduce the risk that someone will be killed or seriously harmed by an unanticipated side effect. How far should we reduce the risk? Not *too* far, because there are costs as well as benefits attached to additional testing. A major cost will be the lives lost and the suffering not relieved because the drug isn't available while it's being tested.

How will an FDA commissioner evaluate these two costs: the lives lost through premature introduction and the lives lost through excessive delay in introduction of new drugs? People will blame the FDA if an approved drug turns out to have disastrous side effects, and they will applaud the FDA if it refuses to approve a drug that subsequently turns out to have disastrous side effects in other countries. But almost no one condemns the FDA for lives lost while a drug is being tested or applauds the FDA for cutting the testing period short in order to get a new drug on the market. The conclusion is obvious. FDA commissioners will find it in the public interest to test drugs beyond the point at which the marginal benefit equals the marginal cost.

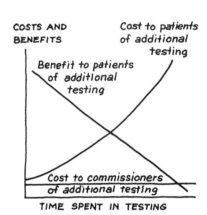

If all this is unsettling to those for whom it is an article of faith that the government takes care of the public interest, it may be time to question this article of faith. Perhaps it stems from the habit of equating "government" with "nation" and extending to the former the reverence felt for the latter. Or it may be a result of our belief that government is the last resort and therefore must be an effective resort, since we don't like to admit to any insoluble problems. There's a popular bit of deductive reasoning that also leads toward this conclusion. It asserts that all social problems are the result of human behavior, that human behavior can be altered by law, and that government makes the laws, from which the argument concludes that government can solve all social problems.

Alexis de Tocqueville offered a more realistic view in *Democracy in America*: "There is no country in which everything can be provided for by the laws, or in which political institutions can prove a substitute for common sense and public morality."[2]

Once Over Lightly

Economic theory assumes that the actions of government follow from the expectations of citizens and government officials about the marginal costs and marginal benefits to themselves of alternative courses of action.

The distinguishing characteristic of government is its generally conceded and exclusive right to use coercion. To coerce means to induce cooperation by reducing people's options. Voluntary cooperation relies exclusively on persuasion, which secures desired behavior by offering additional options.

Coercion is useful to the members of a society, because it can sometimes secure the production of goods that everyone values at more than the cost of supplying them, but which would not be supplied through purely voluntary cooperation.

Coercion may be able to secure the supply of such goods by lowering transaction costs. These are deadweight costs incurred in the process of carrying through an exchange.

Coercion may also be able to overcome the interrelated problems of free riders, positive externalities, and public goods. Free riders are those who enjoy benefits but refuse to pay the costs. This becomes possible when the production of goods generates positive externalities—benefits that spill over to others. Public goods are those that cannot be supplied exclusively to those who pay, because their production generates positive externalities. The use of coercion can provide adequate incentive for the supply of public goods by denying people the option of behaving as free riders.

The traditional activities of government turn out upon examination to be largely actions aimed at reducing transaction costs and overcoming free-rider problems.

The coercive activities of government presuppose voluntary cooperation. Persuasion is prior to coercion because, in the last analysis, citizens and government officials must be persuaded to employ coercion in particular ways. This implies that the limits on the effectiveness of voluntary cooperation that justify coercive action by government are limitations also on the effectiveness of the government's coercive action.

Positive externalities thoroughly permeate the political processes in a democratic government. They make it unlikely that citizen voters will be adequately informed or that elected

---

2. Book I, Chapter VIII.

officials will consistently act in the way that the information available to them tells them they ought to act.

QUESTIONS FOR DISCUSSION

1. In each of the following cases, what are the significant differences between government-owned and nongovernment-owned enterprises? Why do you think the government owns the enterprises mentioned? What different forms does competition take in the case of government-owned enterprises? In what different ways do they operate because of their government ownership?
   a. Investor-owned utilities and utilities owned by states or municipalities
   b. State colleges and private colleges
   c. City-owned intraurban bus companies and interurban bus companies like Greyhound and Trailways
   d. Forest Service campgrounds and privately owned campgrounds
   e. Public libraries and private bookstores
2. A frequent argument in support of government-produced goods is that they are vital to social welfare and therefore their provision cannot safely be left to the "whims" of the marketplace. Does this explain why parks and libraries are usually municipal services, while food and medical care are usually secured through the market? Can you suggest a better explanation to account for these cases?
3. Is competition more common in business than in government? Is it more common in business than in colleges or universities? Is it more common in capitalist countries than in socialist ones?
4. Does the chief executive officer of a large corporation with widely diversified ownership (Exxon, General Motors, American Telephone and Telegraph) make decisions in the public interest or decisions intended to maximize profits? What other objectives than the two mentioned would be likely to influence the decisions of these executives? What considerations guide the decisions of college and university presidents?
5. A feature story in the *Wall Street Journal* of May 23, 1979 carries the headline, "Washington PR Staffs Dream Up Ways to Get Agencies' Stories Out."
   a. How does a director of public affairs in a government agency differ from the director of advertising or public relations for a soap manufacturer?
   b. Why do the Department of Defense, the Department of Transportation, the Department of Agriculture, and other departments of the federal government spend millions of dollars trying to influence public opinion? Isn't it the case, at least in a democracy, that public opinion is supposed to control the actions of government agencies?
6. Each of the 10 families on a suburban block is likely to have its own gasoline-powered lawn mower. Why don't families more often share a single lawn mower? Try to enumerate the principal transaction costs that stand in the way of such a cooperative arrangement.
7. Most Parent-Teacher Associations have a hard time getting people to attend

meetings and do other work for the association.

    a. Why does this not imply either that parents don't care about their children's education or that they don't think the PTA accomplishes anything?

    b. Why is attendance usually better among teachers than among parents?

    c. Why do a few parents choose to be very actively involved in the PTA?

8. "Of the 34,937 members in the cooperative eligible to vote, only 737 voted in the election of trustees, and 483 of these cast absentee ballots." Do these data indicate that the members don't support the cooperative? Do you think better trustees would be selected if more members voted?

9. Most automobile drivers probably exceed the legal speed limits somewhat when they think they can get away with it. Does this imply that they would vote for higher speed limits if given a chance?

10. Why do some people who drink alcoholic beverages vote in favor of legal prohibition?

11. Visualize a city composed entirely of green (one half) and purple (one-half) citizens. No one objects to living next door to someone of the opposite color. But they all object to having neighbors of the opposite color *on both sides* and will move if they find themselves in that position. Will a segregated or integrated housing pattern emerge under a system of voluntary exchange? Why? If integrated housing is considered a good thing, how could it be achieved under these circumstances?

  Suppose the people in a neighborhood band together in an association that tries to enforce racial quotas. They attempt to prevent black families from purchasing homes in areas where the black-white ratio is above the citywide average. Are they promoting segregation or integration?

12. Who receives the benefits when people paint and fix up the exterior of houses that they own? In what ways are homeowners induced to internalize some of the positive externalities from making the exterior of their homes more attractive? Would coercion secure a closer-to-optimal amount of home beautification?

13. Should the members of a volunteer fire department refuse to put out a fire in the home of someone who has refused to contribute to the fire-fighting service? What damage would they be doing by putting out the fire?

14. Why do people obey the law? Is it always in their interest to obey the law? Do people obey the law when it is not in their interest to do so?

15. If running laps around the football field improves the conditioning of athletes and makes them more effective players, why do so many players try to get away with running fewer laps than the coach orders? Who receives the benefits and who bears the cost of such conditioning activities? Are coaches likely to order their players to run a more-than-optimal number of laps?

16. When a government agency requires households or businesses to submit detailed reports on their activities, the costs are borne by those who must prepare the reports and the benefits (in the form of additional information) are received entirely by the agency.

    a. How does this explain the expansion of government-required paperwork despite a general consensus that such paperwork is already excessive?

    b. Do you think the requirements would decline if agencies were required to use funds from their budget allocations to compensate those who must submit the forms?

c. Should teachers be required to read and comment on all papers that they require their students to write?

17. If positive externalities create free-rider problems to the extent suggested by the text in its analysis of charitable programs, why do United Way campaigns work as well as they do in so many American cities? Are there elements of coercion in United Way fund drives, either in obtaining people to work on the campaign or in inducing people to contribute? What might be the advantages and disadvantages of having local government assume the welfare functions currently performed through the United Way?

18. The free-rider analysis applied to political life provides an argument for fining citizens who fail to vote in a general election. Would you support such a law? Would you prefer that citizens be paid to cast a ballot? Would the latter be noncoercive?

19. Do the decisions of people now living take any account of the demands of future generations for natural resources? Do these decisions take *adequate* account of the demands of future generations? Is government likely to take *better* account of the demands of future generations? Evaluate the contention that government must serve as the steward of natural resources for future generations.

20. The Council on Wage and Price Stability frequently criticizes the Environmental Protection Agency for issuing antipollution regulations that are allegedly too costly. Why does this occur despite the fact that both are agencies of the federal government and both are supposed to be looking out for the public interest? If someone hired to do benefit-cost analysis transfers from the EPA to the CWPS, how do his incentives change?

21. Many informed Americans are beginning to express concern about imminent shortages of electricity, especially in the northeastern United States. Many of the same people have argued in the past against strip mining of coal, coal-burning electrical power plants, imports of oil (because of the danger of spills), construction of nuclear power plants, and the building of the Alaska pipeline. How should this conflict between competing social concerns be resolved?

22. Whether or not to develop nuclear power as an energy source is a highly controversial issue in our society. Scores of experts have volunteered their testimony on both sides. Why are the experts in such fundamental disagreement?

23. Would you agree that the U.S. Constitution describes the property rights of the President, members of Congress, and Supreme Court justices?

a. Why does the Constitution prohibit Congress from lowering the salaries of the President or of federal judges during their term of office?

b. Are we likely to be governed better or worse during a president's first term than during the second? (The Constitution prohibits a third term.)

c. Would you expect more statesmanlike decisions from members of the House of Representatives, who must stand for reelection every two years, or from justices of the Supreme Court, who are appointed for life?

24. Does the umpire in a baseball game secure cooperation among the players by persuasion or by coercion? Upon what must your answer depend? Are employers using persuasion or coercion when they threaten to fire you if you don't get to work on time? Upon what must your answer depend?

25. The Constitution of the United States gives Congress the power to establish post offices.
   a. Can you think of any reasons why the government should assume responsibility for providing a system of postal service? Were there better reasons in 1789 than there are today?
   b. Congress has passed "private-express statutes" which give the Postal Service a legal monopoly over letter carrying. Why should the government prevent firms from competing with the United States Postal Service in the delivery of letters?
   c. Who would be likely to put pressure on Congress to defeat any bill that was introduced to repeal the private-express statutes?

26. Does either persuasion or coercion enjoy any inherent advantages over the other as a way of inducing cooperation?
   a. Does one tend gradually to displace the other in the course of social evolution?
   b. People who are cooperating because they have been persuaded usually want to maintain the relationship. Those who have been coerced will typically be looking for ways to sever the relationship. What does this imply about the level of transaction costs that will be associated with cooperative endeavors in each case?
   c. Coercion can be used to deny people the opportunity to engage in voluntary cooperation. Does this occur? Are the private-express statutes, which prohibit people from delivering letters for other people, an example? Why should anyone want to use coercion to prevent others from cooperating on a voluntary basis? If anyone wanted to do it, how could they expect to get away with doing it?
   d. Why is coercion so much more effective than persuasion as a way for sellers to eliminate competitors?

27. By using the concepts of this chapter, can you explain the continuing use of violence (war) as a way of resolving disputes between nations?

Inflation, Recession, Unemployment:
An Introduction

There is one responsibility of government that receives about as much attention these days from the press and public as all of the others put together: the responsibility of the federal government to prevent, cure, or otherwise control inflations and recessions. Except for an incidental mention, Chapter 14 ignored this responsibility in examining the functions of government. We'll make up for that omission now. The remainder of this book will be devoted almost entirely to the issue of aggregate economic fluctuations and government stabilization policies.

Why do we regard periods of inflation and recession as *problems*? Some readers will be thinking at this point that anyone who has to ask a question like that is too stupid to understand the answer. Inflation means a rise in the cost of living, and anything that makes it more costly for people to live is obviously a problem. As for recessions, they cause a loss of income and of jobs, and no one has to be told why both of those are problems. But matters are not that simple.

Dollar Prices and Real Costs

In the case of inflation, matters are not that way at all. *Inflation is not a rise in the cost of living.* Inflation is basically a fall in the value or purchasing power of money. Looking at it in another way, we can say that inflation is a rise in the money price of goods. You may even, if you wish, speak of inflation as a rise in the money cost of living. But the key word is *money*. A $2 hamburger this year really costs no more than a $1 hamburger last year if the cost of obtaining a dollar has been cut in half since last year.

The cost of obtaining anything is the value of what must be given up to obtain it. We get so into the habit of expressing the value of sacrificed opportunities in the common denominator of money that we sometimes forget to check on whether the value of the common denominator has changed. But that is precisely what inflation is. It's not an increase in the height of everything we're measuring—it's a decrease in the length of the rule that we're using to do our measuring.

Of course, everything is finally relative to everything else. It's logically possible to insist that money has maintained a constant value in recent years and everything else has gone up. But that would be as sensible as arguing that the price of a barrel of crude oil remained unchanged throughout 1979, while the value of everything else declined by about 50 percent. When we find oil prices moving relative to everything else, common sense tells us to look for the explanation in changes that have occurred in the conditions of supply or demand for oil—not for "everything else." When we see money prices moving relative to everything else, common sense ought to dictate the same course of inquiry.

Perhaps we would be more likely to look to money as the explanation for inflation if we stopped to realize that *inflation simply could not occur in the absence of money*. If all exchanges occurred through barter, there would be absolutely no way in which we could experience inflation. You may have to think about it for a moment to convince yourself. But inflation is a logical impossibility in a society relying entirely on barter.

OPEC has often been blamed for causing much of the inflation experienced by the U.S. and other nations during the 1970s. The truth is that OPEC has done something far worse: it has raised our cost of living. OPEC requires us to give up a much larger quantity of valuable goods to obtain a barrel of their oil now than we had to give up prior to 1973. We must either work harder, therefore, or give up more of some other goods that we're currently enjoying if we want to continue consuming as much OPEC oil as we used to.

OPEC has a lot of power to manipulate the price of oil by controlling its production. But the power to manipulate the price of the dollar lies primarily in the hands of those in the United States who control the production of dollars. OPEC's manipulations make life more difficult for the dollar producers, it is true, and may even put them under substantial political pressure to increase the supply of dollars.

But we are confusing the issue if we try to summarize the situation by saying that OPEC's price increases have caused our inflation. To understand the causes of inflation, we shall have to ask about the supply and demand for money, not for oil. How money is supplied, why it is demanded, and the ways in which money affects the rest of the economy will be major topics for consideration throughout the rest of this book.

The Real Costs of Inflation

The problems that inflation creates are almost entirely caused by uncertainty. Uncertainty about the rate and timing of increases in particular money prices leads to arbitrary redistributions of wealth, to costly efforts by people to protect themselves against losses in wealth, and—perhaps most serious of all—to mounting levels of resentment that can eventually cripple a society's capacity to maintain cooperation among its members.

If the price of everything increases in equal proportion, then nothing has really become more expensive. The cost of living is the same for everyone as it was before the price increases. Money has simply become cheaper. Note carefully that "everything" includes the services of wage and salary workers as well as financial assets of every kind, from mortgages through bank deposits to the "entitlements" of people drawing pensions or social security benefits. Of course, all prices do not increase in equal proportion during an inflation, so that some goods do become more expensive in real terms. But it is a logical corollary that other goods then become less expensive in real terms. Unless this has other effects, the losses must balance the gains. Insofar as inflation simply means a decrease in the purchasing power of money, it does not make the society as a whole worse off.

Redistributions of Wealth

But inflation does tend to redistribute wealth and income, for all prices and wages will not increase in the same proportion and at the same time when the value of money declines. Some prices are set for only short periods of time and can move up quickly in response to increased demand: examples are the prices of farm products and many of the raw materials used in industrial production. Other prices, like those at a retail grocery chain, are revised less frequently and so respond less quickly to changed circumstances. Commercial and residential rents are usually set by contract and often cannot be changed for long periods; although there are ways for landlords to compel a reopening of the contract in order to negotiate a higher rental, these procedures entail additonal costs to the landlord. Wages and salaries are typically established by agreements that are supposed to extend over longer periods of time; these agreements can also be renegotiated during the contract period, and some will even contain formal clauses calling for renegotiaton if certain conditions change. Wages and salaries, however, tend to be less quickly responsive to changed conditions than retail prices, though more responsive than rental prices. There are many prices that cannot be raised quickly because to do so requires the consent of a regulatory body that may move with glacial speed: railroads, gas and electric utilities, and telephone companies all complain of their inability to respond quickly enough to changed circumstances. Then there are creditors who have made long-term loans and cannot raise the payments they receive for that service until the loan matures—which might be 25 years in the future. On the other hand, consider the happy position of the federal government, selling us national defense and a variety of social services and charging a price (the personal income tax) that not only increases but increases at a progressive rate as we all spend and take in more money because the value of money has fallen. The net result of all this is that inflation redistributes income.

Prices that respond more slowly don't necessarily increase less; they just take longer to get where they're going. But that still means income is redistributed during the transitional period so that some people will have lost out even after they have caught up. The redistributive effects of inflation depend heavily on how rapidly the inflation occurs, because this affects the ability of different people to anticipate and adjust to it. From 1967 to 1973, for example, the Consumer Price Index rose 41.4 percent, while the mean hourly wage of production workers in private industry rose 46.5 percent. So wages more than kept pace. But when the price level spurted up 16.1 percent from January 1973 to July 1974, the mean hourly wage increased only 11.9 percent, so that the real hourly wage declined.

These redistributions of wealth are hardly enough to account for the public's hostility toward inflation. The strength of the popular pressure on government to control inflation (or at least seem to be controlling it) can only be appreciated if one understands why the beneficiaries of inflation so often join the victims in denouncing it. The principal reason is that they mistakenly think they are victims.

There is no better example than residential rents. In any period of rapid inflation, rents will lag well behind the rate of increase in other prices, including the "price" of labor as measured by average hourly wage rates. The result is that inflation redistributes wealth from landlords to tenants. But tenants do not realize this. They notice the increases in their rents. They do not notice that their rent is increasing at a lower percentage rate than the prices of everything else and their own incomes. So they conclude they are being hurt by inflation, when in fact they are its beneficiaries.

Many of us are also inclined somewhat to exaggerate our own merit and the value of our contribution to the welfare of the world. So when we look back and notice that our annual income has gone up 120 percent over the last decade, we tend to regard that as a 120 percent increase in the world's appreciation of our worth. When someone points out to us that the official index of consumer prices shows a 100 percent increase over the same period, we do not deflate that generous estimate of our own improvement. We still think we earned a 120 percent increase in our income, and we resent the fact that we have to pay twice as much nowadays for the things we buy.

Protection Costs

Illusion thus plays a major role in making inflation unpopular and creating pressure on governments to do something about it. But the costs of inflation to a society as a whole are not completely illusory. Imagine a situation in which the various state governments controlled the standards for weights and measures. Suppose that the only way to effect a shift to the metric system was to be sneaky about it—to expand the inch gradually until it measured 1/36 of a meter. So at periodic but unpredictable intervals over the next 10 years, the officials of various states announced to their jurisdictions an official increase in the length of the inch–"never enough to notice," as they were fond of saying, but enough to increase the inch from its former length of .0254 meters to the desired length of .027⅞ meters.

Where would the costs of such a procedure show up? In resources devoted to guessing the timing and rate of changes and ensuring against the consequences of mistakes; in resources spent on translating measurements when goods produced in one state are used in another; in resources employed to fit tools conforming to older specifications to products made to newer specifications; in resources wasted on the correction of mistakes arising from the increased uncertainty and the complexity of the coordinating task.

The real costs of inflation to a society are like the costs just described. We suggested a few paragraphs back that inflation is a change in the length of the measuring instrument. That doesn't mean inflation has no real costs. An elastic measuring instrument is a serious problem whenever decisions have to be coordinated over space and time. A large real cost of inflation is the effort and other resources that people devote to "beating" it. As evidence, thumb through a few of the unbelievable number of paperback books published in the last few years telling people how to come out ahead or at least stay even during periods of inflation.

Inflation and Social Conflict

The most serious cost of inflation to a society such as ours, however, may be the damage it does to our resources of mutual trust and good will. We have tried to call your attention on several occasions to a fact that was well appreciated by Adam Smith, but which his modern successors in the economics profession too often slight. The cooperation that is the essence of society and of civilization presupposes a substantial amount of self restraint on the part of its members, or a willingness to include the interests of others in the conception of one's own interests. If people come to believe that they are being defrauded, they will more readily throw off the constraints of ethics and do unto others what they think is being done unto them. When the illusory losses of inflation are added to the actual redistributions of wealth that inflation causes, the aggregate sense of injustice may rise to a critical level.

If people then organize into groups to secure a redress of their grievances through coercion, they feed the anger and resentment of others. School teachers striking in protest against salaries that don't keep pace with inflation add to citizen dissatisfaction with the school system and the taxes required to support it. The inflation that convinces tenants they are the victims of landlord exploitation—but which actually reduces the relative price of renting—creates low vacancy rates. This makes it appear that higher prices are producing less rental housing. Meanwhile, the net revenue of landlords will be falling, bringing with it the predictable consequences for maintenance, new construction, and the state of landlord-tenant feelings. Demands become more strident when people believe they are being victimized, and the total of claims that groups start to insist upon as their right climbs well above 100 percent. These demands tend to become concentrated upon government, which is increasingly thought to have the duty and the power to set all things right. Elected officials will find themselves under pressure to do something, even if that something provides only short term symptomatic relief and worsens the problem in the long run. Every action taken by government in response to mounting levels of citizen discontent creates a reason for doing more, either in response to the next interest group or to remedy the unanticipated problems caused by the last response. When the sum of the expectations by far exceeds the sum of what is available to satisfy them—and people begin using coercion to satisfy their expectations—

something must give way. It could too easily be the consensus upon which the society itself is founded.

What Happens in a Recession?

Recession is related to *recede*, which means to withdraw or retreat. A recession is a retreat from earlier rates of growth in the total output of the economy. By a general consent earned over many years, the National Bureau of Economic Research, a private, nonprofit research organization, has the privilege of deciding officially when a slowdown in growth has become a recession. But would every substantial slowdown in growth have to be a recession? Is perpetual growth the only possible norm?

That implication is avoided when we realize that *the costs of a recession are largely the costs of disappointed expectations.* The point is fundamental. If we lose sight of the relationship between recession and disappointment, we will find ourselves unable to distinguish between unemployment and leisure, or between changes that leave people worse off than before and changes that add to human welfare. We may also miss seeing the crucial role that uncertainty plays in causing recessions and thereby conclude that recessions can be cured with remedies that are more likely to aggravate the disease.

If a recession were merely a slowdown in the rate of economic growth, recessions would be popular with advocates of zero economic growth and all those who think we should reduce our emphasis on the production of marketable goods. But recessions are not popular with these groups or anyone else, because they entail *unintended and therefore disruptive slowdowns* in the rate of economic growth. Bare statistics on aggregate output, like the data on gross national product that we'll be using later, are incapable of revealing disappointed expectations. We may be able to infer widespread disappointment from such statistics, but aggregate data could truly measure a recession only if they could somehow measure the gaps between the output that people had counted on producing and what they finally decided to produce.

Producer's expectations are frustrated every day, of course. But every day some other producers are delighted to discover that events have turned out *better* than they had expected. A recession occurs when, for some reason, the number and depth of the disappointments increase, without any compensating increase in the quantity and quality of delightful surprises. Why that occurs and what can be done about it will be a major question in the chapters ahead.

We described the phenomenon of recession just now by referring to output or production. The costs and causes of

U.S. output in 1939 was almost exactly the same as it had been in 1929. Was the 1930's a decade of "zero economic growth"?

recessions, however, are better described in terms of income. It is the lost income that finally disappoints producers, and it is declining income that induces producers to cut back on the rate of output. The owners or managers of business firms count on selling some quantity of their product at some anticipated price. But when sales prove disappointing, inventories of unsold goods pile up, costs run ahead of revenues, and so production is slowed down or stopped altogether for awhile. Net income is the criterion that guides these decisions.

When business firms reduce their rate of production below what they had intended earlier, they often lay workers off and thereby create unemployment. This is the problem that first comes to mind when we think about recessions: a rising rate of unemployment. But what exactly is the problem? Once again we must ask for patience from the reader who thinks the question is stupid because the answer is obvious. The answer is obvious only until we begin thinking about it carefully.

When Is Unemployment a Problem?

Recessions do indeed cause unemployment to increase. But it doesn't increase from zero, and it doesn't fall back to zero when the recession is over. Even in the year 1944, when one-sixth of the entire labor force was in the armed forces, and people were being urged to leave school and take a job, to come out of retirement, to work six- and seven-day weeks, 1.2 percent of the labor force was classified as unemployed. No one who lived through those labor-hungry years would believe that 1.2 percent of the labor force could not find jobs in 1944.

There is some amount of unemployment that no one worries about because it isn't a problem. How much is that? What is an acceptable unemployment rate? How can we distinguish problem unemployment from nonproblem unemployment? The distinction is important, because when unemployment reaches a "problem level," political pressure to do something about it begins to build. What the federal government does in response to these pressures will definitely have costs and may have other undesirable consequences, especially if unemployment is, in reality, not above the critical "problem level." But where is that level and how do we recognize it?

In some circles it is still common practice to duck the whole question by saying something like this: Unemployment becomes a problem when it rises above the level of purely "frictional" unemployment. And "frictional" unemployment is that amount of unemployment which poses no problem because it represents ordinary labor-market turnover. This might be a satisfactory procedure if we had reason to believe that "ordinary labor-market turnover" was some identifiable constant over time. Quite to the contrary, however, we have excellent reasons for supposing that "ordinary labor-market turnover" is a variable, rather than a constant, and that it changes in response to a variety of factors that have shifted substantially in recent years.

What we would really like to do is find some way to distinguish clearly between those who are *unemployed* and those who are merely *not employed*. The extreme cases are easy to distinguish. Some people would do almost anything to find satisfactory employment, whereas there is almost nothing that would persuade others to accept a job. But did you spot the fudge factors in that preceding sentence? People who would describe themselves as "desperate" for work will nonetheless decline *some* job opportunities in the expectation of finding something better. And very few of those who say they "absolutely" don't want a job would decline *every* offer that might come their way. People who say they "can't find a job" mean they can't find a job at which they're willing to work. Those who say they "don't want to work" mean that they don't want to work at any job they can find. In some cases, the difference between those two situations isn't going to be discernible to an outside observer.

Measuring Unemployment

The outside observers on whom we depend to make this distinction for us are some very highly trained employees of the U.S. government. The official data on U.S. unemployment are published by the Bureau of Labor Statistics (BLS), an agency in the United States Department of Labor. The source of the data is the *Current Population Survey*, a sample survey of households which the Bureau of the Census conducts on behalf of the BLS. The sample consists of 56,000 households, selected to represent the entire population, and interviewed monthly. (The data are *not* derived, as many people think, from claims for unemployment compensation.) The household survey provides information on the labor force activity of every person in the population who is 16 years old or over and not in an institution, such as a hospital or prison.

The illustrative numbers we will use in looking closely at unemployment are the BLS averages through the first three months of 1979, which was the last quarter before the beginning of the 1979 slowdown. All numbers will be rounded to the nearest thousand. If the components don't quite sum to the totals, that will reflect detail lost in the rounding process. Before beginning we should also note that the data have been *seasonally adjusted*. This means that they have been corrected to eliminate the effects of variations caused entirely by seasonal factors—the closing of schools in June, extra hiring in December, major holidays, and so on. Seasonal adjustment lets us detect trends that would otherwise be concealed or exaggerated by purely seasonal fluctuations.

Employed, Not Employed, and Unemployed

The average population of the United States during the first quarter of 1979 was very close to 220 million. The number of people counted by the BLS as employed was 96,596,000, to the nearest thousand, which includes not only those who received wages and salaries but also the self-employed and unpaid family workers. We can conclude, therefore, that almost 125 million Americans were *not employed*.

But *not employed* isn't the same as *unemployed*. To be counted as unemployed, a person must first be in *the noninstitutional population: the total of those who are 16 years of age or older and not in an institution*. The noninstitutional population in the 1st quarter of 1979 was 162,663,000. Subtracting from this total the number in the armed forces (2,093,000) leaves *the civilian noninstitutional population*: 160,570,000.

Each person in the civilian noninstitutional population is classified as either employed, unemployed, or not in the labor force. Deciding who is employed presents no serious problems. But what is the distinction between someone who is *unemployed* and someone who is "not in the labor force" and therefore merely *not employed*? The BLS has developed precise criteria for distinguishing between these two groups and measures the size of each with considerable confidence. Measurement is not the problem. The problem is the significance of the distinction, especially in light of the highly diverse and changing costs to particular people of being "not in the labor force" or being officially unemployed.

Let's look more closely. To be classified in the household survey as unemployed, an individual must (1) be in the civilian noninstitutional population; (2) have been without employment during the survey week; (3) have made specific efforts to find employment sometime during the preceding four weeks; and (4) be presently available for work. (Persons who are on layoff or are waiting to start a new job within 30 days are counted as unemployed without meeting the third criterion above, which requires that they be actively looking for employment.) The total number satisfying these criteria in the first quarter of 1979 was 5,878,000. That was 5.7 percent of *the civilian labor force*, which is *the sum of the employed and the unemployed* (102,475,000). The unemployed divided by the civilian labor force yields the official unemployment rate, which makes the newspapers and the newscasts when the BLS publishes it each month.

Total population

− under 16 or institutionalized

= Noninstitutional population

− armed forces

= Civilian noninstitutional population

− not in the labor force

= Civilian labor force

− employed

= unemployed

What about all those people in the civilian noninstitutional population—58,095,000 of them—who are "not in the labor force" because they are counted neither as employed nor as unemployed? Let's examine the data on them. The BLS divides them into two categories: those who say they do not want a job at the present time and those who say they do want a job. Those who do not want a job now (53,942,000) are asked to state their current activity. Those who do want a job now (5,262,000) are asked why they are not looking for one. Remember that this second group would be counted in the unemployed, rather than among those who are not in the labor force, if they were actively seeking the employment they say they want.

The current activities of those who are not in the labor force because they do not want a job at the present time are Keeping House (55 percent), Retirement (18 percent), Going to School (11 percent), Illness or Disability (9 percent), and "Other" (7 percent).

The reasons given for not looking by those who say they want a job are School Attendance (25 percent), Home Responsibilities (23 percent), Illness or Disability (14 percent), Belief That They Cannot Get a Job (14 percent), and "Other Reasons" (23 percent).

The most interesting subset is composed of those people who are not employed, are not actively seeking employment, say they want a job, and give as their reason for not looking their belief that they cannot get a job. They are called *discouraged workers*. The BLS counted 724,000 such discouraged workers in the first quarter of 1979. It divided them further into those who gave job-market factors (483,000) and those who gave personal factors (241,000) as their reason for believing they could not get a job.

Details of this sort don't make very exciting reading. But it is crucial that we know what people must do or not do in order to meet the BLS criteria for being unemployed. There is simply no way to understand the significance of unemployment or the nature of the problem it presents unless we know something about the cost of that status to those who choose it.

Labor-Market Decisions

Choose it? The notion that people choose to be unemployed seems at first to contradict the very concept of unemployment. But economic theory tries to explain *all* behavior as the consequence of choice. Insofar as people have no discernible or significant amount of choice in a situation, economic theory has nothing useful to say about what's going on. Our instinctive hostility to the assertion that people choose unemployment is probably rooted in an erroneous equation of *choice* with *free choice*—or an equally erroneous assumption that everyone has

Civilian
noninstitutional
population

seeks
employment
(in labor force)

does not seek
employment
(not in labor force)

accepts
employment
(employed)

does not accept
employment
(unemployed)

some *good* choices available. To choose simply means to select the best available alternative, on the basis of one's expectations regarding relative costs and benefits.

The BLS definition makes quite clear the specific choices that produce the status called "unemployed": (1) a decision to look actively for employment, and (2) a decision not to accept the employment opportunities offered. Both clearly are choices people make. The first decision stands at the fork that leads either to being unemployed or to being out of the labor force. The second decision marks the fork that leads to employment or to continued unemployment. For large numbers of people, the anticipated benefits and costs of particular decisions at those forks have changed considerably in recent years. As a result, particular unemployment rates do not mean what they meant 25 years ago or even 10 years ago.

Once we start looking closely at the BLS data, it becomes apparent that people are facing and making different choices in the labor market from those they made just a decade ago. Suppose we compare the first quarter of 1979 with the year 1969. The unemployment rate in 1969 was 3.5 percent, the lowest annual rate experienced in this country since 1953. The 5.7 percent rate in the first quarter of 1979, in comparison, looks very high. But is it really?

Suppose that we compare the number *employed* during each period. Civilian employment in 1969 was 77,902,000. In the first quarter of 1979, it was 96,596,000. Higher unemployment in 1979 was accompanied by higher employment, too. But does this mean anything except that the population increased during these years? We can control for population changes by dividing the number employed by the civilian noninstitutional population in each period to obtain an employment *rate*. If we do that, we find that 58 percent of the civilian noninstitutional population was employed in 1969 when the unemployment rate was 3.5 percent. In the first quarter of 1979, with the unemployment rate at 5.7 percent, the employment rate was 60.2 percent.

There is no contradiction in this. It means that a much higher proportion of the population chose to enter the labor force in 1979 than in 1969. The civilian labor force participation rate (the civilian labor force divided by the civilian noninstitutional population) was 60.1 percent in 1969, a record-high level up to that time. But in the first quarter of 1979 it stood at 63.8 percent. A higher percentage of the population is looking for employment today than at any previous time in US history.

Costs and Decisions

They are looking for employment; but that does not mean they are willing to accept the particular job offers currently available to them. Nor does the fact that they won't take a particu-

lar job that's been offered to them mean that they don't really
want a job. It more commonly means that they expect to find
something better if they continue searching.

We must beware of aggregation. Both the cost of taking a
job and the cost of not taking one will differ considerably from
one person to another, depending on such factors as skill,
experience, age, family responsibilities, other sources of income, and the attitudes of those whose opinions the person
respects.

Consider the situation of teen-agers living with their families. They often want jobs and may actively seek them in ways
that qualify them for inclusion in the ranks of the officially
unemployed. But if they are currently attending school, they
are "presently available" for a very limited number of jobs. If
they are on summer vacation, employers won't want to hire
them for jobs that require a lot of training, so they aren't really
"available" for these jobs either. If they are out of high school
but trying to make up their minds about college, they will be
reluctant to accept any job that requires a commitment. Moreover, the job opportunities available to them will tend to be
relatively unattractive, because employers don't want to pay
much to teen-agers, who tend to be unskilled and who quit
before the employer has recovered the cost of training them.

But someone receiving free room and board can afford to
search a long time—or to quit a job that proves unsatisfactory
and start looking again. Any job will begin to seem unsatisfactory to teen-agers who discover that they must work while their
friends are partying. When we put all this together, we see that
the cost of taking and keeping a job is high for teen-agers, and
that the cost of continuing to look is relatively low. Should we
be either surprised or disturbed, then, to discover that the
unemployment rate among people 16 to 19 years old was 15.8
percent in the first quarter of 1979?

If we found an unemployment rate like that among adults
with families entirely dependent on their earnings for income,
we would have grounds for astonishment and concern. That
was indeed the case during the Great Depression of the 1930s,
traumatic years that have left their mark on all our thinking
about unemployment. But that has not been the case at any
time since World War II. Even in 1975, at the peak of the
unemployment caused by this country's deepest recession
since the 1930s, the overall unemployment rate never reached 9
percent. More to the present point, the unemployment rate
among principal family earners was well below the overall rate.
The BLS actually has no separate category for principal family
earners. But the unemployment rate among married men living
with their spouses never climbed above 5.7 percent in any
month of 1975. In the first quarter of 1979, it was 2.6 percent.

The unemployment rate among "women who head families" was a lot higher than that: 8.1 percent in the first quarter of 1979. But we must use care in drawing inferences from this fact. The cost of taking a job is the value of the other opportunities given up. Women who head families with small children must find another way of caring for those children when they accept employment. Consequently they would not want to accept some jobs that might readily be taken by others without parental responsibilities. The cost of *not* taking a job is largely the value of the earnings forgone. The value of those earnings to a woman who heads a family will depend on other sources of income available to her, including some (child support payments, cash and in-kind welfare assistance) that may decline as her earnings increase.

What may we infer from the fact that the unemployment rate for men 20 years old and over was 4.0 percent in the first quarter of 1979, but was 5.7 percent for women 20 years old and over? Does this prove that employers discriminate against women? There can be no doubt that many employers discriminate against women, but the different unemployment rates for men and women cannot be used as evidence for that fact. *Less* discrimination against women might well produce a *higher* rate of unemployment among them. If declining discrimination encourages more women to look for work, the unemployment rate could rise. This would be especially likely if the family income of these new labor force participants was already high, so that they could easily afford to keep searching until they found something they liked. It's worth noting in this context that the civilian labor force participation rate of women was 50.3 percent in the first quarter of 1979; in 1969 it had been only 42.7 percent.

A Summing Up

We don't want to point out so many trees that you lose sight of the forest. The principal thesis we've been trying to establish is that *unemployment is not simply a consequence of recession.* In a recession, the demand for labor decreases, and this causes unemployment to rise. The recovery after a recession increases the demand for labor, and unemployment falls. But it does not follow from this that all unemployment is the result of an inadequate demand for labor. Unemployment rates are the product of complex decisions by both demanders and suppliers of labor, all of whom pay attention to the expected opportunity costs of their decisions to supply or to demand.

Moreover, the costs of unemployment do not fall with equal severity on every unemployed person and do not take the same form from one person to another. For some, the lost income is the principal cost of unemployment. For others, the cost of unemployment will be the loss of goods that they value more highly than money income: a sense of contributing, a daily discipline, workplace associations, challenge and variety. For some people the sum of these costs will be crushing; for others the costs will be negligible; and for a few who receive unemployment compensation and live in families with more than one earner, the costs can even be negative.

There is no undifferentiated mass called *The Unemployed*, upon whom the burdens of unemployment fall. There is no constant number above which unemployment first begins to be a problem. There is no single policy suitable for reducing all unemployment. There is no clear line that divides the unemployed from those who happen to be only not employed. In the last analysis, the distinction between suffering unemployment and enjoying leisure can be made only by the person who calculates the relative net advantages of taking and of not taking a job.

Table 15A summarizes labor-force activity in the United States in each year since 1947. That's a good cut-off year, because in 1947 the BLS revised its definition of the noninstitutional population to exclude persons 14 and 15 years old. We'll be looking at data from earlier years in Chapter 18, when we examine U.S. experience during the Great Depression and the lessons drawn from that experience.

National Output and Income

The experience of the Great Depression lent added impetus to efforts to compile reliable information on the overall performance of the economy, which had begun in the United States around 1920. The best-known statistical series evolving out of these efforts is the National Income and Product Accounts, compiled by the Bureau of Economic Analysis (BEA) in the United States Department of Commerce. If you read only the front page of the daily newspaper, you will have heard about gross national product. This is the most comprehensive item in the Department of Commerce accounts and the one most frequently cited. Some people watch the behavior of GNP, as it is familiarly known, with the intensity of children listening to the weather report on the morning of a picnic.

What is the *gross national product?* It is *the market value of all the final goods produced in the entire economy over a given period, usually taken to be one year*. When quarterly data are presented—the data are not available more often than quarterly—they are stated on an annual basis, indicating what GNP would be for the year if that quarter's rate of production were maintained for four quarters.

As the name of the accounts suggests, GNP can be calcu-

TABLE 15A LABOR FORCE ACTIVITY

	1	2	3	4	5	6	7
Year	Civilian Noninsti-tutional Population	Civilian Labor Force	Civilian Labor Force Partici-pation Rate (1) ÷ (2)	Employ-ment	Employ-ment Rate (1) ÷ (4)	Unemploy-ment	Unemploy-ment Rate (2) ÷ (6)
1947	101,827	59,350	58.3%	57,038	56.0%	2,311	3.9%
1948	103,068	50,621	58.8	58,343	56.6	2,276	3.8
1949	103,994	61,286	58.9	57,651	55.4	3,637	5.9
1950	104,995	62,208	59.2	58,918	56.1	3,288	5.3
1951	104,621	62,017	59.3	59,961	57.3	2,055	3.3
1952	105,231	62,138	59.0	60,250	57.3	1,883	3.0
1953	107,056	63,015	58.9	61,179	57.1	1,834	2.9
1954	108,321	63,643	58.8	60,109	55.5	3,532	5.5
1955	109,683	65,023	59.3	62,170	56.7	2,852	4.4
1956	110,954	66,552	60.0	63,799	57.5	2,750	4.1
1957	112,265	66,929	59.6	64,071	57.1	2,859	4.3
1958	113,727	67,639	59.5	63,036	55.4	4,602	6.8
1959	115,329	68,369	59.3	64,630	56.0	3,740	5.5
1960	117,245	69,628	59.4	65,778	56.1	3,852	5.5
1961	118,771	70,459	59.3	65,746	55.4	4,714	6.7
1962	120,153	70,614	58.8	66,702	55.5	3,911	5.5
1963	122,416	71,833	58.7	67,762	55.4	4,070	5.7
1964	124,485	73,091	58.7	69,305	55.7	3,786	5.2
1965	126,513	74,455	58.9	71,088	56.2	3,366	4.5
1966	128,057	75,770	59.2	72,895	56.9	2,875	3.8
1967	129,873	77,347	59.6	74,372	57.3	2,975	3.8
1968	132,027	78,737	59.6	75,920	57.5	2,817	3.6
1969	134,335	80,734	60.1	77,902	58.0	2,832	3.5
1970	136,994	82,715	60.4	78,627	57.4	4,088	4.9
1971	139,779	84,113	60.2	79,120	56.6	4,993	5.9
1972	143,326	86,542	60.4	81,702	57.0	4,840	5.6
1973	145,937	88,714	60.8	84,409	57.8	4,304	4.9
1974	148,598	91,011	61.2	85,935	57.8	5,076	5.6
1975	151,269	92,613	61.2	84,783	56.0	7,830	8.5
1976	153,904	94,773	61.6	87,485	56.8	7,288	7.7
1977	156,426	97,401	62.3	90,546	57.9	6,855	7.0
1978	158,941	100,420	63.2	94,373	59.4	6,047	6.0

SOURCE: Bureau of Labor Statistics. All data are stated in thousands. Components may not sum to totals because of rounding.

lated either as the national income or as the national product or output. The national output is the sum of all the value added at each stage of the production process. In the case of bread, for example, it's the value added successively by the wheat farmer, the miller, the baker, the distributor and the retailer as the loaf wends its way toward the consumer's shopping cart. The national income is the sum of all the payments made in the course of the production process to those who did the producing: the owners of labor, of capital, and of land. The value of the national output must necessarily equal the value of the national income, when properly calculated, because every dollar paid for output becomes income for someone. An apparent exception would be the amount of tax, such as sales tax, paid on a purchase. But this is income, too; it's income for government, which uses it to pay for the labor, capital, and land that government employs in the process of producing goods.

Another question might arise about unsold goods. They are part of the year's output, but since they aren't sold, they don't generate income for anyone. This is handled in the accounts by assuming that the business firm that produced the goods also bought them. It surely had to pay to get them produced. Maybe it hadn't intended to buy them itself. But goods produced and not sold are indeed added, however reluctantly, to the inventories of the firm that produced them.

Thus we can actually measure gross national product in *three* ways, all of which would yield the same total if we made no errors in counting: (1) The value added by each producer in the course of contributing to the year's total output of final goods. (2) The total income received, in the form of wages and salaries, interest, rent, and profits, by those who contributed the resources used to produce the year's total output. (3) The total purchases of final goods by consumers, investors, and government, plus the purchases of foreigners in excess of what the foreigners sold us in return. When unsold goods are counted as additions to inventory and added to investment purchases, the sum of consumer, investor, government and (net) foreign expenditures on final goods must add up exactly to the total value of the goods produced.

Gross national product is
— the sum of all the value added by producers at each stage of the production process,

or

— the total income received by those producers,

or

— total purchases of newly produced final goods.

Some Limitations of National Income Accounting

Never make the mistake of confusing the gross natonal product with gross national well-being. The concept of gross national product is based on so many conventions, with so many essentially arbitrary inclusions and omissions, that it will never be used by any intelligent, responsible, and thinking person to compare the well-being of different nations. The most it can do is indicate whether we're going faster or slowing down. And even there it gives misleading indications if we try to make comparisons over a long period of time.

Two examples may be enough to teach you caution. Among the services not counted by the Department of Commerce statisticians in the calculation of gross national product are the services of the spouse who maintains the home. It is too difficult to evaluate them despite their enormous importance, so they are completely excluded from the accounts. But the value of hired housekeepers' services *can* be measured by the payments made to obtain them; hence they do enter into the accounts. As a result, gross national product will tend to decline as a direct consequence of marriages and increase with a rising divorce rate. It is doubtful that real welfare moves in the same direction.

TABLE 15B GROSS NATIONAL PRODUCT (IN BILLIONS OF $) AND THE PRICE LEVEL

Year	Gross National Product	Personal Consumption Expenditures	Gross Private Domestic Investment	Net Exports of Goods	Gov't Purchases of Goods	Gross National Product in 1972 Prices	Implicit GNP Deflator (1972 = 100)	Consumer Price Index (1967 = 100)	Producer Price Index (1967 = 100)	Year
1947	232.8	161.7	34.0	11.6	25.5	468.3	49.7	66.9	76.5	1947
1948	259.1	174.7	45.9	6.5	32.0	487.7	53.1	72.1	82.8	1948
1949	258.0	178.1	35.3	6.2	38.4	490.7	52.6	71.4	78.7	1949
1950	286.2	192.0	53.8	1.9	38.5	533.5	53.6	72.1	81.8	1950
1951	330.2	207.1	59.2	3.8	60.1	576.5	57.3	77.8	91.1	1951
1952	347.2	217.1	52.1	2.4	75.6	598.5	58.0	79.5	88.6	1952
1953	366.1	229.7	53.3	.6	82.5	621.8	58.9	80.1	87.4	1953
1954	366.3	235.8	52.7	2.0	75.8	613.7	59.7	80.5	87.6	1954
1955	399.3	253.7	68.4	2.2	75.0	654.8	61.0	80.2	87.8	1955
1956	420.7	266.0	71.0	4.3	79.4	668.8	62.9	81.4	90.7	1956
1957	442.8	280.4	69.2	6.1	87.1	680.9	65.0	84.3	93.3	1957
1958	448.9	289.5	61.9	2.5	95.0	679.5	66.1	86.6	94.6	1958
1959	486.5	310.8	77.6	.6	97.6	720.4	67.5	87.3	94.8	1959
1960	506.0	324.9	76.4	4.4	100.3	736.8	68.7	88.7	94.9	1960
1961	523.3	335.0	74.3	5.8	108.2	755.3	69.3	89.6	94.5	1961
1962	563.8	355.2	85.2	5.4	118.0	799.1	70.6	90.6	94.8	1962
1963	594.7	374.6	90.2	6.3	123.7	830.7	71.6	91.7	94.5	1963
1964	635.7	400.4	96.6	8.9	129.8	874.4	72.7	92.9	94.7	1964
1965	688.1	430.2	112.0	7.6	138.4	925.9	74.3	94.5	96.6	1965
1966	753.0	464.8	124.5	5.1	158.7	981.0	76.8	97.2	99.8	1966
1967	796.3	490.4	120.8	4.9	180.2	1,007.7	79.0	100.0	100.0	1967
1968	868.5	535.9	131.5	2.3	198.7	1,051.8	82.6	104.2	102.5	1968
1969	935.5	579.7	146.2	1.8	207.9	1,078.8	86.7	109.8	106.5	1969
1970	982.4	618.8	140.8	3.9	218.9	1,075.3	91.4	116.3	110.4	1970
1971	1,063.4	668.2	160.0	1.6	233.7	1,107.5	96.0	121.3	133.9	1971
1972	1,171.1	733.0	188.3	-3.3	253.1	1,171.1	100.0	125.3	119.1	1972
1973	1,306.3	808.5	220.5	7.4	269.9	1,235.0	105.9	133.1	134.7	1973
1974	1,406.9	885.9	212.2	7.7	301.1	1,217.8	116.2	147.7	160.1	1974
1975	1,498.8	963.8	182.6	21.2	331.2	1,202.3	126.4	161.2	174.9	1975
1976	1,700.1	1,090.2	243.0	7.4	359.5	1,271.0	133.76	170.5	183.0	1976
1977	1,887.2	1,206.5	297.8	-11.1	394.0	1,332.7	141.61	181.5	194.2	1977
1978	2,107.6	1,340.1	345.6	-12.0	433.9	1,385.7	152.09	195.3	209.3	1978

SOURCES: Bureau of Economic Analysis and Bureau of Labor Statistics.

When a coal-burning station generates electricity, its output enters GNP. When people are hired to clean and paint as a consequence of the sooty fallout from the generating plant, GNP rises once more. Overcounting obviously occurs in this case. It would make sense, if we were interested in welfare, to deduct the cost of the cleaning from the value of the electricity generated. If Chapter 13 did not put you sufficiently on guard, then be warned once more: the consequences for human welfare of particular economic decisions are not always what they seem at first glance. Systems for keeping score are useful, but they inevitably harbor deficiencies that must be kept in mind by those who use them. And the good life is far more (or is it far less?) than the simple sum of the values that enter into the National Income and Product Accounts.

Nominal and Real Gross National Product

GNP data overstate the rate of increase in national output and income in one way that the Bureau of Economic Analysis knows about and corrects for. Since GNP expresses the *market* value of output, any decline in the value of money will show up as an increase in GNP. But that isn't an increase in output or real income. It is a purely nominal increase, an increase in name only, because it really represents a decline in the value of money. The Bureau consequently calculates *deflators* for gross national product that indicate by how much any given year's GNP overstates the value of output, relative to some base year, because of the inflation that has occurred since the base year.

To illustrate, GNP in 1978 was $2,107.6 billion. But if we valued 1978's output at the market prices that prevailed in 1972, the current base year used by the Bureau of Economic Analysis, then GNP in 1978 would be only $1,385.7 billion. Dividing 1,385.7 into 2,107.6 gives us 152.09,[1] which tells us that the average price of the goods entering into GNP in 1978 had gone up 52 percent since 1972. To calculate actual changes in output from year to year, therefore, we must divide gross national product by the implicit GNP deflator for each year.

Table 15B shows nominal gross national product; consumer, investor, government, and net foreign expenditures on gross national product; gross national product in 1972 dollars; and the implicit GNP deflator for each year from 1947 through 1978.

---

1. If your calculator yields 152.10, to the nearest hundredth, you have been victimized by an error due to rounding off the data. The officially calculated deflator for 1978 was 152.09 in the month when this was written. That last qualification had to be added, because the Bureau of Economic Analysis often goes back and revises old data on the basis of more accurate information that has become available.

The table also presents two other indexes of inflation that are more commonly quoted than the GNP deflator because the Bureau of Labor Statistics calculates and publishes them monthly, while the GNP deflator is only available at quarterly intervals (and even then with a time lag of several months). The best known BLS index is the Consumer Price Index, which hits the front page of the newspapers every month whenever there is substantial public concern about inflation. The Consumer Price Index tracks changes in the money price of goods that enter into the budget of typical urban consumers.

Another BLS index, and one more useful for a few purposes, is the Producer Price Index, which long went by the highly misleading name, Wholesale Price Index. The name was changed recently to remove the implication that the index measured prices paid by retailers. The Producer Price Index is a measure of changes in the market prices of a long list of basic agricultural and industrial commodities, such as processed foods and feeds, textile products, hides, fuels, chemicals, lumber, metals, machinery, and so on. (The BLS currently uses 1967 as its base year, in contrast with the BEA's use of 1972).

Once Over Lightly

Inflation is an increase in the average money price of goods. It is not an increase in the cost of living but a decrease in the purchasing power of money.

Inflation does impose real burdens on a society. It redistributes wealth, induces people to spend resources trying to anticipate its effects, and stimulates dissatisfaction and conflict among people who believe, rightly or wrongly, that they are being harmed by inflation. All of these are effects of the increased uncertainty that inflation introduces into people's estimates of future prices.

A recession is an unanticipated and disruptive slowdown in the rate of increase in total output and income.

Recessions add to unemployment by causing the demand for some goods—and hence for the labor of those who produce the goods—to fall short of expectations.

The level of unemployment depends on the supply of labor as well as the demand. The Bureau of Labor Statistics (BLS) counts as unemployed all those who are not currently employed and are actively seeking employment. Both the decision to enter the labor force and the decision not to accept particular job offers will depend on people's estimates of the relative advantages of alternative opportunities.

Different unemployment rates for different population groups do not merely reflect differences in the demand for the labor services of the people in those groups. They also reflect variations in the cost to different people of searching for, accepting, and retaining employment.

Unemployment rates have been high in the 1970s in comparison with unemployment rates in the 1950s and 1960s. But labor-force participation rates and employment rates also rose during the 1970s to record-high levels.

Changes in total output and income are most commonly measured by changes in gross national product (GNP). GNP is an attempt to measure the market vaue of all final goods produced in a year. It is equal by definition to the total income received by those who produced the year's output and to the sum of expenditures on new final goods by consumers, investors, and government, plus net exports.

Measuring GNP in dollars of current purchasing power overstates the rate of growth in output when the level of money prices is rising. Nominal GNP must be divided by the appropriate price deflator to obtain real GNP.

The GNP Deflator is published quarterly by the Bureau of Economic Analysis (BEA). The Bureau of Labor Statistics publishes two monthly indexes of general price level changes: the Consumer Price Index, measuring changes in the prices of goods purchased by urban consumers, and the Producer Price Index, measuring changes in the prices of major industrial inputs.

QUESTIONS FOR DISCUSSION

1. Numerous public opinion surveys in the 1970s showed that the majority of Americans regard inflation as a more serious threat than unemployment.
   a. Does this imply that the majority of Americans would rather be unemployed in a period of stable prices than employed in a time of rising prices?
   b. If the management of a firm allowed employees to vote on whether the firm should lay off 10 percent of the employees or reduce wage rates by 5 percent, how do you think they would vote? Do you think the outcome of the vote would depend on whether the employees knew in advance exactly who would be laid off?
2. If inflation redistributes income and wealth, there will be gainers as well as losers. Which classes and categories of people are most likely to gain and lose from an inflation? What difference does it make how well the inflation is anticipated?
3. An article in the *Wall Street Journal* of July 16, 1979 described some of the ways in which Argentines have learned to live with annual inflation rates as high as 150 percent. An Argentine economist quoted in the article comments that the economy has become one of speculation rather than of production.

How does this illustrate one of the genuine social costs of inflation?

4. Professor Plato received an annual salary of $12,000 in 1967 and $22,000 in 1978.

   a. How did his real income change from 1967 to 1978?

   b. Is Professor Plato likely to think that his additional experience entitled him to a much larger salary in 1978?

   c. Do you think it was inflation or changed conditions of supply and demand that caused Professor Plato's real income to fall between 1967 and 1978?

   d. Professor Plato's college classmate, Rock Igneous, was also earning $12,000 a year in 1967, working as a mining engineer. In 1978 Rock's salary was $48,000. Why do you suppose that he fared so much better than Professor Plato in this inflationary period?

   e. Do you think it would have been easier or harder for the college to reduce Plato's salary from $12,000 to $11,265 in a period of stable prices than to raise it from $12,000 to $22,000 in a period when prices rose 95 percent? Why?

5. The items included in the Consumer Price Index don't all increase at the same rate during an inflation. Here are the approximate percentage increases from 1967 to 1978 in the prices of several important categories of goods included in the CPI: Food, 125 percent; Residential Rents, 70 percent; Fuels, 155 percent; House Furnishings, 60 percent; Clothing 55 percent.

   a. How will these changes in relative prices affect people's purchases of these various items?

   b. Would you expect people in 1978 to be buying the same quantities of these goods as they were buying in 1967?

   c. How does a price index exaggerate the effects of inflation on people's budgets if it's based on the assumption that households always purchase the same quantities of goods, regardless of changes in their relative prices?

6. The Federal Reserve System calculates indexes of production for various industries. The overall index declined 8.9 percent from 1974 to 1975. Here are the percentages by which the index changed from 1974 to 1975 in selected industries:

Iron and steel	−20.0%
Electrical machinery	−19.0
Transportation equipment	−10.4
Lumber and products	−7.4
Printing and publishing	−4.1
Foods	−0.5

   a. How would you account for these differences? Would you expect *every* recession to affect the food industry very little but hit the iron and steel industry very hard?

   b. From 1969 to 1970 the overall index declined 3.0 percent. Here are the percentages in the index for the same industries:

Iron and steel	−7.0%
Electrical machinery	−3.4
Transportation equipment	−17.4
Lumber and products	−2.1
Printing and publishing	−0.4
Foods	+2.6

Why do you suppose the transportation equipment industry did so much worse in the 1970 than in the 1975 recession?

7. Can there be "overfull" employment?
   a. Suppose that the vacancy rate on apartments in a large city is less than 1 percent. What undesirable consequences might be associated with such a full level of apartment employment? Would you enjoy moving to a city with such a low vacancy rate?
   b. If you are driving on only 80 percent of the automobile tires you own, is the spare tire unemployed? Would you like to be driving with your tires at "full employment"? Across the Great Salt Lake Desert?

8. Jones is a tool and die maker earning $12 an hour. He is suddenly laid off.
   a. He frequents employment agencies, reads want ads, and follows up leads on tool and die making jobs for two weeks. Is he unemployed during this time?
   b. At the end of the two weeks he is offered a job driving a bread truck that pays $4.50 an hour. He turns it down. Is he unemployed?
   c. He receives an offer of a job as a tool and die maker in a city 125 miles away. He turns it down because his teen-age children don't want to change high schools. Is he unemployed?
   d. After three months of searching, Jones becomes discouraged and quits looking. Is he unemployed?

9. A woman who is laid off from her job goes to work for herself (becomes self-employed) "producing" information about alternative job opportunities. How long she will remain self-employed in this way depends on her "productivity" (is she generating what she considers valuable information?) and the opportunity cost of this self-employment. (She'll want to continue as long as her anticipated marginal revenue exceeds anticipated marginal cost.) How will the duration of measured unemployment be affected by
   a. unemployment compensation?
   b. food-stamp programs?
   c. persistent rumors that many large firms are beginning to hire?
   d. a spirit of confidence and optimism?

10. Should the hypothetical individuals who made each of the statements below be classified as unemployed or as not in the labor force? Which of them is voluntarily rather than involuntarily unemployed?
    a. "I quit my job and I'm going to remain unemployed until I find a job that pays $1000 for 10 hours' work a week."
    b. "I was laid off last month. I had a great job as marketing consultant to a franchising chain. They paid me $1000 a week for about 10 hours of work. I'm going to keep looking until I find another job like that one."

c. "I decided I could no longer be a part of the military-industrial complex, so I quit my job. I'm looking now for an engineer's position that doesn't require me to participate in murder, pollution, and mind-raping."

d. "When they laid me off, I figured I could easily find another job in engineering. But now I don't care. I'll take any job at all that pays what I used to get."

e. "I've been out of work for six months, and I'm pretty desperate. I'll do anything that's legal to get food for my family. But I have an invalid wife and five small children, so I can't take any job that pays less than $100 a week."

f. "I could get any one of a dozen jobs tomorrow. But I don't want to. I'm eligible for three more months of unemployment compensation, so I'm just going to take it easy until the checks run out. Oh, if something really good turned up, I'd take it, of course."

g. "I could get any one of a dozen jobs tomorrow. But I don't want to. I'm eligible for three more months of unemployment compensation, so I'm just going to spend my time really looking. I'm going to use those three months to find the very best job I can possibly get."

11. The Bureau of Labor Statistics divides the unemployed into four groups on the basis of what it calls the reason for unemployment: job losers, job leavers, reentrants into the labor force, and new entrants into the labor force. The percentage of the total number unemployed who were job losers was 39 percent in 1973, 43 percent in 1974, and 55 percent in 1975. After 1975 this percentage declined again: to 50 percent in 1976, 45 percent in 1977, and 42 percent in 1978. How would you relate these figures to the data of Table 15B, showing annual changes in real gross national product?

12. Why can't a society's output increase faster than its income? Could a society's income increase faster than its output?

13. The Department of Commerce statisticians strive to avoid double counting in their calculations of gross national product. Why would there be double counting if the total output of new steel products and the total output of automobiles in a given year were both included in gross national product? Do you understand how double counting is avoided by *not* counting sales of intermediate products or by counting only the value *added* by producers?

14. List some ways in which increased *inefficiency* could cause gross national product to rise. Are there any goods contributing to the total of gross national product whose rising output clearly reflects *reduced* welfare?

15. Are government purchases of commodities and services consumption expenditures or investment expenditures? They must be one or the other. Why do you suppose the Bureau of Economic Analysis groups them separately?

16. Why must total expenditures for new goods and services, by consumers, investors, government, and foreigners, necessarily equal gross national product? What if some of the year's output is not sold?

17. If it could be shown that a rising gross national product promotes a rising level of anxiety, tension, and conflict in the population, would you favor deducting these psychological costs to obtain the true value of gross national product? How would you do so?

18. Would you favor including the services of housewives in the calculation of gross national product? What arguments could be given for doing so? Are there any good reasons for continuing to exclude these services from the calculation of GNP?

19. As an economy industrializes, a larger percentage of its population tends to enter the labor force as conventionally measured. Fewer goods intended for use in the home are produced in the home, and a larger proportion of total product passes through the marketplace. What does this imply about the validity of GNP data in industrializing societies? Will estimates of per capita income derived from GNP data tend to overstate or understate improvement over time?

20. To be certain that you understand the relationship between nominal GNP, real GNP, and the price level, try deriving either the level of GNP in current dollars, the level of GNP in 1972 dollars, or the Implicit GNP Deflator from the other two for any given year.

Chapter **16**

The Supply of Money

Inflation is a fall in the value or price or purchasing power of money. We ought to be able to explain inflation, then, in terms of changes in the demand for, and supply of, money. That won't adequately explain inflation, because we will still have to ask what causes the supply or the demand to change in ways that produce a fall in the value of money. But understanding money—what it is, how it is supplied, why it's demanded—is the indispensable first step. Changes in the supply of and demand for money also have something to do, as we shall see, with recession. Some people believe that the supply of money can be managed in ways that will reduce the severity of recessions. Others believe that the supply of money is rather consistently mismanaged in ways that aggravate recessions. All of this gives us additional reasons for wanting to understand the phenomenon of money.

Money as a Unit of Accounting

You probably didn't even notice that we have come this far without discussing money. The previous chapters, after all, were replete with dollar signs, and dollars are money. But the dollars referred to so far were simply conventional units for discussing values—a common denominator that enabled us to compare and add apples and oranges, convenient transportation and unpolluted air, goods in the hand and goods in the bush, the services of engineers and the gains from exchange.

One important function of money in a social system is to provide such a unit for accounting. We might have used any other common denominator, such as bread or human labor. We could have stated the values of gasoline and sugar in terms of the number of standard loaves for which a gallon of one and a pound of the other will exchange. Or we could have expressed the gross national product as the equivalent of so many hours of "average" labor time. But we're all accustomed to thinking and talking about values in terms of dollars because we have had a lot of practice in translating the values of diverse commodities and services into dollar terms. Money functions effectively as a unit of accounting because of all the experience we've had with its more important function as a medium of exchange.

Money as a Medium of Exchange

A "medium of exchange" is just what the words say: a middle-thing used in the process of exchanging one good for another. The alternative to employing a medium of exchange is barter: exchanging the goods at our command directly for the goods we want to obtain. What do we use in the United States as our medium of exchange?

Most people who think about money think immediately of green pieces of paper, called Federal Reserve notes, and coins in various sizes and colors. Economists lump these all together and call it the currency component of the money supply. But what else do we use as a medium of exchange?

The most widely used medium of exchange is not currency but deposit credits in commercial banks, usually called checking accounts, but officially known as *demand deposits*. (Because they are deposits that can be withdrawn or transferred on demand. Savings accounts are called *time deposits*, because banks may legally require advance notification of withdrawal.)

Students often have trouble at first seeing that demand deposits really are money. They themselves may handle all their transactions by means of currency, and when they receive a check, they cash it; that is, they obtain currency for the check and spend the currency. But student habits are in no way typical of the transaction procedures employed by business firms, government units, and households. The overwhelming majority of exchanges, measured in dollar value, employ demand deposits as the medium of exchange. Purchasers instruct their banks to transfer ownership of a portion of the purchasers' deposits to sellers: they write a check, in other words. Sellers typically deposit the checks rather than cash them, thereby instructing their own banks to collect the ownership whose transfer was ordered by the check writer. No currency at all will change hands. The bank in which the check is deposited will make an entry in its books; the bank on which the check is written will make an equal but opposite entry in its books.

It isn't hard to imagine a situation in which demand deposits are the only medium of exchange. As credit cards become more common, people will carry less currency and pay for more of their purchases with monthly checks. Couldn't all transactions be handled in this way? It would be possible, even though inconvenient in some cases. But currency could disappear from existence without any reduction in our use of money as a medium of exchange.

Currency plus demand deposits. Is that all? Suppose someone asks, "How much money do you have?" You would calculate the currency in your possession. Having read this far you would then add the balance in your checking account. Should you also add what you have in your savings account? You can get it out quickly or transfer it to your checking account. It's available for spending, even though savings accounts cannot be used directly as a medium of exchange. But then what of the deposit you have in a savings and loan institution? You could also convert that amount into "ready cash." And why not also the government bonds you own? They can be cashed too. How far shall we go in calculating how much money you have? Your automobile could also be converted into currency or a demand deposit. Is it therefore money?

Money as Liquidity

Notice what we've done now. We have shifted the definition of money from "the commonly employed medium of exchange" to "assets that can be exchanged in order to obtain other goods." But any asset at all, under the right circumstances, can be exchanged for other goods. Is every good therefore to be included in the money supply?

The distinguishing characteristic of money is its *liquidity*. Money is a liquid asset. The more liquid something is, the more moneylike it is. When an asset is completely liquid, it has attained the zenith of moneyness.

What do we mean by liquidity? *The liquidity of an asset refers to the cost of exchanging it for other assets.* An asset that can be exchanged for any other asset at a zero cost is a completely liquid asset. The Federal Reserve note in your wallet is an excellent example. It's an asset you can give in exchange for

```
┌─────────────────────────────┐
│        We accept            │
│   Federal Reserve Notes     │
│        (eagerly)            │
└─────────────────────────────┘
```

```
┌─────────────────────────────┐
│           No                │
│   Personal  Toothbrushes    │
│        Accepted             │
└─────────────────────────────┘
```

a great variety of other things you might want; sellers of every sort are willing to accept it without question *and without discounting it.* An asset that cannot be exchanged at all, because no one else would be willing to give anything in exchange for it, would be a completely illiquid asset. (Your toothbrush?) If you own a government savings bond, you can exchange it for other assets; but first you'll have to incur the cost of a trip to the bank where you exchange the bond for currency. So government savings bonds are liquid assets, but they're not as liquid as Federal Reserve notes. Are they money? Just how liquid does an asset have to be to qualify as money? That turns out to be a difficult question on which competent people disagree. In this world of continuous variables and every shade of gray, assets will rarely hit either end of the liquid-illiquid continuum. Most assets are somewhat liquid. The point to remember is that an asset becomes more moneylike as it becomes more liquid, as the cost of exchanging it for other assets approaches zero.

The concept of liquidity is important in the economist's way of looking at the world. To possess liquid assets is to have a greater range of choices, better opportunities, and hence more wealth. Your wealth, by which we always mean the range of options available to you, will depend among other things upon the precise forms in which you're currently holding the goods you own, or in the useful jargon of finance, upon the *composition of your asset portfolio.* Suppose, for example, that you're in a strange city with a checkbook but no currency, and you're hungry. The restaurant signs "No Checks Accepted" establish that you are at the moment not as wealthy as you would be with $20 less in your checking account and a $20 bill in your wallet. You may also be driving an expensive sports car. But exchanging it for a meal (plus other assets) would almost certainly entail a substantial loss of wealth, because sports cars are not fully liquid assets.

How Money Creates Wealth

The advantages of using money rather than employing a barter system are enormous. The cost of exchanging would be far greater, and social wealth as a consequence far less, if there were no money to facilitate the process. In an economic system limited to barter, people would have to spend an inordinate amount of time searching for others with whom they could advantageously exchange. A violin maker would have to find a grocer, a haberdasher, an electrical utility, and a glue supplier, among many others, all willing to accept violins in return for the goods they sell. All that time devoted to searching would be time not available for violin making, and the production of violins would fall. Aware of the high costs of exchanging, people would increasingly try to produce goods for their own use, thus avoiding the necessity of searching out others from whom they can buy and to whom they can sell. Specialization would decline dramatically in a society confined to barter. And that means, of course, that people would lose the benefits that accrue from the systematic and widespread exploitation of comparative advantage. The evolution of some kind of money system in almost every known society, even when conditions were extremely unfavorable for it, is eloquent testimony to the advantages of having a generally accepted medium of exchange.

Defining the Money Stock

So the moneyness of particular assets is a matter of degree. How then are we going to define the money supply in the United States? The answer is: somewhat arbitrarily. There just is no completely satisfactory way to decide what should be counted in the money supply and what should be excluded. A substantial number of economists believe that changes in the rate at which the money supply grows are the most important single factor causing recessions and inflations. Their contention is difficult to prove or disprove because they cannot agree on what counts as money. That isn't because they're a disputatious lot. The appropriate definition of money is a function of financial institutions and social practices that evolve over time, usually very slowly, but sometimes with dramatic suddenness. You might even say that scholars cannot agree on the best definition of money because the public, whose practices make something money, does not itself know what it will be using next year as a medium of exchange.

If we adhered strictly to the definition of money as the common medium of exchange, we would want to define the money supply in the United States as the total of currency in circulation plus demand deposits at commercial banks. For that is what we use to pay for almost all our transactions. To avoid double counting we must include only the currency which is in circulation or outside the banking system. Thus when someone deposits a $20 bill in a checking account, the money supply does not change. The demand deposit component rises by $20, but currency in circulation falls by $20. If we continued to count as money the currency now in the bank's possession, we would come to the highly misleading conclusion that deposits or withdrawals of currency from checking accounts change the quantity of the exchange medium held by the community. But they obviously don't; they only change the *form* in which it is held. After you've written a check for "cash," you have exactly as much money as before, and so does everyone else.

But do we want to define money strictly as that which actually functions as the common medium of exchange? What we're really going to be after in these chapters is insight into the determinants of aggregate money demand or total monetary expenditures for other goods. That will partially depend, as we shall see, upon the amount of money people are holding relative to the quantities of other goods that they own or would like to acquire. The more money people possess, other things being equal, the more likely are they to surrender some portion of it in exchange for an alternate good when an attractive opportunity presents itself. Now it is quite clear that most people do not just look at their present stock of currency and demand deposits in deciding how much money they have. Savings held in commercial banks as time deposits and savings held in nonbank thrift institutions, such as savings and loan associations, would be regarded by most people as "available cash." So shouldn't we include these deposits in our working definition of the money supply?

The central bank of the United States, the Federal Reserve System, calculates the money supply in three principal ways and publishes each set of figures as M_1, M_2, and M_3.

M_1 is demand deposits plus currency in circulation.

M_2 is M_1 plus time deposits in commercial banks—those banks which provide checking account service as well as accepting the deposits of savers, making loans, selling money orders, and so on.

M_3 is M_2 plus deposits in mutual savings banks and savings and loan associations—sometimes called nonbank thrift institutions.

Table 16A gives you some notion of the magnitude of each of these measures of the money stock. Since the quantity of money can and does fluctuate considerably from day to day, figures are usually expressed as averages over some period of time. The numbers below are in billions of dollars and give the averages of daily figures throughout the year. Next to each number, in italics, is the percentage by which that measure of the money stock increased (or decreased) from the preceding year.

The stock of money, no matter in which of the three ways we measure it, has increased substantially since 1960. The average annual rate of increase from 1960 to 1978 was 5.1 percent for M_1, 8 percent for M_2, and 8.9 percent for M_3. Moreover, the percentage rates of increase varied considerably, both among the three measures of the money stock and from year to

Year	M_1		M_2		M_3	
1960	143.5	−0.1	212.6	1.0	310.3	3.5
1961	146.5	2.1	223.7	5.2	331.9	7.0
1962	149.7	2.2	236.7	5.8	356.8	7.5
1963	154.1	2.9	252.0	6.5	386.8	8.4
1964	160.3	4.0	267.8	6.3	417.7	8.0
1965	167.1	4.2	289.2	8.0	453.5	8.6
1966	174.9	4.7	311.9	7.8	486.0	7.2
1967	181.8	3.9	335.9	7.7	522.6	7.5
1968	194.8	7.2	366.0	9.0	566.7	8.4
1969	206.6	6.1	389.8	6.5	601.8	6.2
1970	214.5	3.8	406.0	4.2	627.5	4.3
1971	228.8	6.7	453.1	11.6	707.7	12.8
1972	245.0	7.1	500.9	10.5	798.3	12.8
1973	263.3	7.5	549.1	9.6	884.8	10.8
1974	277.7	5.5	595.4	8.4	954.3	7.9
1975	289.8	4.4	641.3	7.7	1,041.6	9.1
1976	305.1	5.3	704.6	9.9	1,167.8	12.1
1977	327.3	7.3	779.7	10.7	1,312.8	12.4
1978	352.9	7.8	846.7	8.6	1,441.9	9.8

SOURCE: Annual U.S. Economic Data, prepared by Federal Reserve Bank of St. Louis.

year within each measure. Why? How has this come about?
Where did all this additional money come from?

Commercial Bank Lending and the Creation of Money

The basic answer is that it came about through a net expansion
of commercial bank loans. *The money stock increases when
commercial banks make loans to their customers and decreases
when customers repay the loans obtained from commercial
banks.* That's the short of the story. The long of it is a bit more
complicated but not really difficult to grasp.

Suppose your application for a loan of $500 from the First
National Bank is approved. The lending officer will make out a
deposit slip in your name for $500, initial it, and hand it to a
teller who will then credit your checking account with an additional $500. Demand deposits will have risen by $500. The
money stock will be larger by that amount.

Where did the $500 come from? The bank *created* the $500
to lend you. Out of thin air? Not really. But the raw material
isn't as important at this point as the fact that the bank really
did create new money in making you a loan.

But suppose you don't have a checking account at First
National? Then the bank can open one and start you off with a
$500 balance. But suppose you don't want a demand deposit:
you want the money? Slips! A demand deposit *is* money. You

can use it to buy whatever it is you borrowed for. All right, but suppose you decide to withdraw your $500 right away in $20 bills? Fine. The teller will accommodate you. The total of demand deposits will fall by $500, but the total of currency in circulation will increase by $500. The bank takes the currency from its vault, where it is *not* money, and gives it to you, whereupon it becomes currency held by the nonbank public or currency in circulation and hence *is* money.

Does it all seem too simple? Why don't banks keep on doing that indefinitely? It seems just like having your own money machine in the basement. We'll see in a moment that banks are limited in their ability to make loans and thus add to the money stock. But first let's see how the stock of money is decreased.

One year later your note comes due. In the interim you've built up your money balance to be able to pay off the loan on time. You have $500 (plus the interest due, which we neglect for present purposes) either in your checking account or your cookie jar. If it's in the cookie jar, you turn it over to the bank on the due date and money in circulation drops by $500. Note again that currency counts as money when and only when it is held outside the banking system.

If, as is more likely, you have the $500 in your checking account, you write a check for that amount to the bank. The bank subtracts $500 from your demand deposit balance. The money stock goes down by $500.

If you have grasped this simple process, you understand how money, defined as M_1, is created and destroyed. Changes in the size of M_2 and M_3 are the consequence of the public's preferences regarding the form in which it wants to hold its stock of money assets. If you transferred the $500 you had borrowed out of your checking account and into a savings account at the bank where you borrowed, M_1 would fall by $500. But M_2 would be unchanged, because M_2 includes everything in M_1; the $500 contributes just as much to the total of M_2 when it's in a checking account as when it's in a savings account. If you subsequently transferred the $500 into an account at a savings and loan association, M_3 and M_1 would not change, but M_2 would fall by $500. In short, commercial bank lending increases M_1. The public's desire to hold more or less of its assets in demand deposits, time deposits, or savings accounts in nonbank thrift institutions will determine the different rates of growth among M_1, M_2, and M_3.

But you must be wondering what has been left out. Surely private, commercial bankers cannot create money without constraint. And you are right: they cannot. First of all, the bankers must find people willing to borrow on the terms at which the banks are willing to lend. Secondly, each bank must

COMMERCIAL BANK

ASSETS	LIABILITIES
+ Your $500 IOU	+ $500 Demand deposit

COMMERCIAL BANK

ASSETS	LIABILITIES
− $500 Currency from vault	− $500 Demand deposit

COMMERCIAL BANK

ASSETS	LIABILITIES
− Your $500 IOU + $500 Currency from your cookie jar	

COMMERCIAL BANK

ASSETS	LIABILITIES
− Your $500 IOU	− $500 Demand deposit

operate within the constraint imposed by its reserves. That's the constraint which government authorities use in their efforts to exercise control over bank lending and hence over the process of money creation. Every bank is legally required to hold reserves in forms specified by law. A bank may make new loans, and thus create money, only when it has free reserves, that is, reserves greater than the minimum amount it is legally obligated to hold. And the Fed (the common name for the Federal Reserve System) has the power to increase or decrease the reserves of the banking system.

The Central Bank

The Federal Reserve System is the central bank of the United States, created by an act of Congress in 1913. Although technically owned by the commercial banks that are its members, the Fed is in practical fact a government agency. Its board of governors in Washington is appointed by the President of the United States, with the consent of the Senate. And the board effectively controls the policies of the twelve banks that make up the system. We seem to have 12 central banks, but this is only an appearance, a legacy from the days when much of the country harbored a populist suspicion of Easterners, Wall Streeters, and men in striped pants with cutaway coats. These suspicions were allayed by scattering banks around the country. But the Fed has actually been a single bank (with branches) at least since the legislative changes enacted by Congress in the 1930s. The power of any one of the 12 branch banks depends pretty much on the amount of influence it is able to exert on policy formation through its executive officers and research staff.

Many of the commercial banks in the United States are not subject to the rules of the Federal Reserve System. Banks holding charters from the federal government have the right to put the word "National" in their name and the obligation to join the Federal Reserve System. But many banks hold state government charters; they are permitted but not required to join the system. If they choose not to join, they operate in accordance with state definitions of reserves and state established legal reserve minima. Although less than half of all the commercial banks in the United States belong to the Federal Reserve System, member banks have more than three quarters of the total assets of the entire commercial banking system. We're going to simplify this account by pretending that all banks are subject to the rules and regulations of the Fed. Since the Fed indirectly but powerfully influences the position of all banks and not just those subject to its direct regulation, this assumption won't yield a seriously misleading picture. We should note in passing, however, that the percentage of banks holding membership in the system has been decreasing in recent years, and that Fed officials believe this trend may be interfering with their ability to exercise a sufficiently precise control over the money supply.

Bank Reserves as Constraints on Money Creation

Because of its power to fix legal reserve requirements for member banks (within wide limits set by Congress) and its power to expand or contract the dollar volume of reserves, the Fed controls the lending activities of the commercial banking system and thus the process of money creation. Reserve requirements differ for time deposits and demand deposits; moreover, the legal reserve requirement on demand deposits currently varies between 7 and 16¼ percent, depending upon the size of a particular bank's demand deposit liabilities. (Note that demand deposits are bank *liabilities*: your bank owes you the amount in your checking account.) The Fed also decides what may count as legal reserves. Since 1960 it has been the banks' vault cash plus the deposits the commercial banks themselves have at the Federal Reserve Bank of their district. To see what all this has to do with changes in the money stock, we'll come in for a close-up look at the First National Bank of Anywhere.

Suppose that First National Bank is holding $10 million in vault cash, has $30 million on deposit with the Federal Reserve Bank, and is required by law to hold $38 million in reserves against its outstanding liabilities. That $38 million will be the sum and product of a lot of complex calculations involving different percentage reserve requirements for different liabilities. But we don't have to get into all the arithmetic, because it's irrelevant to our purposes. All we have to know is that First National Bank has $2 million in *excess reserves*. At least they're excess from the legal point of view. If First National has a reason of its own for holding $2 million more in reserves than it's legally required to hold, those won't really be excess reserves—any more than the amount in your checking account is an excess reserve because you aren't *legally* required to hold anything in your checking account.

But we're going to assume that First National has no desire to hold more reserves than the law says it must. So First National is indeed holding $2 million in excess reserves. Banks make use of excess reserves by lending them. First National can make new loans totaling $2 million if it can find acceptable borrowers. Let's assume it finds them and watch what happens as a result.

First National makes the loans by creating new demand deposits for its borrowers. The moment it does so, the stock of money increases by $2 million. All participants are happier than before. First National has additional income earning assets in the form of the borrowers' IOU's, and the borrowers have the money that they wanted badly enough to pay interest for it.

The story doesn't end here, however. The bank loans transformed $2 mllion of excess reserves into a $2 mllion addition to the stock of M_1. But what will now happen to the $2 million in the checking accounts of the borrowers? Since people usually borrow in order to spend, we'll assume that's what these borrowers do, too. They write checks totaling $2 million.

The Dispersion of Excess Reserves

When the payees receive the checks, they deposit them in their own banks. Run the process through in your mind to convince yourself that no money is created or destroyed in this process. If borrower A writes a $100 check to the order of payee B, and B deposits that check in Second National Bank, Second National will add $100 to B's checking account and send the check to the Federal Reserve Bank for clearing. The Federal Reserve Bank will credit Second National with an additional $100 in its reserve account, will subtract $100 from the amount it has credited on its books to the reserve account of First National, and will send the check to First National. First National will subtract $100 from A's checking account. At the end of the process, the $100 of recently created money will be in B's checking account, and $100 of First National's excess reserves will have been added to the reserves of Second National.

But now Second National will have excess reserves! It acquired $100 in new liabilities and $100 in new reserves. But under our fractional reserve system, *at least* $83.75 of those new reserves will be excess reserves, because the *maximum* reserve requirement is 16¼ percent. So Second National will have an additional $83.75 or more to lend.

All around the commercial banking system, wherever the checks sent out by the borrowers are being deposited by payees, new additions are being made in this manner to the excess reserves of commercial banks. Some reserves will probably even find their way right back into First National, because some of the payees are almost certain to be depositors of First National Bank. All these new excess reserves permit further loans, which in turn create more M_1. And when these further additions to the stock of M_1 are spent by the borrowers and redeposited by payees, still more additions are made to the excess reserves of the commercial banking system.

The conclusion of the matter is this: *a dollar of original excess reserves can create several dollars in additional money* as banks use their excess reserves to acquire interest-paying assets. Exactly how many dollars of additional money will be generated from one additional dollar of excess reserves? We don't know. The ratio of new money to new reserves will depend on the legal reserve requirements in force, the size of the banks into which deposits move, the distribution of the deposits between member and nonmember banks of the Federal Reserve System, the public's preferences about the form in which it wants to hold new money, the lending policies and practices of banks, cash management procedures of the federal government, the balance between exports and imports, and even the monetary policies of foreign central banks. The answer will also depend, of course, on what we're including in our definition of money. During the 1970s, M_1 tended to increase a little over $2 for each $1 increase in bank reserves, while M_2 rose almost $7 for each $1 added to reserves.

We know at least that the commercial banks cannot continue indefinitely to create new money out of a given quantity of new reserves. Additional lending creates additional liabilities against which reserves must be held, so that continual lending will eventually "use up" the excess reserves upon which the lending was based. Moreover, the public will tend to withdraw larger quantities of money from the banking system as the stock of money increases, and every dollar of currency that moves into circulation reduces bank reserves by a dollar.

The discussion has been carried on in terms of excess reserves, additional loans, and more money. The process also works in reverse. When a bank's reserves fall below the legal minimum, it reduces its rate of new loans below the rate at which old loans are being repaid, in order to acquire the additional required reserves. If the entire banking system is doing this, the result is a net contraction of loans and hence a reduction in the money stock. Eventually, through the acquisition by the commercial banks of additional currency formerly in the hands of the public and the reduction of demand deposits as the public repays loans, the legal minimum reserve-to-deposit ratio will be reached. The process of contraction will stop.

It should be clear from all this that excess reserves plus a demand for bank loans on the part of eligible borrowers are the two factors jointly controlling the expansion of the money stock. The Fed can therefore influence the growth of the money stock either by changing the legal reserve requirements or by somehow changing the dollar volume of bank reserves. The latter is in fact the Fed's regular operating lever in money management.

The Tools Used by the Fed

How does the Fed actually go at the job of expanding or contracting the money supply? The most powerful tool and the one that sets the stage for the rest is the authority to establish legal reserve requirements. Changes in reserve requirements are generally viewed by Fed officials as a blunt weapon, not suitable for the delicate surgery that monetary management usually requires. They prefer to take the reserve requirements as the framework and alter the volume of reserves.

How is that done? The briefest explanation is that the Fed creates and destroys reserves in the same way that commercial banks create and destroy money: by extending and contracting loans.

The Fed can extend a loan to a commercial bank directly. It does so by crediting the bank's reserve account and taking in return the bank's IOU or someone else's IOU (a government bond, for example) that happens to be in the bank's portfolio—just as a commercial bank lends to its customers by creating a deposit balance in return for an IOU. The interest rate at which such loans are made is called the *discount rate*. It's a financial page celebrity, because many people look upon it as a sign of current Fed policy. It probably is more of a symbol than a genuine rationing device, since the Fed is selective about the banks to which it will lend. Official Fed policy is to accommodate special circumstances, rather than lend to any bank willing to pay the rate, and to behave more like a Dutch uncle than a profit-seeking lender. But that's what most people look for from a central bank.

The principal technique that the Fed employs is the purchase and sale of United States government securities in what are called *open market operations*. The Fed currently holds a portfolio of government securities worth more than $100 billion. When it increases its holdings by purchasing securities through dealers in government bonds, it writes checks for the amount of the purchases on its own credit. These checks are deposited in commercial banks. When the banks forward the checks to their Federal Reserve Bank, they are credited with additions to their reserve balances.

In short, the acquisition by the Federal Reserve Banks of new earning assets, which is the same thing as the extension of credit to someone, whether the government or banks, increases commercial bank reserves by that amount. And that, as we have seen, enables commercial banks to increase their own loans and thereby the money stock.

The entire process is reversible. The Fed can withdraw credit from member banks or sell some of the government securities already in its asset portfolio. This results in a reduction of commercial bank reserves. For example, when the Fed sells a $1000 government bond, the bond winds up in the hands of someone who pays the bond dealer with a check. But the dealer in turn pays the Fed with a check, and the amount of the check is deducted from the reserve account of the bank on

FEDERAL RESERVE BANKS

ASSETS	LIABILITIES
+ Government bonds	+ Commercial bank reserves

COMMERCIAL BANKS

ASSETS	LIABILITIES
+ Reserve accounts	+ Demand deposits

which it is drawn. That wipes out a portion of the total reserves of the banking system.

Who Is Really in Charge?

Open-market operations, as we said, are the principal working tool of monetary management. A special committee, made up of the seven members of the board of governors and five of the twelve Reserve Bank presidents, sits as the Open Market Committee and continuously determines the direction of monetary policy. The question of the effectiveness with which the Open Market Committee manages the money supply has long been debated by friends and critics of the Fed, both among economists and politicians.

There are two main questions. One is the determination of policy. Does the Fed set appropriate goals? Does it try to do what it ought to be doing? The other is the execution of policy. Does the Fed do an effective job of achieving the goals it sets for itself? The questions are related, of course, because intelligent policy formulation presupposes a realistic assessment of technical capabilities. The football coach who orders a passing strategy when his team is two touchdowns behind in the fourth quarter is making a poor policy decision if the quarterback has a rubber arm and all the receivers have butterfingers. Beware of textbook accounts which, like football plays on the blackboard, gloss over problems of execution and assume that the opposition isn't doing any planning of its own. It's a gross oversimplification to suppose that the Fed has a monetary brake and a monetary accelerator with which it adjusts the money stock as quickly and surely as you slow down and speed up your car in traffic. Monetary management may be more like driving a balky mule train that sometimes refuses to go and sometimes won't stop going even when firmly ordered to halt. To make matters worse, there is a bunch of bickering back seat drivers on the wagon, and some of them aren't above shouting their own instructions or even trying to grab the reins. We'll return to these problems in later chapters when we examine monetary policy.

Why Should Banks Hold Reserves?

Throughout our description of money and the banking system, we have treated reserves as constraints upon the power of banks to make loans and thus to expand the money supply. That seems to have little or nothing to do with the concept of a reserve fund, something that can be drawn upon in an emergency. But legal reserves do not in fact perform a significant reserve function. The reserve requirement is today primarily a limitation on the ability of the commercial banking system to expand the money stock.

But isn't it necessary for the banks to hold reserves against the possibility of a "run" by depositors? If a lot of depositors suddenly lost confidence in a bank for some reason and tried to withdraw their deposits in currency, the bank would be unable to honor those withdrawals. And if that happened, the loss of confidence might spread to other banks and bring down a large part of the banking system.

There actually hasn't been a financial panic like that in the United States for over 45 years. The reason, however, has little to do with the level of bank reserves. Bank customers no longer rush to withdraw their deposits on every rumor of financial trouble because their deposits are now insured by the Federal Deposit Insurance Corporation. If a bank closes, for whatever reason, its depositors can expect reimbursement within a few days. Some critics argued when the FDIC was established in 1935 that the premiums it charged banks to insure their deposits were far too low, and that the FDIC would go broke trying to pay off depositors when banks closed their doors. But the very existence of the FDIC ended the phenomenon of bank runs; and in the absence of runs, banks no longer failed the way they formerly did. The FDIC premiums have thus proved more than adequate. And the institution of the FDIC has turned out to be probably the single most stabilizing reform of the 1930s.

Some credit must also go to improved Federal Reserve procedures since the 1930s. The Fed now understands clearly that it has the responsibility to provide short term liquidity to the banking system, without regard to the amounts banks happen to be holding as reserves. Thus a bank today can meet any demand for currency, however large, by securing additional currency from the Fed. If the bank were to use up its entire reserve balance, the Federal Reserve Bank would simply loan the bank additional reserves, taking as collateral some of the IOU's in the asset portfolio of the borrowing bank. Banks are granted access to this "discount privilege" whenever they have a legitimate demand for additional reserves; and this has made the whole banking and monetary system more flexible in response to changing conditions as well as more resistant to crises and temporary dislocations.

What about Gold?

But hasn't something important still been left out of all this? If reserves aren't really reserves, what is it that provides backing for money? Doesn't money have to have some kind of backing? And where does gold fit into the picture?

The conviction that money must have "backing" if it is to have value raises an interesting question. What stands behind the backing to give it value? And behind the backing of the backing? But the whole set of questions is misdirected. In economics, value is the consequence of scarcity. And scarcity is the result of demand plus limited availability. It is clear enough why there exists a demand for money: it can be used to obtain all sorts of other things that people want, which is to say that it is accepted as a medium of exchange. The other part of the picture, limited availability, is taken care of, more or less effectively, by the monetary managers. No "backing" is required. If this makes you nervous or causes you to doubt the value of your currency or checking account, you can easily shore up your faith by "selling" your money to others. You will find that they are willing to take it and to give you other valuable assets in exchange.

The critical factor in preserving the value of money is limited availability and confidence that the supply will continue to be limited. Nature has made gold relatively rare. It's up to the Fed to keep Federal Reserve notes and demand deposits relatively rare. But some people have more confidence in the reliability of nature than in the reliability of central bankers and governments. That is why some intelligent and well informed people would like to see us return to a genuine gold standard, under which currency could be exchanged for gold at some fixed ratio. It is not because they think that money must have backing, but because they distrust governmental money managers. If the government were required to maintain the convertibility of demand deposits into currency, and currency into gold at predetermined exchange ratios, the limited availability of gold would severely restrict the power to increase the money stock.

As a matter of fact, governments are often tempted, especially in wartime, to create additional money as a way of financing expenditures without the painful necessity of openly levying taxes. And they haven't always resisted the temptation. The consequence has usually been inflation, a more concealed but hardly a more equitable way for the government to finance its expenditures. Urging a return to the gold standard would seem to be a counsel of despair, however. A government so irresponsible that it must be reined in by gold would be most unlikely to adopt a gold standard and even more unlikely to respond to the pressure of such a rein. The problem of irresponsible government is a weighty one; but we cannot believe that the problem could be solved through a return to the gold standard.

Once Over Lightly

Money is a social institution that increases wealth by lowering costs of exchange, thereby enabling people to specialize more fully in accordance with their own comparative advantages.

The moneyness of any asset is a matter of degree. An asset is money insofar as it is liquid. An asset is completely liquid when it can be exchanged for other goods at no cost. Whatever assets everyone freely accepts as a medium of exchange make up a society's stock of money.

In the United States today the stock of money is primarily the total of currency held outside the banking system plus the demand-deposit liabilities of commercial banks. But other assets, such as time deposits, which can be converted into currency or demand deposits at negligible cost, also contribute to overall liquidity and ought to be included in more comprehensive measurements of the money stock.

The money stock increases or decreases primarily as commercial banks expand or contract their lending.

The managers of the Federal Reserve System have the responsibility for regulating the size of the money stock. The Fed does so by controlling bank lending through its power to set the legal ratio between commercial bank liabilities and reserves and to expand or contract those reserves through loans to commercial banks and through open market operations.

The idea that money must have "backing" to have value is not correct. Money must only be acceptable as a medium of exchange to have value. Limited availability is a necessary condition for continued acceptability of any functioning medium of exchange.

QUESTIONS FOR DISCUSSION

1. Would your existence be more or less secure if we had a barter economy, rather than one employing money? Why would we all be poorer if we had to rely exclusively on barter? Is a very poor family subject to 5 percent fluctuations in its income more or less secure than a wealthy family subject to 50 percent fluctuations in its income?
2. Can you think of any ways in which concentration on money obscures the real working and effects of economic events? What about an argument that the government of India could attack poverty by printing more rupees and distributing them to the poorest people?
3. Shares of common stock listed on a major exchange can be sold quickly—that is, exchanged for other assets. Is stock as liquid as money? Why might people hold part of their wealth in common stocks and part in money? Why might they shift the composition of their portfolios in order to hold more of one asset and less of the other?
4. If you were to ask some people how much money they have in the bank, they might not distinguish in answering between their checking-account and

savings-account balances. Why would economists want to distinguish between the two?

5. At any moment some already printed Federal Reserve notes will be in (a) the wallets of the public, (b) the vaults and tills of commercial banks, (c) the vaults of Federal Reserve Banks. How does each enter into or otherwise affect the total money supply?

6. If money is created by bank lending, is it also created by the lending of savings and loan associations, credit unions, and consumer credit companies?

7. How does a withdrawal of currency from checking accounts affect the money stock? How does it affect a bank's reserves? How does it affect excess reserves? What effect might this withdrawal subsequently have on the money stock?

8. People cannot spend the deposits they hold in commercial-bank savings accounts or savings and loan institutions without first withdrawing the funds; that is, converting them into currency or demand deposits. But since they are able to do that at almost no cost, these deposits are assets almost as liquid as checking-account balances.
   a. Does it follow that total spending ought to be more closely correlated with M_3 than with M_1?
   b. What does a faster rate of increase in M_3 than in M_1 suggest about the public's spending *intentions* in the short run?
   c. How will your answers to this question have to be changed if savings and loan institutions allow customers to pay bills through telephone transfers of their deposits to the accounts of others?

9. If bankers can create money, why can't you? Is it against the law for you to create an accepted medium of exchange? Can you think of a situation in which you might succeed in creating a little money? (Hint: Demand deposits, which serve as money, are liabilities of commercial banks; suppose your promissory notes were considered in the community "as good as gold"?) Have you "created" any money if someone to whom you have written a check holds it a long time before depositing it?

10. To an employee, a bank is a place, people, and activities. But to an economist banks are often nothing but assets and liabilities in motion. Simplified asset and liability statements are given below for the Federal Reserve Banks and the Commercial Banking System, each viewed as a single composite bank.

Federal Reserve Banks

assets	liabilities
_____	_____
_____	_____
_____	_____
_____	_____

Commercial Bank System

assets	liabilities
_____	_____
_____	_____
_____	_____
_____	_____

a. Insert each of the following dollar amounts (in billions) into the appropriate place or places above. (Don't worry if the assets aren't equal to liabilities; these are only partial statements of bank positions.)

  $80 U.S. government securities owned by the Fed
   55 U.S. government securities owned by commercial banks
    3 U.S. Treasury deposits with the Fed
  215 Demand deposits owned by the public
    8 Federal Reserve notes in commercial bank vaults
  200 IOU's of customers who have borrowed from commercial banks
    2 Member bank borrowings from the Fed
   30 Member bank reserves on deposit with the Fed
   65 Currency in circulation outside the banking system
    4 Treasury tax and loan account at commercial banks

b. How large is M_1?

c. The public decides to increase its holding of currency to $70 billion by reducing demand deposits to $210 billion. How might this additional currency be supplied and how would that affect the asset and liability components above?

d. What would be the effects of a Fed purchase of $2 billion in government securities from the commercial banks? What would be the effects of a purchase from the nonbanking public?

e. Trace the effects on various assets and liabilities if the Treasury borrows an additional $5 billion from the Fed and subsequently spends that amount for goods purchased from the public? What difference would it make if the Treasury borrowed from the commercial banks?

f. What would be the effect if the Treasury borrowed from the Fed and just kept the borrowed funds idle in its account at the Fed? Suppose it kept the borrowed funds idle in its tax and loan accounts with the commercial banks?

g. Where else could the Treasury go to borrow? What effects would you expect on the bank asset and liability statements if the Treasury spent money after borrowing it from the nonbank public?

11. If the Treasury were to sell bonds to the Fed and then purchase commodities or services with the proceeds, the money stock would increase. If resources in the economy were already "fully employed," where would the goods purchased by the government come from? What would happen to prices? Do you agree that "inflation is a tax"?

12. Many people worry about the size of the national debt. (We'll examine that concern in a later chapter.) The marketable debt of the United States government (the savings bonds that many individuals own are not marketable, because they cannot be bought and sold on the open market) currently stands at around $500 billion. Suppose the Fed, a government agency, bought up all outstanding marketable securities, so that—in a sense—the government only owed the debt to itself. How could this be done? What would happen as a result? (The Fed already owns more than $100 billion of the outstanding marketable debt.)

13. You're the manager of a commercial bank and you want to increase your bank's free reserves. Perhaps you currently have *negative* excess reserves—in which case your bank is borrowing from the Fed and the Fed may be putting pressure on you to remove that debt. Or you may simply believe that your bank would be in a more advantageous position with a somewhat higher level of free reserves. What policies could you pursue to reach your objective? What effects would these policies have on the banking and monetary system?

14. Why does the Fed use open market operations as its principal tool of monetary management rather than changes in legal reserve requirements?

15. Why might the Fed find it significantly easier to expand the money stock in a period of prosperity than in a period of falling output and rising unemployment?

16. There were 14,390 insured commercial banks in the United States as of September 30, 1978. Of these 8810 were not members of the Federal Reserve System. Do you think membership should be required for all banks? How would you assess the political chances for such a proposal? Do you think that the Constitution, in giving to Congress the right to "coin money," implicitly gave it the right to regulate banks when they become the society's principal issuers of money?

17. If it is *not* essential that money have "backing" of some kind, why do so many people believe otherwise?

18. "Nature has made gold rare, but people have made it scarce." Explain.

19. On July 19, 1979 the price of gold climbed for the first time in history above $300 an ounce. If you had bought gold 40 years earlier at $35 an ounce, would you have made a profit by holding gold over this period? If you had invested your $35 in some very safe asset, such as a bank certificate of deposit, which paid 6 percent interest compounded annually, how many dollars would you have had after 40 years? Would it be more correct to say that the value of gold has increased over the last decade, or to say that the value of the dollar has fallen? How could you decide?

20. Money gets a lot of attention but tends to have a bad press. Are the authors of the following statements talking about money as we have defined it? Or are they using money as a synonym or symbol for something else? What is that "something else" in each case where you conclude that money is not really the subject of discussion?

a. "The love of money is the root of all evil" (often misquoted as "Money is the root of all evil.")
b. "Health is . . . a blessing that money cannot buy."
c. "If this be not love, it is madness, and then it is pardonable. Nay, yet a more certain sign than all this: I give thee my money."
d. "Wine maketh merry; but money answereth all things."
e. "Words are the tokens current and accepted for conceits, as moneys are for values."
f. "Money speaks sense in a language all nations understand."
g. "Americans are too interested in money."
h. "Protecting our natural environment is more important than making money."

Chapter **17**

The Demand for Money

In the preceding chapter we saw how money comes to be supplied. To understand why the price or purchasing power of money changes, we must also look at the demand side. In the course of doing so, we'll begin to see how changes in the supply or demand for money affect total spending for other goods. And that will begin to link money with the phenomenon of recession as well as inflation.

The phrase, "demand for money," strikes most people as a little odd when they first hear it. The demand for anything, such as raspberry jam, refers to the quantities people will want to purchase during a specified time period at various prices. At higher prices, people will shift toward substitutes for raspberry jam; at lower prices, they'll substitute raspberry jam more frequently for other goods. But what sense do those sentences make if we insert "money" in place of "raspberry jam"?

They make excellent and important sense if we remember two things. (1) Money is not the same as income. (2) While the demand for raspberry jam is a demand to acquire and consume, the demand for money is a demand to *hold* an asset, not to "consume" it.

Money Is a Stock, Not a Flow

You will never understand the important concept of the demand for money if you identify money with money income. *Money income is a flow*, and so must always be stated with reference to some time period: $4 per hour, $800 per month, $12,000 per year. But *money itself is a stock*; it is a certain amount in existence at some time. Because the size of the stock varies from day to day, we can measure only with respect to some point in time. But it is *at a point* in time that we try to measure the size of a stock, while we measure the size of a flow *during a period* of time.

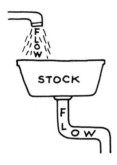

Thus if an employee says, "I'm going in to see the boss this afternoon and demand more money," what is really meant is that he or she is going to insist on more money income: a larger flow of money per month. That is *not* what we're talking about in this chapter. The amount of money that people hold (as a stock) will usually be related closely to the amount of money income they receive regularly (as a flow). But it's certainly possible for one to go up while the other is going down.

The way to understand this is to think it through. How much money, defined as M_1, are you currently holding? In other words, what is the sum of your checking account balance and the currency plus coin that you have in your pocket, purse, billfold, and bureau drawer? Whatever it is, what must you do in order to increase or decrease this amount? To decrease it, you must exchange money for other assets (we'll assume you don't lose it or throw it away). These assets could be anything from food for immediate consumption to shares of stock in AT&T. To increase the amount of M_1 you're currently holding, you must give up other assets in exchange for currency or an addition to your checking account balance (we'll rule out finding money or stealing it).

Meat eaten per year is a flow.
Meat in the freezer is a stock.

The stock can be increased by purchasing more than is eaten for a time.

Now let's suppose you've been working 20 hours a week for $4 an hour. You've been exchanging 20 hours of your time each week for $80, yielding a money income of $80 per week. Then you decide to spend more time studying, so you cut your hours to 15 per week and your income to $60 per week. If at the same time you reduce your expenditures by more than $20 per week (you eliminate a lot of recreation activities, let's say, in order to increase your study time), you will be adding to the stock of money you hold, even though your income has decreased.

The desire to hold more meat in the freezer does not necessarily imply a desire to eat more meat per year.

It all seems too obvious to summarize. But we're going to use these basic relationships, and they should be clear in your mind. People add to the stock of money they hold, to their money balances, by reducing their expenditures below their income. They reduce the stock of money they hold, or their money balances, by raising their expenditures above their income.

Why Do People Hold Money Balances?

The demand for money, we said, is a demand to *hold* money, not to consume it. Money isn't unique in this respect. Lots of goods yield services by being held: fine art, shares of stock, and houses are examples. The demand for all of them should be understood, therefore, as a demand to hold the good in question, not to "use it up." It's clear how paintings, corporate stock, and houses yield services by being held or owned. But isn't it true that money provides a service only when it's spent? It is *not* true. Money does provide services when it's spent, which is why people want to hold money in the first place. They're looking forward to the enjoyment of what they expect the money to buy them.

But money also provides a service while it is being held. If it did not, no one would hold it, because holding money is costly. While holding money, we're sacrificing the valuable current services that other goods would yield us if we bought them with the money: the interest on a government bond, the pleasure of a Woody Allen movie, a comfortable arm chair in which to relax. Since present goods are more valuable than future goods, why don't people immediately spend their money income when they receive it and maintain their stock of money balances at zero? They obviously don't do this. And that implies, correctly, that holding money yields a valuable service, a service valuable enough in comparison with the cost of holding money to persuade people to hold those amounts that they do hold.

That service, quite simply, is flexibility. By holding money rather than some other asset, you increase your freedom to maneuver. You make it easier for yourself to buy what you want when you want it, to take advantage of opportunities that you don't know about yet, or to escape from an unexpected misfortune. Moreover, you make these things possible for yourself without the trouble and expense of first taking a trip to the bank or making a visit to your stockbroker. A synonym for flexibility is *liquidity*, a concept introduced in the preceding chapter to describe money. An asset that can be exchanged at any time at its full value for any other asset is a completely liquid asset. Money is, by definition, the most liquid asset in a society. The demand for money is the demand for liquidity.

But liquidity, like most other goods, must be purchased at a price. There is, as we already pointed out, a cost associated with holding money. It will be the value of the opportunities forgone through the decision to hold money, rather than alter-

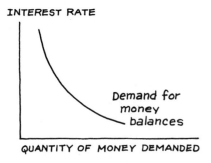

native assets. Two specific costs associated with the holding of money are worth singling out for special examination.

Two Costs of Holding Money

The first is the rate of interest. By holding your wealth in currency or demand deposits, you give up at minimum an opportunity to earn the current rate of interest. We're thinking of the rate of interest on essentially riskless assets, such as short-term government bonds or interest-earning bank deposits. The quantity of money the public will want to hold (the quantity demanded) will be inversely related to the rate of interest (one cost of holding money). The demand for money, in other words, slopes downward to the right, just like all other properly behaved demand curves.

Another important cost associated with holding money is the risk of loss through a decline in its value. That's a risk associated with holding any good, of course; but for two reasons it's not as important in the case of most other goods as it is in the case of money. First of all, the resale value of most goods we buy is not our prime consideration in acquiring them. You don't give a thought to what anchovy pizza may be selling for next year when you place your order, because you intend to consume it, not hold it for resale. You give much more thought to the probable future price when you consider buying a house. But if you're buying it for your own use and you intend to live there a long time, your principal concern will be the service that the house is expected to provide you while you own it.

However, in the case of an asset acquired because it's a medium of exchange, resale value is everything. People who hold onto a house even though they think its market value is going to fall may be perfectly rational in doing so: they enjoy living there. But people will not want to hold onto money when they believe its market value is going to decline. They'll look for something better to hold. In general, the quantity of money people want to hold, other things being equal, will decrease the faster they expect its value to fall and the more confidently they expect it to fall. The reverse of this is also true. People will become eager to hold money if they believe its value is likely to increase substantially in the future.

The other reason why the risk of loss has so much to do with people's willingness to hold money is that it has such a low cost of production. If most of your wealth was tied up in an office building that you owned, an office-building construction boom could make you substantially poorer. But it costs a lot to erect new office buildings, so they aren't going to spring up like mushrooms unless builders also expect a large increase in the demand for them. (You would have more cause for concern if the city government decided to subsidize the construction of new office buildings.) In the case of money, the marginal cost of production is so low that very rapid increases in the amount supplied are a distinct possibility. When people fear that this will happen, they become much less willing to hold any considerable part of their wealth in money.

Actual and Preferred Money Balances

Whatever the quantity of money the public *prefers* to hold, the quantity it *actually* holds will be the quantity supplied. This is a simple but important point to keep in mind. The size of the money stock at any time, however measured, will necessarily be equal to the quantity of money balances the public is holding at that time. But *actual money balances may not be equal to preferred money balances.* If the stock of money increased at a time when the public was satisfied with its current money holdings, some people would have to find themselves holding larger money balances than they preferred to hold. And so they would take steps to reduce their money balances back to the preferred level. If the money stock declined when people were holding their preferred amounts of money, they would try to raise their balances back up to the previous level. They would make these adjustments in the way we've already described, by changing the relationship between their income and their expenditures.

 Let's use some numbers to illustrate what happens when the public tries to make actual money balances conform to preferred money balances. In 1970 the U.S. stock of money measured as M_2 (currency in circulation, demand deposits, and time deposits in commercial banks) was $406 billion. M_2 then increased to $453.1 billion in 1971, to $500.9 billion in 1972, and to $549.1 billion in 1973. These were annual increases of 11.6 percent, 10.5 percent, and 9.6 percent respectively—or a compounded annual rate of change of 10.6 percent. By way of contrast, M_2 had increased by just 4.2 percent from 1969 to 1970 and had shown an average annual rate of increase of 6.7 percent through the decade of the sixties. So the increases from 1970 to 1973 were substantial in comparison with the rates of increase to which the public was accustomed.

 How were people persuaded to begin holding so much more money than they had been accustomed to hold, about 35 percent more in 1973 than they had been holding in 1970? If you dismiss the question as silly on the grounds that no one has to be persuaded to accept additional money, you've missed the point by confusing the flow of money income with the stock of money balances. People will indeed be quite happy to accept as much additional money as others choose to give them. But they won't necessarily *hang onto it!* They are in fact much more likely to spend it, or at least most of it, just as you would

M is the quantity of money supplied and the quantity being held.

Quantity actually held must equal M.

Quantity public would prefer to hold may be greater or less than M.

probably do if you unexpectedly won a $50 door prize at the local pizzeria. Our question is: What induced people to hold 35 percent more M_2 in 1973 than they were holding in 1970?

The basic answer is that increases in people's incomes did the trick. In 1970 total income and total expenditure on new goods in the U.S., measured by gross national product, was $982.4 billion. In 1973 it was $1,036.6 billion. The public was willing to hold 35 percent more M_2 in 1973 than in 1970 because aggregate money income and expenditures increased by about that much (by 33 percent) over the period.

It's plausible to assume that the quantity of money people want to hold will be closely related to their current incomes and their anticipated expenditures. Unless something occurs to change the cost of holding money balances, we would expect the ratio between preferred money holdings and money income or expenditures to be fairly constant for a group as large as the U.S. public. The data bear this out. The quantity of M_2 held by the public, expressed as a percentage of gross national product, was 41.3 percent in 1970, 42.6 percent in 1971, 42.8 percent in 1972, and 42.0 percent in 1973.

How More Money Produces a Larger GNP

But we've left something out, as we hope you've already noticed. What caused the gross national product to rise as it did? If people are persuaded by a one-third increase in income to hold one-third more money, what explains the fact that income increased by one-third? The answer is that the one-third increase in the quantity of money supplied to the public *caused* gross national product to rise by one-third.

When additional money is supplied to a public that is already holding the amount it prefers to hold, the public will attempt to exchange that additional money for other goods. This will increase the aggregate demand for goods other than money. An increased demand will produce higher prices in the case of goods in perfectly inelastic supply, increased output in the case of goods with perfectly elastic supply curves, and some combination of higher prices and increased output in the case of all those goods with supply elasticities somewhere in between zero and infinity.

Gross national product can thus be expected to increase, through some combination of higher prices and increased output, in response to an increase in demand for new goods that was prompted in turn by an increase in the quantity of money supplied to a public already holding its preferred amount of money balances. Gross national product will continue to rise in this way as long as spending for new goods keeps increasing. Spending will continue to increase as long as people are still holding more money than they want to hold. The attempt by individuals to reduce their money holdings by increasing their expenditures on other goods adds to the money holdings of others; it does not reduce the money stock. The public's attempt to reduce its money balances cannot succeed, because all the money that's supplied must be held by someone. What happens instead is that the attempt to reduce actual money balances to the level of preferred money balances causes total money income to rise, until the public prefers to hold balances equal to the quantity that's been supplied.

It's all harder to explain than it is to understand. The logic of it is simple and really rather obvious once you think it through. More money produces more spending, which produces money incomes that rise until people become willing to hold that additional amount of money. The key assumption that makes it all work is that the quantity of money the public prefers to hold and will attempt to hold is some stable percentage of money income or expenditures.

The attempt to exchange money for other assets increases nominal GNP.

The quantity of money the public wants to hold increases when nominal GNP increases.

Nominal GNP increases until the public is willing to hold the quantity of money supplied by the Fed.

How Stable Is the Demand for Money?

How accurate is that assumption? Table 17A provides a partial answer. It shows M_1, M_2, and M_3 for each year from 1960 to 1978 as a percentage of the gross national product in that year.

As you study the table, you'll notice that when we chose M_2 to illustrate our analysis, it wasn't because M_2 is half-way between M_1 and M_3. We chose it because the relationship between the money stock and gross national product shows the greatest stability when we define money as M_2. The stability in the case of M_3 also seems too remarkable to explain, except on the assumption of a causal link between M_3 and gross national product. Even M_1 displays a closer connection with GNP than the percentages of Table 17A might at first suggest. While the public's holdings of M_1, expressed as a percentage of GNP, declined significantly over these years, they declined in a rather steady way; that suggests a stable and predictable, if not constant, relationship.

The relationship between the quantity of money the public wants to hold and the gross national product expresses the demand for money. If that relationship is stable and predictable, then the demand for money is stable and predictable. And if the demand for money is stable and predictable, it follows that changes in total income and output, or nominal gross national product, can be explained as the effect of changes in the supply of money. The stability or instability of the demand for money is therefore a question of the utmost importance for the understanding of fluctuations in gross national product and policies to control them.

Keep in mind that a stable demand curve does not imply a

**TABLE 17A   THE STOCK OF MONEY
AS PERCENTAGE OF GROSS
NATIONAL PRODUCT**

Year	M_1	M_2	M_3
1960	28.4%	42.0%	61.3%
1961	28.0	42.7	63.4
1962	26.6	42.0	63.3
1963	25.9	42.4	65.0
1964	25.2	42.1	65.7
1965	24.3	42.0	65.9
1966	23.2	41.4	64.5
1967	22.8	42.2	65.6
1968	22.4	42.1	65.3
1969	22.1	41.7	64.3
1970	21.8	41.3	63.9
1971	21.5	42.6	66.6
1972	20.9	42.8	68.2
1973	20.2	42.0	67.7
1974	19.7	42.1	67.5
1975	19.0	41.9	68.1
1976	17.9	41.4	68.7
1977	17.3	41.3	69.6
1978	16.7	40.2	68.4

SOURCE: Bureau of Economic Analysis and Board of Governors, Federal Reserve System.

stable quantity demanded. A stable demand for raspberry jam implies that the quantity demanded will decrease and increase as its price rises and falls. Similarly, a stable demand for money is consistent with decreases or increases in the percentage people want to hold, relative to income, *if the cost of holding money rises or falls*. Let's consider the two major costs of holding money that we discussed earlier.

Hyperinflation and the Demand for Money

If the monetary authorities were to let the money stock increase so rapidly that almost everyone came to expect large increases in the price level, the quantity of money the public wants to hold would almost certainly fall. Money would then be an asset whose future value, relative to other assets, was expected to decline rapidly. People would therefore want to exchange money for other goods before this happened. Expenditures would increase sharply, thereby pulling up prices and confirming their fears of inflation. It's even possible in such a situation that the quantity of money demanded could fall virtually to zero, as money became like the Old Maid card that all players try to pass on the moment it enters their hands.

In such a situation, where no one wants to hold money, money is useless; the monetary system disintegrates, and ex-

The demand for money depends upon its expected value.

If people expect its value to decline rapidly, they will not want to hold money.

When everyone is trying to avoid holding money, its value plummets — hyperinflation occurs.

change must occur through the cumbersome processes of barter. That's what occurred in the German hyperinflation of the 1920s. The German situation was considerably aggravated by the monetary authorities' adoption of a curious argument. Noticing that the rapidly increasing rate of money expenditure was causing the value of money to fall, the monetary authorities concluded that a greater quantity was required to make up for the loss of its value. So they supplied still more money, prompting an even greater reluctance to hold money and ever more rapid inflation until, toward the end, people quit work early in the day to spend their money income because they expected it to be worthless by nightfall.

The lesson in all this can be briefly stated. There is some rate of increase in the stock of money that will cause the value of money to begin falling at an accelerating rate. When changes in the supply of money are so great that they cause sudden, large changes in the quantity the public wants to hold, then relatively modest price level changes can suddenly turn into spectacularly large changes. Rates of growth above 10 percent annually for M_2 and M_3 did not trigger this effect in the U.S. economy in the 1970s. The percentage of gross national product that the public wanted to hold in the combined forms of currency, demand deposits, and time deposits—or in these three forms plus savings accounts in nonbank thrift institutions—did not decline significantly. But the record shown in Table 17A does not prove that the quantity of money demanded, relative to GNP, would not fall if the money-stock growth rates of the 1970s were repeated in the 1980s. The key factor is people's expectations, and the money-stock growth rates of the 1970s probably surprised most people. The public may be less willing, after its experience in the 1970s, to conclude in the future that large spurts in the money-stock growth rates are aberrations that will quickly be corrected.

Interest and the Cost of Holding "Cash"

The steady decline over this period in the quantity of M_1 held by the public, relative to GNP, certainly suggests that people are not altogether passive in deciding upon their money holdings. An important cost of holding currency or demand deposits is the interest forgone. Because savings accounts pay interest, people may have been choosing to hold a larger proportion of their "ready cash" in commercial bank time deposits or nonbank savings accounts. This option became increasingly attractive during the 1970s as financial institutions made it easier and less costly for people to shift funds quickly out of savings deposits into an immediately spendable form. It may well be, therefore, that M_2 or M_3 has become a better indicator than M_1 of the public's spending intentions, and that the rate of growth in M_1 is now much less significant than the rate of growth in M_2 or even M_3.

A Warning against Policy Conclusions

Nothing in this discussion should lead you to conclude that there is a fairly tight linkage between changes in the size of the money stock and changes either in the price level or in the rate of growth in output. Such an inference is erroneous. It is also dangerous, because it suggests to the unwary that the Fed can control inflation, recession, or both by using its power to control the money stock.

To begin with, the relative stability shown in Table 17A is a stability in the relationship between the money stock and *nominal* gross national product. Nominal gross national product reflects two factors simultaneously: real output and the money prices at which that output is valued. The important policy question is not how a change in the rate of growth of the money stock will affect nominal gross national product, but how it will affect each of its components—real output and the price level. That is a much more difficult question than any of the ones we've tried to answer in this chapter.

In the second place, the stable relationships shown in Table 17A are long-term ones. If we were to break down the data for 1970 to 1973 into quarterly components, the percentage of GNP held by the public as M_2 would fluctuate far outside the limits of 41.3 and 42.8 percent. It is one thing to say that nominal GNP tends, over the course of a year, to run at a rate between 2.34 and 2.49 times the size of M_2. It is an altogether different matter to suppose that changes in M_2 are a policy lever that can be used to alter GNP by 2.34 to 2.49 dollars for every dollar change in M_2.

Not only is the short-run relationship less stable and predictable than the long-run relationship has recently proved to be; in addition, the stability and predictability of the long-run relationship may well depend on our not using it as a short-run policy instrument. The world of human relationships is full of examples of correlations that break down as soon as someone tries to use them for "policy purposes." For example, if the head of the economics department authorizes a higher grading curve in 8 o'clock sections than in 10 o'clock ones because the statistics show that the former attract better students, more poor students will enroll at 8 o'clock (assuming the word gets out), and the relationship on which the grading policy was based will no longer hold. The word does get out about what the monetary authorities are trying to do, and the adjustments that some people will make in response to such information might well turn stable relationships into unpredictable ones.

A third reason for extreme caution about policy inferences

at this point is the growing difficulty that the monetary authorities seem to be having in controlling the stock of money. Chapter 16 showed that the Fed does not control the stock of money directly—only indirectly through its power to change bank reserves and reserve requirements. This chapter has underscored the limitations upon the precision of Fed control by emphasizing the public's ability to shift about among the various components of the money stock. When we come to consider the relationships between international exchange and domestic stabilization policies, we will discover even more ways for the public to frustrate the intentions of the monetary authorities. Innovative means to facilitate exchange seem to be evolving more rapidly today than they can be recognized, understood, and brought under control.

Finally, the money stock cannot be used effectively as a tool to get us from where we are to where we want to be if we don't know where we are. As we shall see in painful detail when we start to assess some of the policies that have been recommended for controlling inflation and checking recession, we never know where we are or even the direction in which we're headed until quite a while afterwards. That may be much too late to do anything about it.

Once Over Lightly

The price, or purchasing power, of money depends upon the demand for money, as well as upon the quantity of money supplied.

Money is a stock and must be carefully distinguished from money income, which is a flow.

The demand for money is a demand to hold money. People want to hold money balances because liquidity provides enhanced flexibility to those who are holding money, rather than alternative assets.

People adjust their holdings of money balances up or down by altering the relationship between their money income and their expenditures.

Other things remaining equal, the quantity of money the public wants to hold will decrease when the cost of holding money rises and increase when the cost of holding it falls.

Two important factors in the cost of holding money are the interest forgone and the loss (or gain) that occurs when the purchasing power of money falls (or rises).

The quantity of money the public wants to hold is best stated not as some quantity of nominal dollars but as a percentage figure related to income or expenditures. The demand for money in the U.S. has shown long-run stability since World War II.

The more stable and predictable the demand for money,

the more closely will changes in the rate at which money is supplied control the rate of growth in nominal gross national product.

Because nominal gross national product reflects changes in both real output and the price level, even the most precise control over nominal GNP would not be enough to provide control over inflation or recession.

QUESTIONS FOR DISCUSSION

1. Analogies must be used with care. But this one may help you visualize the major relationships between the two flows of income and of expenditures and the stock of money. Imagine a lake formed by a dammed-up river. Let the lake represent the stock of money someone is holding. The river above the lake represents income, the river below the lake represents expenditures.
   a. What must be done to raise or to lower the lake level?
   b. How could the lake level be raised, even though the flow above the lake is declining? How could the lake level be lowered, even though the flow above the lake is increasing?
   c. If the dam operator anticipates a late-summer drought and wants to prevent the lake from falling below some desired level, what might be done during the spring?
2. List the major factors you consider in deciding how large a stock of money balances you want to hold at any time.
3. Many people insist that consumers could stop inflation if they launched a consumer strike against higher prices.
   a. What would happen to your stock of money balances if you decided to do your part in fighting inflation by reducing your expenditures?
   b. How likely is it that large numbers of people will choose their preferred level of money balances by neglecting their personal interests and considering instead the contribution they might make to checking inflation?
   c. What would happen to the value of your stock of money balances if inflation continued?
4. Would money function as a medium of exchange if people were unwilling to hold it, even for very short periods of time? Is there any difference between a barter economy and an economy in which people hold no money balances?
5. The demand for some goods—we have mentioned fine art, shares of stock, and houses, in addition to money—is primarily a demand to hold the good. Why is the supply of such goods not the same as their current rate of production? Could the number of shares of stock offered for sale at a given price increase, even though the corporation that originally issued them had issued no additional shares? What could cause the number of houses listed for sale in a particular city to increase, even though no new construction had been completed?
6. You want to buy a used sailboat if the right one comes along at the right price. You think you'll be able to get a better deal if you can offer the seller

immediate cash. What are some good options for you to consider as alternatives to holding M_1 while you're searching for the sailboat?

7. We describe the demand for most goods by referring to prices and the number of units that would be demanded at those prices. But economists describe the demand for money by referring to the price (or cost) of holding money and *some percentage of income.*
   a. Why is the quantity demanded expressed as a percentage in the case of money, rather than as a number of units?
   b. Would you be willing to say that someone's demand for money had not changed if that person held the same quantity of dollars when his money income had doubled and the purchasing power of dollars had fallen 50 percent?

8. Suppose that every household and business firm decided to spend on Tuesday every dollar it was holding.
   a. What would be the effect on the stock of money balances held on Wednesday by households and business firms?
   b. What other effects would you predict from such a mass decision to unload money balances?
   c. Suppose this decision resulted from a sudden conviction that money was going to be worthless by the end of the week. What do you think would happen?

9. Assume that the public wants to hold money balances, in the form of M_2, equal to 40 percent of nominal gross national product.
   a. How large will GNP have to be to persuade the public to hold $800 billion of M_2?
   b. If M_2 rises by $80 billion, by how much will GNP have to rise to induce the public to hold this additional amount of money?
   c. Will this increase in GNP mean greater prosperity?

10. Anyone who reads extensively in economic history will encounter periodic complaints from merchants about a *scarcity of money* in the hands of the public.
    a. What observations by a merchant might prompt such a complaint?
    b. What might cause a widespread increase in the incidence of such complaints from merchants?
    c. Why do you suppose it is that so many merchants throughout history have associated an abundance of money with prosperity and a scarcity of it with hard times?
    d. If more money in the possession of a particular merchant's customers will produce prosperity for that merchant, will more money in everyone's hands produce greater prosperity for all merchants?

11. What effect does inflation have on the value of people's money balances? What will happen if the monetary authorities, in an effort to maintain the real value of the public's money holdings, increase the stock of money when inflation occurs?

Chapter **18**

The Great Depression
and Keynesian Analysis

Much of our thinking about recession and unemployment is still shaped by the experiences of the Great Depression. Anyone who lived through the 1930s will readily understand how the events of a single decade could have such an enduring impact. For those who don't remember the 1930s (which includes most of us) Table 18A provides a statistical sketch of the years from 1929 to 1939 for the United States, the leading industrial nation of the world.

The Great Depression

For four successive years, beginning in 1930, real output and income declined. It declined by huge amounts: 9 percent in 1930, 8 percent in 1931, 14 percent in 1932, and another 2 percent in 1933. Compare that record with the performance of the U.S. economy since World War II. On only one occasion, up to 1978, did total output decline in two successive years. It fell in 1974 and again in 1975. But the percentage declines were only 1.4 percent and 1.3 percent, almost unnoticeable by the standards of the Great Depression.

Moreover, recovery was slow in coming in the 1930s. In the three years after the 1974–75 recession, output increased by 5.7, 4.9, and 4.0 percent, making up much of the ground lost during the recession. If we combine the five years of recession and then recovery from 1974 to 1978, the average annual rate of growth

**TABLE 18A   THE GREAT DEPRESSION—
OUTPUT, PRICES, AND UNEMPLOYMENT**

Year	Gross National Product in Current Dollars (billions)	Implicit GNP Deflator (1972 = 100)	Gross National Product in 1972 Dollars (billions)	Unemployment as Percent of Civilian Labor Force
1929	103.4	32.87	314.7	3.2
1930	90.7	31.81	285.2	8.7
1931	76.1	28.89	263.3	15.9
1932	58.3	25.69	226.8	23.6
1933	55.8	25.13	222.1	24.9
1934	65.3	27.27	239.4	21.7
1935	72.5	27.80	260.8	20.1
1936	82.7	27.94	296.1	16.9
1937	90.7	29.29	309.8	14.3
1938	85.0	28.59	297.1	19.0
1939	90.8	28.40	319.7	17.2

SOURCE: Bureau of Economic Analysis and the Bureau of Labor Statistics.

in output was 2.3 percent. But six years after the trough of the Great Depression was finally reached in 1933, total output and income were only 1½ percent above what they had been in 1929. With a population 7½ percent greater in 1939 than it had been in 1929, that tiny increase in output and income over the decade was far below what would have been required just to restore predepression levels of prosperity. The per capita after-tax income of Americans actually fell by 7 percent from 1929 to 1939. (It had fallen by almost 30 percent from 1929 to 1933.) The Great Depression even featured a recession within a depression, as real output and income dropped 4 percent from 1937 to 1938.

The most vividly remembered experience of those who lived through the 1930s is the experience of massive, stubborn unemployment. The unemployment column in Table 18A should be compared with the unemployment percentages of Table 15A. In every single year during the 1930s unemployment was higher than it has been in any recession year since World War II. If we leave out 1930, when unemployment was still growing, the unemployment rates of the 1930s *averaged* more than 19 percent. That is one out of every five members of the labor force.

The depth of the recession from 1929 to 1933 was unprecedented in U.S. history. Just as unsettling, however, was the persistent failure of the economy to recover fully after the decline ended. Economists had long known about recessions. They had even made some progress toward understanding why they occurred and what might be done to reduce their severity. But a basic assumption in all theorizing about recessions was that they were *temporary* disturbances. Recessions were the consequence of mistaken decisions based on misleading or erroneous expectations, and they ran their course as those mistakes were corrected. When the corrections had been made, recovery was supposed to begin and carry total output and income up to new heights. Recessions were temporary interruptions within an overall pattern of long-term growth. The experience of the 1930s raised grave doubts, for obvious reasons, about the adequacy of that analysis.

Keynes and *The General Theory*

One man did so much to crystallize economists' rethinking of recessions during and after the 1930s that his name is frequently attached to the "new economics" that emerged. John Maynard Keynes (rhymes with *gains*) was a British economist who lived from 1883 to 1946. He enjoyed a brilliant and diversified career as investor, editor, teacher, writer, government servant, and architect of systems for the reconstructing of international finance. But he is chiefly remembered today as the author of a book published at the beginning of 1936, entitled *The General Theory of Employment, Interest and Money*.

The General Theory, to give it the abbreviated title by which it's usually known, is by common agreement an obscure and badly organized book. "What *The General Theory* Means" was a topic for innumerable essays and symposia in the years immediately following its publication, evidence that its message was deemed important, but that no one quite knew what the essential message was. Books and articles about what Keynes *really* meant continue to appear today, more than four decades after the publication of *The General Theory*. But consensus at least exists on this much: Keynes believed that the traditional approach of economists to the question of recession came close to assuming the problem away, and that modern industrial economies such as those of Great Britain or the United States did not incline automatically toward full employment.

Order and Disorder in Economic Systems

One of the characteristics of economic theory about which Keynes had misgivings was its tendency to be *a theory of orderly coordination*. But if recessions resulted from a breakdown of the coordinative mechanism, no satisfactory explanation or remedy for recessions would be obtained from a theory which *assumed* that the mechanism was working.

Traditional economic analysis looked upon recessions as periods of temporary surplus, for that seems to be what we

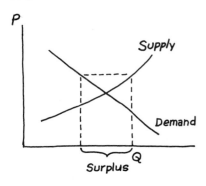

observe in a recession. Workers are unable to find jobs and products cannot be sold; the quantities of labor and produced goods being supplied are greater than the quantities currently demanded. The economist's solution to a surplus is a lower price. If workers cannot find jobs, it's because they're holding out for a wage that's above their value to employers; at some lower wage all those who want work will be able to find it. If producers cannot sell their entire output, it's again because they're asking too high a price; useful goods can always be sold at a sufficiently low price. It's a matter of supply and demand. A recession is simply a temporary disequilibrium. It will come to an end when prices and wages move to their equilibrium or market-clearing levels.

But how long will this take? It only happens instantaneously on the supply and demand graphs of economists. In the real world, market clearing prices must be searched for, and that process may take weeks, months, or even longer. In the interim the world does not stand still. Unemployed workers reduce their spending because they are no longer receiving income, which further reduces the demand for goods. Producers who find themselves with unwanted additions to their inventories cut back production, laying off more workers and reducing the demand for the other goods they use as inputs. Might not an excess supply of labor and produced goods cause a downward spiral in income and demand before prices had fallen far enough to eliminate the surpluses? In that case, prices would have to fall still further to close the gap between supply and demand. Don't recessions, in fact, display just such a cumulative pattern of declining production, reduced income, further declines in production, and further reduced income?

The timeless equilibrium analysis of the traditional economics in which Keynes had been trained did not examine the groping process by which new equilibrium positions are found. It assumed, in effect, an instantaneous leap to a new equilibrium whenever an old equilibrium was disturbed. But if the causes of recessions are to be found in what happens while the economy is out of equilibrium, then the traditional analysis had indeed assumed the problem away.

The importance of expectations in shaping economic decisions also impressed Keynes very strongly. An emphasis on expectations meant an emphasis on the uncertainty of decision making, the frequency of mistakes, the need for time in which to adjust to unanticipated events, and the disorder of economic systems. None of this was captured in the timeless, orderly, errorless world of traditional equilibrium analysis. In *The General Theory* Keynes sought to explain the phenomenon of recession by taking into account the consequences of uncertainty and the processes of adjustment over time. This was the origin of income-expenditures analysis.

A Simple Keynesian Model

In order to present the logic of income-expenditures analysis, we're going to construct a very simplified economic system in which the relationships between key variables are clearly specified. (Economists refer to such systems as *models*.) We shall postulate an economy with no government and no foreign trade. There are only households and business firms. The households supply productive resources to the business firms which produce all goods, and the business firms in return pay out all income to the households. The goods produced will either be purchased by the households for consumption or purchased by business firms themselves for investment. (Thus we're abstracting from any investment expenditures by households.) The income paid out to households will either be consumed or saved.

The production decisions of business firms are made in anticipation of demand, both from the households as consumers and from other business firms as investors. Suppose that business produces $450 billion of consumption goods and $100 billion of investment goods. By definition, since the value of income is identical to the value of output, $550 billion of income is paid out to households. If the households save $100 billion of this amount and spend the other $450 billion on the consumption goods that were produced, and if business firms borrow that $100 billion of saving and spend it on the investment goods that were produced, all will be well. Everything produced for sale was purchased. There was no excess supply or excess demand at the end of the "period."

But now suppose that producers had failed to anticipate demand correctly, and that business firms only want to purchase $80 billion of investment goods. (Firms for the most part purchase investment goods from other firms.) Twenty billion dollars of the total $550 billion in output will consequently not be sold as planned. It will become an unintended addition to the inventories of the producing firms. Because additions to inventory are investment, actual as distinct from intended investment will still be $100 billion. But now all will not be well. Some business firms clearly made mistakes. There was an excess supply of goods that showed up in undesired additions to business inventories.

The Response to Unintended Investment

What is likely to happen? The firms whose inventories are now excessive will want to cut back production in the next period. How far they cut it back will depend upon their new estimates of future demand. Suppose they decide that the unexpectedly low demand in the previous period was due to unique condi-

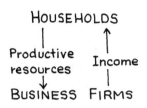

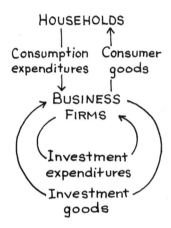

$$\text{INCOME} \equiv \text{Consumption} + \text{Saving}$$

$$\text{OUTPUT} \equiv \text{Consumption} + \text{Investment}$$

OUTPUT: 550

CONSUMPTION: 450
INTENDED
INVESTMENT: 80
UNINTENDED
INVESTMENT: 20
                      550

SAVING: 100

OUTPUT: 530

CONSUMPTION: 450
INVESTMENT
PURCHASES: 100
INVENTORIES: −20
                530
SAVING: 80

marginal propensity to consume:

$$\frac{change\ in\ consumption}{change\ in\ income}$$

tions that won't be repeated and so they again plan to offer $450 billion of consumption goods and $100 billion of investment goods. They will nonetheless *produce* only $80 billion of investment goods (plus $450 billion of consumption goods) and plan to make up the difference out of the inventories reluctantly accumulated during the previous period.

This could work out as planned. Total income will be $530 billion with output reduced to that level. If households purchase $450 billion of consumption goods and save $80 billion, while business firms purchase the expected $100 billion of investment goods, producer expectations will be fulfilled. There will be no excess supply or demand. Note that total investment will be only $80 billion, matching total saving, because the $20 billion reduction in inventories is negative investment.

The Consumption Function

But is such an outcome at all likely? In particular, with household income reduced by $20 billion as a result of reduced production, can we expect consumption to hold at $450 billion? Keynes asserted that we could not expect this because aggregate consumption spending in any period will depend primarily upon the aggregate income of that period. Consumption spending will change in the same direction as income changes, though by a somewhat smaller amount than the change in income. He called this relationship the *propensity to consume* or *consumption function*. It is a key to the income-expenditures model.

Suppose that for every $100 change in aggregate income, aggregate consumption expenditure changes by $75. The *marginal propensity to consume* (the change in consumption divided by the change in income) is then .75. With a marginal propensity to consume of .75, aggregate consumption will be only $435 billion rather than the $450 billion anticipated by the firms selling consumption goods. And so there will again be some unintended investment. Total business inventories will not be reduced to the desired level.

Let's summarize the outcome during this period in two columns, the first showing what business firms planned for and the second showing what actually occurred.

Intended output:	$530 billion	Actual income:	$530 billion
Planned sales of consumption goods:	450	Actual sales of consumption goods:	435
Intended investment:	80	Actual investment	95

The *intended* investment total is made up of $100 billion in expenditures for new investment goods minus a $20 billion reduction in inventories from the preceding period. The *actual* investment total results from a net reduction of inventories by only $5 billion, as a result of the decline in consumption spending caused by the decline in income that resulted from the reduced output that was a response to an excess output of investment goods in the preceding period.

Note once again that actual investment is equal to actual saving: $530 billion in income minus $435 billion in consumption expenditures equals $95 billion of saving. Business firms implicitly expected households to reduce their aggregate saving by $20 billion in response to that $20 billion fall in income, for that is the only way in which consumption could have held at the hoped for level of $450 billion. But that assumes a marginal propensity to consume of zero: a change in income leading to no change in consumption. With an actual marginal propensity to consume of .75, the marginal propensity to save is .25 rather than 1.0. Saving falls by only $5 billion when income falls by $20 billion, and so $15 billion of expected sales to consumers fails to materialize, and business inventories at the end of the period are consequently $15 billion larger than intended.

As a result the economy is still out of equilibrium. What will happen next under the assumptions we're using? Business firms will again curtail production in an effort to reduce inventories to desired levels. But that will further reduce income, which will induce a further fall in consumption, which will again frustrate the sales expectations of business firms.

The income-expenditures model which we have just described in a very summary form presents a variant type of supply and demand analysis in which supply and demand are allowed to influence one another. A change in demand does not encounter an unchanged supply curve to bring about a new equilibrium. Rather the change in demand changes supply, the changed supply affects income and hence demand, the further change in demand once again changes supply, and equilibrium is finally reached through a series of mutual accommodations. The model describes a process of mounting frustration for participants in the economic system rather than the rapid accommodation to changed circumstances, largely through price changes, that would occur if decision makers had perfect information. It explains how output can fall and unemployment can rise contrary to anyone's intentions.

The Unstable Force: Investment Spending

The initiating cause of aggregate fluctuations in output and income, in the Keynesian framework, is a change in the desired rate of investment expenditure. Recall what investment means.

To invest is to purchase a good for the sake of the future income it is expected to yield. A business firm is investing, therefore, when it purchases machinery, just as you would be investing if you purchased corporate stock. But we must distinguish between those two kinds of investment, because we're interested now in investment as a process of adding to the quantity of real goods in the society. Your purchase of corporate stock would merely be a transfer of financial assets, from the viewpoint of society as a whole. Even if you bought *new* stock, issued so that the corporation could purchase additional machinery, your surrender of money to acquire stock would be a financial transfer only. The real investment would occur when the corporation purchased the new machinery with the funds you supplied. Investment in this sense is one of the four components of total expenditures on gross national product—along with consumption expenditures, government purchases of new commodities and services, and net exports.

Notice again that the distinction between an *investment expenditure* and a *consumption expenditure* will inevitably be somewhat arbitrary. An amateur tennis player purchases a racket for the sake of the future services he expects it to provide. Is the racket a consumption or an investment good? Family automobiles are also purchased for the sake of future services. A kitchen blender is an investment inasmuch as it is obtained for the sake of the goods it will produce in the future. Nevertheless, the National Income and Product Accounts classify all these purchases as consumption expenditures unless they are made by business firms. If you buy a water cooler for your patio, that's a consumption expenditure. If one is purchased for the office where you work, that's an investment expenditure. The only such purchase by households that qualifies as investment in these accounts is the purchase of new housing. Here the stream of services extends so far into the future that it seems unduly misleading to count the purchase of a new residence as consumption. But the difference between automobiles and residences is only one of degree. Customers, of course, usually don't worry about these fine accounting distinctions, and consider the purchase of a durable household good as an investment. Thus people say, quite correctly, that they "invested" in a clothes dryer, or a dining room set, or new carpeting. That is completely consistent with our definition of investment. But accountants must make distinctions even if they seem to be arbitrary, in order to measure.

The components of investment in the National Income and Product Accounts are (a) residential construction, (b) purchases of new business structures (offices, factories, stores), (c) purchases by business firms of new durable equipment (machinery), and (d) net additions to business inventories. The last item makes sure that everything produced is counted as purchased by someone. If a business firm finds itself unable to sell all the output it had hoped to sell, it is considered to have purchased that output itself and added it, reluctantly, to inventory.

Investment is so important for the understanding of recessions, because investment spending is far less stable than consumption spending. There's no mystery about why that should be the case. It's usually easier to postpone the purchase of capital goods than to postpone the purchase of consumer goods. People are therefore likely to maintain consumption spending at a fairly steady rate, but to "bunch" investment spending at what they consider appropriate times. Moreover, the purchase of any good that's expected to yield its services over a long period of time entails additional uncertainty. Will the stream of services turn out to be as large as it's currently expected to be? Will some new method of securing these services appear soon and make this investment obsolete? Will a more opportune time come along later, perhaps a time when funds can be borrowed more cheaply or when capital goods producers are offering lower prices? Continually changing conditions can act upon the uncertain expectations of investors to produce waves of postponed or accelerated investment expenditures.

Are Fluctuations Self-Correcting?

There was nothing unusual in 1936 about focusing on investment decisions as the principal trigger of economic fluctuations. The big question was and still is: What happens next? *Does the economic system moderate or does it magnify the initial effects* of the change in investment expenditures? Most economists up to the time of Keynes believed that the economic system operated to check and reverse destabilizing decisions. Keynes found it more probable, at least in mature industrial economies, that the system would magnify disturbances and would demonstrate little capacity to generate a recovery from recessions. Which view is correct?

Almost anyone looking back from 1939 at the performance of the American economy over the previous decade would incline toward the Keynesian view. Whatever forces were supposed to arrest a decline in output and income certainly didn't seem to be working from 1929 to 1933. And if a recession was indeed a time for correcting mistakes, after which growth could resume again on a sounder basis, the payoff seemed terribly slow in coming.

Let's look at some of the stabilizing forces that were supposed to dampen recessions and initiate recoveries, then at Keynes's reasons for doubting their effectiveness. One such force was falling prices. Recessions had historically meant a falling price level, or a rising value for money. When people *expect* prices to fall, they become more eager to hold money. But once prices *have* fallen, the real value of the public's money balances is larger. Moreover, prices that have already fallen will be more widely expected to rise than to fall further. These two situations brought about by a recession—larger money holdings in terms of purchasing power and an increased expectation of rising prices—should prompt people to begin reducing their money balances by increasing their rate of expenditures above their incomes. This will bring about recovery.

But suppose the recession produces a sizable fall in output with very little change in prices? The public will still find its stock of money balances growing, relative to income and expenditures. At some point the public will decide it's holding all the money it wants to hold, in view of the lower gross national product, and will begin exchanging money for other goods. This will launch a recovery.

A decline in investment spending also implies less demand for loans, which in turn implies a decrease in the cost of borrowing. But as the cost of borrowing falls, the incentive to invest increases. Some investment projects that had been postponed will now be undertaken in response to better credit terms, and aggregate investment will revive. This will promote recovery.

The idle resources that begin to appear in a recession also provide opportunities for entrepreneurs who were waiting for the right location, a favorable lease, or more advantageous terms from suppliers. Thus the recession itself encourages new initiatives, increased production, and additional investment. All of this works to slow down the decline in a recession and generate a recovery. But Keynes had reasons for suspecting that none of these countering forces might be sufficient, especially in a wealthy, industrialized economy.

Keynesian Doubts

Prices often did not fall in response to decreased demand. The market power of larger sellers, the wage-fixing practices of labor unions, and the existence of long-term contracts all tended to put a floor under the existing level of prices. With prices rigid in a downward direction, decreases in aggregate demand would not raise the value of money. Decreases in demand would operate almost exclusively to reduce total output.

While it is true that the public's money holdings increase when its expenditures decrease, that assumes other things remain equal. But they don't remain equal if income falls as fast as expenditures. And a reduction in total output entails a simultaneous reduction in total income.

If the stock of money does not change while gross national product is falling, the ratio between the public's cash balances and its income will rise, of course. But this does not necessarily mean the public will find itself holding larger money balances than it prefers to hold. The demand for money might increase substantially because of the public's apprehension about the coming recession and the expectation that the value of money is going to increase.

The lower interest rates and other reduced costs that recessions tend to bring in their wake do indeed tend to spur investment and production. But will their combined effect be enough to offset the gloomy expectations that recession creates? How much stimulus is a one-point reduction in the interest rate to entrepreneurs who fear that there will be no demand for their output?

Some of the most interesting passages in *The General Theory* present Keynes's thoughts (usually quite unsystematic) on the importance of expectations. It is expectations, as you know by now, that guide economic decisions. The relevant expectations will not be based exclusively on the decision makers' appraisals of their own particular prospects. Larger and more vague considerations will also enter in, such as the state of the economy, the political climate, the social milieu, and even (as Keynes suggests in one place) the nerves, hysteria, digestions, and reactions to the weather of potential investors.

Expectations and the state of confidence were especially important to Keynes's interpretation of the role that money played (or failed to play) in restraining a recession and promoting a recovery. Remember that the monetary authorities can increase the excess reserves of the banking system but cannot compel the commercial banks to extend loans and thereby turn those reserves into money. Moreover, the creation of a larger money stock will not produce an increase in spending if the public responds simply by building up its money balances.

In a recession, everyone tends to become more pessimistic and more cautious. Banks scrutinize potential borrowers more rigorously before extending loans and refuse to renew some loans that come due. Borrowers are less eager to apply for loans because short-term profit prospects seem unfavorable. People look for ways to increase their liquidity as a precautionary move. The expectation of declining prices also adds to the public's preference for holding money rather than assets whose value relative to money is likely to fall. In short, a recession can create a crisis of confidence that worsens the recession by prompting a sharp increase in the demand for money. The monetary authorities may find it difficult to satisfy this demand or to induce people to begin spending their idle balances.

United States monetary statistics from the 1930s provide an interesting commentary on all of this. The total reserves of banks that were members of the Federal Reserve System averaged $2,395 million in December of 1929; $2,347 million of these were legally required reserves against bank liabilities; banks held only $48 million in excess reserves. Four years later, at the bottom of the recession, total reserves were $2,588 million; but excess reserves had grown to $766 million. In December 1939, after all sorts of reserve-expanding policies had been pursued in an effort to stimulate recovery, the total reserves of member banks were $11,473 million; but excess reserves had grown to $5,011 million. It certainly seemed as if efforts by the central bank to halt a recession or to spur a recovery were no more effective than pushing on a string. "Pushing on a string" became, in fact, a common way of characterizing the impotence of monetary authorities in dealing with recessions.

The conclusions seemed rather clear to most observers by the end of the 1930s. Relatively small changes in demand can cause substantial changes in output and employment through the cumulative interaction of income and expenditures. This "multiplier process," as the Keynesians called it, can transform minor disturbances into major disruptions, because the economic system does not contain stabilizing forces of sufficient strength. The adjustments of consumers, investors, and producers to changed circumstances do not necessarily push the economy back toward full employment when it begins to slip toward recession. On the contrary, the economy can settle down indefinitely at a rate of output far below capacity and with high unemployment.

Saving and Economic Growth

Keynes liked to emphasize the implications of all this for the way we regard the act of saving. In the Keynesian perspective, saving is not the unmixed blessing that economists have traditionally assumed it to be. If intended investment falls, the attempt by savers to continue their current rate of saving will prevent consumption expenditure from picking up the slack. The result will be unsold goods, reduced output and reduced incomes—until savers have been compelled by falling income to scale down their rate of saving to what investors want to spend. This comes close to reversing the traditional argument that high rates of saving are necessary to permit high rates of investment.

It has long been a fundamental tenet of economics that a nation's income and wealth grow roughly in proportion to the growth in its stock of capital. Investment is the process that adds to the capital stock. A higher rate of investment therefore means a faster rate of economic growth, a more rapid rise in national income, and a speedier improvement in living levels. But what determines the rate of investment? The classical answer was: the rate of saving. There is no way for a society to produce capital goods except by withdrawing some of its resources from the production of consumer goods. Those who save abstain from current consumption and either purchase capital goods themselves or turn their income over to others who purchase capital goods. Without saving there can be no investment. (If investment is financed by borrowing from abroad, foreigners must do the saving.) The incentive to save must therefore be preserved and extended, according to the classical argument; it is the root cause of social progress.

Keynes suspected that this line of reasoning might be altogether inapplicable to societies in advanced stages of economic growth. Economic growth, Keynes believed, had two effects that jointly made the practice of thrift an increasingly doubtful virtue. On the one hand, the accumulation of capital in the course of economic growth meant that the most profitable investment opportunities were steadily used up. Further additions to the capital stock had to go toward projects with lower expected rates of return for investors. The incentive to invest consequently tended to fall as economic growth proceeded.

On the other hand, the incentive to save tended to become stronger. Saving, Keynes maintained, is dependent primarily upon income; people will tend to save more as their income rises and will in fact tend to save a higher proportion of their income as that income increases. Because economic growth increases people's incomes, therefore, it increases the amounts that they desire to save relative to their income.

The implication is that in wealthy, industrialized economies the desire to save will be continually pushing out ahead of the desire to invest. But if people wish to save a larger amount than investors are willing to spend, the savers cannot succeed. Their purpose will be frustrated by an insufficient aggregate demand, which will lead to lower output and higher unemployment, until the reduced incomes of savers finally persuade them to save no more than investors are willing to spend.

The outcome might even be worse. A chronic tendency toward insufficient demand, created by persistent efforts to save more than investors want to spend, may so damage the "state of confidence" that the aggregate desire to invest actually decreases. Here would be a strange outcome indeed, one which came to be known as the "paradox of thrift" among those who thought that the 1930s had shown it to be much more

The traditional perspective:

INCOME

CONSUMPTION   SAVINGS

INVESTMENT

HIGHER OUTPUT
AND INCOME

The Keynesian perspective:

INCOME

CONSUMPTION   SAVINGS

LESS DEMAND

LOWER OUTPUT
AND INCOME

than a mere logical possibility. An increased desire to save so damages the incentive to invest that output and income fall below the level at which savers can even maintain their previously desired rate of saving. The attempt to save more results in less actual saving. The public would actually succeed in increasing the amount it saves if it determined to save less—and thus spent more.

This would not mean, it's important to note, that *anyone* can save more by spending more. And that's what counts. A household or business firm that wants to increase its rate of saving will *not* achieve that end by reducing its rate of saving. The paradox of thrift applies to the actions of savers and investors *as a whole*. But saving and investment decisions are not made by "wholes." They are made by persons who don't assume, and quite correctly don't assume, that their own actions will induce others to behave in the same way.

A Case for Government Intervention

Does that argument sound familiar? It should, because we have once again run into the problem of *externalities*. The Keynesian analysis suggests that individuals, paying attention only to the costs and benefits that they expect their decisions to create for themselves, are induced to take actions that make everyone, including themselves, worse off. It would be useless in such a situation to urge that people throw caution to the winds, reduce their money holdings, and start spending freely on new goods in order to bring about prosperity. That kind of cheerleading does in fact occur. But it's never been known to accomplish anything, because almost everybody behaves like a free rider. Households and business firms will continue to pursue the course that seems most advantageous to their own interests, while hoping that others will engage in those beneficial bursts of spending. These prudent households and business firms may even join the cheerleading squad in an effort to get others to do what they themselves don't want to do. Thus we might *all* end up cheering for actions that *none* of us is willing to take.

Free-rider problems create a case for government intervention. More vigorous and effective intervention by government was certainly one of the objectives that Keynes had in mind when he published *The General Theory*. A more active role for the central bank was one of his recommendations. But because action by the monetary authorities might be ineffective against recessions, especially severe ones, Keynes lent his considerable persuasive talents heavily to the task of making a case for what he called "loan expenditure" on the part of government. Income-expenditures analysis would not have caught on with economists as rapidly as it did after 1936 had it only offered a diagnosis. But it seemed also to suggest a way out of the mire. If the private sector was unwilling to invest as much as it wanted to save, government could step in to borrow and spend.

But questions of monetary and fiscal policy must be postponed until we have looked at some additional complications created by the fact that national policies have international effects.

Once Over Lightly

Economic theory is primarily a theory of order, showing how independent decisions are coordinated through market inter-relationships. The experience of the Great Depression persuaded many economists that recessions could not be adequately explained by any theory that postulated a self-adjusting system.

The most influential effort in the 1930s to show how uncertainty and imperfect coordination interfere with the maintenance of full employment is associated with the name of John Maynard Keynes and *The General Theory of Employment, Interest and Money*.

The income-expenditures analysis developed by Keynes and his successors offers a theory of aggregate supply and aggregate demand in which surpluses lead to declining demand rather than to the reduced prices upon which economic theory usually depends for a solution to problems of excess supply.

In income-expenditures analysis, the cumulative effects of a "disequilibrium" are transmitted through the consumption function. Consumption is assumed to change as income changes, and in the same direction, but by a smaller amount. When producers reduce output because their sales fail to reach expected levels, they also reduce incomes. Lower incomes mean less consumption and therefore a further decline in sales.

Aggregate "equilibrium" is achieved in income expenditures analysis when the level of income is consistent with the intentions of savers and the intentions of investors. Income will fall as long as savers try to withhold from consumption more income than investors want to spend. Eventually income will fall far enough so that savers will no longer want to save more than investors intend to invest.

Instability is introduced into the flow of income and expenditures primarily through fluctuations in investment spending. Because investment decisions depend so heavily on a reading of the uncertain future, the rate of aggregate investment expenditure will display fluctuations over time.

Economic theorists had traditionally assumed that recessions generate self correcting pressures. Keynes argued that these pressures were weaker than had been widely supposed, and that an economy might not recover fully or quickly from a recession if left to its own devices.

The progressive accumulation of capital in a society raises people's incomes and makes them want to save more out of their income. But the same accumulation of capital, according to Keynes, reduces the expected rate of return from investment and so diminishes the desire of investors to spend as much as savers want to hold back from consumption. The result, Keynes argued, may be a chronic insufficiency of aggregate demand in highly developed economies.

Keynes cast special doubt upon the ability of increases in the money stock to promote a revival of spending and an economic recovery. He suggested that the collapse of confidence and the dismal expectations associated with recession might require strong government initiatives to restore adequate rates of aggregate spending on new goods.

QUESTIONS FOR DISCUSSION

1. What caused the recession that began in the U.S. in 1929? Why did the decline continue for four years? Why did the decline occur at such a steep rate? Why did real output not regain its 1929 level until 1939? Why did the unemployment rate remain so extraordinarily high throughout the 1930s? Why has no recession or depression of even remotely comparable severity occurred since World War II? Substantial disagreement still exists among economic theorists and economic historians on how these questions are to be answered. Some suggestions pointing toward partial answers will be found in Chapters 20 and 21. How one evaluates the long-run importance of Keynes's contribution to economic theory will depend largely on the answers given to these questions.

2. The table below shows gross private domestic investment in the U.S. in dollars of that year's purchasing power, for each year from 1929 through 1934. It also shows one critical component of total investment expenditures: the net change in business inventories. The figures are in millions of dollars. Interpret these data in the light of this chapter's analysis of investment and recession.

Year	Investment	Inventory Change
1929	$16,197	$1,714
1930	10,249	−352
1931	5,620	−1,148
1932	965	−2,480
1933	1,406	−1,564
1934	3,328	−735

3. Can an economy be at equilibrium if much of its industrial capacity is standing idle and a large percentage of its labor force is unemployed? Is that a question about fact or a disguised argument about the proper way to use the concept of equilibrium?

4. Suppose that consumer demand for the following goods turns out to be less than the producers anticipated, so that the goods already produced cannot all be sold at current prices. What consequences would you predict in the case of each good? Would prices or production levels be likely to fall first? How long will the sequence of adjustments take?
   a. automobiles
   b. beef cattle
   c. secondary school teachers

5. How long must a recession continue or a recovery be delayed before we are justified in assuming that recessions are not *temporary* disturbances?

6. If total expenditures on new goods fall below total income, so that aggregate saving increases, what happens to these savings?

7. In the following passage from Adam Smith's *Wealth of Nations*, the word *stock* refers either to a stock of goods or to a stock of money that can be used to acquire goods.

   > In all countries where there is tolerable security, every man of common understanding will endeavor to employ whatever stock he can command, in procuring either present enjoyment or future profit. . . . A man must be perfectly crazy who, where there is tolerable security, does not employ all the stock which he commands [in one of these ways].

   a. Does this passage imply that all income will be either consumed or invested?
   b. Is this passage compatible with Keynes's analysis of the saving-investment relationship?

8. Is it true, as Keynes assumed in describing the consumption function, that people increase their consumption as their income increases but not by as much as the increase in their income? Does consumption in one period (a month, for example) depend upon income in that particular period? Would you expect a salesman receiving a highly variable monthly income to vary his consumption as his income varies?

9. If saving suddenly and unexpectedly increases, unintended investment will rise by enough to keep actual saving and investment equal.
   a. What form does this unintended investment take?
   b. What further consequences will this unintended investment have?
   c. Suppose that saving suddenly and unexpectedly *decreased*. Would such an occurrence be capable of creating a temporary inequality between saving and investment? Explain what might happen.

10. Consumer expenditures on durable goods fluctuate far more from year to year than do consumer expenditures on nondurable commodities or on services. How does this support the contention that investment expenditures are less stable than consumption expenditures?

11. Do fluctuations in spending for particular goods necessarily cause fluctuations in the output of those goods? Do you think that production rates in the toy industry fluctuate as much as consumer expenditures for toys fluctuate?

Under what circumstances can a smooth flow of production be reconciled with variations in expenditure on that output? When are reductions in expenditure most likely to cause production cutbacks and unemployment in a particular firm or industry?

12. Would the following transactions be classified in the National Income and Product Accounts as consumption, as investment, or as neither. If a transaction is neither, what is it?
    a. Your purchase of two new baseball bats.
    b. Your purchase of two used baseball bats.
    c. The New York Yankees' purchase of two new baseball bats.
    d. Your purchase of Ford Motor Company Stock.
    e. The New York Yankees' purchase of Ford Motor Company stock.
    f. Your purchase of a new automobile.
    g. The Ford Motor Company's production of a new automobile that no one purchases.

13. The following questions all deal with the relationship between investment and interest rates.
    a. How do interest rates affect investment spending?
    b. How do higher interest rates affect residential construction?
    c. "Shall we maintain production and allow our inventories of unsold goods to rise or should we shut down production until we've managed to sell off most of the finished goods now in the warehouses?" How might the level of interest rates enter into this decision?
    d. An electric utility postpones construction of a new generating plant because the market price of its bonds is disappointingly low. How does this illustrate the relationship between investment and the interest rate?
    e. A corporation plans to begin a huge capital expansion program, using proceeds from a sale of new stock. But common stock prices decline and the firm postpones the stock sale and the investment program it was intended to finance. Does that have anything to do with interest rates?
    f. "Higher interest rates don't deter any business firm that has a profitable use for the money. If we can make 30 percent on an investment, we're going to invest whether we can borrow at 3 percent or have to pay 12 percent." Evaluate this statement.
    g. "The higher the interest rate I can get, the more I'm going to invest. Investment increases as interest rates rise." Is that right?
    h. "Interest rates tend to be higher in booms than in recessions. But investment spending is usually greater in booms than in recessions. This implies that high interest rates encourage investment spending and low interest rates discourage it." Criticize that argument.

14. Does investment depend on saving? Can investment occur if there has been no saving? What are the real differences between the older view that investment could only be maintained by maintaining saving and Keynes's view that a high rate of investment might be a precondition for a high rate of saving?

15. Does the "paradox of thrift" imply that saving is an antisocial act and consumption an act that benefits society?

National Policies and International Exchange

The movement of money and other goods across national boundaries is both a problem and an opportunity for government officials charged with stabilizing their domestic economies. That's why this chapter on international exchange comes before the two chapters that will examine national policies for dealing with recession and inflation.

Perhaps the insertion of this chapter *within* the chapters on national policies can also serve as a reminder that international economic policies are constructed by national states. There is no "international government" today with the will and the capacity to establish rules for the governance of international exchange. We often hear that nationalism is obsolete in the era of jet planes, rockets, space exploration, satellite communication, and nuclear weapons. But that is the statement of an ideal, not a description of reality. The present reality is this—that any actual international economic order will be produced by the interactions of people whose allegiance is *not* to "the community of nations." And no international economic system will be supported by a nation unless that support is seen to be in the best interest of those who head national governments.

It is an unpleasant truth that national policies are often constructed on the premise that foreigners are enemies rather than participants in mutually advantageous exchange. That occurs because it is so often in the interest of those who govern nation-states to behave as if that premise were true. So it is that the governments of national states attempt to bend the flow of international exchange to fit the goals of domestic policy. But they are not altogether successful. International exchange often escapes from the channels to which national policies have tried to confine it, and frustrates the intentions of domestic policymakers.

Comparative Advantage and International Trade

The principle of comparative advantage received its first explicit statement in the early nineteenth century as an explanation of the gains to be obtained from international trade. But the principle has never fared well in the area where it originated. "Everyone knows" that imports hurt domestic firms and destroy jobs, while exports generate profits for domestic producers and create additional jobs. Policies aimed at restricting imports and subsidizing exports have consequently had a strong political appeal for centuries, and never more so than when a recession is cutting into sales and adding to the level of unemployment.

The argument that imports destroy jobs has the seductive appeal of a half-truth. When Americans buy Japanese radios, they do not buy as many domestically made radios. An increase in radio imports can therefore lead to production cutbacks and layoffs in the domestic radio industry. So the owners and employees of radio manufacturing firms have an obvious interest in restricting imports. And when they go to Congress to request taxes or quotas on radio imports, they have a handy slogan with which to claim that such protection is good for the country: it protects American jobs. But the argument is misleading.

In the first place, jobs are created by the production of export goods, as well as the production of goods that compete with imports. And American firms cannot continue indefinitely to sell abroad if foreigners are not allowed to sell in the United States. Trade is a two-way street.

Second, jobs should not automatically be treated as goods. Some jobs no doubt are intrinsically satisfying and worth doing for themselves without regard to the commodities or services that result. But that's certainly rare. The justification for jobs generally is the income they provide for workers and the corresponding benefit to others in the form of useful goods. The "protect American jobs" argument ignores the gains in real income that come from specialization. If the Japanese can make better radios and sell them at lower prices than American manufacturers can, Americans ought to produce other products and buy their radios from Japan. The attempt to justify the protection of less efficient producers on the grounds that this will preserve jobs runs quickly into absurdity. Why not push the argument further and produce domestically all the coffee we consume? American soil, climate, and geography are not as well suited for the production of coffee trees as are large areas of Brazil and Colombia. But think of all the jobs we could create by building and operating huge greenhouses in which we try to duplicate the favorable growing conditions in those countries! And why stop with goods currently imported? Think of how many new jobs we could create by outlawing the use of automated equipment in the telephone industry!

Producer Interests and the National Interest

For two centuries, economists have been arguing along these lines against the proponents of restrictions on imports, but not with great success. A French pamphleteer-economist named Frederic Bastiat (1801–1850) wrote a witty satire in 1845 in the form of a petition by the French candlemakers for protection against the unfair competition of the sun. Their request to the Chamber of Deputies for legislation that would protect the jobs of candlemakers by prohibiting windows brilliantly exposes the absurdity of protectionist logic. Bastiat's satire has been reprinted numerous times; the arguments he ridiculed do not disappear.

Part of the explanation must be found in the resistance of special interest groups to mere logic. People are readily persuaded by arguments in which they want to believe and have more difficulty understanding arguments that run counter to their interests. And the political process almost guarantees that those who stand to benefit from restrictions on international trade will have a louder voice in policy formation than will the larger group that stands to lose. Transaction costs prevent radio purchasers from organizing effectively to oppose domestic producers; and the foreign producers obviously have little influence on domestic policy. The externalities of the political process in a democracy make it almost certain that when government officials come to the point of choosing between the interests of American buyers of radios and Americn producers of radios, they will be surrounded by the clamor of producers but will hear almost nothing from consumers. Officials who wish to survive in their jobs pay attention to that kind of pressure.

A consumer who works against import restrictions cannot hope to receive more than a tiny fraction of the benefits. A producer lobbying for restrictions hopes for a very large benefit.

A limited but legitimate argument for protection against imports can be constructed from the costs of change. The closing down of an industry unable to meet foreign competition entails losses for its owners and employees. The more narrowly specialized the displaced resources, the greater the losses. There may be a case for protection in such circumstances. Notice, however, that the argument can be applied to the case of an industry hurt by domestic competition as well as foreign. Domestic competitors have political influence, of course, and are therefore harder to exclude by special legislation. Nonetheless, if resources were attracted to an industry because of government restrictions on imports, it may be unfair to jerk that protection away suddenly. So there is a case for the maintenance of prior and long continued restrictions on imports, or at least for their reduction (in the interest of efficiency) at a slow rate (in the interest of equity). Equity considerations along with political realities may also suggest a policy of transitional subsidies, designed to reduce the loss to workers and owners or to help them find new opportunities. But this argument cannot support the introduction of new or additional restrictions against imports.

There is no limit to the number of bad arguments that can be constructed in support of import restrictions, and it would be an exercise in futility to attempt to anticipate and refute each one. The fact that there is a kernel of validity in most such arguments complicates the task of their analysis. The valid reasoning must be winnowed from the chaff that surrounds it before the limitations of its applicability can be shown. Nothing would contribute more toward raising the quality of public discussion in this area than a firm grasp of the principle of comparative advantage.

The principle of comparative advantage shows why and how exchange creates wealth. It keeps insisting that the cost of a transaction is the value of what is given up and the benefit is the value of what is obtained, so that it is nonsense to claim that a country can grow wealthy by exporting more than it imports. The principle of comparative advantage undercuts the claim that one country may be more efficient than another in the production of everything: the logical impossibility of that is apparent from the very definition of efficiency as a ratio between the value of what is produced and what is consequently not produced, between the goods obtained and the goods that had to be sacrificed because their production entails genuine opportunity costs. By focusing on the real factors involved in production and trade, the principle of comparative advantage disperses the fog that creeps in when trade policy is discussed exclusively in monetary terms.

"But then we'd be losing dollars!" So? Dollars cost almost nothing to produce. If other countries want to trade transistor radios for dollars, that's a marvelous swap from our point of view, so marvelous, in fact, that other nations can be counted on not to do it for long. This becomes obvious as soon as one understands the concept of the balance of international payments. Unfortunately, the balance of payments is more often invoked to confuse than to clarify the issue.

The balance of payments always and necessarily balances. You might be a bit surprised to hear that, since we are told so often that we must do this or cannot do that "because of the balance of payments." The implication is that its balance is precarious, and that we are in danger of disastrously losing our equilibrium. But if patriotism is the last refuge of a scoundrel, as Samuel Johnson suggested, the balance of payments is today very often the last refuge of Dr. Johnson's patriots. Special-interest groups looking for favors look also for a way to wrap themselves in the balance of payments. A little clarity on the meaning of the balance of payments can therefore go a long way toward locating the public interest amid the confusing claims of competing partial interests.

Balance-of-payments accounting is an attempt to keep track of international transactions by dividing them into transactions that earn foreign exchange, called credits, and transactions that use up foreign exchange, called debits. If you keep this basic definition in mind you should have no trouble deciding under which column to list a particular item.

Exports are credit items in the balance of payments. Foreigners who want to purchase our products must ultimately pay dollars to the American sellers. This results either in the reacquisition by Americans of dollars previously held by foreigners, in the acquisition of foreign currency used to purchase dollars, or in the acquisition of some other medium of international exchange that can be used to purchase dollars. U.S. imports simply reverse this flow. To purchase the products of some other country we must either turn over previously acquired holdings of that country's currency, obtain some by giving up dollars in exchange, or use up our stocks of some other accepted international exchange medium to obtain the required currency.

That's all there is to the balance of payments—if we define exports and imports broadly enough. Imports, for example, must include not only commodities like magnesium and tape recorders, but also services like the Geneva hotel room used by an American tourist or the entertainment provided in Fort Worth by an English rock group. Payment for these services entails the using up of foreign exchange, and so they are debit items in the U.S. balance of payments.

What about gold? Gold sales or exports are credit items, just like any other exports; gold purchases or imports are debit items. Gold sales are a way of acquiring foreign exchange, just as are sales of wheat. Momentary confusion may arise from the fact that gold is itself considered a medium of international exchange. Treat it like any other commodity, however, and you'll get it in the correct column.

We must also include under imports the "purchase" of whatever it is we obtain when our government extends foreign aid or Americans send money to relatives in Europe. If it seems inappropriate to think of either activity as "importing," the fact remains that any payments made to foreigners by the United States government, private organizations, or individuals use up foreign exchange and must therefore be classified as debits. These payments may be used in turn to purchase American exports (sometimes that's a condition of the grant); if so, the export is a credit item; but the gift, grant, pension, or other remittance that made it possible goes under the debit column. Gifts to us by foreigners or payments made to Americans by Lloyds of London in settlement of insurance claims are correspondingly credit items in our balance of payments. And the sizable income that we receive each year as a return on our overseas investments goes into the credit column, because it is a source of foreign exchange earnings for the United States.

What about the original acts of investing? Capital flows can be treated like commodities and services if attention is focused on the stock, bond, or other evidence of indebtedness that changes hands. Thus foreign investment by Americans amounts to importing securities. Investment by foreigners in the United States is a U.S. export of securities. If this way of describing the matter strikes you as strained, you can keep the effects of foreign investment clear by concentrating on the basic definition of credits and debits. Investment by Americans in the French economy is a debit item in our balance of payments because Americans must purchase French francs to buy an interest in French companies. And Britons buying shares of General Motors contribute to the credit side of our balance of payments because they must obtain dollars to complete the purchase.

To invest abroad is to import securities.

Why Credits Always Equal Debits

Suppose now that we sum the values of all the debits in the course of a year, then of all the credits, and find that they are not equal. We conclude in such a case that we made a mistake in record keeping! Errors and omissions are inevitable, of course, when one is trying to keep track of *all* international transactions. The value of some transactions can only be guessed at, as when the balance-of-payments accountants tacked on $40 million in the 1920s for imports of bootleg liquor. And the value of many perfectly legal transactions is estimated from incomplete records, inaccurate data, and partial samples. So measured credits and debits never do turn out to be precisely equal in balance of payments statements. The keepers of the accounts rise to the occasion by adding the difference to the smaller of the two totals and labeling it Net Errors and Omissions.

"Aha!" says the voice from the rear. "It's all a trick. The balance of payments always balances because the Bureau of Economic Analysis puts in a fudge factor. Outside the artificial world of double-entry bookkeeping, however, it's perfectly possible for Americans to buy more from foreigners than they buy from us. Real world deficits can and do occur."

But the accounting conventions used to keep track of international exchanges are not arbitrary. They are based on the assumption that an exchange is in fact an exchange, so that every international transaction is properly entered on the ledger as simultaneously a "getting" and a "giving up." Credits are made to equal debits to reflect the fact that sales of goods are also receipts of payments. A Japanese radio imported into the United States means something was exported from the United States to Japan, whether commodities, services, dollars, yen, gold, or promises to pay later. And for accounting purposes, goods exchanged for each other have the same value.

The Ambiguity of "Disequilibrium"

But what do informed people mean, then, when they talk about deficits or surpluses in the balance of payments? And why are they ever concerned about disequilibrium in the balance of payments if in fact it always balances? The answer is that a deficit or a surplus is a discrepancy between what *actually* happened and what people *intended* to happen. That is always the meaning of a disequilibrium in the economic way of thinking and you've encountered it before.

A disequilibrium price for wheat does not show up as a difference between actual sales and purchases (which are necessarily identical) but as a difference between intended or desired sales and purchases. A disequilibrium in income-expenditures analysis does not mean that actual saving and investment are unequal (they cannot be) but that intended saving and investment are unequal. The implication of a disequilibrium is that matters will not continue in this way because intentions are not being realized, and so adjustments are going to occur. It follows that we cannot use the concept of equilibrium or disequilibrium unless we have a clear notion of intended or desired results that we can contrast with actual results.

The concept of a balance-of-payments disequilibrium is so extraordinarily ambiguous that we would probably be better off if we discarded the notion altogether. There are just too many intentions of too many different kinds entering into the aggregate of international transactions for anyone to assert

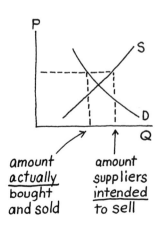

amount
actually
bought
and sold

amount
suppliers
intended
to sell

that intended credits are larger or smaller than intended debits—which is the meaning of a disequilibrium. In general, the larger the universe to which we try to apply the equilibrium concept, the more vague and uncertain is its meaning—and the more likely is it to obscure rather than clarify the problems at which we're looking.

A Dialogue about a Deficit

To claim that the U.S. balance of payments is in disequilibrium is to claim that something undesired is occurring. But from whose point of view is this claim made? Didn't the importers want to purchase whatever they purchased? Didn't banks want to loan whatever they loaned? Didn't the government, corporations, or individuals want to offer the gifts or grants they sent abroad? Who were the people for whom the results of international trade turned out to be inconsistent with what they had intended?

A simple little question should always be addressed to anyone who claims that the balance of payments is in deficit: "How do you know that?" The answer, if followed up properly, will tell you what it is that the speaker disapproves.

"We're losing gold." That was a common answer in the 1960s. But why call that a deficit? It was actually the way in which we paid for some of our purchases and so *avoided* a deficit.

"True," comes back the answer; "but a country cannot continue indefinitely to pay for its imports by drawing on its gold stock." And that's correct. But neither can a country continue indefinitely to pay for its imports by drawing down its stock of mineral resources. Nonetheless, no one regards Venezuelan oil exports or Malaysian tungsten exports as evidence of a deficit in those countries' balance of payments. Why single out gold for special treatment?

"Because if we lose all our monetary gold, we'll be forced to let the dollar depreciate." The United States government maintained the value of the dollar relative to gold up until the early 1970s by standing ready to exchange an ounce of gold for $35. If too many purchasers bought gold at that price, the U.S. would run out of gold and would have to allow the gold price of the dollar to fall. But why should we care if the price of gold rises to $40, $80, $300, or anything else?

"It isn't the price of gold we care about but the price of the dollar. We must maintain the dollar's value in terms of gold, because the dollar is the major international medium of exchange. The whole world uses dollars because it has confidence in the value of the dollar. If we let the gold price of the dollar go down, we'll betray the world's confidence. Then what will there be to take the dollar's place as the medium of inter-national exchange?" The argument is getting more complex, which is one of the points we've been trying to make: The assertion that the balance of payments is in disequilibrium is a way of saying that something undesirable is going to occur. The assertion is a deceptively simple way of making a very complex and uncertain argument without having to defend the steps in that argument or even acknowledge the actual goal. But now we can raise all sorts of critical questions. Foreigners were holding far more dollars in the late 1960s than we could redeem in gold at $35 an ounce. They knew that; nevertheless they continued to accumulate and hold dollars. Is the real value of the dollar determined by the quantity of gold it will purchase or by the quantity of useful goods and income-earning assets for which it exchanges? Foreigners want dollars for essentially the same reason as Americans: because they can be used to obtain Chevrolets, shares of IBM, and rib-eye steaks. The value of the dollar has not gone down unless its general purchasing power has decreased. Why the obsession with the amount of gold that a dollar will purchase?

"You've put your finger on the problem. The value of the dollar has been declining in the terms you've described. We must maintain its gold value as evidence that the United States intends to maintain the general purchasing power of the dollar. We cannot let the value of the dollar decline relative to other currencies." But why not? What difference does it make whether the dollar buys 400 Japanese yen or only 200, 3 German marks or 2?

International Exchange Rates

Our dialogue has brought us finally to the issue of exchange rates. Since the special problems of international economics are so closely bound up with the fact of different national currencies, it's important to understand what determines the rate at which one currency exchanges for another and what the consequences are of changes in these rates. We'll simplify the explanation by assuming that there are only two nations in the world, Germany and the United States. The United States uses dollars, and Germany uses marks as the domestic medium of exchange. Americans who want to purchase German goods must therefore exchange dollars for marks, and Germans must exchange marks for dollars in order to purchase American goods. At what rate will they be exchanged for one another?

Suppose that 1 dollar exchanges for 2 marks. This ex-change rate will determine the price to Americans of German goods and the price to Germans of American goods. A Volks-wagen, for example, that carries a factory price tag of 10,000

$$\frac{10,000 \ marks}{2.1 \ marks \ per \ \$} = \$4762$$

$$\$5000 \times 2.1 \ marks \ per \ \$ = 10,500 \ marks$$

marks will also carry an implicit price of 5000 dollars. If the exchange rate moved to 1 dollar for 2.1 marks, that 10,000 mark price tag would be a price of 4762 dollars, because that's how many dollars it would now take to buy 10,000 marks. Meanwhile, a U.S. factory price tag of $5000 on a Chevrolet is read by Germans as 10,000 marks when the exchange rate is 2 marks for 1 dollar. The price becomes 10,500 marks when the exchange rate moves to 2.1 marks per dollar.

It follows that the attractiveness of foreign goods will depend on the applicable exchange rate, as well as the price levels in each country. A depreciation of the dollar, which is identical with an appreciation of the mark in our simplified case, causes German goods to look less attractive to Americans and American goods to look more attractive to Germans.[1] With a depreciation of the dollar against the mark, German imports (equals American exports) would tend to increase, and American imports (equals German exports) would tend to decrease.

The exchange rate, in short, is a relative price that ties together two sets of relative prices. The existing exchange rate between two currencies will primarily express the relative purchasing power of the two currencies. If it takes 50 cents to buy a mark but only half a cent to buy a Japanese yen, you know that 1 dollar, 2 marks, and 200 yen will all buy approximately the same amount of goods in the U.S., Germany, and Japan, respectively.

Don't neglect the word *approximately*. Since the range of goods available in the three countries isn't the same, we can't actually say that a certain number of dollars has the same purchasing power in the U.S. as some particular number of marks or yen have in Germany or Japan. Moreover, exchange rates are more responsive to the relative prices of internationally traded goods (farm commodities, machinery, petroleum, automobiles) than to the relative price of *all* goods, including those that are rarely exported or imported (housing, most services).

Most importantly, however, international exchange rates won't express the current purchasing power of currencies when their relative purchasing power is expected to change. A belief that the U.S. will experience more rapid inflation than Germany in the coming year is a belief that the German mark will lose less value than the U.S. dollar during the year. That belief increases the present demand for marks, relative to the demand for dollars, and causes the current value of the mark to rise relative to the value of the dollar.

---

1. Students are often confused by the fact that a depreciation sometimes looks at first glance like an appreciation. You have to think about it for a moment to see that, when the mark goes from 45 to 50 cents, this is a depreciation of the dollar—and an appreciation of the mark, of course.

The exchange rate between marks and dollars, then, ultimately expresses the demand for each currency by holders of the other. An exchange rate cannot persist unless it clears the market, so that the quantity of dollars demanded by Germans is equal to the quantity of dollars supplied by Americans who want to buy marks. An equivalent way of stating it is that the quantity of marks demanded by Americans must be equal to the quantity of marks supplied by Germans who want to buy dollars. An inequality will mean either a shortage of dollars (equals a surplus of marks) or a surplus of dollars (equals a shortage of marks). Shortages and surpluses, as we saw in Chapter 4, can always be created by inappropriate prices. The price in this case is the exchange rate, or the price of one currency in terms of the other.

On the Manipulation of Exchange Rates

It is important to note what the preceding argument does not assert. It does not suggest that a country can increase its exports and decrease its imports simply by manipulating the rate at which its domestic currency exchanges for the currency of other countries. The argument actually runs in the other direction: a particular exchange rate must be consistent with underlying supply and demand conditions, or it cannot be maintained for long. We've already noted the tendency for nations to push their exports while restricting imports. Devaluing their currency is a route they have often taken. But it isn't likely to succeed.

Suppose that an exchange rate of 50 cents per mark is currently clearing the market. But German exporters begin complaining that they can't sell in the United States the way they used to, because it costs Americans so much more these days to purchase marks. The German exporters recall the "good old days" when Americans had to pay only 25 cents for a mark, and they urge their government to do something to protect the export markets of German manufacturers. So the German central bank starts buying dollars with marks, thereby raising the mark price of the dollar. The dollar rises, as a result of this price-fixing operation, from a price of 2 marks to 2.2 marks. (Viewed from the other side, the mark falls from 50 cents to 45.45 cents.) And sure enough, U.S. imports of German goods increase, because German goods are now cheaper for Americans to buy. Moreover, U.S. exports to Germany fall, because U.S. goods are now more expensive to Germans.

If 2.2 marks are worth 1 dollar, 1 mark is worth 45.45¢ (1 ÷ 2.2)

But can this situation persist? The German central bank must continue buying dollars to keep the price up to 2.2 marks. As it does so, it keeps increasing the quantity of marks in circulation, because it buys those dollars by supplying marks.

Eventually the increased stock of marks created by this policy will raise the domestic price level. But when German prices rise 10 percent, the competitive advantage created for German exporters by the 10 percent devaluation is wiped out, and German goods no longer enjoy any price advantage over U.S. goods. Will German prices necessarily rise by that much? Until they do rise by enough to cancel out the effect of the devaluation, the German central bank will have to continue increasing the stock of marks in the hands of the public—or else abandon its effort to fix the dollar-mark exchange rate.

The crucial point is that this kind of exchange-rate manipulation will not secure a permanent increase in Germany's exports or decrease in its imports—an impossible goal in the first place, because no country (or person) finally sells without also buying. Manipulating exchange rates in this way merely generates enough inflation to correct for the artificially maintained exchange rate. Exchange rates cannot be set arbitrarily; they must finally be consistent with underlying patterns of supply and demand. If governments nonetheless attempt, under the pressure of special interests, to secure advantages for their own industries by manipulating exchange rates, they will either fail to control the exchange rate or they'll produce side-effects (like the inflation just described) that cancel out the supposed benefits. A tailor cannot cut the cloth arbitrarily if the suit is to fit the customer. In the tailoring shop of national policies on international trade, the practice is unfortunately common of cutting the cloth arbitrarily and then performing surgery on the customer to make the suit fit.

The Bretton Woods System

It was largely in order to prevent this kind of "competitive devaluation" that the Western nations established the International Monetary Fund (IMF) after World War II. The IMF was supposed to assist any member nation whose currency was tending to depreciate and to advise on devaluation when it appeared that existing exchange rates seriously overstated the currency's value. With varying rates of economic growth from country to country and different rates of domestic inflation, exchange rates might have to be altered occasionally. But the objective of the Bretton Woods system (named after the town in New Hampshire where the international monetary agreements were negotiated in 1944) was *fixed* exchange rates. Each nation was supposed to buy and sell its currency in order to keep it pegged at the officially established rate of exchange. (Other currencies were pegged to the dollar, and the dollar was pegged to gold.) Out of all this, it was hoped, would develop an expansion of international trade.

The system was not a failure. International trade did expand under the Bretton Woods system, at roughly twice the rate of increase in domestic production. And the advantages of international specialization contributed substantially to rising levels of real income. But an international monetary system with fixed exchange rates is difficult to maintain among governments pursuing divergent domestic policies. Those policies inevitably produced different patterns of growth in industrial and agricultural production, different movements in the structure of relative prices between countries, different rates of inflation, and consequently large fluctuations in the international demand for different countries' currencies. Surpluses or deficits in a country's balance of payments became a chronic occurrence, because prices could not adjust in ways that would prevent such surpluses or deficits.

The standard substitute for adjustments achieved through relative price changes became restrictions on the free movement of goods. Thus the United States at various times in the 1960s raised the cost to American tourists of bringing back foreign merchandise, placed a tax on money borrowed by foreign corporations from U.S. sources, restricted foreign lending by U.S. banks, imposed first voluntary and later mandatory controls on direct investment abroad by U.S. corporations, recalled the dependents of American servicemen stationed overseas, threatened to impose quotas unless particular countries "voluntarily" curtailed their exports to us, and in a variety of smaller ways tried to discourage imports and encourage exports. All this was done to "protect the dollar" against the balance of payments "deficits" that supposedly threatened the international monetary order. The irony is that the United States wanted to preserve the international monetary order as a way of promoting the advantageous exchanges that we were preventing as a way of preserving the international monetary order!

Fixed versus Floating Exchange Rates

In 1971 the United States suspended the convertibility of the dollar into gold, and other countries more or less reluctantly gave up the effort to maintain an established rate of exchange between their currencies and the dollar. Some experts immediately announced the breakdown of the international monetary system and the onset of a world monetary crisis. They called for emergency conferences to create a new system that would restore order before the flow of trade and exchange broke down in chaos. But other experts rejoiced in the disappearance of the old system. The first group's crisis was the second group's solution. Some had long argued that the real

A sudden appreciation in the dollar relative to the yen makes Japanese goods cheaper to Americans — and threatens U.S. producers selling in competition with Japanese producers.

problems in the international monetary system arose from that system itself, from the attempt to maintain fixed exchange rates, rather than allowing them to float with changing conditions of supply and demand.

Outside of academic circles, however, and especially among the economists working for central banks, floating exchange rates were regarded as unworkable, if desirable, and undesirable, if workable. They would increase uncertainty for foreign traders and investors, it was argued. But they would also create additional uncertainty for domestic producers and investors, because a change in exchange rates could quickly and radically change the potential profitability of industries producing import-competitive goods, as well as goods that might be exported. Moreover, governments were not likely to remain passive when a sudden depreciation in the currency of a major trading country led to an unexpected surge of imports or threatened established export markets. Governments would far more likely retaliate with trade and exchange controls that could eventually lead to a breakdown of international exchange.

Advocates of floating exchange rates replied that government attempts to maintain fixed rates had demonstrably failed. Such attempts did not, in fact, make it easier for international traders and investors to predict the future. On the contrary, they led governments into all sorts of trade and exchange restrictions, as price controls of any sort inevitably do. And they did not subject domestic policy to any "balance of payments discipline," because countries were always willing to devalue anyway when attention to the balance of payments might threaten cherished domestic objectives. In short, fixed exchange rates offered the worst of all possible worlds: increased uncertainty in the name of greater stability, restrictions on trade for the sake of free trade, and a "discipline" that inhibited flexibility while allowing irresponsibility.

The advocates of floating rates have generally had their way since 1971. This was more by default than by design; conflicting national interests prevented governments from agreeing on the structure of a new fixed-exchange-rate system. Most countries do not allow their currencies to float freely, however, but try to keep them in some loose relationship with another major currency or set of currencies. A variety of limited international agreements, such as the European Monetary System that was haltingly launched in 1979, have aimed at reducing fluctuations in exchange rates—at least among countries that trade extensively with each other.

What difference does it finally make whether the dollar buys 400 Japanese yen or only 200, 3 German marks or 2? That was the question that eventually emerged from our dialogue on the meaning of a "deficit" in the balance of payments. In order to answer that question, we had to examine the determinants of exchange rates and their effects on the flows of international trade. We see now that there is no simple answer to that question, because cause and effect aren't as neatly distinguishable as the question assumes. The rates at which currencies trade for each other direct the flow of international exchange. But the flow of international exchange also establishes the rates at which currencies will trade for each other. Everything depends on everything else. And the policies of national governments are a very important part of the interaction.

The Falling Dollar

From June 1976 through January 1979, the international value of the dollar declined rather steadily. We have to generalize cautiously, because the dollar didn't decline in value during this period relative to *all* currencies. It rose in value relative to the Canadian dollar, the Australian dollar, the Italian lira, and many currencies of little importance in international trade. But it fell substantially relative to the German mark, the Japanese yen, and the Swiss franc, and by lesser amounts relative to other important currencies. When the effects of all these exchange rate variations are weighted by each currency's importance to U.S. trade and then averaged together, the value of the U.S. dollar declined about 18 percent over this 2½ year period.

Why? In January 1979, the people to whom it mattered estimated the value of a dollar relative to the average value of other national currencies about 18 percent lower than they had estimated it in June 1976. That's the complete answer. It's not a very satisfactory answer, because we really want to know why their estimate of the dollar's relative value declined by so much over this period. To that question, however, no brief answer can be given. The relative purchasing power of the different currencies, as affected by the rates of inflation in their home countries, is one factor. Expected rates of inflation are also important, because holders of liquid assets can and do gravitate toward currencies that they think are most likely to appreciate over time. The policies of national governments are therefore also important, because these policies affect the rate at which currencies are supplied and the prospective return on investments made through the medium of those currencies.

Purchases and sales of foreign exchange by central banks are probably unimportant in all of this, except insofar as they provide a clue to the direction of future government policies. Although central bankers sometimes pretend that they can control exchange rates through intervention in the foreign exchange markets, no one can support the price of beans by purchasing beans with money derived from the sale of beans. The Fed supports the dollar by purchasing dollars with a stock of reserve assets that must ultimately be replenished either by selling dollars, which cancels out the effect of the purchases, or by selling other goods. But it's the reluctance of foreigners to buy those other goods in adequate amounts that causes the original decline of the dollar. To assume that foreigners will change their habits because we want them to is assuming the problem away.

Working in the opposite direction, the Fed lowers the international value of the dollar by buying foreign currencies. As it does so, it increases the size of the U.S. money stock, which will cause the value of the dollar to decline if other things remain equal. And that's the key to the whole matter. It is the demand for and the supply of dollars that determines the value of the dollar in the U.S. and therefore also finally its value throughout the world. That reality can be temporarily disguised, but it will always assert itself in the end.

You should, therefore, look skeptically at any assertion that the decline of the dollar causes inflation by making us pay more for imports. That's probably confusing a symptom with a cause. It is usually more correct to say that inflation caused the decline of the dollar by making imports too cheap to Americans (and our exports too expensive to foreigners). International disturbances are a convenient scapegoat for domestic policymakers, but the causes of international problems can usually be found in domestic policies.

Eurodollars and Alien-Currencies

All of this might seem to imply that when Fed officials sally forth to "defend the dollar," they're behaving like the wolf who joins a posse to search for Little Red Riding Hood. But central bankers are not completely free to pursue the goals they prefer, and they are not completely capable of reaching the goals they pursue. There is one important way in which international exchange seems to be making the work of monetary authorities increasingly difficult.

Perhaps you've encountered the word "Eurodollars." Eurodollars are dollar liabilities of European banks. An easy way to understand what Eurodollars are is to compare them with some "Americoyen" that you might conceivably acquire. Suppose your business firm exports to Japan so that you regularly acquire yen in payment from the Japanese importers. Instead of converting those yen into dollars and depositing the dollars, suppose you deposited the yen directly and persuaded your bank to give you a checking account denominated in yen. Then you could pay your bills or make other purchases with a

"a-mér-i-co-yen": Deposits in American banks denominated in yen.

check drawn either on your dollar account or on your yen account. You would have to find sellers willing to accept checks denominated in yen. But if the firms from which you buy are fairly sophisticated and also expect the yen to retain its value better than the dollar in the immediate future, that would be possible. Moreover, the larger the number of firms willing to accept yen as a medium of exchange, especially for large transactions, the less will be the reluctance of other firms to begin accepting them. Do you see how yen might come in this way to function as a domestic medium of exchange, at least for interfirm transactions, in the United States?

Eurodollars are like these hypothetical Americoyen. Dollars came to be accepted and widely used in this fashion in Europe after World War II, largely because so many Europeans had more confidence in the dollar than in the future value of the currencies issued by their own war-battered governments. As a result, the size of the relevant money stock in European countries could not be estimated by counting merely the quantity of domestic money in the public's possession. Holdings of Eurodollars had to be counted, too.

The use of *alien-currencies*, if we may employ that as a generic term to cover all bank deposits denominated in the currencies of other nations, obviously presents a challenge to central bankers trying to exercise precise control over their domestic money stock. The challenge is greatly intensified by the ability of the banks that hold these deposits to use them as the basis for the creation of more alien-currency. Banks can and do lend alien-currencies by creating demand deposits, thereby adding to the size of the effective money stock. Information on such alien-currency money creation is not very accurate, and the process is generally beyond the effective control of monetary authorities. Those two facts are related. It's hard to control what you can't see, and easier to see what you have under control.

Could new legislation bring all this under the control of the appropriate monetary authorities? Assuming that the benefits of such a move would exceed its costs, it isn't clear that anyone knows how to draft legislation that would do the job. If Americoyen are prohibited by law, Americans can hold yen accounts in banks in Japan. A medium of exchange cannot be legislated into existence if people choose not to use it. And a medium of exchange cannot easily be legislated out of existence if people have found its use advantageous.

Governments have always had problems catching smugglers. The problems increase immeasurably when the good whose international movements a government is trying to control can be transferred in quantities of almost any size by a telephone call. That's the case with money. There is mounting

evidence that money is becoming increasingly international-
ized, and that new mediums of exchange can be devised and
put to use far faster than anyone can learn to understand them
well enough to legislate controls.

Private Interests, National Interests, Public Interests

All of this will suggest to some people that there is no longer any
international economic order. That might be true for those who
equate order with legislated systems and international order
with negotiated treaties. But it would not be true for those who
see order simply in the continuation and extension of international exchange. It sometimes happens that we become so
absorbed in our search for solutions that we forget what the
problem was. Is it our goal that consumers, investors, producers, tourists, and bagpipe players—people, in short—be enabled to cooperate more freely across the barriers that national
boundaries raise? Or is that the problem—namely, that people
are engaging in international transactions that interfere with
the goals of national governments?

It is certainly possible that the interests of the larger public
might require some restrictions on international exchange. But
a thoughtful person will wonder why the national interest
seems so regularly to require that more be given away than is
received in return; that jobs be preferred to goods; that
efficient producers be hobbled to prevent them from using
their advantage to the detriment of less efficient producers; and
that in general people be prevented from increasing their
wealth by exchanging freely. The skeptic should be pardoned
for concluding that the public interest may be something quite
different from the national interest, at least as the national
interest is usually defined by those who shape international
economic policy.

Once Over Lightly

The movement of goods and financial assets across international boundaries can either frustrate or promote the domestic
policies of national governments. Government stabilization
policies have particularly close interconnections with international trade policies.

The principle of comparative advantage has not fared well
in the area of international trade against well-organized producer interests, economic nationalism, and the enduring belief
that imports cause unemployment.

The total credits in the balance of international payments
always equal the debits. Any discrepancy can only be due to
errors in record keeping.

A disequilibrium in the balance of payments implies that *desired* credits and debits (desired by whom?) are not equal. To assert that the balance of payments is in deficit is to imply that some credit items were unintended, cannot be expected to continue, or should not have been allowed to occur. The assertion of a balance-of-payments disequilibrium is usually a complex policy judgment disguised as a simple statement of obvious fact.

A common meaning for "balance of payments disequilibrium" is "a situation inconsistent with maintenance of present exchange rates."

If they are to persist, exchange rates between national currencies must reflect underlying forces of supply and demand. The ability of national governments to achieve domestic objectives by altering exchange rates is thus severely limited.

A government that tries to peg its currency at a price below its market value promotes domestic inflation, which only succeeds in bringing the market value of the currency down to its pegged rate.

Exchange rates can be set arbitrarily only by governments able to enforce arbitrary prohibitions on international exchange.

Governments finally control the international value of their currencies by controlling the domestic values of those currencies, which means by regulating the supply in relation to the demand.

The increasing ability of firms to use a variety of foreign currencies as their medium of exchange and the ability of commercial banks to expand the stock of alien-currencies through loans have made the task of money-supply management more difficult for central bankers.

QUESTIONS FOR DISCUSSION

1. In order to take advantage of lower production costs, a Massachusetts textile manufacturer builds a factory in North Carolina, and a United States television manufacturing firm opens an assembly plant in Mexico.
   a. In what ways is the action by the television firm different from the action by the textile firm?
   b. Is either action contrary to the national interest?
   c. Is either action likely to encounter effective political opposition?
2. Why cannot one country have a comparative advantage over another country in the production of everything if the first country has excellent natural resources, a huge capital stock, a highly skilled labor force, and ingenious technicians and managers, while the second country is poor in all four areas?

3. What evidence exists to support the view that Japan has a comparative advantage over against the United States in the production of small automobiles? How would you account for this comparative advantage? How would you explain the fact that the United States in general seems to have a comparative advantage in the production of large automobiles but a comparative disadvantage in the production of smaller ones?

4. How does the theory of external benefits and "free riders" help explain the generally greater legislative influence of producers than of consumers?

5. Estimates published in 1972 predicted that the Concorde SST would not repay its development costs, would create environmental problems, and would not generate sufficient additional revenue to cover the associated costs for the airlines that purchase them. These were essentially the objections that led to cancellation of government financing for an American SST. A counterargument in both cases had been that these planes would provide many additional jobs, help the balance of payments, and prevent other countries from gaining an advantage. How would you evaluate these counterarguments?

6. Everyone will agree that *some* policies that would create more jobs for Americans are nonetheless not in the national interest. For example, no one recommends that we build highways without using heavy machinery, even though many more jobs would be created if highways were built entirely with hand tools. When is the job-creation argument actually used? Are there any circumstances in which it's a defensible argument?

7. What is meant by "a favorable balance of trade," a term that has been in common use for several centuries? What is favorable about it? To whom?

8. Can a country export more than it imports? Be clear in your definition of exports and imports (for example, are financial securities and gold included in exports and imports?).

9. If the value of Canada's merchandise imports is 20 percent greater than the value of its merchandise exports, does Canada have a deficit in its balance of payments?
   a. If the difference is covered by 20-year loans?
   b. If the difference is covered by one-year loans?
   c. If the difference is covered by selling gold from the national treasury?
   d. If the difference is covered by selling newly mined gold?
   e. Suppose that merchandise imports are 400 percent greater than merchandise exports, *excluding petroleum*, and the difference is made up by selling newly extracted "black gold"?

10. An American sends a $100 check as a gift to a relative in Vienna. This action counts as a debit in the U.S. balance of payments. Where does the balancing credit item appear as the following events unfold?
    a. The Austrian relative exchanges the dollars for schillings at a Vienna bank. The bank holds the dollars, because it has customers who frequently want to buy dollars with schillings.
    b. The Vienna bank sells the dollars to the Austrian central bank in exchange for schillings.
    c. The Austrian central bank gives the dollars to the German central bank in exchange for schillings that the German central bank had been holding.

d. The German central bank sells the dollars to the Volkswagen Company in exchange for marks.

e. The Volkswagen Company gives the dollars as expense money to a company executive who is taking a business trip to Pennsylvania. He spends them at a motel in Scranton.

f. If the dollars had remained permanently in Europe, would this imply that the U.S. had a deficit in its balance of international payments?

11. One step taken by the U.S. government in the 1960s to correct the "balance of payments problem" was to restrict foreign investment by U.S. firms and banks. If it had been effective, how would such a program have influenced U.S. debits and credits? Would the long-term consequences be different from the short-run consequences?

12. What might induce foreign commercial banks to hold large quantities of dollars, accumulated through purchase from exporters, rather than sell those dollars for their own domestic currencies? How would holding or selling affect the exchange rate between the dollar and the other currency?

13. In the late 1960s the Fed tried to keep short-term interest rates up in order to "protect the U.S. balance of payments." How would this affect the balance of payments? The Fed simultaneously tried to keep long-term interest rates low to encourage investment and economic growth. Where is the line between the short term and the long term? Can the "line" be crossed?

14. Charles DeGaulle rejected U.S. complaints about French purchases of gold in the 1960s by stating that France could not be expected to finance an American takeover of French industry. Is France making loans to the U.S. if the French central bank holds dollars that it acquired by giving francs to former owners of French corporations who have sold their shares to American corporations?

15. Do exporters care whether their currency depreciates or appreciates in international exchange? Explain why. How do importers feel about exchange-rate changes? Why?

16. "Floating exchange rates free a nation to pursue the domestic policies it prefers." Is that true?

17. Is it harmful to U.S. prestige when the dollar depreciates? Why do you suppose that governments usually express more official alarm over depreciation than over appreciation of their currencies?

18. What is the difference between exchange rates that are free to fluctuate in response to conditions of supply and demand, and exchange rates that are fixed but are periodically altered in accordance with changed conditions of supply and demand?

19. Suppose that the Japanese yen is significantly undervalued in international exchange, but that the Japanese government refuses to revalue it upward (that is, change the price at which it pegs the yen to other currencies). What effects will this have on Japanese exports and imports of merchandise? What effect will it have on the Japanese domestic price level? (Hint: As Japanese exporters acquire foreign currencies, they turn them in to the central bank for yen.) What if the central bank sold Japanese government bonds in the same amount? (This is called "sterilization.")

20. How can U.S. imports reduce the domestic money supply? How can the Fed

prevent this from occurring? What would be the consequences of such "neutralization" actions by the monetary authorities?

21. What happens to the price Americans pay for imported oil when the dollar declines in value, relative to the average of other major national currencies?

22. Why are "alien-currencies" like Eurodollars used? What are the essential conditions that would have to be satisfied before you could pay your bills using Swiss francs?

23. The table below shows the compounded annual rate of change in the implicit GNP deflator for seven different countries over three recent time periods.

	1968–73	1973–75	1975–78
United States	5.1%	9.6%	6.2%
Canada	5.3	12.9	7.8
France	5.6	12.4	9.6
Germany	6.0	6.8	3.6
Switzerland	6.9	6.9	1.8
Japan	6.3	14.2	5.3
United Kingdom	7.9	22.3	11.9

a. What evidence does the table provide in support of the argument that OPEC was responsible for the worldwide inflation of the 1970s?

b. What evidence does the table provide against the argument that OPEC was responsible for inflation after 1973?

24. Why do so many Americans believe that this country would be endangered by Arab ownership of "essential" U.S. industries, but do not believe that U.S. ownership of foreign industries poses a threat to the national security of those countries? Why are U.S.-owned foreign enterprises thought to be at the mercy of foreign governments and the United States at the mercy of foreigners who own U.S. enterprises? Who in the United States benefits and who is harmed if OPEC citizens purchase U.S. agricultural land?

Fiscal and Monetary Policy

Can the federal government prevent or moderate recessions? Can it prevent or halt inflation? Those are the large and difficult questions to which we now turn.

Total spending by households, business firms, and government clearly affects gross national product. It is equally clear that the federal government can take actions that will increase or decrease total dollar expenditures on new commodities and services. But consensus begins to dissolve rapidly once we move beyond these two rather obvious assertions.

Real Output and the Price Level

We must begin by distinguishing once more between nominal and real gross national product. Nominal GNP measures total expenditure or total output in dollars of *current* purchasing power. Real GNP measures the value of that output in dollars of *constant* purchasing power. Nominal GNP is the product of real output and the price level—and consequently can increase even when real output is falling, if the price level is rising fast enough. That's exactly what occurred during 1974 and 1975. Nominal gross national product rose at an annual rate of 8.2 percent, but it did so despite a 1.3 percent annual rate of decline in real output because of a 9.6 percent annual rate of inflation. Inflation is hardly compensation for recession. Even if the federal government could control with precision the

TABLE 20A   OUTPUT AND THE PRICE LEVEL:
PERCENTAGE CHANGE FROM
PRECEDING YEAR

Year	GNP in 1972 Dollars (Q)	Implicit GNP Deflator (P)
1960	2.3%	1.7%
1961	2.5	0.9
1962	5.8	1.8
1963	4.0	1.5
1964	5.3	1.6
1965	5.9	2.2
1966	6.0	3.3
1967	2.7	2.9
1968	4.4	4.5
1969	2.6	5.0
1970	—0.3	5.4
1971	3.0	5.1
1972	5.7	4.1
1973	5.5	5.8
1974	—1.4	9.7
1975	—1.3	9.6
1976	5.7	5.2
1977	4.9	5.9
1978	4.0	7.4

rate of growth in current dollar spending, it might be unable to control either recession or inflation. Their control presupposes the ability to affect separately the rate of growth in real output and the rate of change in the price level.

Table 20A shows the percentage changes in real output and in the price level for each year from 1960 through 1978. Real output increased at an average rate of 5.4 percent in the five years after 1961, well above the long term trend for the American economy (which is somewhere between 3 and 3.5 percent). At a 5.4 percent rate of increase, real output doubles in a little over 13 years. But the growth rate faltered after 1966, averaging only 2.5 percent from 1966 through 1971, while fluctuating between 4.4 percent in 1968 and —0.3 percent in the recession year of 1970. A strong revival of growth in 1972 and 1973 was interrupted by two years of decline, followed again by three years of fairly rapid growth. The average rate of growth from 1971 through 1978 was 3.3 percent. Within those years, however, the U.S. experienced its deepest recession since the 1930s. It was an *unstable* decade.

For many people, the problem of aggregate economic growth shows up much more clearly and forcefully in unemployment figures. Unemployment expressed as a percentage of the civilian labor force tended to decline through the decade of the 1960s. (The detailed data are in Table 15A.) It rose sharply in the early 1970s, however, and averaged over 6.2 percent from 1970 through 1978.

Uneven growth rates and rising unemployment were only part of the problem in the 1970s. From 1970 through 1978, the average annual increase in the price level, as measured by the GNP deflator, was 6.6 percent.[1] At that rate of increase, the purchasing power of a dollar is cut in half every eleven years.

The most unsettling years in this period were 1974 and 1975. Real output declined by 1.4 percent and 1.3 percent, while the price level rose 9.7 and 9.6 percent. Inflation of that magnitude coupled with recession was unprecedented in U.S. experience. Prices were supposed to fall during recessions, or at least stop rising. They certainly weren't supposed to rise at rates approaching 10 percent a year. This is the historical context in which the question is now being asked: What should the government do to prevent or moderate recessions and to prevent or halt inflation?

Aggregate Demand Management

This chapter focuses on *aggregate demand management*. What are the techniques that the government might use to expand or contract total spending on newly produced commodities and services? How precise is the control that these techniques afford over total spending? Can this control be used effectively to correct or compensate for changes in private sector spending so that the federal government is able to prevent or reverse recessions and to prevent or stop inflations?

Aggregate demand management takes two principal forms: fiscal policy and monetary policy. *Fiscal policy* means budget policy. In this context, *fiscal policy is policy aimed at controlling undesired fluctuations in aggregate demand through changes in government expenditures and taxes.*

Monetary policy is policy aimed at controlling undesired fluctuations in aggregate demand through changes in commercial bank reserves or legal reserve requirements.

Two Frameworks for Thinking

Total dollar expenditures on gross national product, which is what we shall mean by aggregate demand, can be thought about in two different ways. One is to classify total expendi-

---

1. We're going to use the GNP Deflator rather than the more popular Consumer Price Index as our measure of inflation, because the GNP Deflator provides a more accurate summary of what's happening to the price level. The Consumer Price Index employs weights based on consumer expenditure patterns during a past survey period, and thus assumes that relative price changes don't induce people to alter the pattern of their expenditures.

tures as the Bureau of Economic Analysis does, dividing them into personal consumption expenditures, private domestic investment expenditures, government purchases of commodities and services, and net exports.

Alternatively, we can ignore these divisions and think of total dollar expenditures on GNP as the money stock multiplied by the GNP velocity of money, which is the average number of times each unit of money changes hands in the course of expenditures for GNP. There is obviously no procedure by which we can actually measure the GNP velocity of money. It can only be calculated by dividing the money stock for any year into the nominal gross national product for that year. The velocity with which money circulates for GNP expenditures is therefore nothing but the inverted ratio of the money stock to GNP, the ratio whose stability we discussed extensively in Chapter 17.

We can use abbreviations to summarize these two ways of looking at aggregate demand. Using C to represent personal consumption expenditures, I to represent gross private domestic investment, G to represent government purchases of goods, and E_n to represent net exports, we can write the equality:

$$PQ \equiv C + I + G + E_n$$

P stands for the price level, measured by the GNP deflator, and Q stands for real output, or GNP in dollars of constant purchasing power. P times Q is therefore nominal gross national product. If you look carefully at the equation above, you will see that the equal sign has three bars, which means that the equality is an identity. *PQ* is *equal by definition* to the sum of C, I, G, and E_n. This isn't some empirical statement that we could go out and test; it's a way of thinking about a relationship between total spending on the one hand and the price level and real output on the other.

The second way of thinking about this relationship is summarized in the following equality:

$$PQ \equiv MV$$

M stands for the money stock and V for the GNP velocity, or the average number of times each unit of money changes hands in expenditures for GNP. Since V can be calculated only by dividing M into PQ, this equality is also an identity, or true by definition.

The first of these frameworks was popularized as a result of the Keynesian reformulation of economic theory. In the simple form that we are using, it contains no variable to represent the stock of money, because Keynesians did not think that monetary policy was an effective technique for stimulating aggregate demand. Rather its emphasis is on the consumption-income (or saving-income) relationship which magnifies the effect of any changes in desired expenditure, on investment spending as the unstable factor which triggers fluctuations in aggregate demand, and on government as the agency that can use its budget to compensate for undesirable changes in private spending.

The second framework completely ignores the composition of total spending, in order to focus on the stock of money through which that spending occurs. The emphasis in this case is upon the stability of demand for money balances, or the velocity of circulation, and the consequent link between changes in the size of the money stock and changes in total spending.

From Theory to Practice

The belief that fiscal policy can be a useful stabilization tool is closely associated with the first way of thinking about the determinants of aggregate demand. The argument for fiscal policy is simple and straightforward. If recessions occur because investors are unwilling to spend as much as everyone is trying to save, why can't the government take steps to correct the imbalance? Why allow an insufficient demand to reduce production and raise unemployment? The government is not bound by the narrow considerations that guide private spending and saving decisions. It can engage in compensatory finance, either by expanding its own purchases of goods or by stimulating private spending through tax cuts or increases in transfer payments. If we know what amount of total spending, by consumers, investors, government and foreign buyers, would generate a level of gross national product consistent with "full" employment, is there any excuse for allowing the economy to operate below capacity?

Beginning students of economics are easily impressed by the simple mechanics of income-expenditures analysis. "If current demand is inadequate, the government has the power to raise aggregate demand to the appropriate level." That sounds straightforward and sensible. But it is, in reality, an extremely abstract assertion. When we leave the safe ground of high abstraction and come down to actual practice, we discover severe limitations on the effectiveness of either fiscal or monetary policy as tools for the stabilization of aggregate demand.

We're going to reserve for Chapter 21 most of the dilemmas created for aggregate demand management by the fact that even perfect control over total spending would not entail control over the actual targets of stabilization policy, which are real output and the price level. But this is clearly a major difficulty for fiscal or for monetary policy, because expanding or contracting aggregate demand may cause the wrong component to move.

Another large set of difficulties comes into view the moment we remember that government is not like Aladdin's marvelous genie, always obedient to command and always able to accomplish its assignments. The agencies of government, for all their power and importance, are still made up of people, managed by people, run for people. And people here does not mean The People, another potentially misleading abstraction. It means people like us, who are neither omniscient nor omnipotent and are sometimes even guilty of defining the public interest in suspiciously self-serving ways.

The people in government do not have knowledge or capabilities beyond the knowledge and capabilities of mere mortals. "Raise aggregate demand to the appropriate level." That's excellent counsel. But who knows the current level of aggregate demand, the appropriate level, and the actions that will move aggregate demand from the wrong to precisely the right level? Who knows all the unintended side effects of such actions, and how to prevent the undesirable ones while bringing about all those that are desired? And what good will it do to know, if one lacks the power to compel action? Power in a democracy is shared by many people with different perspectives and ideals and what sometimes even look like conflicting interests. Among those human beings who are neither omniscient nor omnipotent, we must regrettably include Federal Reserve officials, Senators and Representatives, members of the administration up to and including the chief executive, and even the professional economists who serve on their research staffs or function as their council of advisers (or as their critics!).

Timing is crucial if aggregate demand management is to be an effective stabilizing technique. Time will inevitably elapse between the appearance of a problem and its recognition, between recognition and analysis, between analysis and decision, between decision and action, and between action and its ultimate consequences. When we add to all this the effects of scarce information and conflicting interests, the prospects for steering the economy neatly onto the full employment track through aggregate demand management no longer look as bright as they do when we're considering hypothetical cases where all the data are known and all the responses are completely predictable.

Are the Lags Inherently Unpredictable?

The time lag between a fiscal or monetary policy action and its full effects on total spending is a particularly troublesome one.

Estimates of the length of these lags range from a few months to several years, and diligent research efforts designed to nail down the time distribution of the effects have not produced a workable consensus. The lags may even turn out to vary in some way we can't predict, in which case economists would be trying to measure something that actually has no standard length.

There are good reasons for supposing that the time lags between fiscal or monetary policy actions and their effects are not some constant that can be measured and then relied upon. The operating procedures of commercial banks, the payment practices of business firms, the perceptions of households and corporations with respect to the advantages of holding assets in one form or another, international monetary transactions, and even the public's efforts to anticipate the effects of government actions will all play a part in determining the distribution over time of any policy's impact on total spending. The problem is that these factors are continually changing. And they are especially likely to change in response to any improvement in our ability to forecast them! It is a case in which forecasts falsify themselves by altering the stock of information that had to be assumed in order to make the forecast. Here's a simple example: If we knew with confidence the pattern that some stock's market price would trace over the coming year, it wouldn't trace that pattern. This is the paradox with which sciences of human behavior must live. Predicting the future changes the future, because the people whose actions create the future read the predictions.

We can't even assume that the fiscal or monetary authorities at least know the effect they *want* to have on total spending. They presumably know what effect they *think* they want to have on total spending. But this opinion will be based on a reading of statistical indicators that don't provide wholly adequate information. Data on the current performance of the economy will necessarily be data on its performance in some past period. The data required for stabilization policy, however, are data on the *future* performance of the economy. Today's policy actions can't compensate for yesterday's deficient or excessive aggregate demand. Today's actions aim, rather, at compensating for tomorrow's deficiency or excess. Stabilization policy is necessarily based, therefore, on forecasting. And economic forecasting is far from an exact science.

The Federal Budget as a Policy Tool

When we turn specifically to fiscal policy, an additional difficulty emerges. There is at least a touch of comedy in the belief that the federal government can use its budget as a stabilization tool when almost all observers agree that Congress no longer has effective control over the budget. The spending programs of the federal government are so many and so complex that no one can even begin to evaluate all of them for the purpose of determining annual appropriations. As a result, next year's budget begins by taking this year's budget for granted and adding on. Once a program gets in, it is almost impossible to dislodge, because its beneficiaries form a knowledgeable and determined lobby for its continuance, and no one on Capitol Hill has the time, energy, and interest to accumulate the evidence that could justify its removal.

Fiscal policy is not something under the control of the Council of Economic Advisers. A change in government expenditures or in federal taxes requires action by the House of Representatives and then the Senate, with committee meetings before and often after, and a presidential signature at the end. That takes time and timing, as we said, is crucial. The discussions will be complicated and prolonged by the fact that, even if Congress were to agree quickly on the desirability of a change in expenditures or taxes of a particular amount, it would still have to decide whose taxes will be changed and which expenditures. Conflicting interests will be involved and alternative theories about the expansionary or contractionary effects of particular actions. Is it better to cut the taxes of low-income people or to give tax credits for investment? Which will have a greater impact on employment? And are we talking about the long run or the short run? Meanwhile some members of Congress will certainly decide that an important tax or expenditure bill provides an opportunity to eliminate the depletion allowance for oil producers, give a bonus to retired people on social security, prop up the housing industry through a special subsidy, or take a slap at multinational corporations—to mention only some of the concerns that managed to achieve expression in the March 1975 "antirecessionary" tax bill.

The more in a hurry Congress and the president are, the more likely they are to produce fiscal policy actions that few competent and impartial observers will be able to defend. The imperative of haste tends to enhance the power of those who are willing to enforce their demands by threatening to block any action at all. But due deliberation, the careful assessment of alternatives, and the weighing of the probable short- and long-term outcomes may require so much time that the moment for action passes before any action is taken. The 1974–75 recession probably began late in 1973. Congress passed an antirecessionary tax-cut bill at the end of March in 1975; even at that late date, the bill contained evidence of undue haste.

Whether or when the federal government will use fiscal

policy in response to the 1979 slowdown cannot be known as these words are being written, although we shall see later why a shrewd bettor would give odds that it *will* be used. But the reductions in expenditure that led to the 1979 slowdown began in the autumn of 1978. It was not until July 1979, when the decline had already gained considerable momentum, that members of Congress and the Administration first started *thinking and talking* about the desirability of a tax cut to counter the decline. A recession of average length would have pretty well run its course before such thinking and talking could become legislation and the legislation could translate itself into actual increases in private or government expenditure.

Advocates of stabilization through fiscal policy who are not mesmerized by the genie conception of government have long been aware of these difficulties. They know that the protracted discussions which precede any congressional action on taxes and expenditures could easily make fiscal policy unworkable: action might not be possible until the time for it has passed. They have consequently looked around for ways to speed up the process. One proposal recommended by some economists and urged by President John Kennedy was that Congress authorize unilateral action by the President. Appropriations for particular projects could be approved by Congress and then put on the shelf, to be taken off whenever the President and his advisers decided that the stimulus of increased government expenditures was called for. Congress could also authorize the President to increase or decrease tax rates within narrow limits when aggregate demand seemed excessive or inadequate.

This proposal doesn't exactly assume a genie: it attempts to create one. If you're wondering why Congress never acted on such a "sensible" recommendation, think for a moment about the political power that a president would command if he could unilaterally determine the timing of tax decreases and the placement of expenditure projects. Congress is not likely to grant that kind of power to any President, not even to a trusted President who is a member of the same political party as the majority in both houses of Congress. Some Senators and Representatives will be deterred by the constitutional principle of a balance of power among the branches of government, some by respect for Lord Acton's maxim that absolute power corrupts absolutely. But all will know that such power in the hands of a president substantially diminishes their own power and influence. The conclusion, therefore, is that fiscal policy will continue to be a stabilization tool that doesn't become available until the appropriate time for its use has passed.

But isn't this negative verdict on fiscal policy inconsistent with the historical record? Hasn't fiscal policy actually been used effectively to fight recessions?

Stabilization versus Stimulus

The rather common belief that fiscal policy has proved its effectiveness as a stabilization tool seems to be based largely on a failure to distinguish between the ability to stabilize aggregate demand and the ability to change it. But stabilization requires more than the power to change aggregate demand—it presupposes the power to control it by fairly precise amounts and with close timing. There is ample evidence that increased government spending with no increase in taxes, or reduced taxes with no reductions in government spending, can, under the right circumstances, stimulate total spending. World War II seems to be the clearest demonstration of fiscal policy's potency. The Great Depression finally ended when the federal government, responding to the imperatives of wartime, threw fiscal caution aside and began running huge deficits. Federal government expenditures increased 105 percent from 1940 to 1941, by an additional 175 percent in 1942, and by yet another 50 percent in 1943. In 1944 federal government expenditures, even after adjustment for changes in the price level, were six and one-half times what they had been in 1940. The federal budget deficit, measured in 1972 dollars, grew from about $6 billion in 1940 to $165 billion in 1944.

The economy responded to this stimulus much as income-expenditures analysis suggested that it would. Jolted out of the doldrums of the Great Depression by the massive fiscal stimulus of wartime expenditures, the economy produced almost as much real output in 1944 just for the government sector as it had produced for the combined private and government sectors in 1939 (94 percent as much). The total real output of the economy in 1944 was more than 75 percent greater than it had been in 1939.

In this colossal but undesigned test of fiscal policy's *stimulative* capabilities, there was no real test of its effectiveness for *stabilization* purposes. Nor could there by any such test until at least a majority in Congress and the President were persuaded to make the experiment. That situation certainly did not exist before 1964. In that year Congress enacted and the President signed a tax-reduction bill that had been argued for largely on Keynesian grounds. Lower taxes without any accompanying reduction in federal government expenditures were supposed to stimulate the economy and reduce the high unemployment rate that had developed and persisted since 1958.

Unemployment did decline after the tax cut. But even if we

could be certain that it declined because the tax cut stimulated aggregate demand, we would once again have evidence for no more than the stimulative potential of fiscal policy. A glance at the first column in Table 20A shows clearly that the economy was not in any recession in 1964 and consequently could not be pulled out of one by a compensatory federal budget deficit. The 1964 tax cut actually supports the point we are making, that fiscal policy cannot be used effectively to counter fluctuations in private spending, because of the long time lags associated with its use. The Keynesian argument for a tax cut that culminated in the tax reduction of 1964 *began to be made in the recession of 1960.*

Nondiscretionary Fiscal Policy

We have been arguing that the federal government did not, in fact, use changes in tax rates or expenditures as a *stabilization* tool—at least not until sometime *after* 1964. We now want to argue that the fiscal policy of the federal government after World War II may nonetheless have contributed significantly to economic stabilization. The second statement doesn't contradict the first, because a stabilizing fiscal policy does not necessarily require legislated changes in tax rates or expenditures. Fiscal policy can be automatic, as well as discretionary. Only discretionary fiscal policy is incapacitated by the severe time lags associated with its use.

When an economic downturn begins, tax receipts fall automatically as corporate and personal incomes decline. Because the applicable rates on these two principal sources of federal revenue are progressive, taking a higher percentage of higher incomes, a decline in income actually leads to an even faster decline in taxes. The government also puts some additional income into the hands of the public during a recession whenever the economic decline leads to an automatic increase in unemployment compensation and welfare benefits. These automatic responses to a recession presumably function as stabilizers, dampening fluctuations in income and thereby reducing fluctuations in private spending.

Allowing budget deficits or surpluses to appear and doing nothing about them is also fiscal policy. It must be distinguished from another view that was widely advocated prior to the 1930s and the publication of Keynes's *General Theory*. The older position held that government should retrench in a recession, deliberately cutting its expenditures and increasing tax rates if necessary in order to preserve a balanced budget. Such a policy, if adopted, would be the exact reverse of what Keynes recommended. But it would be a discretionary fiscal policy, not an automatic one, and it would be subject as a result to the same problems of timing that make any discretionary fiscal policy an inappropriate instrument for stabilization.

Automatic fiscal policy was clearly at work, whether by design or by inadvertence, in the 1958 recession. The federal government's 1957 budget surplus of $3.5 billion (in 1972 dollars) turned into a $15.6 billion deficit in 1958. This happened not because Congress and the President chose to cut taxes or to increase expenditures, but because federal tax receipts fell in response to the recession, while federal expenditures continued on their previously targeted course.

What contribution did this kind of passive fiscal policy make toward the relative stability of the economy in the years after World War II? We really have no good way of knowing. It can be argued that automatic fiscal policy is bound to increase stability, because it diminishes the impact that changes in investment expenditure have on the income of consumers. With consumer income buffered to some extent against fluctuations in output, the multiplier effect of destabilizing events is reduced. Automatic fiscal policy provides shock absorbers for the economy and probably ought to receive at least part of the credit for the smoother "ride" of the years after World War II.

The Revival of Monetary Policy

It has only been within the last 15 years or so that monetary policy has achieved anything like equal status with fiscal policy in the thinking of economists. The impotence of monetary policy as a means of restoring prosperity seemed to many to have been adequately demonstrated in the Great Depression, when the Fed pursued an "easy money" policy but could not stir a revival of bank lending and private spending. The power of fiscal policy had seemingly been just as clearly demonstrated by the "fiscal experiment" of 1940–1944. When the urgencies of war finally overcame concern for a balanced budget and the federal government began spending profusely, private spending also revived. And once restored by a massive injection of federal spending, private consumption and investment were able to take up the slack when government expenditures fell sharply after the war.

Monetary policy inched its way back into esteem through a concurrence of events. One was the unexpected mildness of recessions in the postwar period and the persistence of inflation. Inflation was a problem against which monetary policy might be more effective because, in the metaphor widely used, one could pull a balloon down with a string even though pushing on the string would not make it *rise*. As a practical matter, it was much easier to tighten up on money growth than to get tax increases or spending reductions through Congress. So the monetary managers were able to practice their stabilization skills to some extent by trying to control inflation. These experiments in turn persuaded many observers that monetary policy, though perhaps impotent at the depth of a severe depression, might well be effective as an expansionary tool in mild recessions. One further reason for the revival of monetary policy was the research done during this period by economists who were convinced that changes in the money stock had a more predictable impact on total spending than the advocates of fiscal policy believed.

The impact of changes in the size of the money stock on total spending will be stable and predictable if the quantity of money that the public wants to hold is a stable and predictable percentage of total spending. If the demand for money remains unchanged, increases in the stock of money will induce an expansion of total spending. This expansion will continue until gross national product is large enough to persuade the public to hold the full quantity of money supplied to it by the monetary authorities and the banking system. All that was explained in Chapter 17.

Time Lags in Monetary Policy

The effectiveness of monetary policy is limited by the fact that the stable demand for money upon which its effectiveness depends is a long-run stability. But policies aimed at compensating for fluctuations in aggregate demand must depend on a short-run link between the policy tool and the target, because fluctuations are essentially short-run phenomena. It may help if you think about the distinction between the average water level in a reservoir and the action of the waves. Monetary policy can operate the gates in the dam to affect the average level of water in the reservoir, but it cannot prevent the wind from stirring up the waves and causing the level of the reservoir to vary substantially from one point to another.

Federal Reserve officials do not face timing problems as severe as those that Congress and the President encounter when trying to use fiscal policy. Because Federal Reserve policy-making is much more insulated from political pressures than is government budget-making, the Fed can act far more quickly once it spots a problem. But the Fed cannot avoid the difficulties presented by the time lags between the origin of a problem and its recognition or, even more important, between action and consequences. The effects of any change in the rate of growth of the money stock are felt with long, variable, and perhaps inherently uncertain time lags.

Loose Links in Monetary Policy

It's also important to remember how far the members of the Open Market Committee are removed from their target, total dollar expenditures on new commodities and services. (That still isn't their *ultimate* target. We remind you again that the object of concern is *P and Q*, even though aggregate demand management operates only on *PQ*.) The Fed has direct control only over commercial bank reserves and legal reserve requirements. Beyond that point, the preferences of the banking and non-banking public take over. We can get a sense of the uncertainty which this introduces into monetary policy by comparing changes from year to year in nominal gross national product, the money stock, and the adjusted monetary base.

Since you haven't yet encountered the monetary base, a word of introduction is in order. The monetary base is sometimes called "high-powered money," because a dollar of it can potentially be used as reserves by the commercial banking system to create several dollars of money. (The process was described in Chapter 16.) *The monetary base is the sum of the currency held by banks and the public plus the reserve deposits of Federal Reserve System member banks.* The *adjusted* monetary base refers to calculations of this sum that have been adjusted to take account of changes in legal reserve requirements. That adjustment is important, because the power of any dollar of high-powered money depends fundamentally on the legal reserve requirements to which bank deposits are subject. The adjusted monetary base is the variable over which the Open Market Committee has direct control. It is the lever, one might say, on which the hand of the monetary authorities actually rests.

Table 20B shows the annual percentage changes in the adjusted monetary base, in the three principal measures of the money stock, and in the nominal gross national product from 1970 to 1978. However long it takes for changes in the monetary base to work their way through changes in the money stock to affect changes in total spending, *the linkage is loose*. The Fed does not possess the precise control over the money stock, much less over total spending, that it would have to possess if it were to compensate effectively for fluctuations in aggregate demand.

For all of these reasons, it sometimes happens that the monetary authorities end up regretting what they have done. The political time lags that hamper fiscal policy but from which monetary policy is largely free turn out to be not altogether an advantage of monetary policy. The speed with which the Open Market Committee can act enables it also to make more frequent mistakes. Of course, it can quickly reverse direction when it learns it made an error. But sharp reversals of direction

TABLE 20B ANNUAL PERCENTAGE CHANGES IN
MONETARY AGGREGATES AND TOTAL SPENDING

Year	Adjusted Monetary Base	M_1	M_2	M_3	Nominal Gross National Product
1970	5.6%	3.8%	4.2%	4.3%	5.0%
1971	7.9	6.7	11.6	12.8	8.2
1972	7.3	7.1	10.5	12.8	10.1
1973	8.7	7.5	9.6	10.8	11.6
1974	8.5	5.5	8.4	7.9	8.1
1975	7.9	4.4	7.7	9.1	8.2
1976	8.4	5.3	9.9	12.1	11.2
1977	8.4	7.3	10.7	12.4	11.0
1978	9.4	7.8	8.6	9.8	11.7

SOURCE: Calculations by Federal Reserve Bank of St. Louis.

by an institution as powerful as the Open Market Committee
can themselves be a destabilizing force.

Interrelations between Fiscal and Monetary Policy

We have so far looked at aggregate demand management in
terms of fiscal policy *or* monetary policy. Most economists
today prefer to think of themselves as eclectics, willing to use
fiscal *and* monetary policy rather than debate their respective
merits. This may be evidence of an admirable openminded-
ness. Or it may be simple prudence in the face of the difficulties
encountered when one tries to measure their effects. These
difficulties are compounded by the fact that fiscal policies will
usually have monetary repercussions whether or not they're
intended. A fan of fiscal policy can then credit his preferred
tools while the fan of monetary policy attributes the effects
to the changes that the fiscal action induced in monetary
conditions.

Why does fiscal policy inevitably have an impact on the
monetary sector? Consider the case of the government decision
in 1975 to provide a fiscal stimulus by cutting taxes while
maintaining or even increasing expenditures. The Treasury
must obtain money in order to spend. There are basically two
ways to get it. The Treasury can either have new money created
or it can borrow from the stock of already existing money.
Whichever course is chosen, the fiscal actions will have monetary effects. Let's try to sort out the possibilities.

The Treasury does not ordinarily create new money on its
own. As we saw in Chapter 16 the creation of additional money
comes about through credit expansion by commercial banks
and the Federal Reserve. We can therefore set the problem up

in terms of the three sources from which the Treasury may borrow: the Fed, commercial banks, or the nonbank public.

Suppose the Treasury borrows from the Fed in order to secure the funds to finance expenditures not covered by taxes. The Fed in effect gives the Treasury additional deposits in exchange for government securities. When the Treasury then spends these deposits, they flow into the bank accounts or currency holdings of defense contractors, welfare recipients, government employees, or whoever is on the receiving end of the expenditures. The money stock consequently increases.

These new deposits are also new reserves for the commercial banking system. Banks will therefore find their lending power increased. If they can locate eligible borrowers, the commercial banks will, by expanding their loans, create a further addition to the money stock.

It follows that the money stock could increase by the entire amount of the deficit even though the Fed directly financed only a portion of the deficit. A $50 billion deficit, for example, could be handled through some combination like a Fed purchase of $15 billion in new government securities and commercial bank purchases of $35 billion. The Fed purchase, by supplying new reserves to the banking system, enables the commercial banks to acquire additional government securities by creating new demand deposits.

Now suppose that the Fed wants to prevent any growth of the money stock while the Treasury is borrowing. Insofar as the Fed is successful, the Treasury will be forced to compete with other borrowers for use of the existing money stock. Unless there are idle funds around, interest rates will consequently rise, until the higher cost of borrowing squeezes out the excess demand. The net effect, then, will be an expansion of government spending and a compensating reduction of private spending. But this defeats the original purpose of the government's policy; an increase in government spending that is exactly matched by a decrease in private spending provides no stimulus to total expenditures.

There's one other possibility. Suppose the public is holding large money balances simply because consumers and investors are fearful of the future and don't trust available financial assets. People might be persuaded to exchange those balances for government securities. That would give the Treasury the money it wants without an increase in the measured money stock. More spending would then occur with no increase in M, because the government would be spending previously idle balances that the public had been persuaded to exchange for government bonds. But is that very likely outside a period of deep depression? Perhaps in the 1930s public confidence was so low that deficit spending could tap large idle money balances.

But that doesn't seem to describe the situation at any time since World War II.

The conclusion is a simple one. Deficit spending by the government affects the monetary sector. It results in some combination of an enlarged money stock and higher interest rates. Insofar as the Fed tries to prevent public expenditures from crowding out private expenditures by making more credit available when the Treasury is borrowing, it causes a growth in the money stock. If the Fed tries to prevent such an increase, it will force private borrowers to bid against the Treasury for the limited supply of credit. Fiscal policy is therefore inseparable from monetary policy.

Monetary policy, on the other hand, might be conducted independently of fiscal policy. Government spending uses money, but more money can be created and spent independently of any changes in the government budget. It doesn't follow, however, that fiscal policy cannot be a useful aid to monetary policy. Remember that the Fed does not directly control the size of the money stock. It can increase the available reserves of the banking system, but it cannot force anyone to borrow and thereby convert free reserves into money. Government borrowing and expenditure is one way to increase the money stock and to increase it rapidly. And in a period of low confidence, when consumers and investors don't want to borrow, fiscal policy might be the only way to make monetary policy effective. The 1930s come immediately to mind.

All of this has one very practical implication. The sometimes vehement debates in recent years over the respective roles of fiscal and monetary policy in causing inflation were largely debates over a nonissue. The federal government has been running very large deficits in recent years. To ask whether this would have caused inflation if the Fed had not simultaneously allowed a rapid expansion in the money stock is a somewhat pointless question; an expansion of the money stock was inevitable given the size of the deficits and the unwillingness of both the Fed and the Treasury to let mounting federal expenditures crowd out private spending.

The Causes of Continuing Inflation

If you have grown impatient waiting for a firm conclusion, you may have found one at last. We seem to have located the cause of the inflation that has beset the U.S. economy since about 1968. The rate of inflation rose in 1968 to 4.5 percent, the first time since 1951 that the price level had increased by more than 3½ percent in any year. The outbreak of the Korean War caused a rapid rise in prices in 1951 (6.8 percent), but the inflation rate quickly subsided and did not exceed 1½ percent in any of the three succeeding years. The 4.5 percent inflation rate of 1968 was only the beginning, however. As Table 20A shows, the annual inflation rate has been *less* than 4.5 percent in only a single year since 1968—it was 4.1 percent in 1972—and it averaged over 6 percent from 1968 to 1978.

This kind of inflation is the inevitable consequence of the fiscal and monetary policies that the United States has followed since the late 1960s. The federal government ran sizable deficits in every year but one since 1967. Because the value of the dollar has fallen so rapidly since 1967, current dollar figures understate the significance of these deficits. A better way to look at them is as a percentage of gross national product. The combined deficits of the federal government in the years from 1967 through 1978 come to almost 1.8 percent of the gross national product in those years. That may seem small. But 1.8 percent of the 1978 gross national product was $38 billion. That can be thought of as the average amount, in 1978 dollars, by which the federal government has outspent its income in each year from 1967 through 1978.

This expansionary fiscal policy was matched by an expansionary monetary policy. Whatever measure of the money stock we use, the rate of increase since 1968 has been well above the rate at which real output could be expected to grow. The annual rate of change in M_1 from 1968 to 1978 was 6.1 percent. For M_2 it was 8.7 percent, and it was 9.8 percent for M_3. The monetary base increased over this period at an annual rate of 7.8 percent. Real output cannot possibly grow at even the lowest of those rates over any extended number of years. The consequence is inevitable: When aggregate demand rises faster than real output can increase, the price level must rise to make up the difference. Aggregate demand, or gross national product in current dollars, rose at an annual rate of 9.3 percent from 1968 to 1978, a rate just about midway between the growth rates of M_2 and M_3. But real output increased at an average annual rate of only 2.8 percent. The 6.3 percent inflation rate over this period requires no further explanation.

What does require an explanation are these excessive growth rates in the monetary aggregates and these large and persistent federal budget deficits. Why has the federal government pursued fiscal and monetary policies that were bound to cause inflation? That is a question to which we'll return in Chapter 21. Before concluding this chapter, however, we ought to look at an issue that disturbs a large number of people: the issue of the national debt.

The National Debt

Conversations about deficit spending always come around eventually to the question of the national debt. This looms so large (if rather vaguely) in the public mind as a serious problem that Congress has placed a legal ceiling on the debt. It's an odd sort of ceiling, because the president periodically asks that it be raised and Congress always cooperates. But the existence of a statutory ceiling, even a flexible one, at least persuades people that someone has an eye on the problem.

What kind of problem is it? How large can the debt grow before we encounter disaster? Surely the government can't go on indefinitely living beyond its means, can it? When will the debt have to be repaid? And how? Direct answers for direct questions.

Very few knowledgeable people worry about the national debt or consider it much of a problem. It could probably grow to several times its present size without presenting any unmanageable difficulties. The federal government can, if it chooses, live beyond its means indefinitely. The debt doesn't ever have to be repaid. The question of how to retire the debt is academic, in view of the fact that it will probably never be retired.

Nothing in that paragraph should alarm you or arouse the suspicion that the government is a welsher. No debtor has to pay back creditors, as long as the creditors don't demand repayment. And the individuals or institutions to whom the federal government is indebted are not holding government bonds out of either patriotism or necessity, but out of concern for their own financial welfare. They purchased the bonds because they decided the best thing they could do with their money was lend it to the government. Moreover, should they change their minds, they would find that the government cheerfully redeems certain bonds on demand and others at maturity, and that there exists an active market for the latter, through which some other party can easily be found to take the bond and return the original purchaser's principal.

Refinancing the Debt

Despite the fact that bonds regularly fall due, requiring the federal government to repay the principal, the debt is never retired. The government secures the funds to repay the principal basically by selling more bonds. As long as it can find purchasers, the government faces no problems. And finding purchasers isn't difficult. If a particular issue of new bonds doesn't sell out, that means the Treasury Department has been stingy in setting the yield. A slightly lower price for the bonds, which comes to the same thing as a slightly higher interest rate, will bring a surge of additional offers to purchase.

You could do the same thing if you enjoyed an adequate credit rating, and many private firms and individuals do. They borrow for a set term, then extend the loan when it falls due. In effect they are paying the interest and borrowing the funds to repay the principal. Lenders are glad to cooperate because they earn their income by lending; the repaying of principal is a nuisance requiring the lender to find a new borrower, especially if the borrower is considered a good risk and the lender has little fear of default on the loan.

The federal government enjoys a uniquely high credit rating among lenders. Lenders do not request an audit of the government's books, demand collateral, raise embarrassing questions about the efficiency with which the government manages its business, or insist upon evidence that the government plans soon to begin living within its means. For they know that the federal government has the power to collect revenue by coercion and, even more importantly, that it enjoys a constitutional monopoly of the right to print currency. State and local governments can and do default on their obligations at times, as do some of the largest corporations, when their revenues fall short of expectations. But the federal government in such a fix could simply create the money with which to pay its debts. In a pinch it can always count on the cooperation of the Federal Reserve Banks. This power makes the bonds of the federal government uniquely safe and guarantees that buyers can be found at the right price. Are we to conclude, then, that the national debt is neither a problem nor a burden? That would be going too far.

Dangers in the Debt

In the first place, increases in the debt mean that the government is either expanding the money stock or competing with private borrowers for available credit. If the economy is operating close to capacity, deficit financing may be inflationary. Of course, if the economy is in a depression, an increase in the debt may be the stimulus to demand that restores prosperity. It is thus not the absolute size of the debt so much as the direction in which it is changing that ought to be carefully watched.

Second, government borrowing isn't confined in practice to times when the economy is in a recession and idle resources are consequently available. Most of the time, at least in recent years, government borrowing has pulled resources away from private into public uses. Taxation has the same effect, of course. But taxes have a greater political impact, and expenditures undertaken out of tax revenues therefore tend to be scrutinized more critically than expenditures financed through borrowing. Whether this is a point for or against government borrowing depends on how one evaluates the relative importance of public and private spending. Some students of American society maintain that we spend far too much on goods for private consumption (automobiles, houses, filet mignon) and far too little on the goods whose provision is largely left to government (education, public parks, national defense). But there are others who maintain just as insistently that government expenditure promotes social welfare less efficiently than does private expenditure. However you stand on that issue, the ability to increase expenditures without increasing taxes almost certainly enables governments to spend more than they otherwise would.

The Burden of the Debt

The often-heard argument that deficit financing pushes the burden of present expenditures onto our descendants is almost wholly mistaken. The debt that passes on to future generations is for the most part matched by the bonds that we bequeath them. We leave them assets as well as liabilities, and hence no net burden of indebtedness.

When you stop to think about it, you realize that current expenditures, however they are financed, require the use of current real resources. Wars, for example, can be financed by borrowing, but they must be fought by drawing upon the current population and using the productive capabilities of the current economy. Highways, schools, and dams all require for their construction the use of current resources, resources that are consequently not available to provide other goods for the current generation —regardless of how these projects are financed. In fact, deficit financing may well make future generations better off. If the borrowed funds are wisely used in the construction of projects that will yield large future services, the current generation is sacrificing the present enjoyment of real resources in order to provide a larger real income to later generations. We are benefiting right now from past government expenditures on schools, roads, public buildings, parks, dams, irrigation projects, and other public investments, just as we are currently enjoying the fruits of past private investment in the form of a larger output of privately produced commodities and services.

There is one partial exception to all this. If a government borrows from foreigners to finance current expenditures, then it is attempting to use the current resources of foreigners, rather than of its own citizens. And future generations will be left with the obligation to repay that borrowing by giving up some of their resources to foreign bondholders. Of course, if the projects for which the government borrows are good investments, they will augment the real income of future generations by more than enough to repay the resources originally borrowed from abroad. We see again that the wisdom of the project for which the borrowing is undertaken is more important than the mere fact that the expenditure is financed by borrowing. And this agrees with everything we know about private spending and borrowing. A business firm or a household will gain from going into debt whenever the project financed by borrowing increases the flow of future goods (income) by more than it increases the stream of future payments on principal and interest.

Numbers and Alarms

This discussion of the national debt has stayed away from actual numbers because the principles are more important than the numbers, however dramatic the latter can sometimes be made to appear. Some people are apparently thrilled in a terrifying sort of way by the news that if Alexander the Great had started to spend money after the Battle of Issus at the rate of $400 a minute, he would not yet today have spent a sum equal to the total of the national debt. But what does that mean? Do we gain a relevant sense of proportion from such numbers? Or are they like estimating the relative importance of mosquitoes and elephants by figuring out how many mosquitoes would have to be put on a scale to balance one elephant?

The interest paid by the federal government annually on the national debt may be a more meaningful measure of its significance, since the interest is rather like the "carrying charge" on the debt. It's currently close to 2 percent of the gross national product. That's a substantial sum; but it hardly spells fiscal ruin. Another way to put the debt into perspective is to note that in 1945, at the end of World War II, it was approximately equal to the total national income. Thirty years later the debt was more than twice as large but was less than 40 percent of the value of our annual national output.

In short, the national debt is not a major problem. If you've been worrying about it in a vaguely fearful way, we encourage you to discard your anxieties or transfer them to some social problem more deserving of your concern.

Once Over Lightly

In the 1970s the U.S. economy experienced three recessions, high average unemployment rates, and record rates of inflation for peacetime years. This experience has given additional urgency to the question of the federal government's responsibility for controlling inflation and recession.

Those who want the federal government to assume more responsibility for stabilizing the economy usually emphasize the task of aggregate demand management.

Fiscal policy and monetary policy are the principal techniques of aggregate demand management available to officials of the federal government. Fiscal policy aims at controlling fluctuations in aggregate demand through compensatory budget deficits or surpluses. Monetary policy works toward the same goal through changes in commercial bank reserves or legal reserve requirements.

Timing is crucial in any effective stabilization policy. The time lags that will inevitably occur between the appearance and the recognition of a problem, the recognition and the decision to take a particular action, and the action and its ultimate effects combine to make aggregate demand management less stabilizing in practice than on paper.

Attempts to stabilize aggregate demand through fiscal or monetary policy actions must predict accurately if they are to be successful. But economic forecasting is an undeveloped art. It is made especially hazardous by the fact that the people whose behavior is to be controlled try to anticipate and adjust for the controls.

The political delays inevitably associated with its use create especially acute timing problems for fiscal policy.

While there is little evidence for the position that discretionary fiscal policy is an effective stabilization tool, a strong case can be made for its power to change aggregate demand under appropriate circumstances.

Nondiscretionary fiscal policy, operating through changes in taxes or government outlays that occur automatically in response to changing levels of output and income, may have contributed significantly to the post-World War II stability of the U.S. economy.

Monetary policy shares with discretionary fiscal policy a better demonstrated capacity to change than to stabilize aggregate demand.

The special problem of monetary policy is that the Fed cannot control the quantity of the exchange medium with precision. Moreover, the Fed's ability to control it seems to be diminishing.

Fiscal and monetary policies are interdependent, because government borrowing affects the monetary sector. Responsibility for inflation in the United States since the late 1960s may therefore be assigned to them jointly.

The size of the national debt is a less important issue than the size and timing of changes in the debt and the purposes to which the borrowed funds are put.

QUESTIONS FOR DISCUSSION

1. If the assertions that PQ equals $C + I + G + E_n$ and that PQ equals MV are both true by definition, can they convey any useful information? If they're both true by definition, how can they be competing ways of thinking about the effect of aggregate demand changes on output and prices?

2. How much time elapsed between the beginning of the 1979 slowdown and (a) the suspicion, (b) the growing conviction, and (c) the official recognition that the economy was in a recession? If Congress wants to use fiscal policy to counter recessions, should it cut taxes when the recession is a suspicion, when it's a widespread conviction, or when it's officially announced?

3. Assume that Congress and the President want to cut taxes by $5 billion to stimulate the economy in a period of recession. Does it matter whether they cut personal income taxes or corporate income taxes? Whether the cuts in personal income taxes are concentrated among low-income groups or more widely distributed? What difference does it make and to whom does it make a difference?

4. During the depression of the 1930s, increases in federal government expenditures were often accompanied by promises (threats?) of future tax increases to hold down the size of the budget deficit. Do you think this policy had any effect on investment spending?

5. Would you favor the proposal, mentioned in the text, to give the President authority to change tax rates or authorize expenditures on his own (within congressionally designated limits) as a way of making fiscal policy more flexible? Why or why not?

6. The columns below present a partial history of the 1974–75 recession. The first column shows the annual rate of change in real output for each quarter from the 4th quarter of 1973 through the 1st quarter of 1976. The second column shows, also at an annual rate, the federal government deficit for that quarter.

Quarter	% Change in Q (Annual Basis)	Federal Deficit (Annual Basis)
4th –73	2.1%	$2.3 billion
1st –74	−3.9	4.1
2nd–74	−1.8	7.6
3rd –74	−2.5	9.0
4th –74	−5.5	25.3
1st –75	−9.0	48.5
2nd–75	6.4	99.2
3rd –75	10.5	65.5
4th –75	2.6	67.6
1st –76	9.3	60.3

a. Congress passed an antirecessionary tax cut at the end of the 1st quarter of 1975. Do you think this tax cut helped end the recession?

b. Do these data provide any evidence that nondiscretionary fiscal policy might have had a stabilizing effect?

7. If tax cuts stimulate aggregate demand, is it possible that they also stimulate aggregate supply? How could a reduction in corporate or personal income tax rates affect the supply curves of goods?

8. President John Kennedy's proposal in his 1962 Economic Report that Congress grant the President stand-by authority to reduce tax rates in a recession contemplated only temporary reductions. Do you think people are more

likely to spend or to save tax reductions that they know will be temporary? What difference does the answer make to the effectiveness of fiscal policy as a stabilization tool?

9. On which monetary aggregate should the Open Market Committee focus in its efforts to manage the money supply: the monetary base, the monetary base adjusted for reserve requirement changes, M_1, M_2, or M_3? Why?

10. "An increase or decrease in government spending will usually entail an offsetting decrease or increase in private spending." Under what circumstances would you expect that statement to be true? Why? Under what circumstances would you expect that statement to be false? Why?

11. The late Senator Hubert Humphrey said shortly after the March 1975 tax cuts that "common sense" told him federal borrowing would not raise interest rates and crowd out private borrowers. "To a large extent this credit-market question takes care of itself," he said. "Private demands for credit go down when unemployment is high. This makes room in the credit market for government demand which goes up." Do you agree?

12. Can you think of any experiment by which we might test the proposition that fiscal policy affects total spending regardless of what is happening to the money supply?

13. Does monetary policy require assistance from fiscal policy to be effective?

14. Here are the average annual percentage changes from 1959 through 1967 of several economic variables whose performance after 1967 is discussed in the text.

Adjusted monetary base: 4.1%
M_1: 3.0%
M_2: 6.0%
M_3: 7.2%
Nominal gross national product: 6.4%
Real gross national product: 4.3%
Price level: 2.0%

Do these data support the contention that inflation after 1968 was produced by an excessive rate of growth in the stock of money?

15. "The size of the national debt is not as important as the size of changes in the debt." Evaluate that assertion.

16. What would be the consequences of a systematic effort by the federal government to retire the national debt over a period of 20 years?

17. What would be the consequences if the Federal Reserve Banks purchased from the public all the outstanding marketable debt of the United States government? (The value at maturity of all U.S. government marketable securities rose above one-half trillion dollars in March 1979.)

18. When a corporation successfully sells additional bonds or a new issue of common stock, it goes more deeply into debt. Is this evidence that the corporation is failing or that it's succeeding? How well do analogies from the area of business indebtedness apply to questions of government indebtedness? Where do such analogies present a misleading picture and why?

Chapter **21**

Inflation, Recession, and Political Economy

In March of 1975, Congress passed, and President Gerald Ford signed, a bill reducing federal taxes despite the fact that projected deficits for the current and succeeding fiscal years would be the largest peacetime deficits in our history. There was no outcry of disbelief or indignation: the economy was in a recession in 1975, and tax cuts were widely considered a proper remedy, regardless of the state of the federal budget.

The United States economy was in a far deeper and more prolonged recession in 1932 when Franklin D. Roosevelt campaigned for the presidency on a promise to balance the federal budget if elected. The deficit at which Roosevelt was looking, adjusted for changes in the value of the dollar, was less than one-fifth the size of the smallest deficit being projected at the time of the 1975 tax cut.

Shifting Public Opinion

Public thinking about deficits and recessions has obviously changed. Prior to the 1930s, the orthodox view was that government should actually retrench in a recession, cutting its expenditures and increasing tax rates if necessary to preserve a balanced budget. A balanced budget, in turn, was viewed as the test of responsible government and the surest indicator to the business community of the government's determination to maintain or restore "confidence." And confidence was seen as the key to recovery.

As for creating additional money to stimulate recovery —that was considered the very depth of irresponsibility. Downturns were supposedly the inevitable consequence of previous actions based on overly optimistic expectations; they had to be suffered because they were the appropriate penance for previous excesses, the means by which mistakes were cleared away so that solid foundations could be laid for subsequent advance. Once the mistakes had been corrected— through bankruptcies, forced sales, writing down of assets, readjustments of expectations—confidence would return and a new advance could begin. We are not saying that everyone held these positions, for the historical record shows that there were many who disputed the wisdom of such counsel. It was, nonetheless, the viewpoint that pretty much controlled the policy thinking of governments in the industrialized nations of the Western world prior to the 1930s.

The dominant view today is that government has a responsibility for the management of aggregate demand, and that the federal budget and the supply of money are tools which the government may use to fulfill those responsibilities. The question now is not *whether* but *how*. How can the government use its control over expenditures and tax receipts to stabilize the aggregate level of economic activity? That is the question of *fiscal policy*. How can the government, and primarily the central bank, use its control over the money stock to stabilize the economy? That is the question of *monetary policy*.

A Survey of the Terrain

Fiscal and monetary policy, at least when used jointly, are powerful techniques for changing aggregate demand. But that does not make them effective stabilization tools. The principal conclusion that emerged from the preceding chapter is that the stabilization of aggregate demand requires finer adjustments than we know how to make with the powerful but nonetheless blunt-edged instruments of fiscal or monetary policy. That doesn't imply, however, that the instruments will not be used. We shall see in this chapter why it is that they are very likely to be used as stabilization tools, even if it is widely agreed that they aren't effective.

Further complications are presented by the fact that inflation and recession are not opposites. While rapid inflation can appropriately be viewed as the consequence of excessive aggregate demand, recession is seriously misconceived when thought of as the consequence of inadequate aggregate demand. We'll have much more to say about all that in the present chapter.

Finally, we must acknowledge the possibility that government will be unable to prevent inflation or moderate recessions because the people in control of government policies don't want to do so. This is not to suggest that any policymaker prefers inflation to price stability, or frequent and deep recessions to steady levels of production and employment. It suggests only that policymakers may not find it in their interest to do what must be done if periods of recession and inflation are to be avoided.

Inflation versus Unemployment

Nothing contributed more strongly to the public's sudden disillusionment with economists in the early 1970s than the appearance of rapid inflation combined with high and rising unemployment. That wasn't supposed to happen, according to the public's notion of what economists were teaching, because inflation and recession are opposites.

Inflation and recession are not actually opposites, of course. The opposite of inflation is deflation, a falling rather than a rising price level. There is no generally accepted term for the opposite of recession, but *boom* comes close: a period of increasing output and employment, mixed possibly but not necessarily with rising prices. But if inflation and recession aren't opposites in the strict sense, they have been considered opposites in the sense of sunshine and rain: the two are not expected to occur in the same place at the same time. The simultaneous occurrence in the 1970s, therefore, of rapid inflation and a severe recession was surprising as well as disturbing.

Professional economists weren't as embarrassed by it all as some journalists and television commentators, perhaps too eager to proclaim a crisis, claimed they were. But it was true that the economics textbooks had for some years been analyzing inflation and recession as if they were the result of opposite forces and therefore could not occur simultaneously. The textbooks spoke of "gaps" between what aggregate demand was and what it ought to be. An inflationary gap meant that everyone together was trying to purchase more goods than the economic system could produce and bidding up the price level in the process. A deflationary or recessionary gap meant that spending intentions were falling short of what producers wanted to supply, so that either prices were starting to fall, or, far more likely given the general sluggishness of prices under downward pressure, output and employment were declining.

This way of setting up the problem leaves the impression that inflation will not occur when a deflationary gap exists and recession cannot occur in the presence of an inflationary gap, so that inflation and unemployment are indeed opposites. If they are caused, respectively, by an excessive and inadequate level of aggregate demand, we should not expect to observe both at the same time. Moreover, the way to deal with inflation is clearly to "close" the inflationary gap by reducing spending. Recession calls for closing the gap by increasing spending. But then what does inflation *with* recession call for? It calls above all for some other way of looking at the problem.

The argument based on aggregate-demand gaps can be supplemented to allow for *some* inflation coexisting with high unemployment. Suppose the economy has been in a recession and is now recovering. We would not expect all prices and wages to stand still until rising aggregate demand had restored the entire economy to "full capacity" operation. Demand will expand faster in some areas than others, and sometimes more rapidly in sectors already operating close to capacity than in sectors where idle resources are especially large. And so some prices and wages will rise before unemployment has been reduced to the target level. In such a case policymakers might have to choose between less unemployment and less inflation; within a certain range, at least, one could not be reduced without increasing the other. This analysis is one source of the widely held view that high employment levels and price stability are *alternatives* between which we must choose by assessing the relative impact of each on social welfare.

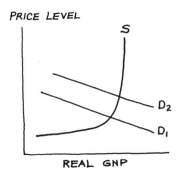

PRICE LEVEL

REAL GNP

The Phillips Curve: Use and Abuse

In 1958 a British economist named A. W. Phillips published a study on "The Relationship between Unemployment and the Rate of Change of Money Wage Rates in the United Kingdom, 1861–1957," and invented the "Phillips Curve." Phillips showed that there was a stable relationship during the period he studied between the unemployment rate and the rate at which the average money wage increased. Unemployment was greater when money wage rates were increasing more slowly, and fell in periods when money wage rates were rising rapidly. That seems thoroughly plausible. During periods of high demand for labor, employers will tend to bid up wage rates to obtain and keep the employees they want. In periods of high unemployment, employers will not have to bid so energetically for labor, and wage rates will increase less.

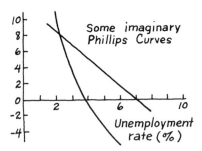

% RATE OF CHANGE IN MONEY WAGES (per year)

Some imaginary Phillips Curves

Unemployment rate (%)

But the argument was subsequently extended to suggest that unemployment might be reduced by allowing an inflationary rate of increase in money wages and, by extension, in the average of all prices. The Phillips Curve of this latter argument purports to show that there is a general trade-off between inflation and unemployment, so that less of one can be obtained by accepting more of the other. But the conclusion does not follow either from A. W. Phillips' data or from reflection on the causes of inflation and unemployment. And the notion that government policymakers can reduce the rate of unemployment by deliberately causing inflation is an extremely hazardous one.

It is probably true that prices and wages will be more likely to drift upward when the economy is close to "full" employment. The economic system always contains a great deal of internal movement: industries grow, others decline, firms rise and fall, new production techniques are introduced, the composition of demand changes, people enter and exit from the labor force. Resources must therefore be attracted continuously into particular employments through the offer of acceptable employment terms. But employers and employees do not have perfect information. They must search for what they want and incur the costs of that search.

In a period of low unemployment, the cost of finding a new job will, on the average, be lower for employees than during a period of high unemployment. Employees will therefore be more ready to give up a job when they think the wage is unsatisfactory and begin searching for another. So employers will find it difficult to reduce wages.

Search costs for employers are higher in periods of full employment. And so employers will offer higher wages than they might otherwise be willing to offer in order to avoid making an extensive and costly search for the new employees they want and to reduce the risk of losing present employees, who would be expensive to replace.

The same argument applies to prices in product markets. When the economy is operating close to capacity, excess supplies are generally hard to find, and buyers will pay higher prices, rather than search for alternative sources of supply. In a period of high unemployment and substantial excess capacity, sellers will be shaving prices, because buyers are hard to find.

The identical conclusion emerges whichever way we look at it. "Full" employment fosters an upward creep in prices and wages; substantial unemployment and excess capacity encourages a downward drift in prices and wages.

The basic argument asserts that the direction of drift in price and wage movements is a response to tightness or slackness in markets. In other words, the level of employment is the cause and price-wage movement the effect. But we cannot assume that because full employment causes inflation, inflation will bring about full employment. When there is a big crowd at the basketball game, the gymnasium temperature rises because of body heat; but the athletic department cannot make a crowd come to watch a losing basketball team by overheating the gymnasium.

Reducing Unemployment by Illusion

Nonetheless, the policy of deliberately stepping up inflation probably would lower the unemployment rate—temporarily. People are unemployed because they don't find the job opportunities of which they're aware sufficiently attractive. It follows that if the level of real wages could somehow be increased across the board, all employment opportunities would become more attractive and employment would increase—except for the fact that employers would then demand less labor at those higher real wage rates. The quantity supplied would increase, but the quantity demanded would fall. When money wages and prices advance together, however, as they do in a general inflation, real wages don't actually increase. But workers will think they have increased, and that may be enough to lower the unemployment rate.

A policy of deliberate inflation makes job opportunities seem more attractive by raising the money wage rate offers of employers. And this is how inflation might reduce unemployment. But the higher wage rate offers are only seemingly more attractive. As long as potential employees don't realize that the job opportunities they're now accepting are in reality no better than the opportunities they previously rejected, employment will indeed rise. But it will subsequently fall back down to its previous level when employees discover what's happening: that inflation is creating the illusion of more attractive wage offers. No permanent reduction in unemployment will have occurred, but the economy will be undergoing more rapid inflation.

A deliberate policy of pursuing lower unemployment by accepting a higher rate of inflation calls, then, for continuously increasing the inflation rate *so that workers always expect less than the actual rate of inflation.* In that way they can be made to overestimate continuously the real value of the money wages they are being offered. Or else the policy assumes that employees pay exclusive attention to money wage rates, never to real wage rates. This is a superficially plausible assumption, since we know that few employees consult the most recent changes in the Consumer Price Index before deciding whether a wage offer is adequate. They look at *money* wage rates, in other words. But they also learn after a while that their wages buy less and adjust their perception of the wage rate's real value. An extreme example will make the point. In 1960 workers stood in line for jobs in manufacturing offering $3 an hour. In 1980 manufacturers can find almost no one who will accept employment at that wage. Employees do know, even if they've never heard of price indexes, that $3 is a much lower hourly wage today than it was twenty years ago.

Policy cannot be constructed on the assumption that workers will be permanently fooled, for people learn from experience. And the simultaneous existence of high unemployment with very rapid inflation in the 1970s ought to be sufficient evidence that people have learned. When they begin to assume continued inflation, they no longer suffer from the illusion that money wages and real wages are the same thing.

But suppose a government tried this approach to the unemployment problem, found that it couldn't actually lower unemployment, and decided to abandon the policy. It had been causing inflation by applying fiscal and monetary stimulus, and it now eases up. After a lag of some length, total spending will stop increasing so rapidly, and producers will be unable to sell at the prices they had anticipated; so inventories will mount, production will be curtailed, and unemployment will rise. Eventually sellers will learn not to expect such a rapid rise in prices, they will adjust downward the prices they ask and the prices they offer to pay for inputs, sales will revive, inventories will decline, production will start up again, and unemployment will fall. But that won't all happen within a week or even a month. The higher unemployment that will result from an attempt to slow down the rate of inflation will be temporary; but temporary can be a long time.

Switzerland: A Case Study

It's always hazardous to draw inferences about what will happen in the United States from what has actually happened in some other country. Economic systems differ vastly, and the differences between the Swiss economy with its 6 million people and the U.S. economy with 220 million people are bound to be enormous. Nonetheless, Swiss experience provides a striking case study for anyone interested in the problem of slowing down a rapid inflation.

The price-level column has been inserted twice into Table 21A to help you visualize it first as a growing problem, then as a problem resolved. The 4.8 percent inflation rate in 1970 was no great surprise; that happens to be the average inflation rate in Switzerland during the 1960s. But the almost 10 percent inflation rates of 1971 and 1972 were quite high by Swiss standards. Inflation had clearly been fueled by excessively rapid increases in the money stock. In 1973 and 1974, the rate of money growth was drastically reduced in an effort to bring inflation under control.

Total spending didn't decline immediately. In 1973, when

TABLE 21A   SWITZERLAND'S
PERCENTAGE RATES OF CHANGE

Year	Price Level	Money Stock	Nominal GNP	Real GNP	Price Level
1970	4.8	10.0%	11.8%	6.7%	4.8%
1971	9.0	18.5	13.4	4.0	9.0
1972	9.6	13.4	13.1	3.2	9.6
1973	8.3	—0.3	11.6	3.2	8.3
1974	7.1	—1.7	8.9	1.7	7.1
1975	6.7	2.2	—1.3	—7.5	6.7
1976	2.4	6.9	1.8	—0.6	2.4
1977	0.4	4.7	3.1	2.6	0.4

SOURCE: International Monetary Fund, International Financial Statistics.
Prepared by Reserve Bank of St. Louis.

the money stock fell 0.3 percent, total expenditure as measured by nominal gross national product increased 11.6 percent. It increased again, by 8.9 percent, in 1974. In 1975 the effect of slamming on the monetary brake finally showed up in nominal GNP, which declined 1.3 percent.

But look now at Q and at P. The price level continued to climb steeply in 1975, at a rate of 6.7 percent. With the demand for new goods down 1.3 percent from the preceding year, output tumbled 7.5 percent. Real GNP continued to decline, though at a much more moderate rate, in 1976; and finally, in 1976, the rate of inflation fell sharply. By 1977 the inflation had finally been brought to a halt.

The experience of Switzerland is consistent with the analysis presented above. The introduction of fiscal-monetary restraint to deal with inflation has its first effects on output—the effect on prices comes later. In the Swiss case, quarterly data show that the policy of sharply reducing the rate of growth in the money stock began late in 1972. Consumer prices didn't stop rising rapidly until the middle of 1975. But the rate of growth in industrial production came to a halt in the first quarter of 1974 and declined steeply throughout the year and on into 1975. The Swiss economy went through a major recession before the policy of reduced monetary growth was able finally to halt inflation.

Conclusions and Implications

Let's try to summarize the conclusions that have emerged so far from our examination of the relationship between inflation and unemployment.

1. A movement from a situation of low employment to one of high or "full" employment will generally be accompanied by a rising price level. Increased demand will bid up some

prices and wages even before "full" employment is achieved. Increases in aggregate demand when the economy is already operating in the vicinity of "full" employment will have their principal impact on the price-wage level.

2. An economy operating in the vicinity of "full" employment tends to experience creeping inflation. By lowering search costs for sellers, both of products and labor, and raising them for buyers, "full" employment promotes an upward drift in the terms of price and wage bargains.

3. The unemployment rate is affected by *changes* in the rate of inflation. An unanticipated increase in the inflation rate tends to reduce unemployment by making available job offers look more attractive than they actually are. An unanticipated decrease in the inflation rate tends to increase unemployment until sellers of products and labor services learn to adjust their expectations. But a constant rate of inflation, because it's presumably fully anticipated, probably has no effect on the unemployment rate.

There are some important policy lessons tucked away in those conclusions for anyone who dislikes both high unemployment rates and inflation.

1. Avoid recessions if you want to avoid inflation, because the process of recovery from a recession usually entails inflation.

2. Try not to let inflation get started if you want to prevent high unemployment, because slowing down the rate of inflation will ordinarily cause unemployment to increase.

3. Creeping inflation is probably the price that a society must pay for all the gains that accrue from continuous operation at or near the economy's capacity.

4. The Phillips Curve is a dangerous concept insofar as it encourages the illusion that a permanently lower unemployment rate can be "purchased" by accepting a higher rate of inflation.

Points 3 and 4 are not contradictory. Point 3 merely acknowledges the fact that upward price adjustments will dominate downward adjustments, leading to a slow upward drift in the price level, when an economic system is operating with very little slack. It warns, you might say, against the pursuit of perfection. Point 4 warns against confusing cause and effect by assuming that since high employment generates inflation, more inflation will generate higher employment.

Points 1 and 2 are lessons of doubtful value if we don't know how to avoid recessions or increases in the rate of inflation. A fiscal-monetary activist might extract from them a recommendation for what has come to be called *fine-tuning.* A fiscal-monetary passivist, on the other hand, will argue that the attempt to fine-tune is a principal cause of recessions and inflation, and will see in these lessons a case for restraint in the practice of demand management. It's time to face the much debated issue of fine-tuning and its equally debated opposite, the abandonment of discretionary fiscal or monetary policies.

Fine-Tuning or Blindman's Buff?

We have reminded you repeatedly that economic decisions are always made on the basis of expected and therefore uncertain costs and benefits that may turn out to be mistaken. That's also true for the makers of fiscal and monetary policy.

A sucessful program of aggregate demand management will require extensive information. Policymaking today can take advantage of the vast strides we have made in recent years in the accumulation of statistical data on the economy's performance. But information of this sort will always be approximate as well as highly aggregative. Moreover, all the information available will be dated. It will summarize some situation in the past. But even very recent and reliable data aren't enough. Since any policy action will impinge on future situations the challenge is to obtain data on the future by extrapolating from the past. And that requires considerable theorizing to accompany the data.

What we really want to know is what will happen if various policy actions are taken. What will be the effects of the actions, direct and indirect, and how long will they take to make themselves felt? How long does it take for a purchase of government securities by the Fed to transform itself into an increased demand for consumption and investment goods? How much of the impact will come almost at once, perhaps as a reaction to the mere news of an easier monetary policy? How will the rest of the impact be distributed over time? Fiscal actions raise the same questions. The actual multiplier effect of a change in government expenditures or taxes can't be determined by arithmetic manipulations of various marginal propensities because we don't really know the future values of these propensities. Public attitudes toward tax and expenditure changes may bring about a shift in spending or saving plans so that the relevant multiplier changes when the policy action is announced. And the distribution of the multiplier effects over time is a crucial piece of information if stabilization policy is not to become destabilization policy.

Knowledge about the time lags between monetary or fiscal actions and their effects has been extremely hard to obtain, as we pointed out in Chapter 20. There is no way to deduce the distribution of lags from pure theory; we have to rely on empirical measurements. But how are we going to sort out the effects of a particular fiscal or monetary stimulus from the effects of all the other forces that will be impinging on the economy? There are good reasons for believing that the lags have no set length. To ask how long it will take for a particular fiscal or monetary stimulus to have 80 percent of its effects may be like asking how long it will take for 80 percent of the people to learn the news. Which news? Which people? Who already knows? Is it important news? To whom? What media of communication are available? Who has access to them? Who has an interest in spreading the news? Who might want to suppress or distort it?

Is It Better to Have Tried and Failed?

It has become increasingly obvious in recent years that we do not have the knowledge that would be required to steer the economy on a steady course of full employment with price stability. But are we better off than we would have been if we hadn't tried? Most economists now agree that fine-tuning has been somewhat oversold, that we have been too optimistic about our ability to reduce aggregate fluctuations through demand management. A smaller number go further: they argue that the attempt to stabilize has increased both unemployment and inflation.

How could this occur? The key element in the argument is the relationship between unemployment and uncertainty. Unemployment occurs largely because mistakes are made and subsequently have to be accepted and corrected. It follows that anything which increases the probability of mistakes, of decisions based on a faulty anticipation of future events, will increase the average level of unemployment. The question then becomes: Has the behavior of the federal budget and of the money supply in recent years made the future more predictable? Or has it increased the uncertainties confronting economic decision makers?

Stabilizing Factors

We cannot jump from the fact that there have been no major recessions since the 1930s to the conclusion that the net effect of government stabilization efforts was greater stability. Other factors have been at work. We earlier discussed (in Chapter 16) the importance of the Federal Deposit Insurance Corporation in eliminating the phenomenon of bank runs and the supporting role of the Fed as the guarantor of short-run liquidity to the banking system. Between them they have eliminated the panics that once swept regularly through the financial sector; and with financial panics a thing of the past, the economy has not again had to go through anything even remotely approaching the 25 percent contraction in the money stock experienced between 1929 and 1933.

Another stabilizing factor seems to have been the tendency for personal consumption expenditures after World War II to maintain their own steady rate of increase, with relative disregard for fluctuations in income. Some of this should probably be attributed to relatively high wealth levels, which enable people to maintain their spending during periods of temporarily reduced income. Some of it can also be credited to our system of progressive taxes on personal and corporate income that cushion income against fluctuations in gross national product. The fact that government transfer payments move inversely to GNP has an added cushioning effect on aggregate consumption spending.

Destabilizing Factors

If personal consumption expenditures have been a steady and stabilizing component of aggregate demand, investment expenditures have not. You can go back to Table 15B to see just how unstable private investment spending has been. But did fiscal and monetary policy compensate for this instability, or were they a major *cause* of the instability? The construction component of investment is sensitive to monetary policy shifts, and changing monetary policies do seem to have destabilized the building industry. What about the policy of shifting between tax surcharges to dampen inflation and special tax credits for investment spending to promote employment? Since there is usually considerable discretion about the timing of investment expenditures, couldn't government policy reversals be largely responsible for the large fluctuations from year to year in private investment? It's true that policymakers intended to reduce fluctuations through shifting tax policies; but it wouldn't be the only time a tax program hit something other than its target.

What have been the overall effects of government programs? Remember that an unanticipated change in the composition of spending will cause unemployment even though total spending does not change. When the government makes a decision to send men to the moon, to produce a particular military plane, to restrict oil imports, to subsidize a giant railroad system, to enforce high standards of job safety in industry, to become self-sufficient in energy by 1980, to encourage home ownership through government-subsidized loans, to enlarge steel-making capacity by granting special tax refunds for investment—when the government does any of these things, it signals labor and other resources to move in specific directions. It tells people to change their places of residence, to acquire particular knowledge and skills, to sink resources into specific projects. *Any subsequent slackening of government intentions or shift in emphases announces that these resource movements were partly mistaken and thereby creates unemployment.* These changing signals from government may also trigger surges of investment spending by industries trying to make rapid adjustments to revised government policies. How sure can we be that private economic decisions are the unstable factor for which government decisions must compensate?

The Benefits and Costs of Aggregative Theories

It is difficult to discuss the problem of recession and unemployment without using large aggregates such as consumption expenditure, investment expenditure, government expenditure, tax revenues, total demand, national output, and national income. But there is an important sense in which these data conceal the very nature of the problem with which we're trying to deal. Total output is the sum of the outputs of several million firms producing different goods under constantly changing conditions, including conditions of both cost and demand that can change in different directions and at different rates for each separate firm. It is these differences and the uncertainties associated with them that produce the phenomenon of recession in the first place.

Remember that a recession is not a mere slowdown in the rate of economic growth. It is an unintended and therefore disruptive slowdown for a large number of producers (but never all producers!) who discover that their revenue expectations relative to their cost expectations were too optimistic. Recessions begin because imbalances have developed and accumulated over a period of time. Recessions can perhaps be measured with highly aggregative concepts. But they cannot be adequately understood or controlled without paying attention to the changing structure of costs and demand from one industry to another, one region of the country to another, and even one firm to another.

Attempting to counter recessions by stimulating aggregate demand assumes more uniformity and homogeneity within recessions than is actually the case. The enlarged demand must be a demand for the right goods if it's going to check the decline in output *in particular firms and industries*, which is the essence of the recession. It's true that in a recession most industries and perhaps most firms will experience disappointing revenue-cost outcomes. But they won't all do so, and among those who do encounter disappointment, the called-for adjustments will range from minor through major all the way to bankruptcy and reorganization. What can we expect to happen, then, if government responds to a recession by expanding aggregate demand?

Won't the result depend on how this policy affects the relative demand for the inputs and for the outputs of particular firms? Doesn't increased demand often produce higher costs as well as higher revenues? Remember that inputs are not some stockpile of perfectly substitutable resources that can quickly stop producing X and start producing Y when the demand for X goes down and the demand for Y goes up. Won't a policy of stimulating total demand in response to a recession make life easier for some firms but harder for others?

The massive economic breakdown of the Great Depression led to the construction of highly aggregative theories of economic fluctuations. That was certainly understandable. Only a highly aggregative theory is likely to suggest a cure sufficiently simple to be workable. And what was above all desired in the 1930s was a workable solution, something that could quickly be put into practice. Part of the tragedy of the Great Depression may have been the timidity that prevented national governments from taking the heroic measures to expand aggregate demand that the events of the 1930s seemed to require: 1929 to 1933 was no "normal" recession. Whatever the circumstances that produced or aggravated the long and deep decline into the depression of the 1930s, there was abundant evidence by 1933 that bold actions by government to stimulate recovery carried a low risk and a high potential benefit.

But if policymakers in the 1930s were guilty of failure to recognize an economic breakdown and to react appropriately, policymakers today may be guilty of responding in equally inappropriate ways by treating every recession as if it were a breakdown. The continuing confidence that many public officials and much of the electorate have in discretionary fiscal and monetary policy—despite the record of their performance—is hard to explain on any other grounds.

It wasn't until the late 1960s that the United States acquired both a President and a majority in Congress who believed in the effectiveness and desirability of using discretionary fiscal policy along with monetary policy as stabilization techniques. Is the increased instability of the years since then a mere coincidence, to be blamed on external forces beyond the control of policymakers, such as the OPEC cartel and worldwide agricultural failures? That's certainly possible. And those who want to continue advocating discretionary aggregate demand management, especially in response to recessions, will find in those events a plausible explanation for the fact that increased use of these stabilizing techniques has been accompanied by increased instability. Whether you decide it's consequence or coincidence, the fact remains that our most rapid inflation and highest unemployment rates since World War II appeared *after* both major policital parties had committed themselves to fine-tuning of the economy through aggregate demand management.

Discretion and Rules

The alternative to discretionary fiscal and monetary policies is not *no* policy but policy based on firm commitments to known rules. Sometimes this is called automatic or nondiscretionary fiscal and monetary policy. But there is actually nothing automatic about adhering to clearly enunciated rules, and continuing to do so in the face of strong temptations to relax the rules is certainly a discretionary act. The issue is not whether discretion is better than the absence of discretion. The question, rather, is whether anyone can in fact increase the stability of the economy by deliberately moving the government budget between surplus and deficit and deliberately changing bank reserves or reserve requirements. The alternative view is that efforts to stabilize in these ways will actually be destabilizing, because no one has the knowledge and other capabilities, technical and political, to manipulate aggregate demand with the necessary precision. A sufficiently graceful elephant could stabilize a sailboat in rough weather by shifting its weight with delicacy and perfect timing. But the sailing companions of an elephant without these gifts would probably prefer that it remain quietly in the center of the boat.

Those economists who believe that fiscal and monetary policies have aggravated recession and fostered inflation over the last decade offer two recommendations. With respect to fiscal policy, they want the level of expenditures determined without reference to stabilization imperatives, and tax rates set so as to balance the budget over a normal period. In recessions tax receipts will fall and the budget will be in deficit. In a period of boom or when a recovery is well along, tax receipts will be high and will generate a surplus. These recurring deficits and surpluses will function, as we tried to show in Chapter 20, as self-regulating governors, dampening oscillations in the economy. Any additional discretionary policy actions are more likely to aggravate than to reduce instability, because discretionary actions are hard to time appropriately and because anticipation of them creates additional uncertainty for private decision makers.

The critics of so-called discretionary demand management want monetary policy also to enunciate a course and stick to it.

They want the Fed to maintain a steady hand on the stock of money, either holding it constant or allowing it to increase by some definite, known, uniform, and moderate rate, perhaps one equal to the long term average growth rate of real output. There are automatic monetary stabilizers as well as automatic fiscal stabilizers in the economic system. A boom will eventually run against rising interest rates and credit rationing if the monetary managers don't feed the boom by pumping new reserves into the banking system. And during a period of economic decline, lending terms will tend to improve as the demand for credit slackens, thus encouraging some potential investors. More than this, as in the case of fiscal policy, is much more likely to increase than to diminish instability.

Economic Uncertainties and Political Realities

If all the interrelationships that we've been discussing since Chapter 15 were clearly and firmly established, so that we could tie together cause and effect as confidently as chemists do in their laboratories, government stabilization policies would probably be set in the public interest. But the theories of economists with respect to inflation and recession are much less precise and far more debatable than are the theories of chemists. That leaves considerable room for policies to be shaped by the personal interests of elected and appointed officials, who will always be able to find acceptable reasons for pursuing the policies that contribute most effectively to their own continued tenure in office. This perspective yields a pair of predictions: The stabilization policies of the federal government in the 1980s will be actively discretionary policies, not policies based on commitment to preestablished rules; and they will be strongly biased in an expansionary direction. Let's see why.

As soon as any substantial number of voters comes to the conclusion that government action can alleviate a particular problem, government officials acquire an interest in acting. And if the benefits from an action are expected to appear considerably sooner than the costs, the action will be especially attractive to officials whose tenure in office depends upon continuing public approval. The prediction of active and expansionary policies follows from these premises.

You don't have to study economics to find out that it's easier for a legislator to support tax reductions than tax increases and to support enlarged expenditures rather than reduced expenditures. Economic theory explains this in terms of the externalities associated with the democratic political process. With the dice always loaded in this way against surpluses and in favor of deficits, why do surpluses ever appear in any government's budget? The answer is that a number of countervailing pressures operate against deficits.

One is the strong public prejudice that sees deficits as evidence of an irresponsible failure to live within one's means, a prejudice that has produced in some states a constitutional prohibition of budget deficits. In addition, many tax systems are set up so that revenues automatically expand when income increases, which allows expenditures to grow without either a deficit or a legislated tax increase. State and local governments also have to worry about their credit rating. They cannot run a deficit without borrowing; but they will not be able to borrow unless they can convince lenders that the deficit is only temporary. All these factors operate to counter the pressure toward deficit financing that the externalities of the democratic political process create.

The federal government has a tax system that is extraordinarily effective at generating additional revenue when the incomes of taxpayers rise. From 1970 to 1978 the receipts of the federal government rose 125 percent, which is 10 percent more than gross national product increased over the period. Despite this fact, however, the federal government ran budget deficits in every year during the 1970s. Why did this occur?

The first fact to note is that the federal government does not have to be concerned about its credit rating, because it has control of the mechanism through which money, the means of debt payment, is created. The federal government was also not subject during this period to any constitutional limitations on deficit financing. Finally, the widespread prejudice against government deficits is no longer fully operative against federal budget deficits, because the public vaguely "knows" that a budget deficit can be a means for promoting prosperity. The lesson taught by Keynesian analysis was that budgets don't have to be balanced from year to year; they need only to be balanced over the course of the business cycle, with surpluses in periods of prosperity making up for deficits in periods of slump. This new doctrine can be used to argue that a particular deficit is good for the economy, and that anyone who insists upon a balanced federal budget just doesn't understand "modern economics."

Fiscal Policy in a Political Setting

The trouble with this new doctrine is that its actual effect is to permit perennial deficits. There is no fiscal period that can be identified with "the course of the business cycle." As a result, the surplus that is supposed to balance the deficit never has to be budgeted; it can always be promised for next year or the year after. With every effective pressure toward a balanced budget thereby eliminated, the bias of the democratic political process takes over and produces a long and perhaps endless succession of deficits.

The grounds for predicting expansionary fiscal policy in the 1980s become even stronger when we look more closely at the way in which expansionary and contractionary fiscal policies have their effects. Once rapid inflation has got underway, a contractionary policy, entailing a reduction of the deficit and a slowdown in the rate of economic growth, will take many months, perhaps even several years, to restore price stability. The benefits are thus relatively distant. The costs, however, come quickly. Taxes must be raised and expenditures reduced; at the very least, pressure for increasing expenditures must be resisted while the system of progressive personal and corporate income taxes continues to augment tax revenues.

These tax and expenditure policies will not be as popular as expansionary fiscal policies, which call for lower taxes and higher expenditures. When their immediate costs are set against their relatively distant benefits by someone who must soon stand for reelection, a contractionary policy becomes especially difficult to support. If a recession happens to begin while inflation is being fought through reduced budget deficits, whatever congressional and administrative support does exist for continued fiscal contraction will tend to evaporate rapidly. The normal preference of elected officials for deficits over surpluses will be supported by the claim that "modern economics" endorses larger deficits as a way of fighting recession.

From a political standpoint, it does not matter greatly that switching from fiscal contraction to expansion will have its effects on total spending only after a considerable time lag, because the policy actions themselves are pleasing to voters. Tax cuts and increased transfer payments can quickly increase people's income, even if it takes much longer for them to produce the beginnings of an economic recovery. Notice also that the tax cuts or expenditure increases will take even longer to add to the rate of inflation, because an increase or a decrease in aggregate demand affects real output and employment well before it affects the price level.

No matter how we look at it, everything seems to weight the political process toward expansionary fiscal policy. If this produces inflation, the long time lag between the policy action and its impact on the price level almost guarantees that no one will remember what caused the inflation or who supported the policies that fueled it. The fact that no one likes or wants inflation is not enough to prevent it. As long as the people whose decisions make the difference find it in their personal interest to vote for policies that cause inflation, those are the policies we should expect to see followed.

Can Monetary Policy Prevent Inflation?

You may have noticed that we've been paying attention exclusively to fiscal policy in the course of arguing that government demand-management policies will be active and expansionary. What about monetary policy? Couldn't the monetary authorities prevent inflation by refusing to finance government deficits? Suppose that the Fed allowed the monetary base to grow only by 4 percent per year. What would happen? Could large and continuing government budget deficits lead to inflation if the monetary authorities withheld their cooperation?

These are particularly important questions because the managers of the Federal Reserve System are not subject to the political pressures that constrain elected officials. The people who created the Federal Reserve System in 1913 were well aware that popular politics exerts pressure on governments to pursue inflationary policies, and so they put control of the monetary system in the hands of an independent agency of the federal government. Members of the Board of Governors are appointed by law for 14-year terms, so that they can act independently of Congress and the administration. What would happen if the Fed exercised its statutory independence to the extent of directly opposing the government's fiscal policies?

The Fed would lose in an all-out confrontation, because Congress can, finally, take away the independence that it has granted. On the other hand, Congress would be reluctant to take such dramatic steps or to precipitate a public debate in which members of Congress might be seen as advocates of inflation. So the Fed probably could, up to a point, pursue monetary policies designed to neutralize the impact of federal deficits. Nonetheless, it is doubtful that the Fed would persist for very long in any such policy. The reasons are rooted both in uncertainties about the way in which monetary policy works and in the mounting public hostility toward the Fed that such a course would almost surely nurture.

Disagreement about the Conduct of Monetary Policy

You may be surprised to discover after all this discussion of money and monetary policy that the members of the Open Market Committee do not fully agree among themselves on the definition of a restrictive (tight) or expansionary (easy) money policy. The question of the proper target for monetary policy has been a controversial one for a long time. One view holds that the monetary managers should pay attention exclusively to monetary aggregates: measures of the money stock or the monetary base. The money supply is tight or easy according to the rate at which these aggregates are changing. Another view holds that the monetary managers should concentrate on interest rates, using some such measure as the federal funds rate, which is the rate of interest paid by commercial banks to borrow one another's reserves. The money supply is tight or easy according to whether interest rates are high or low.

The disagreement is complicated by the apparently widespread belief that interest rates reflect the scarcity of money, so that rates can be made to fall by increasing the money stock fast enough. We must think carefully about the relationship between monetary policy and interest rates if we are to avoid the error of assuming that high interest rates are conclusive evidence of tight money. When the Fed increases the stock of money, the demand remaining constant, elementary supply and demand analysis tells us that the price of money will fall. But interest is not the price of money! Interest rates can be thought of as the price of credit; but the price of money is the value of money or its purchasing power.

How *does* monetary policy affect interest rates? When the Fed increases bank reserves as part of an easier money policy, banks are enabled to expand their lending. Credit becomes easier to obtain and interest rates consequently tend to move downward. Easier money leads to lower interest rates—at least temporarily.

But we must push the analysis further. What happens to the new money that is created when the Fed adds to bank reserves and the banks make additional loans? The increase in M will tend to increase aggregate demand. If the demand for credit from consumers, investors, and government expands when aggregate demand grows, that will tend to pull interest rates back up. The net effect after a longer period of time cannot easily be predicted, because monetary policy finally influences both the supply and the demand for credit and pushes them both in the same direction.

Nominal versus Real Interest Rates

More importantly, if the expansionary monetary policy leads to an excessive rate of increase in aggregate demand, prices will start to rise. And the expectation of rising prices will cause interest rates to rise. Why? Because if prices are expected to increase by 10 percent per year, lenders will demand an additional 10 percent in interest as compensation for the anticipated decrease in the value or purchasing power (the price) of money. And borrowers with the same expectations of inflation will consent to pay the additional 10 percent because they anticipate repaying the loan with depreciated dollars. The *nominal* interest rate will then exceed the *real* interest rate by 10 percent.

The policy dilemma this poses for the Fed became exceptionally clear in early 1975, when interest rates were falling but some critics of the Fed complained that they were not falling rapidly enough and called for a faster rate of growth in the money stock to get interest rates down more quickly. The basic factual issues, the rate of growth in the money stock and the movement of interest rates, were not at issue. The federal funds rate had fallen from 13.5 to 6 percent between July 1974 and March 1975. The total of currency and demand deposits (M_1) had risen at an annual rate of about 2 percent over this same period. All parties agreed to those facts. Even more interestingly, there was a remarkable consensus among economists inside and outside the Fed that the 2 percent rate of growth in M_1 was definitely too slow. But the commentators were offering two contradictory analyses in March of 1975. One group was saying that the Fed could and should push interest rates down more rapidly by accelerating the rate of growth in the money stock. The other group maintained that nominal interest rates might rise if the Fed increased the rate of growth in the money stock—even though this group also wanted a faster rate of money growth. In other words, one group was saying to the monetary managers: "Increase the money stock until interest rates go down far enough." And the other was saying: "Increase the money stock, but ignore interest rates that might well rise as you do so."

Popular Opinion and Interest Rates

The published reports of the Open Market Committee's policy directives in recent years reveal continuing uncertainty about whether monetary aggregates or interest rates are the proper target at which to aim. But there is very little question about the target at which the general public looks in assessing monetary policy. It looks at interest rates. Moreover, the public looks exclusively at nominal interest rates, the only interest rates that anyone publishes, and sees high interest rates as bad almost without qualification. High interest rates allegedly cause inflation (a rise in interest rates does push up the Consumer Price Index) and recession (a rise in *real* interest rates does tend to reduce investment spending). High interest rates also make it harder for homebuyers to obtain mortgages (rising nominal interest rates do dry up the supply of mortgage credit, but that's because they bump against statutory ceilings on interest rates that make no allowance for the distinction between nominal and real rates). High interest rates also "starve" the economy for credit, "choke off" expansion, "pinch" households and business firms, and perpetrate similar violence. The only people thought to benefit from high interest rates are bankers. And who loves bankers?

The majority of the public believes that the Fed *can* control interest rates and that it has an obligation to keep them at "reasonably" low levels. It can do this, supposedly, by expanding bank reserves whenever interest rates threaten to rise above some "reasonable" level. The upshot of it all is that the Fed will run into enormous public hostility if it tries to tighten its monetary policy at a time when the public is expecting fairly rapid inflation, because those expectations will produce high nominal interest rates that the public will regard as evidence of a monetary policy that is *already too restrictive*. That's exactly what happened, for example, in the last half of 1979. Nominal interest rates were quite high by historic standards in 1979, pulled up by the general expectation of rapid inflation in the immediate future. But newspaper articles and financial commentators rarely pointed out that a 12 percent interest rate when inflation was running at a 13 percent annual rate (as it did for awhile in 1979) was a very low and in fact negative *real* rate of interest.

The published policy directives of the Open Market Committee do little to clarify the situation. These directives regularly speak of maintaining the federal funds rate within some targeted range, as if the Fed had the power to set that rate independently of what was happening to nominal interest rates in the credit market. Remember, however, that the Fed exercises its influence on the federal funds rate through buying and selling government bonds and thereby adding to or subtracting from commercial bank reserves. If the federal funds rate is rising, it is because rising market interest rates are inducing banks to bid more in order to obtain additional reserves that they can lend. To counter this movement, the Fed must supply additional reserves. But could the Fed have pumped large volumes of new reserves into the commercial banking system in mid-1979 without stirring expectations of still more rapid inflation? No action by the Fed can lower interest rates if that action increases the demand for federal funds by even more than it increases the supply.

This fundamental uncertainty about the effect that open market operations will have on interest rates is what has persuaded some economists that the Fed should ignore interest rates and concentrate on monetary aggregates. The attempt to stabilize interest rates, these economists argue, causes the Fed to lose control over the growth rate of the money stock. And it is the rate at which the money stock grows, they maintain, that in the long run determines the rate at which total demand and hence the nominal gross national product will grow.

We can at least be sure of this. It will be politically difficult for the Fed to counter inflationary fiscal policies until the public acquires a better understanding of interest rates—how they function to allocate scarce resources among competing claimants and between present and future; how inflationary expectations raise nominal but not real interest rates; how monetary policy actually influences interest rates; and the limitations on the ability of the monetary authorities to control interest rates. We can also be sure that no effective campaign to educate the public on the significance of interest rates will be possible as long as disagreement on the subject exists even among high-ranking officials in the Federal Reserve System.

There is yet another source of pressure on the Fed to adopt policies with an inflationary impact. Before we examine it, however, we must take a look at a proposed solution to the problem of inflation that has nothing to do with fiscal or monetary policy. This discussion will lead us back to the problems faced by the monetary authorities.

The Popularity of Direct Controls

The general public has never had much trouble believing that inflation is the result of irresponsible behavior on the part of sellers, whether of labor or products. The public looks for villains when things go wrong, and seems to find them in the business firms that announce price increases and the union leaders that call for wage hikes. An excessive rate of increase in demand is a force too abstract and impersonal to be a good candidate for villain, so that corporations and unions tend to be blamed for inflation even when wages and prices are clearly being pulled up by excess demand, not being pushed up by market power. That's why the imposition of wage and price controls during a period of inflation usually encounters an overwhelmingly favorable response from the public, at least initially. A case in point is the wage-price freeze announced in August of 1971.

The popularity of wage and price controls as a way of dealing with inflation makes it all the more urgent that the public understand the mechanisms of inflation. If wages and prices rise after the fiscal or monetary authorities have expanded aggregate demand faster than real output can keep up, or after some disaster (war, oil embargoes, crop failures) has reduced the level of real output, controls are worse than useless. For they suspend the rationing system through which scarce goods get allocated among competing claimants. This means that the goods will have to be allocated by other criteria; buyers will get in line early, cultivate contacts, try to negotiate special agreements, or offer illegal monetary inducements to get around the maximum price. The incentive to hoard goods will increase, because goods are undervalued at their legal prices and because buyers cannot be sure of obtaining supplies in the future. This further aggravates the scarcity.

Producers will have less incentive to expand output and maintain quality. Production will fall further as manufacturers find themselves unable to obtain particular inputs that have suddenly disappeared from suppliers' inventories; they may even have to suspend production and lay workers off. Export controls will be instituted to keep other countries from taking advantage of the controlled prices. Bartering will creep into the supply system, not only decreasing efficiency but also stirring up cries of inequity from those producers who have nothing of value to offer their suppliers. Items will unexpectedly disappear from retail shelves—paper bags, shoe heels, plastic syringes, fertilizer—as shortages multiply and breed further shortages. Relative prices will not be able to change in response to changing relative scarcities, and so the structure of prices will start to give misleading signals to resource users. In short, suppression of the price system suspends the mechanism of economic coordination, leading to inequities, inefficiencies, and disruptions of production that only worsen the imbalance between demand and supply.

Imposing price controls in the face of an inflation caused by too many dollars chasing too few goods aggravates the problem by reducing the supply of goods and diminishing the incentive of demanders to economize in their use. And this is true whether the imbalance was caused by an excessive creation of dollars or a deficient creation of goods. Moreover, it diverts the attention of the public from the actual causes of the inflation and the proper remedies. Of course, a government whose fiscal and monetary policies have fueled an inflation will be only too happy to encourage the public's belief that private avarice is the root of the problem, that public-spirited self-restraint on the part of citizens is the ultimate answer, and that the rascals who have no public spirit must be controlled by law. Congress will rarely admit that its own spending habits are the cause of any ills, and Presidents never locate the cause of inflation in their own earlier policies.

The wage and price controls of World War II are sometimes brought forward as evidence that controls can in fact be effective in preventing excess demand from pulling up prices. But this argument ignores some important facts. It overlooks the public's willingness to put up with shortages and tolerate inequities when they are viewed as temporary necessities. It overlooks the alternative rationing system created by the federal government during World War II to allocate scarce goods among competing claimants: the complex point system, the books of ration stamps, the special gasoline coupons, the priority allocations, and the army of controllers required to make the system work even as well as it did. It overlooks the role of wartime patriotism in securing the voluntary cooperation that kept the system functioning for several years, as well as the illegal and semilegal evasions that sometimes helped the system work by enabling people to circumvent it. And when the controls were removed, as they eventually had to be, the excess money demand dammed up behind them poured out to raise prices 40 percent between 1945 and 1948.

Cost-Push Inflation? The Case of OPEC

It is worse than useless to impose price or wage controls when expansionary fiscal and monetary policies have created a demand for goods that can't be satisfied at prevailing prices. Suppressed inflation creates more inequities and inefficiencies than open inflation. But are inflations always the result of overly expansionary fiscal and monetary policies? Are all inflations caused by the pull of excessive demand? Are they never caused by pressure from the supply side? Is there no such thing as cost-push inflation?

It would be hard to convince any user of petroleum products that OPEC, for example, has played no part in causing the U.S. inflation of the 1970s. The OPEC cartel used its market power to reduce the supply of oil and thereby raise the price of oil substantially to users. Oil and its products enter into the budgets of consumers, directly and indirectly, at innumerable points; every good's production cost was pushed up to some extent by the rise in energy costs. The only question, it would seem, is what portion of the price rises since 1973 can be attributed to OPEC?

We said way back in Chapter 15 that inflation is a fall in the price of money, and that its causes must therefore be sought in the forces affecting the supply and demand for money. That's still true. If the supply of some good is reduced through the action of a cartel, or a drought, or a strike, or any other event, the relative price of that good will rise. The relative prices of goods that use it as an input will consequently also tend to rise. Since oil enters in some fashion as an input into the production of every good, it would then seem to follow that OPEC has the power to raise the relative prices of *all* goods and thus to cause inflation.

But that last sentence is nonsense. The *relative* prices of *all* goods cannot rise, because nothing would be left relative to which they could rise. An increase in the relative price of goods with large inputs of oil in their production processes logically entails a decrease in the relative price of goods with smaller inputs of oil in their production processes. To deny this would be like trying to see whether major league baseball players are better today than they were a generation ago by checking on whether major league clubs win a higher percentage of their games today than they did a generation ago.

Of course, the relative price of all goods *other than money* can rise; that's not a logical impossibility. And OPEC could conceivably be responsible for causing an increase in the price of everything *relative to money*. But don't you find it somewhat odd to focus entirely on oil and to ignore money altogether when the price of *everything* has changed *relative to money*?

Clear the cobwebs for yourself by thinking about the consequences of OPEC's actions in a world without money, where all trade is conducted by barter. OPEC's actions in such a case would have compelled other countries to export more commodities and services per barrel of oil imported. Oil consumers would have had to choose between consuming less oil or sacrificing larger quantities of other goods. With the opportunity cost of acquiring a barrel of oil higher than before, producers would also look for ways to economize. They would produce relatively fewer of those goods that use lots of oil, thereby reducing the supply of these goods and causing an increase in their relative price. What would happen, in summary, is that the relative prices of goods that use lots of oil would rise, and the quantities of them produced and purchased would undergo a relative decline. This necessarily means that the relative prices of goods using very little oil would fall, while the quantities of these goods both produced and purchased would increase.

This is what's actually been happening in the world since 1973. It's been happening in the U.S. in very clumsy and costly ways, because the United States government has chosen to interfere with the movements of relative prices by which these complex processes of reallocation are ordinarily guided. We discussed that issue earlier. The issue here is the way in which all this has been camouflaged by changes in the value of money. We fail to see that the relative prices of some goods have fallen as a consequence of OPEC's successes, because our attention is riveted on the price of everything relative to money. The price of everything (or *almost* everything) relative to money has indeed risen since 1973. But this has occurred because since 1973 the supply of money has increased faster than the demand for money.

Are we saying, then, that OPEC played no part in causing the U.S. or world inflation of the 1970s? Not at all. We are rather trying to find out exactly what that part might have been. And we're getting close. Suppose that the Fed had held M_2 constant in 1973 rather than allowing it to rise during the year, as it did, by 9.6 percent. And suppose the Fed had persisted in allowing no growth in the stock of M_2 during 1974, rather than permitting it to grow by 8.4 percent. What would have occurred? The most probable consequence would have been a strong recession. The U.S. actually did have a recession that began right at the end of 1973 and continued into 1975. But if the Fed had followed a policy of no growth in M_2, or even of substantially slower growth, the recession would almost surely have been more severe.

The reason is that OPEC's actions necessitated large and rapid increases in the relative prices of petroleum-using products. That meant large and rapid decreases in the relative prices of other goods. But prices do not change smoothly and quickly in response to altered conditions of supply and demand. Above all, they do not *fall* smoothly and quickly. The more immediate response is accumulating inventories, which lead to reduced orders, production cutbacks, and increased unemployment. This increased unemployment of labor and other resources continues until relative prices have adjusted to the new circumstances and resources have been reallocated.

The extensive shock that OPEC administered to the U.S. economy in 1973 undoubtedly contributed to the 1974–75 recession. Remember that recessions result from accumulated mistakes; OPEC in 1973 turned a lot of decisions very suddenly into mistakes. OPEC unexpectedly compelled in 1973 an extensive reallocation of resources in the United States, a reallocation that had to be directed by changes in relative prices. The Fed probably made those relative price adjustments easier and the reallocation process consequently quicker by increasing the stock of money rapidly. The increased stock of money permitted the necessary price adjustments to occur without any price having to fall in money terms, because all price adjustments could be upward. The goods whose relative prices were supposed to decrease simply rose, in money terms, less than the average. The Fed promoted inflation in response to OPEC's price increases; but it did so in an effort to counter the reduced output and employment caused by OPEC's unexpected success in cartelization.

Market Power, Unemployment, and Inflation

Here is a major source of pressure on the Fed to pursue inflationary monetary policies. We gave so much space to the question of OPEC's role in the U.S. inflation of the 1970s because the issue illuminates a more general problem. Suppose that a significant number of wage rates are set by collective bargaining and that unions have the ability to obtain wage increases in excess of productivity increases. That would mean that unions (or some unions) can obtain for their members a wage that is above the value of the marginal worker's net contribution to the employer's revenue.

Employers adjust to such a situation by reducing the number of workers they hire. They may not actually lay anyone off; instead they will just refrain from replacing workers as they retire or quit. The result is a reduction in the number of jobs available and an increase in measured unemployment. It makes no difference if we assume that employers can raise their prices and recover the higher labor costs without reducing employment. At higher prices they won't be able to sell as much, and the reduced sales will eventually lead to employment cutbacks. Even if union members realize that higher wages will mean fewer jobs, a majority may vote for the wage increase in the belief that they themselves will be protected by seniority; they are risking the jobs of others.

Rising unemployment caused by this kind of market power puts the Fed under pressure to adopt an expansionary monetary policy. When it does so, prices rise generally. The rise in the price of everything else reduces the relative price of the good whose sales had fallen, its sales expand once more, and employment in that industry is restored. If employers lack the market power to pass the wage increase along to buyers, the increase in the price of all goods does the job for them. The real wage is consequently reduced, and employment is restored to its initial level. The upshot of the matter is that the use of excessive market power creates unemployment problems, and that to deal with the unemployment problems the Fed is forced to cause inflation.

Arthur F. Burns, who became chairman of the board of governors of the Federal Reserve System in 1970, had long maintained, in company with most economists, that the key to a stable price level was monetary and fiscal restraint on the part of government, not wage or price controls. But when he found himself in charge of imposing an important part of that restraint, Burns reluctantly concluded that labor and product markets might not function well enough to let fiscal and monetary policy be effective. He argued that strong unions and business firms with substantial market power were able to raise wages and prices in the absence of any increases in demand. Confronted with this situation, monetary and fiscal authorities had to choose between causing unemployment by refusing to expand total demand or causing inflation by underwriting the wage and price increases.

How did we get into such a bind? Is there a way out? Burns

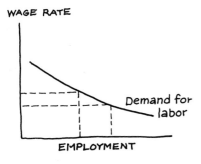

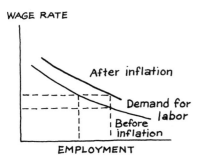

suggested three principal causes of the problem: strong unions, business firms selling in insufficiently competitive markets, and innumerable government regulations that tolerate, encourage, and even require practices which raise costs and reduce efficiency. In the last category Burns included subsidies to farmers, legal restrictions on entry into various trades or professions, import quotas and tariffs, the federal minimum wage law, especially in its application to teen-agers, aspects of our welfare programs, price maintenance laws, and the failure to enforce antitrust legislation. The solution is structural reforms directed toward increasing competition and thereby making wages and prices more responsive to forces of supply and demand.

But reforms of that sort can't be implemented quickly. The active connivance of government in creation of the problems suggests that such reforms will only be possible, if they're possible at all, after a long campaign of public education. In the meantime, if Burns's analysis is correct, we shall have to make do with second-best policies. Some legal controls on prices and wages may be necessary if we are to avoid confronting the nation's fiscal-monetary managers with the unpleasant choice between accepting unemployment or causing inflation.

But even limited wage and price controls are going to pose major difficulties. On whom will they be imposed and how will this be determined? Who will decide when adjustments are called for and by what criteria will they decide? And whatever the economic rationale, will the political system be adequate to such a task? It is essential to note that Arthur Burns assigns much of the blame for the decline of competition to government policies. Is it realistic to expect the same government to undo its own work? Will regulatory agencies that have long taken their function to be the prevention of competition suddenly revise their thinking and procedures? Will state legislators who bow to industry lobbies and create legal cartel arrangements acquire new wisdom or courage? Anticompetitive laws in the areas of agriculture, labor, and international trade continue to command a congressional majority. Why should we expect any of this to change?

Part of the Solution or Part of the Problem?

It's important to maintain our perspective, however. It was not union strength, corporate market power, or anticompetitive government regulations that caused the U.S. inflation rate of the 1970s to be almost three times as high as it was in the 1960s. These anticompetitive forces just didn't become that much stronger from the 1960s to the 1970s—by many indications they actually lost some of their power to push up costs in the absence of increases in demand. OPEC is another matter. The sudden surge to power of the oil exporters' cartel surely did make the task of aggregate demand management much more difficult in the 1970s. On the other hand, government responses to OPEC and the "energy crisis" may have done even more to complicate the task of economic stabilization. The refusal to let relative prices allocate oil, natural gas, and refined petroleum products meant that they had to be allocated by the Department of Energy at high cost, with enormous inefficiency, and with often glaring inequity.

The most damaging consequence of all this "crisis management," however, may be the vastly increased uncertainty that it creates for decision makers. Efficient social coordination becomes more difficult when no one knows the rules of the game or has much confidence that the rules won't be changed tomorrow. And uncertainty is the root cause of recession.

We don't quite want to say that twists and turns in government policies have made the task of economic stabilization more difficult, because this would imply that stabilization policies themselves have not been a part of that twisting and turning. There is considerable evidence that the use of discretionary fiscal and monetary policy to stabilize the economy has actually increased its instability, at least since the late 1960s. This judgment, which cannot be conclusively demonstrated, will be strenuously resisted by those who want to believe that we do possess the knowledge and skills that are required to achieve milder recessions and greater price stability through aggregate demand management. Professional economists probably tend to be biased in favor of this optimistic view, especially if they are specialists in the area of fiscal and monetary policy and therefore likely to be called upon by government for advice and assistance in the tasks of economic stabilization. The fact that stabilization policy obviously failed in the 1970s won't discourage anyone who thinks it failed only because the right people weren't in charge.

But institutions should not be evaluated on the assumption that angels will run them. It is far more likely that government policies will be controlled by politicians than by angels, and that monetary and especially fiscal policies will be formulated in the same political context that produces decisions on import tariffs, flood control projects, and the location of military bases.

Is There Any Social Lever?

The movement for a constitutional amendment to require a balanced federal government budget derives in part from apprehensions on just this score: What happens when aggregate demand management is subject to political control? But balancing the budget annually would be a most difficult task, and preventing changes in the size of the surplus would be impossible given the present state of our knowledge. The attempt to achieve an annual balance between expenditures and receipts would probably require some highly destabilizing actions on the part of government budget makers. And in the last analysis, it still wouldn't prevent the timing and allocation of transfer payments, government purchases, or tax-law changes in ways that destabilize the economy but improve the reelection prospects of incumbents.

While we mustn't expect mortals to be angels, we also mustn't expect miracles from formulas. Consider the recommendation that the monetary authorities adopt a money-growth rule and follow it religiously, as a way of reducing the disruptions created by poorly timed and clumsily executed efforts to "lean against the wind." Do the money managers really know how to make M_1 or M_2 grow at a steady rate? If they admit that they don't, and adopt as their goal a steady rate of growth in the monetary base, can we be sure of a constant or stable relationship between the monetary base and the stock of assets used as mediums of exchange? Money may be as hard to control by formula as by discretionary management.

The Greek physicist Archimedes supposedly said that he could move the earth itself if given one firm spot on which to stand. The thought of such an Archimedean vantage point is alluring to those who worry about economic problems. "There *has* to be a solution. If the economy doesn't work properly, we'll have the government fix it. If the government doesn't work properly, we'll amend the constitution. If we can't get the constitution amended, we'll launch a vast educational campaign. If education doesn't work, we'll transform the whole school system. . . ." There just isn't any firm spot on which an Archimedes can set his fulcrum and lever society into the proper position.

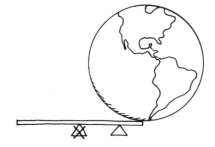

The functioning of the economy, along with the functioning of government and every other social institution, depends finally upon our mutual ability to secure cooperation. We noted on the first page of Chapter 1 how difficult it is for most of us even to recognize the many extraordinary ways in which we successfully cooperate every day. As with an automobile engine, it is only failure that attracts our attention. When the engine is performing well, we don't think about it; we give our attention to the scenery or the road ahead. But because we don't look at our mechanisms of social coordination when they're functioning well, we often fail to discover either how they work or how dependent we are upon their continued smooth performance. And we often conclude erroneously that some simple bit of tinkering will make them function even better.

Wealthy, industrialized economic systems have always experienced periodic fluctuations in production and employment. Is instability an inherent characteristic of an economic system operating without government intervention? That's very probably the case. But how much instability will exist in the absence of government intervention to stabilize aggregate demand? How deep will recessions be? How much time will ordinarily elapse before recovery begins? What will be the costs of recessions? On whom will they fall? Those are important questions.

But so are these. How much instability will exist in the *presence* of government intervention to stabilize aggregate demand? Does anyone really know enough to compensate for fluctuations in private spending? Who will actually be in charge? What interests will guide their decisions? How often will long-term stability be sacrificed for the sake of a short-term performance that improves reelection prospects?

Continuing empirical and theoretical inquiry will eventually give us better answers to these questions. But answering them will not end the controversy. Underneath all these questions, and indeed underneath most significant controversies in economics, lies a much broader question and one far more difficult to resolve: *How well do markets work?* That question is not only and not even primarily whether prices are sufficiently flexible and resources adequately mobile. The question of how satisfactorily markets work is at bottom a question about what kind of society is possible, "taking men as they are and laws as they can be made," to use Rousseau's famous phrase. No one can ever have the *final* answer to that question.

Once Over Lightly

The notion that inflation is caused by excessive aggregate demand and recession by inadequate aggregate demand implies that inflation and recession won't occur together. The fact that they have indeed occurred together in recent years is an argument against focusing exclusively on aggregate demand fluctuations as the cause of rising prices or rising unemployment levels.

Recessions and increased unemployment occur in response to disappointed expectations and can increase regardless of the current rate of inflation. Inflation creates an illusory optimism that will reduce unemployment only so long as people fail to anticipate the inflation correctly. Slowing down the rate of inflation will add to the level of unemployment until people learn to revise the expectations that inflation created.

The closer to its capacity an economic system is operating, the more likely is it that relative search costs for buyers and sellers will generate an upward drift in the nominal level of wages and prices.

There is no convincing evidence that government efforts to produce "full" employment and price stability have actually resulted in lower unemployment rates and less inflation than we would have experienced in the absence of such efforts.

There is evidence to suggest that federal government activities, including some of its stabilization efforts, have been seriously destabilizing in their consequences.

Economists disagree on whether economic fluctuations would increase or decrease if discretionary stabilization policy were abandoned in favor of exclusive reliance on automatic stabilizers.

Some undue optimism about the capabilities of stabilization policy may be fostered by highly aggregative analyses that view the economy as a simple machine. Abstracting from the political process surely fosters a naive over-confidence in the potential benefits of fiscal and monetary policy.

The federal government's budget is a political as well as a stabilization tool. The fiscal policy most likely to produce a steady growth in output and a stable price level is not likely to be identical with the fiscal policy most likely to contribute to the reelection of incumbents.

Public acceptance of federal government budget deficits as an appropriate policy weapon has removed one of the last effective constraints on deficit financing and cleared the way for chronically inflationary fiscal policies.

The ability of monetary policy to counteract the inflationary bias of fiscal policy is also limited to some extent by political factors. Public misunderstanding of interest rates and hostility toward high nominal rates, even when real interest rates are low, makes it especially difficult for the Fed to constrain the growth of the money stock once inflationary demand pressures have built up. The suggestion that technical management of the money stock would be improved if the Fed ignored interest rates is difficult to accept so long as the public focuses on interest rates as indicators of monetary ease or restraint.

The monetary authorities are also under pressure to increase the rate of growth in the money stock whenever relative costs rise significantly in major sectors of the economy. Inflation may prevent unemployment in such cases by permitting all relative price adjustments to be made in an upward direction, and thus more quickly and smoothly.

Price and wage controls might be of some use in promoting high employment without inflation if they were used against groups whose growing political or market power enabled them to raise prices in the absence of any demand increases. This would be a politically controversial policy in practice.

Imposing controls when prices are rising because total monetary demand has increased faster than real output is dealing with symptoms rather than causes, and is likely to aggravate the problems it's intended to solve.

Improved government policy with regard to unemployment and inflation will require better information about many economic relationships of which we are currently uncertain. It may also require that we create a political consensus with regard to the proper goals of economic policy.

QUESTIONS FOR DISCUSSION

1. Evaluate the following assertion: "When aggregate demand is greater than the aggregate capacity of the economy, we get inflation. When it is less, we get recession."
   a. Do firms ever lay off workers when the average price level is rising?
   b. Do firms ever raise their prices during a recession?
   c. How would we know whether the economy was operating at full capacity? Is the aggregate capacity of a single firm ever some definite quantity of output per time period? Think of the college you attend. What would be occurring if it was operating at 100 percent of capacity? Extend the question to an entire industry (e.g., the education industry). Then extend it again to the entire economy.
2. Is aggregate demand inadequate if there is a shortage of automotive mechanics and a surplus of secondary school teachers? Can substantial unemployment exist at a time when listed job vacancies exceed total unemployment? Why will you find help-wanted ads in newspapers even during recessions?
3. Why is the price level likely to be rising more rapidly when the unemployment rate is low than when it is high?
4. Suppose that a corporation suddenly opened a factory employing 5000 workers in a town of 10,000 population. Why would you expect to observe low unemployment, rising wage rates, and rising prices for locally produced goods such as housing and services? What is the causal connection in this case between the town's unemployment rate and its rate of inflation?
5. In the situation described in the preceding question, would you expect prices to start declining if the factory laid off half its labor force? What difference would it make whether the layoff was thought to be temporary or permanent? How much time would it take for a layoff to start bringing down the prices of housing and services in the town?

6. How and why does the attempt to lower the permanent rate of unemployment by deliberately causing inflation depend on the ability to fool people?

7. Why does a slower rate of growth in total demand for new goods, engineered in order to reduce the rate of inflation, usually have an impact on real output before it affects the price level? Can you suggest any ways in which to minimize the effect on real output or accelerate the effect on the price level? How does this sequence of effects make it politically difficult for policy-makers to reduce the inflation rate?

8. You decide to live in an apartment when you return to campus in the fall. Everyone tells you that apartments are extremely hard to find, so you arrive on campus to start searching a week before school begins.

   a. If you find something you like but consider somewhat overpriced, are you likely to take it or to continue looking?

   b. Is the owner likely to hold it for you for several days, while you continue your search, without a nonrefundable deposit?

   c. How would the behavior of tenants and owners be different if recent construction had created a surplus of apartment units near the campus?

9. "There is no danger that a government deficit will cause inflation when unemployment stands at 8 percent of the civilian labor force." Do you agree?

10. Suppose the unemployment rate is 8 percent, and economic statisticians tell the government that 2 of those 8 percentage points are a direct result of sharply reduced purchases of new automobiles. Discuss the advantages and disadvantages in such a situation of offering a tax rebate to purchasers of new automobiles equal to 10 percent of the manufacturers' suggested retail price. Is a dollar of tax reduction offered in this way likely to reduce unemployment more than a dollar of personal income tax reduction? Are the long-run effects on unemployment likely to be different from the short-run effects?

11. If the government decreased spending on highways by $5 billion and simultaneously increased spending on energy development by $5 billion, what effects, if any, would you predict on the level of unemployment?

12. "The basic cause of an excessively high unemployment rate is uncertainty." Explain whether you agree or disagree with that statement and why.

13. Would you expect a different effect on employment from the imposition of a temporary quota against imports than from the imposition of a quota that is expected to be permanent? Why?

14. Can discretionary monetary policy improve upon the automatic monetary stabilizers that would be operative if the Fed simply increased bank reserves at a steady rate? Under what circumstances would discretionary policy be destabilizing in its effects? Under what circumstances would it reenforce the operation of the automatic stabilizers?

15. Suppose we adopted a system under which the federal government made weekly payments to each unemployed member of the labor force for as long as the person remained unemployed. Evaluate the problems such a program would encounter and its probable effects.

16. Suppose we knew that an increase in the budget deficit or in the growth rate of the money stock would have 95 percent of its impact by the end of two

years, 55 percent of its impact within one year, and 20 percent within six months. Would that knowledge solve the timing problems associated with aggregate demand management?

17. "An easy money policy is good for the housing industry in the short run but bad in the long run." Evaluate that argument.

18. Can the monetary authorities raise or lower interest rates by decreasing or increasing the money supply? What limitations exist on their ability to do this?

19. Is a negative interest rate an absurd conception? Can you cite any negative (real!) interest rates in recent years? What was the real rate of interest earned on $100 in a 5 percent savings account in 1974 and 1975? If you were a business executive able to borrow short-term money from the bank at 8 percent, would your decision on whether or not to go ahead with the loan be affected by your expectations regarding the behavior of prices in the coming year?

20. The text asserts that most economic commentators in the spring of 1975 were urging the Fed to increase the rate of growth in the money stock. As long as they agreed in the policy recommendation, why would it matter whether they disagreed over the effect this would have on interest rates?

21. When are interest rates "too high"? What is an appropriate or socially desirable real rate of interest on home mortgages?

22. The concept of *the* interest rate is an abstraction.
   a. Think through the way in which open market operations by the Fed affect (if at all) the interest rate on government bonds, the federal funds rate, the prime rate or rate charged by banks to the most creditworthy borrowers, the rate on automobile loans, the rate on home mortgages, and the finance charge levied by department stores on unpaid credit balances.
   b. In which cases and under what circumstances might the longer-run effects be different from the shorter-run effects?

23. If union-won wage increases add to unemployment and the Fed then expands the money supply to reduce the unemployment rate, who is the villain responsible for inflation?

24. If OPEC is responsible for most of the inflation in the U.S. since 1974, how do you explain the fact that Switzerland, which is far more dependent than the U.S. upon imported oil, has had so much less inflation than the U.S. since 1974?

25. Supply and demand conditions in the market for college professors changed markedly from the 1960s to the 1970s. Is it easy for college administrators to lower salaries when supply increases and demand decreases? What reaction would you expect from professors who were told that market conditions call for a 7 percent reduction in their annual salary? What reaction would you expect from them if they were told that the budget will not allow for any salary increases this year—although the Consumer Price Index has risen 14 percent since last year? Does inflation ease the process of making relative price and wage adjustments?

26. If it is socially irresponsible for sellers to raise their prices in periods of inflation, why did the government raise the price of the annual *Economic Report of the President* from $3.05 in 1974 to $3.25 in 1975?

27. Make up two lists of prices and wages, one containing specific prices and wages that in your judgment are not adequately controlled by competition and the other containing specific wages and prices that you think are adequately controlled by competition. What criteria will you use? What evidence do you have to support your lists?

28. Is it unjust for money wage rates to rise less rapidly than prices? Is it unjust for some money wage rates to rise faster and others more slowly than prices? Can you think of some wage and salary rates that ought to rise less rapidly than prices? On what basis would you answer this question?

29. "A teacher of chemistry should not be paid more than a teacher of history simply because the demand for chemistry teachers is greater relative to the supply. Teachers are not commodities. They are professional persons with family responsibilities who are providing essential public services." Do you agree with that statement? Under what circumstances do you think its principles are most likely to find acceptance? How do issues of this sort complicate a system of wage and price controls?

30. Is it possible to control inflation by having a panel of experts pass on all proposed wage or price increases? Should such panels include an equal number of business, labor, and consumer representatives?

31. In every year throughout the 1970s, the combined budgets of state and local governments showed a surplus, whereas the federal government was in deficit. How would you account for this dramatic difference?

32. Why is it that New York City, when faced with bankruptcy because of continuing budget deficits, can avoid bankruptcy by receiving loan guarantees from the federal government, which has been running even larger deficits?

33. Would you expect to find a relationship between an informed person's attitude toward attempts at fine-tuning and his or her reactions to the following judgments? Explain why.
    a. "Fiscal and monetary managers have better information than business decision makers because they have access to statistical data on the overall performance of the economy and don't have to concern themselves with details."
    b. "The government must establish procedures for national economic planning if we are to avoid the kinds of economic crises experienced in the 1970s."
    c. "The market does not work as it used to. Competition no longer sets prices or allocates resources in the U.S. economy. Most of that is done by organized interest groups with substantial market power."
    d. "The U.S. economy displays an absurd social imbalance. Privately purchased goods are produced in abundance while public sector goods such as education must be content with the leavings."
    e. "Power tends to corrupt, and absolute power corrupts absolutely."

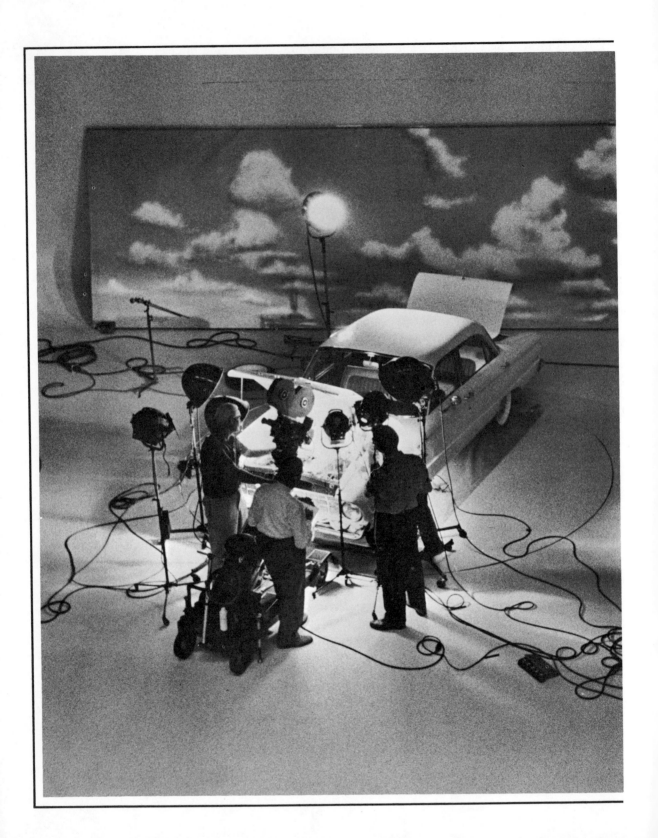

The Limitations of Economics

The possibility of civilization depends largely on how well societies work. What does the economic way of thinking reveal about the the working of society? Is there anything of importance that it conceals?

If you can bring yourself to return to the first chapter of this book, you will find a brief discussion of the biases of economic theory. You might want to read that section again, now that you've completed the book. Are those really biases? Or are they something more like useful working hypotheses?

What Economists Know

The economic way of thinking employs such concepts as demand, opportunity cost, marginal effects, and comparative advantage to order familiar phenomena. The economist knows very little about the real world that is not better known by business executives, artisans, engineers, and others who make things happen. What economists do know is *how things fit together*. The concepts of economics enable us to make better sense out of what we observe, to think more consistently and coherently about a wide range of interrelated phenomena.

This turns out in practice to be a largely negative kind of knowledge. Perhaps you detected, as you read through the chapters of this book, a greater emphasis on what *should not* be done than on what *should* be done. But negative conclusions are important, and they may be especially important in an area like economics. The economist Frank Knight used to defend the heavily negative character of economic reasoning with a quotation: "It ain't ignorance that does the most damage; it's knowin' so derned much that ain't so."

Too many people "know" how to solve pressing social problems. Their mental picture of the economic universe is a simple one, in which intentions can easily be realized and the only obstacle to a better society is therefore a lack of good intentions. But social actions have consequences that run far beyond those that can be easily predicted or foreseen. Restricting textile imports into the United States, for example, does, for the present at least, protect the jobs and income of textile producers; that's clear enough. But it takes a tutored eye to notice that this will shift even more income away from other Americans, by raising textile prices, reducing American export opportunities, and in general inhibiting the exploitation of comparative advantage. Again, it is easy to see that rent controls hold down the money payments that tenants must make to landlords. But how many advocates of such controls are aware of the alternative payments that tenants will have to make, of the new forms of discrimination that will replace discrimination on the basis of money price, and of the short- and long-run effects upon the supply of rental housing?

Nonetheless, people easily become impatient with those who warn against the inadvisability of actions that will make matters worse without proposing solutions of their own. And in a society such as ours, accustomed to the almost miraculous accomplishments of science and technology, the demand for "doing something" tends to exceed by a wide margin the supply of genuine solutions to social problems. We have probably erred in assuming that social problems can be handled in the same way that we manage technological problems. We admit that conflicting interests create hard problems for social policy-makers. But we still underestimate the difficulties in the way of bringing about planned social change, largely because we underestimate the complexity of social systems, of the networks of interaction through which behavior is coordinated in a society and people are induced to cooperate in the achievement of their goals.

Perhaps that's why economic theory often treats proposals for reform of the economic system so unkindly. It is not that economists are themselves uninterested in reform, much less that they are the paid lackeys of the privileged classes. But economic theory, by revealing the interdependence of decisions, calls attention to the unexamined consequences of proposals for change. "It won't work out that way" is the economist's standard response to many well-intentioned policy proposals. Realism is not necessarily conservatism, but it often looks quite similar. And there is a sense in which knowledge promotes conservatism. Even physicists have been accused of hopeless conservatism by would-be inventors of perpetual-motion machines.

Beyond Mere Economics

John Maynard Keynes once proposed a toast to economists, "the keepers of the possibility of civilization." The *possibility* of civilization—that is all. The efficient allocation of resources enlarges the realm of possibility; but it does not by itself guarantee the progress of civilization. A well-coordinated and smoothly functioning society gives individuals more opportunity to choose; it does not guarantee that they will choose well. The economic way of thinking, especially in a democracy, is an important preliminary. But it is no more than that.

Economists are for the most part prepared to admit that the concepts they employ sometimes distort the reality they study. And they are willing to submit their analyses and conclusions to the test of rational criticism. But some point of view is indispensable to any inquiry, in the physical sciences as well as the social sciences. If the economic way of thinking sometimes leads to distortions, to misplaced emphasis, or even to outright error, the appropriate corrective is rational criticism. The application of that corrective has frequently altered the conclusions of economics in the past. It will probably continue to do so in the future.

Index